The "PRESTON" Catalogue

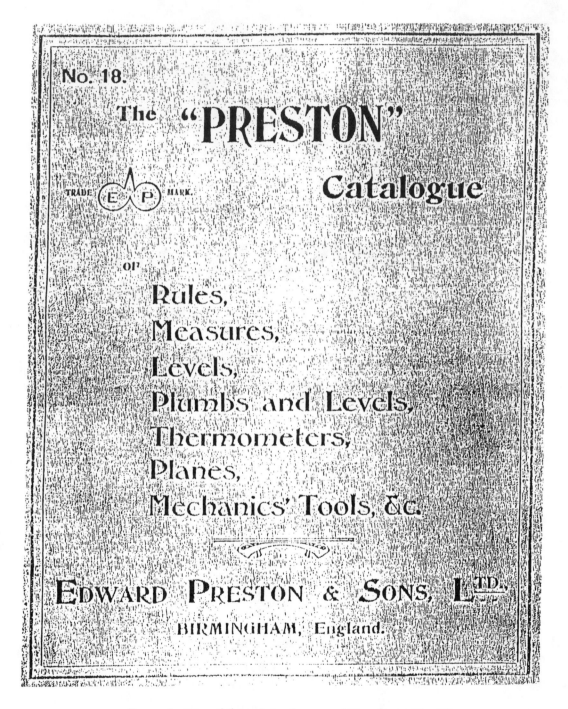

Reproduction of the original cover of Catalogue No. 18.

ESTABLISHED 1825.

AWARDED SILVER MEDAL, MELBOURNE, 1880.

FIRST AWARDS

SYDNEY Exhibition, 1897.

MELBOURNE Exhibition, 1880.

FIRST ORDER OF MERIT, ADELAIDE, 1887.

ILLUSTRATED CATALOGUE

— OF —

RULES, LEVELS, PLUMBS & LEVELS, THERMOMETERS, PLANES, IMPROVED WOODWORKERS' AND MECHANICS' TOOLS, &c.

TRADE

MARK.

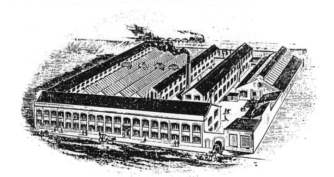

TRADE

MARK.

MANUFACTURED BY

EDWARD PRESTON & SONS, LTD.,
—— WHITTALL WORKS, ——
BIRMINGHAM, ENGLAND.

ENTERED AT STATIONERS' HALL.

CATALOGUE No. **18.—MAY, 1909.**

ALL FORMER LISTS CANCELLED.

D. F TAYLER & CO., LTD., NEW HALL WORKS, BIRMINGHAM.

This catalogue was reprinted from an original edition owned by Jane and Mark Rees. Most of the exhibits illustrated in the Introduction are also reprinted from original material owned by the Rees's, with the exception of Numbers 2, 3, and 4. These come from the prefatory material that was researched and written by Kenneth Roberts, as the Foreword to his reprint of the 1901 Preston catalogue (published in 1979 and now out of print).

Library of Congress Catalogue Card Number: 91-71603
ISBN 0-9618088-9-6

Manufactured in the United States of America

Published by
THE ASTRAGAL PRESS
P.O. Box 239
Mendham, NJ 07945 - 0239

Photo by Whitlook.

Midland Captains of Industry

Mr. Edward Preston Jr.

(from the Gazette Express, September 12, 1908)

EDWARD PRESTON & SONS OF BIRMINGHAM
An outline history
by Mark Rees

The Preston Dynasty

The rise and fall of the firm of Edward Preston is perhaps a microcosm of many British firms—not only enterprises in the field of tool making. Preston was, above everything, a Birmingham firm and was separated not only geographically, but also philosophically from Sheffield, the great centre for tool manufacturing in Britain. This separation and the independence provided by a less traditional environment may be the reason for the willingness to innovate that characterises the firm's history.

Founded in 1825, at first the firm expanded slowly. It was only in the last decades of the nineteenth century that it became a substantial enterprise and subsequently met its demise in 1932, a victim of various factors, including the depression and the intense competition from American tool manufacturers. An outline of the Preston commercial succession is shown in Fig. 1.

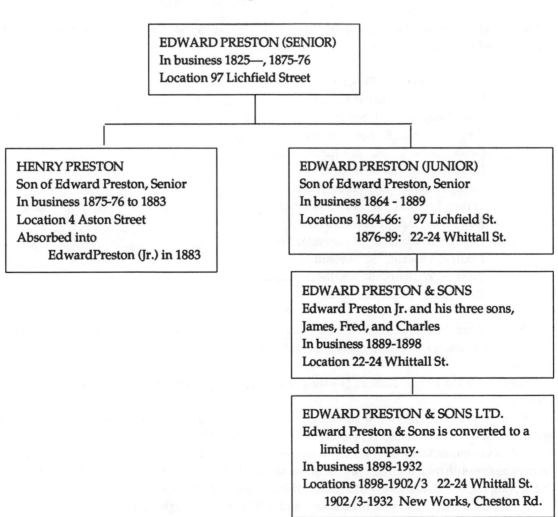

Figure 1. Diagram of the Preston commercial succession.

EDWARD PRESTON (SENIOR)
In business 1825—, 1875-76
Location 97 Lichfield Street

HENRY PRESTON
Son of Edward Preston, Senior
In business 1875-76 to 1883
Location 4 Aston Street
Absorbed into
    EdwardPreston (Jr.) in 1883

EDWARD PRESTON (JUNIOR)
Son of Edward Preston, Senior
In business 1864 - 1889
Locations 1864-66:   97 Lichfield St.
          1876-89:   22-24 Whittall St.

EDWARD PRESTON & SONS
Edward Preston Jr. and his three sons,
James, Fred, and Charles
In business 1889-1898
Location 22-24 Whittall St.

EDWARD PRESTON & SONS LTD.
Edward Preston & Sons is converted to a
    limited company.
In business 1898-1932
Locations 1898-1902/3   22-24 Whittall St.
          1902/3-1932 New Works, Cheston Rd.

One may ask why the firm of Preston has attracted such interest among tool collectors? The answer is that no other firm in Britain produced such a wide range of tools that were of the extra quality that is the characteristic of Preston, and because they expired at just the right moment before modernisation and rationalisation could cheapen their output.

The first decade of the 20th century is surely the era when hand tools were available in the widest possible range, were of the best quality and were still masterpieces of functional design. All this was to end abruptly with the social and industrial changes forced by the first World War. This catalogue (the 1909 together with the 1912 supplement) gives us a view of the diversity and quality of products that were then available to the craftsman.

Origins

In later years, the firm's publicity always claimed that it had been established in 1825, and this is supported by the entries in the various Birmingham commercial directories of that period.

The first reference to a Preston that I have been able to find is in Wrightson's triennial *Directory of Birmingham* of 1825 which contains the following entry:

Preston Wm. Planemaker, 13 Lancaster Street.

The next significant reference is in Piggot & Co.'s *Commercial Directory of Birmingham* 1829, which contains the following list of planemakers:

Brown, Henry, 14 Park Street.
Cox, John, High Street Deritend.
Dale, Joseph, 4 Bell Street.
Davis, George, 8 Court Cheapside.
Gabb, James, & Co., 28 Charlotte Street
Hooper, John, 50 Inge Street
Moss, William, 12 Cannon Street.
Parkes, William, 37 Staniforth Street.
Powell, Samuel, 18 Broad Street.
Preston, Benjamin, 32 Lancaster Street.
Preston, Edward, 55 Stafford Street.*
Preston, William, 57 Steelhouse Lane.
Vale, John, 16 Dubley Street.

*This address does not accord with other, and probably more correct, information which records that in 1827 Edward Preston was already at 77 Lichfield Street.

Neither the list of rule makers (a listing of twenty-five persons) nor the edge tool makers contain a Preston.

It will be seen from this entry that the previously noted William Preston again appears, although now at a different address, and also Benjamin Preston and Edward Preston.

This is a commercial directory and one would expect it to contain only those names of planemakers who were in business on their own account. Of the names listed, all except Joseph Dale and Benjamin and William Preston are known planemakers with recorded examples of their production.

It therefore seems likely that Benjamin and William were working as journeyman planemakers or outworkers (sub-contractors) for the more established firms and at that date had the intention of becoming independent planemakers. However, this apparently was not to be as no planes marked with either of their names have been discovered so far. The inferences that can be drawn from this are that the Preston family (and I do not know what the relationship was between the three—brothers perhaps?) were already well connected with planemaking in Birmingham. Some further evidence to support a close family connection is provided by geography. William is recorded as working (and living?) at 57 Steelhouse Lane which was the next street to Lichfield Street, where at No. 77 (re-numbered 97 in 1855) Edward Preston had his home and business. What, if any, business connection Benjamin and William had with the Edward Preston firm is not known.

It is probable, however, that the William Preston recorded by W.L.Goodman in *British Planemakers from 1700*, firstly in Birmingham (until 1843) and subsequently in Pentonville, London, is the same person as discussed above.

The Early Years

The rating records for the parish of Birmingham record that by 1827 Edward Preston was the tenant of a house and "shops" with a rateable value of £8 13s 4d at 77 Lichfield Street. Lichfield Street was situated in what is now the central area of the city. From the plans of 1854 and photographs taken in 1876, it is known that the premises consisted of a two-storey house situated on the street frontage with attics within the roof space and a shop occupying the front half of the ground floor. As was common in properties of this type in Birmingham, there was an access way through the building from the street to a small court behind which, interpreting from the plans, I believe to have been lined on one side with a row of small workshops.

The 1851 census records Edward Preston, age 54 years, as head of the family and the following children: Sarah, age 24 years; Elizabeth, 17 years; Edward (junior), 15 years, Planemaker; Louise, 10 years; and Henry, 6 years, Scholar; all living at 77 Lichfield Street. Edward is recorded as employing 2 men. Part of the court appears to have been let to a file maker and his wife and part to an instrument maker and his wife.

The whole site area was only 20 feet by 110 feet. In this constricted area it seems that 10 people lived, 3 businesses were carried on, materials stored, and 4 men employed (2 by Edward Preston and 2 by the instrument maker).

The plans to which I have referred above were prepared in 1854 for the purpose of installing a system of public sewers. Before that date it is unlikely that any organised system of below ground drainage existed in that area—conditions must have been truly terrible.

The picture that comes through in 1851 is of a business that, although established for 26 years, had not grown significantly. The principal product was still wooden planes, although from 1841 the firm is listed in commercial directories as toolmakers. However, things were to change.

From the earliest days of industrialization, work was often undertaken by outworkers who would collect workpieces from the proprietor and return them when completed. It is thus quite possible that the 1851 census, which records Edward Preston (senior) as employing two men, gives a somewhat false impression as to the manufacturing capacity of the firm, much of whose business could have been undertaken by a network of outworkers and sub-contractors. It should also be remembered that at this time, and indeed right into the 20th century, many employees were paid piecework only. (Booklets of the piecework rates for the manufacture of planes of all different types, issued by the Birmingham Planemaking Operatives, still survive.)

Edward Junior

Edward had started work as an apprentice planemaker with his father in about 1850 when he was 15 years old.

It seems likely that he fairly quickly perceived that the future lay in expanding the firm into a range of products in addition to planes, such as bevels, squares, spirit levels, etc. Birmingham was by this time the premier centre within Britain for the production of a huge variety of metal goods. These ranged from the smallest products such as jewellery, through silverware and ironmongery, to guns and rifles, including brassware of every description. The Birmingham manufacturers were at the centre of a world-wide export system that distributed these products to almost every corner of the globe. Within the city there existed suppliers of the specialist raw materials needed by such manufacturers; and perhaps more importantly, small manufacturers of part finished goods (castings, screws, rivets, etc.) and the skilled labor needed to produce the finished goods.

By 1864, Edward (junior) had started in business on his own account. His advertisement in the *Birmingham Directory* of that year mentions wood and brass spirit levels, but no other products, (Fig. 2), but by 1866 his advertisement is specifying additional products, including brass plumb bobs and trammel heads (Fig. 3). In 1866, the business transferred out of Lichfield Street, initially to Great Charles Street and then to 26 Newton Street.

In 1866, Edward (senior) was already 70 years of age and had been planemaking for 41 years on his own account. I surmise that he was too old to change and that he came from an older and different school from Edward Junior, who was both a better businessman and more innovative than his father. Once freed from the shackles of the Lichfield Street premises (and the dead hand of father?), Edward Junior's business seems to have developed steadily, shown by increasingly extensive and explanative advertisements in the commercial directories.

By 1867, Edward Junior is describing himself as a wholesale manufacturer of Box and Ivory Rules, etc. (Fig. 4). This advertisement lists three of the new products:

> "Inventor and Sole Manufacturer of the Patent Spring Punch Saw Set;
> Straight and Spiral Spill Machines."

These new products were, in the majority, made of base (cast) iron and well illustrate the leap that had been made in widening the product range from wooden items with perhaps a few brass trimmings into engineered products, largely of metal. Preston was now also making boxwood, ivory and brass rules.

The inventiveness of Edward junior (or at least his inability to resist riding the wave of patenting and design protection that surged through the country after the regularisation of the system in 1851) is illustrated by the list of patents and registered designs shown in Appendices II (Patents) and III (Registered Designs).

The patent spill machine does not appear in Appendix II as it was patented by a J. Machin (in 1865) who presumably then sold the patent to Preston. Also, the Patent for the much advertised saw set has not been traced and may not have ever actually existed. It was quite a common practice to mark goods with the word "patent" when no patent existed. Many patents were refused on the grounds of no originality or were not proceeded with for reasons of cost, and if in such cases were already being sold and marked "patent" why not carry on? It probably deterred or confused some imitators.

In 1875-76, Edward senior, then 79 years of age, left Lichfield Street and went into retirement. The change would seem to have been precipitated by the Birmingham Corporation. Lichfield Street was by this time perceived to be a slum and the area was re-developed with widened and realigned streets. Indeed the site of the Preston premises is now under the Victorian Law Courts building. His younger son, Henry Preston, then 31 years of age, continued the business and, presumably to mark his proprietorship, published the 12 page pocket list which is reproduced in Appendix IV. However, the claim on the title page of this list to be "Manufacturers of every description of Planes and Tools—Wholesale and Retail"—must be taken with a pinch of salt. It is apparent that the nature of the business had changed, and he was factoring a wide range of tools in addition to selling his own production.

In 1883, Edward senior died. It appears that following his death the Henry/Edward Preston (senior) business was amalgamated with the now much larger Edward Preston (junior) enterprise. I have perhaps given the impression in this narrative that the father/son relationship may have been strained, it being the message one gets from the operation of separate businesses. However, it may well be that the schism was

EDWARD PRESTON, Jun.

MANUFACTURER OF

WOOD AND BRASS SPIRIT LEVELS, &c.

97 Lichfield Street, Birmingham.

Figure 2. Edward Preston junior; Advertisement, 1864
1864 Birmingham Directory

97, LICHFIELD STREET,

BIRMINGHAM.

EDWARD PRESTON, Jun.,

MANUFACTURER OF

PLANES, ROUTERS, JOINERS', COACH, GUN,

CABINET, AND CARPENTERS' TOOLS,

Wood, Brass, Plumb Rules, Engineers' Round and Square Tube Spirit Levels, Brass and Lead Plumb Bobs, Trammel Heads, Steel Squares, Boat Builders' Bevils, &c.

☞ *Inventor and Sole Manufacturer of the Patent Spring Punch Saw Set, Straight and Spiral Spill Machines.   Bradawls and Handles.*

Figure 3. Edward Preston junior; Advertisement, 1866
1866 Birmingham Directory

EDWARD PRESTON, JUN.,

WHOLESALE MANUFACTURER OF

BOX AND IVORY RULES,

Wood and Brass Plumb Rules,

ENGINEERS' ROUND & SQUARE TUBE SPIRIT LEVELS,

Brass and Lead Plumb Bobs, Trammel Heads, Steel Squares, Boat Builders' Bevils, T Drawing Squares, &c. Inventor and Sole Manufacturer of the Patent Spring Punch Saw-Set, Straight and Spiral Spill Machines, and of the Patent Awl Handles for the use of Carpenters, Saddlers, and Shoemakers; also, of the Cam Lever Copying Press; Plane Makers' Stops and Plates.

Removed from 97, LICHFIELD STREET to

26, NEWTON STREET, BIRMINGHAM.

Figure 4. Edward Preston junior; Advertisement, 1867
1867 Birmingham Directory

the result of a temporary difference and that after some time, the various businesses operated in parallel and with co-operation. Kenneth Roberts has recorded that Edward (junior) and William were the executors of their father's will, so relations could not have been too bad.[1]

The Developing Business

The last decade of the century saw rapid development of the Preston enterprise. By 1876 the business had moved to larger premises at 22 - 24 Whittall Street. This was a much more mechanised factory, speeding the manufacture and improving the quality of a rapidly expanding range of products. For the first time, the factory was organised on a rational productive basis although it was described later (years after the move to the Cheston Road site) as a "rambling ill-planned edifice." However, for its time (in a trade notorious for its fragmentation and occupancy of numerous small workshops), it represented a step forward in efficiency.

The Preston trade mark is believed to be a visual pun based on the address, Lichfield Street and the spire of Lichfield Cathedral. Application was made to register the mark on 1st February 1876, stating that the trade mark had been in use for six years before 1st January 1876. The trade mark registered between 26th March and 24th April 1877 made reference to all type of goods: spirit levels, planes, etc.

In 1888 the long established rule-making firm of T. Bradburn and Sons was taken over and incorporated into the business. Typically, Preston continued to make rules bearing the distinctive Bradburn lion and compass/dividers trade marks although most of the rules were similar to their own production.

In 1889, the three sons of Edward junior were taken into the firm as partners and the name changed to Edward Preston and Sons.[2] In 1898 the partnership was converted to a limited company. This new status and the continuing expansion of business presumably enabled the firm to finance and undertake the construction of the new factory at Cheston Road. The "New Works" were proudly illustrated on the cover of the July 1901 Illustrated Price List of Rules, Spirit Levels, Planes and Tools, etc. It would seem, however, that the works were not occupied until either 1902 or 1903. This cut was reproduced with the deliberate distortions of scale that are almost universal in such illustrations. Regrettably, today nothing significant remains of the works, and when I visited the site in 1985 the area was vacant. The railway on the embankment at the rear was also disused, but from its position and the position of the road, the size of the site could be assessed. It did not seem to me to be quite the extensive plot that is depicted on the cut! However, such magnifications are just one of the methods which many manufacturers of the late 19th and early 20th century used to depict their firms as large and prospering enterprises. The Preston billheads were also designed to advertise the range of goods and to give the impression of a thriving business (Figs. 5 & 6). Another method was the producton of a large and well illustrated catalogue, and in this respect the firm of Preston was not backward. The 1901 illustrated price list, reprinted in 1979 by K. Roberts Publishing Co., is described as the sixth edition. Regrettably, to date, I have not been able to locate an earlier list. My expectation, based on observations of other catalogues, is that earlier catalogues would have been substantially smaller. The 1901 list demonstrates that by the turn of the century, the firm was producing a huge range of measuring devices and tools. Preston also produced a series of handbills advertising individual or small groups of tools. These were printed on very thin paper for ease of distribution and very few have survived (Figs. 7, 8, 9, & 10).

Decline and Fall

If, in 1912, the reader were to have ordered one of each of the boxwood rules, one of each of the ivory rules, one of each of the brass and steel rules, and one of each of the levels, you would have received the following:

Boxwood rules	362
Ivory rules	64
Brass and steel rules	228
Levels	333

continued on page xii

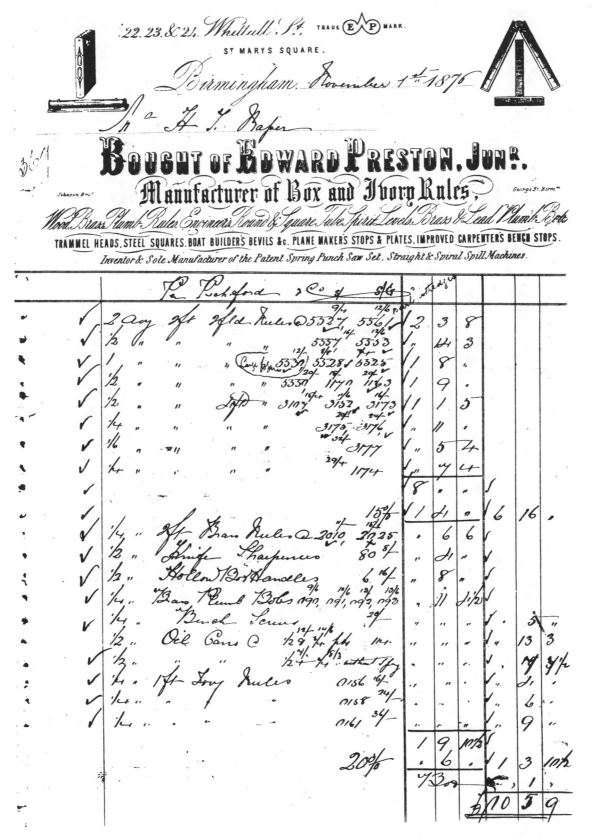

Figure 5. Edward Preston junior; Billhead, 1876

TRADE MARK
E P
REGISTERED

ESTABLISHED 1825.

WHITTALL · WORKS,
22, 23, and 24, Whittall Street,
BIRMINGHAM.

Nov 18 1885

Mr H J Raper   *Kirkgate* *Wakefield*

BoT. of EDWARD PRESTON & SONS,

MANUFACTURERS OF

BOXWOOD, IVORY, BRASS & STEEL MEASURING RULES,

SPIRIT LEVELS, PLANES,

IMPROVED IRON SPOKESHAVES, JOINERS TOOLS, &c.

INVENTORS & SOLE MANUFACTURERS OF

THE PATENT PUNCH SAW SET, THE CARPENTERS IMPROVED BENCH STOP,
& THE IMPROVED IRON SASH, RABBETTING, QUIRK & BEAD ROUTERS.

HIGHEST AWARDS
SYDNEY 1879

HIGHEST AWARDS
MELBOURNE 1880

Thermometers, Plumb Bobs, Trammel Heads, Engineers Steel Squares, Sardine Openers, and other Sundries.

Should any errors or deficiencies be discovered in this Invoice please inform us of same immediately.
Full amount allowed for returned packages if advised and received within 14 days. Half amount allowed if kept.

		Description				£	s	d		£	s	d
✓	1/2	doz 2ft 2fo rules	5530	Large figures	12/		6		✓			
✓	1/4	doz " " "	1161 16/ 1170 18/				8	6	✓			
✓	1/2	doz " " "	5523 13/10 5528 8/6				11	2	✓			
✓	1	doz " " "	5050 8/				8		✓			
✓	1/2	doz " 4fo "	3113 8/3 3114 10/4				9	4	✓			
✓		all rules polished				2	3		✓			
✓				15%			6	5	✓	1	16	7
✓	1/4	doz Trammel Heads	1426 3/				7	9	✓			
✓	1/2	doz 2ft 2fo Brass rules	2010 7/8				3	10	✓			
✓							11	7				
✓				20%			2	4	✓		9	3
✓	1/3	doz 8in Masons Mallets	3/				10	8	✓			
✓	1	Only Web Stretcher	10/				1	3	✓			
							11	11				
				25%			3		✓		8	11
			Bose ??						✓			9
										2	15	6

Figure 6. Edward Preston & Sons; Billhead, 1885

TRADE (E P) MARK.

IMPROVED MALLEABLE IRON

SMOOTHING PLANE,

WITH HANDLE.

No. 1341.

PARALLEL SIDES.   GUN METAL LEVER.

FITTED WITH ROSEWOOD.

WARRANTED CAST STEEL IRONS.

19/6 EACH.

Discount

NOTE:

REVISED PRICE.   FORMER QUOTATIONS CANCELLED.

September 1st, 1889.

KENRICK & JEFFERSON, B'HAM.

Figure 7. Handbill for Smoothing Plane No. 1341; 1st September 1889

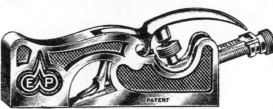

Figure 8. Handbill for Iron Rabbet Plane No. 1368

Figure 9. Handbill for Brewers' Gauging and Dip Rods

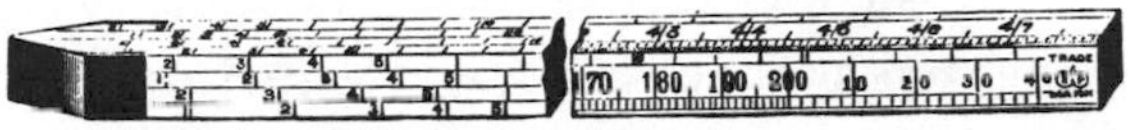

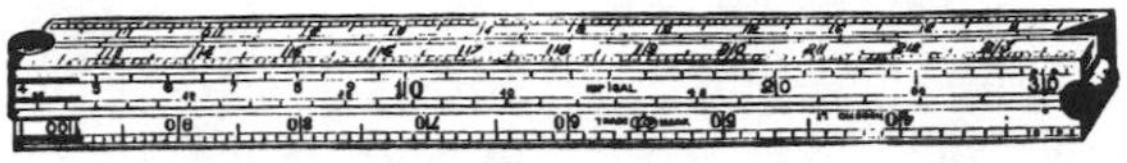

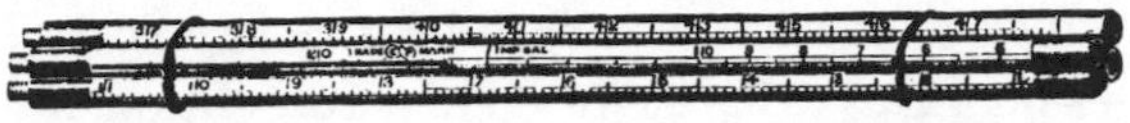

Figure 10. Handbill for Patent Weed Extractor

Herein, I think, lies one of the reasons for the fall of the house of Preston. By the last years of the 19th century, competition within Britain from American tool manufacturers and also, at the cheaper end of the market, from Germany, was intense. This competition extended world-wide, although within the empire trade preferences did give some protection to British manufacturers.

It is obvious from these figures, which demonstrate the immense product range, that few of these products could have been stocked in any quantity, if at all. Had they been, the firm would have been laden with a huge stock much of which never moved. They were made presumably in small numbers as and when orders arrived with, inevitably, high production costs. It was not an efficient operation, certainly not efficient enough to compete in world markets.

In this respect it should be remembered that Preston was not a large firm and, perhaps with the exception of the metal spokeshaves, routers and reeding tools and the various small bullnose and shoulder planes, did not have a dominant market position for any of its products. Birmingham was the principal centre for rule making within the country and indeed huge numbers of boxwood and brass rules were made and exported. This trade was dominated by Rabone with hundreds of workers making more rules than all the other Birmingham makers put together. During the early years of the 20th century the next largest manufacturers of rules were Preston and I. D. Smallwood. They were, however, small fry swimming with a big fish. Rabone was also active and dominant in the level market.

Any collector of Preston tools will vouch for their excellent quality. Indeed this is the major attraction of collecting Preston tools. Preston seems to have refused to reduce the quality of its products even in the face of intensifying competition. Any tool collector who has seen a patent adjustable shoulder plane, unused and gleaming in its original thick nickel plating with each part numbered after hand finishing so that after plating, each plane, including the iron, could be reassembled; or an ebony level, french polished and lacquered to perfection, will appreciate the quality of these tools. This emphasis on quality in the face of the changing times helped lead to Preston's ultimate downfall.

The Final Days

The reasons why a firm goes into liquidation are seldom as simple as they seem.

The intense business depression of the early 1930's was the last nail in the coffin of a firm already weak for the reasons I have outlined. The Preston management may no longer have had the drive and foresight of Edward junior, but as can be seen from the reminiscence which follows, they were certainly not personally profligate. The problem was, I suspect, that which has affected so many old-established firms in many trades. Times had changed; following World War I skilled labour had become scarcer. The firm had not had the foresight or perhaps the capital to install new equipment and rationalise the product line to make it more suitable for production by machine.

It is known that the Birmingham rule makers operated a cartel to mutually defend their interests, and behind the scenes trade between members was probably considerable. I have been told that at some time before the Preston closure, some financial interest in the firm had been taken by Rabone and that the final closure of Preston was due to the withdrawal of this financial support or interest. Whether an indebtedness had arisen in the normal course of trade between the two firms, which was then converted to an interest in the firm, or whether the failing Preston had sought to associate itself with Rabone I am not certain.[3]

The outcome of the closure was that the rule and level business was taken over by Rabone, and the metal plane business was sold to C. & J. Hampton of Sheffield, the manufacturer of Record planes. (Figs. 11, 12, and 13).

Rabone quickly absorbed the Preston rule and level range into its own. Although the Preston range was larger and more diverse than that of Rabone, the vast majority of items were overlapping, and with speedy rationalisation applied, the Preston rule and level range, with few exceptions, quickly disappeared. As an example of this process I would cite the case of the Improved Registered Plumb and Level (Preston pattern Nos. 96 & 98). Production continued for a short while with very few examples of this pattern known bearing

Preston Planes (British Made)

THE Plane bodies are of special close grained grey iron which is thoroughly "seasoned," with rosewood handles fitted with a supporting centre bar.

Cutting Irons are hardened and tempered crucible cast high carbon steel alloy, and are adjustable both laterally and directly. Top iron is shaped as a templet for regrinding the cutting iron.

Bed or Frog is adjustable, enabling varying widths of mouth to be obtain d.

Bright parts are chromium-plated and interchangeable.

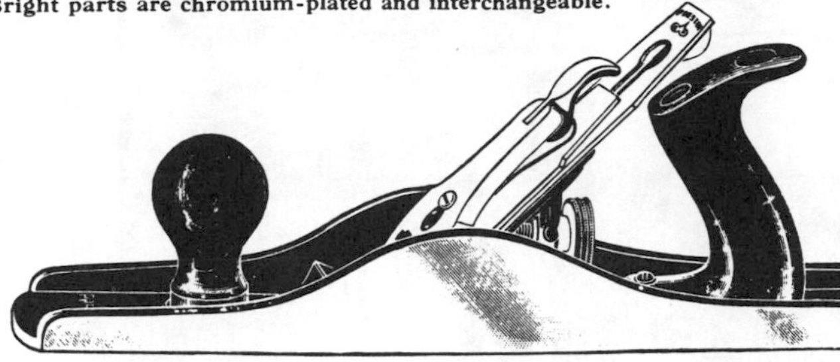

No 16.
Fore or Jointer Plane

No.	Style.	Length, ins.	Cutter, ins.	Price, each.	Extra Irons, each. Single.	Extra Irons, each. Double.
13	Smooth	8	$1\frac{3}{4}$	**12/3**	**2/3**	**3/3**
14	Smooth	9	2	**12/6**	**2/3**	**3/9**
14½	Smooth	10	$2\frac{1}{4}$	**15**	**2/9**	**4/3**
15	Jack	14	2	**15/6**	**2/3**	**3/9**
15½	Jack	15	$2\frac{1}{4}$	**18**	**2/9**	**4/3**
16	Fore or Jointer	18	$2\frac{3}{8}$	**20**	**2/9**	**4/3**
17	Fore or Jointer	22	$2\frac{3}{8}$	**25**	**2/9**	**4/3**
18	Fore or Jointer	24	$2\frac{5}{8}$	**30**	**3/**	**4/6**

No. 14.
Smoothing Plane

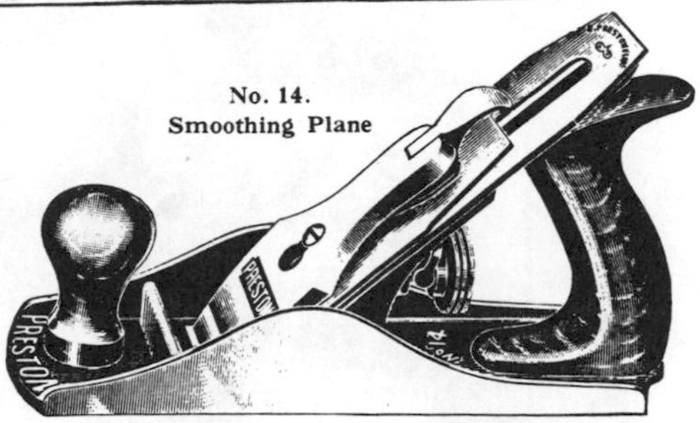

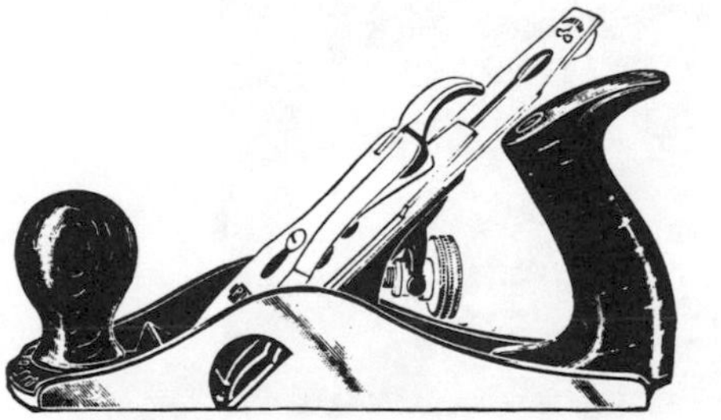

Adjustable Rabbet Plane
Nos. 110½ & 110

Bodies are of malleable iron.

No. 110½. Length, 9 ins. Cutter, $2\frac{1}{8}$ ins.
Price .. .. **21/6 each**

No. 110. Length, 13 ins. Cutter, $2\frac{1}{8}$ ins.
Price .. .. **23/ ,,**

Extra Cutting Irons for Nos. 110½ or 110.
Single .. .. **2/6 each**
Double .. .. **4/ ,,**

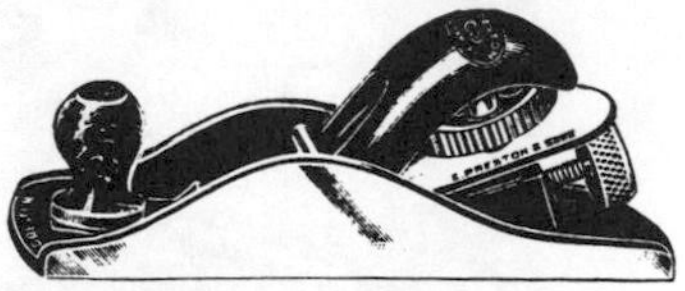

Block Plane

No. 1120. Adjustable, 7 ins. long. Cutting Iron, $1\frac{5}{8}$ ins. **Price** .. .. **5/6 each**
Extra Cutting Irons .. .. **1/3 ,,**
No. 1110. Non-adjustable. **Price** .. .. **3/6 ,,**
Extra Cutting Irons .. .. **1/ ,,**

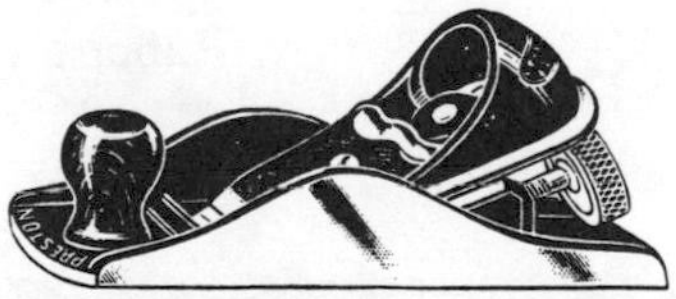

Adjustable Block Plane
No. 1220

Cutter is adjustable endwise and is fastened by cam and lever.

No. 1220. Length, 7 ins. Cutting Iron, $1\frac{5}{8}$ ins. **Price** .. .. **5/6 each**
Extra Cutting Irons .. .. **1/6 ,,**

CHARLES CHURCHILL & CO., LTD., LONDON AND BRANCHES

Figure 11. These illustrations of Preston planes are taken from the 1935 catalogue of Charles Churchill & Co. Ltd. The firm was a wholesaler of hand and machine tools.

Preston had made traditional English steel smoothing planes of dovetail construction from about 1875. In spite of many attempts to produce a cast iron based smoothing plane with adjustment to compete with the Stanley type of plane, Preston did not make a satisfactory competitor until shortly before the firm went into liquidation. In view of the fine range of shoulder planes and bullnosed planes it made, this is a surprising failure. This page shows the range of planes finally produced.

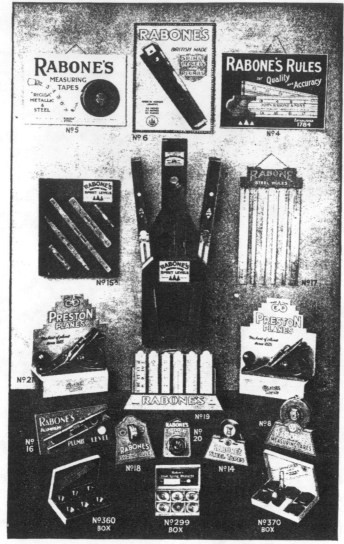

Rabone's Counter Displays (British Made)

A number of very attractive counter and window displays of Rabone goods are available, as illustrated above.

Full particulars will be sent on request

Rabone-Preston Plane Displays (British Made)

This illustration shows one of the Window Displays supplied for Preston Planes.

Full details sent on request

Figures 12 & 13. Rabone counter displays, which include Preston planes, also from the Churchill catalogue.

the Rabone name. This level, which offered improved visibility, though admittedly expensive, was quickly dropped from the line.

The Preston designs for shoulder, bullnose and 3-in-1 planes were adopted by Hampton and form the basis of the design for planes of these types that are still being sold today under the Record and Clico trademarks.

NOTES

1. Roberts, K. *Introduction to Reprint of 1901 Preston Illustrated Price List of Rules, Spirit Levels, Planes and Tools*, etc. Ken Roberts Publishing Co. 1979.
2. James Edward, Frederick William and Charles Henry.
3. Hallam, Douglas J. *The First 200 Years. A short history of Rabone Chesterman Ltd.* Rabone Chesterman Ltd. 1984, pp. 41-42, refer to these events.

ACKNOWLEDGEMENTS

I would like to thank all those who have contributed their knowledge, knowingly or unknowingly, to me and have helped in the writing of this history. In particular I should like to thank the following:

Tudor Somerset — Preston collector to whom I am indebted for the lists of Patents and Registered Designs.

Richard Maude — specialist dealer in Preston tools.

I would also like to thank my wife, Jane, for her help and support.

APPENDIX I.

This vivid and informative reminiscence of the latter days of the Preston firm was written by Mr. F. O. Donnell in 1986. It is reproduced here with minimum editing. Insofar as he contradicts my evidence, I have not altered his version. After all, who is to say which is right?

A REMINISCENCE 1919-1924

I joined the company in 1919 at which time the firm was situated in Cheston Road, Aston, in the vicinity of what we always referred to as the four "A's": Aston Cross, Aston Villa football ground, Aston Station and Ansell's brewery. It was, as many other businesses were at this period, solely a family concern.

Formed some years previously by Mr Edward Preston it was now conducted by three sons and two grandsons of the founder as follows:

Mr James Preston (known as Brains), Mr Fred Preston (known as Rev.) and Mr Charles Henry Preston (known as Chips), Mr James' son (Eddie Preston) and Mr Charles' son (Stanley Preston).

Mr James, the senior director, mainly dealt with finance, the meeting of VIP's and the most important items concerned with the business.

Mr Fred, who seemed more like a vicar than a director and quietly spoken, worked in the thermometer section and also included what small amount of travelling was required.

Mr Charles was the Sergeant Major and works production manager. Mr Eddie and Mr Stanley, who both worked on production, seemed to take less part in the management side, although we thought in those days they had power enough.

(So much for the Board of Directors).

Employees etc.

I would estimate at this period the staff and work force did not exceed 150 to 200 including maintenance etc.

This may seem to be a small number in consideration of the fairly large number of production lines, but where one is now apt to think today in thousands, in those days it was not uncommon to get orders for half doz, quarter doz or even singles of many of the lines particularly in the case of foot gauges, road levels or railway levels although in all these lines a very small stock was held in reserve.

In the case of the making of many of the production lines the amount of machinery was very little to say the least. For instance, laths, T-square heads and blades and all spirit levels woods came into the various making sections straight from the sawmill and one had to really learn to make a spirit level or many other lines from scratch, hand filing, scraping, hand sanding, and even the sideviews in spirit levels were filed out with half round files and smooths. In addition canoe levels came in straight woods that not only were the sideviews hand filed but rasps and files had to be brought into operation to shape them into what they were supposed to represent. It can be now understood how each individual worker had to learn to make a complete article. It can probably now be realised how hard people had to work in those days, in my own case and many others we worked a five and a half day week including Saturday morning; in all a fifty-two hour week for 8 shillings (40 pence present day), but employment was not easy to find and one was very glad to be working full time.

In those days the general lighting of the factory can hardly be described, imagined or even believed by today's workers or standards.

No electric light was available nor, except in offices, were there even gas mantles used. Gas pipes were installed along the back of the work-bench and from these a swinging bracket was attached containing a small jet which gave a kind of fan shaped flame light which had to be brought quite near the work to see what we were doing.

One can well imagine and realise that the setting of all level glass tubes had to be done by daylight. I particularly refer now to the dull days of autumn and winter.

The works heating was by hot water pipes going in suitable positions through the various workshops and offices.

One boiler man (Sparks) was employed for this purpose, but also had other duties to perform to make sure he did a good week's work, cleaning drains, toilets etc.

The Training of Workers

Most employees were trained in various methods and sections of production and were then considered as mobile so that in the case of sickness or any other circumstances, any urgent orders or bottlenecks could be easily executed and completed to the satisfaction of the company and customers by the movement of these experienced people. For instance for the period of time I was employed by E. P. and Sons I spent 3 months mitre blocks, 3 months mallets, 3 months spokeshaves and violin planes and 3 months steel try squares, one of which I made and still possess, and it is as true now as the day I made it 57 years ago with the steel blade going right through the stock.

Conditions of Employment

Stock-taking was organised each year after the Christmas holiday and the required staff for this purpose were notified beforehand, the remainder were away from employment until notified by post or messenger, and it was normally at least two to three weeks without pay before things were back to normal working conditions.

So you can imagine how pleased I was to be chosen as one of the elect the second year and onwards during my employment with the company.

The company's rules for the engagement of personnel or dis-engagement was one hour notice either way. But no matter how long a person had been employed and they received notice to leave through any reason whatsoever, there was not a penny redundancy money paid in those days. I must admit that it was not often that this happened, but I've known it happen on more than one occasion.

It may seem odd that in this period I speak of no-one owned their own car, not even the management, and it was not uncommon to see them travelling by the electric trams, but in the case of Mr Charles and his son Mr Stanley, they came by train from Sutton Coldfield. (As a matter of fact when I moved to John Rabone & Sons at a later date, the same situation existed, Mr Eric Rabone rode to work on his pedal cycle.)

Works canteens did not exist in this age; one managed with cold food and a can of tea or warmed a pre-cooked meal in a basin and placed it in the gas oven although we sometimes managed to bring an egg and fry it over the gas ring to go with our bread and butter.

In Conclusion

As I am drawing near to the conclusion of this report on Edward Preston & Sons, may I say that as I seemed to have got as far as I could progress in my present circumstances I felt that to improve myself I must now get away, and I also had the feeling that all was not going as smoothly for the company as it would have been desired (which later proved correct). My thoughts of course were to try to join John Rabone & Sons Ltd. but knowing full well that an unwritten golden rule existed between the two companies not to engage anyone who had employment with the other, I realised I must take my chance, and I took the bull by the horns and at 12 o'clock I gave one hour's notice to leave at 1 o'clock this being the time of our lunch break. I joined John Rabone & Sons in October 1924.

As time moved forward my fears about Edward Preston & Sons began to take shape. One day while working in the Spirit Level Warehouse at Rabone's, I felt a tap on the shoulder and half turning round to my great surprise it was Mr Eddie Preston (James' son) who shook hands with me and to the astonishment, and I believe annoyance of Mr Eric Rabone (who was with him), asked me how I was getting on. It was not long afterwards I was sent for to go to Mr Eric's office who told me that they were taking E. P. & Sons under our wing. I was also told that I was expected to keep my mouth shut (which I did). Some weeks later Mr Eric sent for me again and from what he said I realised the deal had been completed. He then asked me to write down the most useful workers that I had known at Preston's as he said we were not engaging everyone. All but a few I wrote down came along, but whether the others had found other employment or passed away I knew not. At least fifteen of the Preston employees were engaged and there may have been a few others.

APPENDIX II
LIST OF PATENTS by EDWARD PRESTON and successors.

DATE	NO		OUTLINE DESCRIPTION
1876	986	Edward Preston	Roller skates
1884	13713	"	"Patent Adjustment" <u>Abandoned</u> (see next entry)
1885	12458	"	"Patent Adjustment"
1886	8291	"	Hand Reeder - lever cap (E.P. No. 1393)
1888	1667	"	Small moulding tool (E.P. No. 13938)
1893	7745	"	Shoemakers size stick (E.P. No. 760)
1898	15549	"	Concave/convex slot for adjustment screw
1903	26359	"	Dowel plate - <u>Abandoned</u>
1905	4951	"	Machine for punching holes in slate
1905	10931	"	Mitre box (E.P. No. 566)
1905	16844	"	Picture cramps - <u>Abandoned</u>
1906	339	"	Picture cramps (E.P. No. 0143 & 0144)
1907	21329	"	Router as per E.P. No. 1399 but with fences
1908	8456	"	Human measuring device - <u>Abandoned.</u> Possibly R.D. No. 528202 (1908)
1908	17234	"	Unknown spokeshave
1908	20062	"	Unknown lateral adjustment for spokeshave
1910	8470	"	Bullnose plane (E.P. No. 1347F)
1910	17792	"	Router (E.P. No. 2500)
1911	4202	"	Bullnose plane (E.P. No. 1355C)
1911	13699	"	Unknown spokeshave
1911	26875	"	Addition to Patent No. 4202
1912	20216	Edward Preston and C.E. Saunders	Spokeshave adjustment
1926	247857	Edward Preston	Rule
1928	302209	C.H. Preston	Sliding caliper rule
1928	286042	J.P. Preston	Rule joint
1930	348356	C.H. Preston	Spirit level

APPENDIX III
REGISTERED DESIGNS by EDWARD PRESTON and successors.

DATE	NO		OUTLINE DESCRIPTION
1863 Oct 22	167533	E. Preston (jun.) 97 Lichfield St.	Carpet Stretcher & Tack holder
1864 Apr 27	174137	"	Scissor Sharpener
1864 Oct 18	179890	"	Bradawl Holder
1864 Oct 21	191219	"	Copying Press
1866 Oct 30	203071	E.Preston (jun.) 26 Newton St.	Copying Press
1868 Nov 24	224640	"	Can Opener (E.P. No. 1603)
1869 Feb 25	227434	E.Preston (sen) 97 Lichfield St.	Candle Stick and Match Box
1869 Oct 17	233951	E. Preston (jun) 26 Newton St.	Auger Handle (similar to E.P. No. 1481)
1870 Apr 12	240495	E. Preston (?) 97 Lichfield St.	Not known (*Volume not available at time of research*)
1871 Sep 4	255353	E. Preston (jun) 26 Newton St.	Knife Sharpener
1872 Dec 11	268736	E. Preston (jun) 22/24 Whittall St.	Lever Handle for a Cutter for opening tin or metallic cases (E.P. No. 1631)
1877 Jul 27	312316	"	Cucumber Slicer (similar to E.P. No. 1555)
1878 Dec 27	330676	"	Sardine or Tin Can Opener
1879 Nov 12	342724	"	Tin Can Opener
1893 Jul 25	215628	E. Preston & Sons 22/24 Whittall St.	Shoulder Plane (E.P. No. 1338)
1895 May 15	254794	"	Broom Stick Head Rounding Machine
1896 Jan 20	269393	"	Spirit Level (E.P. Nos. 96, 98-100)
1898 Jul 15	322021	E. Preston & Sons	Spokeshave (E.P. No. 1377)
1898 Oct 25	328028	"	Oveloe Sash Router (body ornamentation exactly as per E.P. No. 1391)
1900 Apr 12	356049	"	Spokeshave (E.P. No. 1373 & 1374)
1901 Mar 29	372093	"	Bullnose Plane (E.P. No. 1363)

1902 Feb 15	387163	"	Bullnose Plane (E.P. No. 1366 & 1367)
1902 May 7	390723	"	Spirit Level (E.P. No. 1010)
1902 May 14	391027	"	Corner Cramps (E.P. No. 0142)
1902 Jun 30	393102	"	Depthing Gauge (E.P. Nos. 56 to 62)
1906 Jan 30	473167	"	Rule for use by the blind
1907 Aug 24	510017	E.Preston & Sons Whittall Works Cheston Rd.	Picture Framers Iron Mitre Box (E.P. No. 569)
1907 Oct 8	513433	"	Engineers Steel Rule with Plumb Bob Hole and Bob
1908 Jul 27	528202	"	Height Measuring Standard
1908 June 15	528844	"	Pattern Makers Cove Box Square & Marker
1909 Dec 12	534243	"	Router (E.P. No. 1397)
1910 Feb 16	557445	"	*Records with Board of Trade*
1911 Dec 2	574449	"	Depthing Gauge (E.P. No. 65)
1911 Jan 18	576670	C.H.Preston Cheston Rd.	Depthing Gauge (E.P. No. 66)
1912 Sep 27	608205	E. Preston & Sons Whittall Works Cheston Rd.	*Records with Board of Trade*
1913 Dec 4	611348	"	"
1916 Nov 17	652729	"	"

APPENDIX IV - 1
Henry Preston Price List of Tools — 1875

PRICE LIST

OF

TOOLS

HENRY PRESTON,

(SON & SUCCESSOR TO E. PRESTON),

LICHFIELD STREET,

BIRMINGHAM.

ESTABLISHED 1825.

Manufacturer of every description of

PLANES AND TOOLS,

WHOLESALE AND RETAIL,

SUITABLE FOR

CARPENTERS' JOINERS' COOPERS' COACHMAKERS', CARRIAGE AND WAGGON BUILDERS', CARVERS', BOATBUILDERS', GUN AND PATTERN MAKERS.

April 15, 1875.

2

SPIRIT LEVELS.

With Brass Tops .... -/9 to 1/6
Engineers' Brass Tube .... 3/- to 5/-
Small Pocket Levels 1/-
Plumb and Straight ditto .... 2/6 to 5/-
,, ,, with Reel combined ... 3/6 each.
Long Levels for Roadmakers' and Contractors' kept in stock or made to order.
Spirit Tubes from 1 to 12, $1\frac{1}{2}$
Warranted correct.

PLANES.

WITH WARRANTED CAST STEEL IRONS.

(With Sarby's, Ward's or Howarth's Irons.)

	To 2	$2\frac{1}{8}$	$2\frac{1}{4}$	$2\frac{3}{8}$	$2\frac{1}{2}$ in.
Smoothing Planes	2/6	2/8	2/9		
Best ,, ...	3/-	3/3	3/6	3/9	4/-
Jack ,, ...	3/-	3/6	3/9		
,, Best	4/-	4/-	4/-	4/6	

Trying Planes .... $2\frac{1}{2}$ inch, 5/-
,, Best .... 5/6 each.
,, or Jointer 26 in., 6/-; 28 in., 6/6; 30 in., 7/6
Compass Smooth Planes .... to $2\frac{1}{4}$ in., 4/-
Compass Smoothing, with Stop .... 6/- ea,
Pannel Planes 5/6
,, ,, Slipped 6/-
Smooth Plane Badgers 5/6
Jack ,, ,, ... 6/6
Bead Planes...... $\frac{1}{8}$ to $\frac{5}{8}$ in., 2/- each
,, ,, ... $\frac{3}{4}$, 2/3 $\frac{7}{8}$, 2/6 1 in 3/- ,,
,, ,, Set of 9 Circular Mouths 20/-
,, ,, Double Box set of 10 .... 28/-
Hollows & Rounds [illegible] Skewmouths 4/- pair
,, ,, ,, ,, $\frac{1}{2}$ set or 9 pr. 36/-

	1	$1\frac{1}{4}$	$1\frac{1}{2}$	$1\frac{3}{4}$	2 in.
Rabbet Planes	2/-	2/3	2/6	2/9	3/-

Common O Gee Planes .... 2/- to 3/-
Grecian ,, ,, ... 3/6 to 5/6
Plough and Irons 14/-
,, ,, with Side Screw 17/6
,, ,, Box Fence ,, ... 20/-
,, ,, Box Screw Stems 25/-
Sash Fillesters .... 10/- to 19/-
,, ,, Box Screw Stems 23/-

3

PLANES—Continued.

Moving Fillester .... 4/- to 9/-
,, ,, Box Faced 11/-
Tooth Planes 3/-
Standing Rabbet Planes with Stop 2/6
Nosing Planes .... 2/6 each.
Coopers' Jointer Planes, 10/-, 14/6, 18/- each.
Ovolo Sash Planes and Templets .... 6/6 pair.
,, ,, and Brass End Templets... 8/- ,,
Lambs Tongue, Sash Plates, and Templets 6/6 ,,
Gothic Sash Planes and Templets .... 6/6 ,,
Grooving or Match Planes .... 4/6 ,,
Moving Grooving, with 3 pairs Irons...... 9/6 ,,
Dado Grooving Planes .... 5/- each.
Scotia Planes .... 2/6 ,,
Table Planes .... 4/6 pair.
Snipe Bills .... 5/6 ,,
Shoulder Box .... 6/6 ,,
Side Rabbets .... 4/6 ,,
Side Rounds .... 4/6 ,,

All Planes are warranted ready for work before sent out.

Every description of Planes made to pattern.

COACHMAKERS' PLANES.

Coach Bead Planes .... 2/- each.
Compass Smoothing Planes .... 3/6 ,,
Concave ,, ,, ... 3/6 ,,
T Rabbet Planes .... 2/6 ,,
T Rabbet Compass Planes .... 3/- ,,
Rounding Planes .... 2/3 ,,
Rabbetted Door Smoothing Planes......... 3/6 ,,
,, ,, ,, with Plated Sides 4/- ,,
Rabbetted Door Jack Planes .... 4/9 ,,
,, ,, ,, with Plated Sides 5/6 ,,
Boxing Routers .... 2/9 ,,
Rounding Tool or Routers .... 5/- ,,
Beading Routers .... 5/- ,,
Extra Irons for ditto .... 10d. pair.
Fence Routers, (Improved) .... 5/6 each.
Jigger Routers, (Improved) .... 10/- ,,
Pistol Routers .... 11/6 pair.
Wheelers Jarvis .... 10/- ,,
Wheelers Rounders .... 1/2 to $1/\frac{1}{8}$

6

SAWS.

Drabble & Sanderson's or Moulson's.

Hand Saws		26-in.	5/- each.
Panel Saws	24-in. 4/9,	26-in.	5/- ,,
Half Rip Saws	28-in. 5/6,	30-in.	6/- ,,

	8	9	10	12	14	16	18 in.
Iron Back Saws	3/-	3/-	3/6	4/-	4/6	5/-	5/9 ea.
Brass Back Saws	3/6	3/6	3/9	4/6	5/6	6/6	7/6 ,,
Compass Saws		1/-	1/3	1/6	1/9		,,
Turning Saw and } Frame }	3/-	3/3	3/9	4/3	5/-		,,

Turning Saw Blades, 4d. 5d. 6d. 7d. 8d. 9d. ,,
Fret or Pad Saw Blades... ... 6d. ,,
Chair Webs, 18 to 26 inches.
Warranted Cast Steel Cross Cut Saws,
 4½ft. 10/- 5ft. 12/- 5½ft. 13/- 6ft. 14/6 each.
Saw Pads, Beech, 1/-, Box, 1/6, Ebony, 1/10 each.
Saw Frame Handles, Beech, 1/-, Box, 1/6 pair.
 Circular Saws.

SAW SETS.

Beech Handled, 10d. Box Handled, 1/- each.
Box Handled, with Brass Guard ... 1/9 ,,
Patent Plyer Saw Sets ... 2/6 ,,
Punch Saw Sets, (PRESTON'S PATENT) ... 5/- ,,
Pit Saw Sets ... from -/6 to 1/6 ,,

CRAMPS.

WROUGHT IRON JOINERS' CRAMPS.

	3ft.	3ft. 6	4ft.	4ft. 6	5ft.	5ft. 6	6ft
	11/-	12/-	13/6	14/6	15/6	16/6	17/6 ea.
Improved	13/-	14/-	15/6	16/6	17/6	18/6	20/- ea.

SASH CRAMPS.

	18	21	24	27	30	33	36 in.
Iron Heads	8/-	9/-	10/-	11/-	12/-	12/6	13/6 pr.
Brass ,,	12/-	13/6	15/6	16/6	18/-	20/-	22/- pr.

COACHMAKERS' HAND CRAMPS.

To take in	5	6	7	8	9	10	11	12 inch.
	4/6	4/9	5/3	5/9	6/-	6/6	7/-	8/- each.

Kimberley's Flooring Dogs or Cramps ... 20/- pair.
Screw Bench Holdfasts ... 5/- each.
Hand Cramps ... 1/-, 1/3 & 1/6 ,,
Coopers' Bick Irons

5

CHISELS AND GOUGES,
Best Cast Steel Warranted.
(WARD'S, or HOWARTH'S.)

CHISELS.	⅛	¼	⅜	½	⅝	¾	⅞	1	1¼	1½	1¾	2in.
Firmer Chisels	-/4	-/4	-/4	-/5	-/5½	-/6	-/6½	-/7	-/10	1/-	1/3	1/6
Firmer ,, Bevilled Edges	-/9	-/9	-/9	-/10	-/10½	-/11	-/11½	1/1	1/5	1/7	1/10	2/1
Coachmakers' Chisels	-/6¼	-/6¼	-/7	-/8	-/9	-/10	-/11	1/-	1/4	1/7	2/-	2/5
Millwrights' Chisels	-/8½	-/8½	-/9	-/10½	1/-	1/2	1/4	1/6	2/-	2/5	2/10	3/6
Socket Chisels (Black)		-/11	-/11	-/11	1/-	1/1	1/2	1/3	1/6	1/9	2/-	2/4
Long Thin Paring Chisels	-/7	-/7	-/8	-/8	-/9	-/10	-/11	1/1	1/5	1/9	2/1	2/6
,, ,, ,, Bevilled Edges		1/-	1/1	1/1	1/2	1/3	1/4	1/6	2/-	2/4	2/11	3/3
Best Mortice Chisels	1/-	1/2	1/5	1/5	1/8	2/-						
Sash Chisels (London Pattern)	1/-	1/2	1/5	1/5	1/8	2/-						
Turning Chisels	-/6	-/6	-/6½	-/6½	-/7½	-/8	-/9	-/10½	1/1	1/5	1/9	2/-
GOUGES.	⅛	¼	⅜	½	⅝	¾	⅞	1	1¼	1½	1¾	2in.
Firmer Gouges	-/4½	-/5	-/5½	-/6	-/6½	-/7	-/8	-/9	1/-	1/3	1/6	1/10
Coachmakers' Gouges		-/10	-/10	-/11	1/-	1/1	1/2	1/3	1/8	2/-	2/4	2/10
Long Thin Paring Gouges		1/-	1/-	1/1	1/1	1/2	1/3	1/4	1/6	2/-	2/3	2/9	3/2
Socket Gouges (Black)			1/3	1/3	1/4	1/5	1/6	1/8	2/-		2/6	
Turning Gouges	-/7	-/7	-/8	-/9	-/10	-/11	1/1	1/2	1/7	2/-	2/6	3/-
Wheeler's Bruzzes			2/9	3/-	3/3	3/6						

4

METAL PLANES.

	2⅜	2¼ inch.
Iron Faced Rosewood Smoothing	8/6	9/- each.
,, ,, Boxwood	11/-	11/6 ,,

Improved Iron Smoothing Planes, 2¼-in. 17/- ,,
Iron Shoulder Planes ... 1½-in. 12/- ,,
Iron Bull Nose Planes ... 1 1/16-in. 5/- ,,
Iron Chariot Planes ... 1¼-in. 5/- ,,
Gun Metal Bull Nose ... 1 1/16-in. 7/- ,,
Gun Metal Chariot ... 1¼-in. 7/- ,,
Iron Shoes for 2¼-in. Smoothing Planes ... 2/3 ,,
Iron Fore Ends, with Cup and Screw ... 1/6 ,,

PLANE IRONS—BEST.
(Wards', Sarby's, or Howarth's.)

	To 1¾	2	2¼	2¼	2⅜	2¼ inch.
Cut Irons	8d.	9d.	10d.	11d.	1/-	1/1 each.
Double Irons	1/3	1/5	1/6	1/7½	1/7¼	1/11 ,,
Parallel Cut Irons	11½d.	1/-	1/1½	1/2¼	1/3	,,
D'ble Parallel ,,	1/9	1/10	2/-	2/2	2/3	,,

T Plane Irons ... 7d. and 8d. each.
Chariot Plane Irons ... 1¼-in. 7d. ,,
Bull Nose Plane Irons, 1 1/16 and 1⅛-in. 9d. ,,
Shoulder Plane Irons ... 1⅛-in. 10½d. ,,
Rabbet Plane Irons, Square, 5d., Skew 6½d. ,,
Sash Fillister Irons ... 6d. ,,
Soft Moulding Irons ... 4d. ,,
Bead Plane Irons ... 6d. ,,
Grooving Plane Irons ... 11d. pair.
Plough Irons ... Set of 8, 4/6, or 7d. each.

CHISELS AND GOUGES.—IN SETS.

Firmer Chisels ... set of 12, 1/16 to 1-in. 5/- set.
 ,, ,, ... set of 14, 1/16 to 1¼-in. 6/9 ,,
Coach Chisels ... set of 12, ⅛ to 2-in. 18/- ,,
Best Mortice Chisels, set of 8, ⅛ to 1 1/16-in. 9/6 ,,
Firmer Gouges ... set of 12, 1/16 to 1-in. 6/- ,,
Chisels and Gouges in sets, Handled.

7

HAMMERS.

Carpenters' Rivetting Hammers,
No. 1 2 3 4 5 6 7 8 9 10 11 12
6d. 7d. 8d. 10d. 1/- 1/2 1/4 1/6 1/8 1/10 2/- 2/3 ea.
Carpenters Rivetting, Handled,
9d. 10d. 1/- 1/2 1/4 1/6 1/8 1/10 2/- 2/2 2/4 2/9 ,,
Best Cast Steel Joiners' Hammers,
1/1 1/2 1/4 1/6 1/9 2/- 2/3 2/6 2/10 3/3 ,,
Best Cast Steel, Handled,
1/4 1/5 1/7 1/9 2/- 2/3 2/6 2/10 3/3 3/8 ,,
Coachmakers' 2-faced Framing Hammers, 9d. per lb. ,,
Ditto ditto Solid Cast Steel 1/4 ,,
Engineers' Best Cast Steel Hammers 1/6 ,,
Upholsterers' Hammers, 1/9 2/- 2/3 2/6 & 2/9 each.
Coach Trimmers' Hammers 2/3 2/6 & 2/9 ,,

AXES.

Coopers' 11d. per lb.
Best Kent and Felling Axes 1/- ,,
Wheelwrights' Axes 1/- ,,
CoachMakers' and other Side Axes 1/1 ,,
Best Cast Steel American Wedge Axes,
2½ to 3 lbs. 1/8; above 3 lbs. 1/6 per lb.

ADZES.

	No. 1	2	3	4	
Coopers'	2/6	2/8	2/10	3/-	each.
Carpenters' Adzes	2/9	3/-	3/3		,,
Boat Builders' Adzes	3/9	4/2	4/6		,,
Wheelwrights' Best					,,

COMPASSES.

Common -/4 to -/9 each
Ditto Wing 1/- 1/3 1/6 1/9 ,,
Beat do. 1/6 to 2/6 pair
Millwrights' 3/8 to 4/6 ,,
Spring Dividers 1/- to 2/- ,,
Drawing Instruments in Cases, 3/- to 10/- per set,
Coopers' Compasses from 6 to 18 inches.

BOXES & TAPS—FOR WOOD SCREWS.

Any size from ⅜ to 2½ inches.

8

BENCH SCREWS.

Black Iron Bench Screws, 18-in. × 1¾-in. 5/6 each.
18 × 1¾-in. 20 × 1¾-in. 22 × 1¼-in.
Bright ditto 7/- 9/- 12/- each.
Beech Bench Screws, 2-in. 1/9 2¼-in 2/3 2½-in. 2/6 ea.
Beech Hand Screws, 12-in. 1/4 14-in. 1/8 16-in. 2/3 ea,
Linen Press Screws to order.

RULES.

2-ft. Arch Joint Boxwood Rules -/9 each.
2-ft. ,, ,, ,, Bevilled edge 1/- ,,
2-ft. do. Extra Thin Double-bevilled 2/6 ,,
2-ft. Box Brass Slide Rules 1/6 & 2/6 ,,
2-ft. do. Routledge's Engineers' Rules 4/- ,,
2-ft. Four-fold Box Rules 1/-, 1/6, 1/9, & 2/- ,,
2-ft. Four-fold ,, with Slides 3/- ,,
3-ft. Four-fold Box Rules 2/3, 2/6, & 3/- ,,
4-ft. Four-fold Coachmakers' Rules 3/- 4/- & 5/- ,,
2-ft. Ironfounders' Contraction Rules, 2/6, & 3/6 ,,
2-ft. Brass Rules 1/2, 1/4 & 2/- ,,
2-ft. Common Iron Rules 6d. ,,
2-ft. Steel Rules, (Chesterman's) 1/3 ,,
1-ft. Engineers Steel Rules,
1/-, 1/3, 1/6, 1/9, 2/-, & 2/6 ,,
1-ft. Box Rules, with Spirit & Plumb Levels 3/6 ,,
1-ft. Ivory Rules 1/9 to 5/- ,,
2-ft. ,, ,, 7/6 to 25/- ,,
12-in. Architects' Scales Box, 2/- Ivory, 7/6 ,,
6-in. ,, ,, ,, 1/- ,, 4/6 ,,
Laths or Rules from 2 feet to 6
Tailors' Squares

TAPE MEASURES.

	33	40	50	66 ft.	
Narrow, in Ass Skin Case,	1/-	1/6	1/9		ea.
,, in Jap'd. Leather Case,	1/9	2/-	2/3	2/6	,,
Broad Linen in Leather ,,	3/3	3/6	3/9	4/6	,,
Chesterman's Metollic Tapes				8/6	,,

9

TURNSCREWS.

Best C. S. London Pattern.
3 4 5 6 8 10 12 inch.
6d. 8d. 10d. 1/- 1/4 1/8 2/- each.
Best Round Blade, Cabinet.
3 4 5 6 8 10 12 inch.
7d. 9d. 1/- 1/2 1/6 2/- 2/6 each.

CHISEL HANDLES.

Octagon, Beech or Ash 1/- doz.
Beech, turned & polished, with Brass Ferrules 1/6 ,,
Boxwood ,, ,, ,, 3/- ,,
Boxwood, Turned with Octagon Centres 3/6 ,,
Beech, Socket Chisel Handles 1½d. ea.
Beech, Mortice Chisel Handles 2d. ,,

PINCERS.

	6	6½	7	7½	8 inch.
Black Tower Pincers	9d.	10d.	11d.	1/-	1/2 pair.
Best Lancashire ,,	1/8	1/10	2/-	2/2	2/4 ,,

MALLETS.

Carpenters' Beech Mallets 1/3, 1/6 & 1/9 each.
,, with Mortice in Hdls. 1/9, 2/- & 2/3 ,,
Carpenters' Iron Mallets 1/3, 1/6 & 1/9 ,,
Tinmens' Round Box -/6 to 1/6 ,,

OIL STONES.

CHARLEY FOREST, 9d. to 2/6 ea. Slips, 4d. to 6d. ea.
Turkey 2/6 to 6/- each. 1/- ea.

GIMBLETS AND BRAD AWLS.

Best C. S. Shell Gimblets 2/9 per dozen.
,, Twist 3/3 ,,
⅛ ¾ ⅞ ½ inch.
Best Spike Gimblets, 6d. 8d. 10d. 1/- each.
Cast Steel Brad Awls 6d. pr. doz.
,, with Oval Polish'd Handles 1/6 ● ,,
PRESTON'S Patent Brad Awls, with 6 Bits 1/- each.
PRESTON'S Hollow Box Handles with 10 Tools 1/6
,, ,, ,, 15 ,, 3/6

APPENDIX IV - 4
Henry Preston Price List of Tools — 1875

10

SQUARES AND BEVELS.

	3	6	9	12 inch.
Plated Rosewood Squares	1/-	1/6	2/-	2/6 each.

Best Plated Ebony Squares.

3	$4\frac{1}{2}$	6	$7\frac{1}{2}$	9	12	15 inch.
1/3	1/6	1/9	2/-	2/6	3/6	4/6 each.

Improved Ebony Sliding Bevels.

6	$7\frac{1}{2}$	9	12 inch.
1/10	2/-	2/6	3/- each.

	8	10	12 in.
Plated Rosewood Mitre Squares	2/3	2/6	3/- ea.
Best Plated Ebony ,, ,,	3/3	3/9	4/6 ,,
Coachmaker's Spider Bevels		2/6	,,
Gun Metal Horizontal Squares		5/-	,,

GAUGES.

Marking Gauges, Beech, 8d. Boxwood, 1/3 each.
Cutting ,, Beech, 10d. Boxwood, 1/6 ,,
Mortice Gauges, Plated Rosewood .... 2/9 ,,
Mortice Gauges, Plated Ebony, Thumb-screw Slide..... .... 4/- ,,
Mortice Gauges, Plated Ebony Turn-screw Slide.................................. 4/- ,,
Mortice Gauges, Oval Ebony Head, Round Brass Stem .... 5/6 ,,
Combined Marking and Mortice Gauges, with Oval Ebony Head.................... 5/- ,,
Ditto ditto, with Brass Head .. .. 5/- ,,

DRAWING KNIVES.

	8	9	10 in.
Carpenters' Drawing Knives	1/6	1/7	1/10
Best ditto....................	1/10	2/-	2/3

Coopers' Drawing Knives, Tiggers' Axes. Adzes, Hammers, &c.

SPOKESHAVES.

	$1\frac{1}{2}$	2	$2\frac{1}{2}$	3	$3\frac{1}{2}$ in.
Best Beech Spokeshaves	9d.	9d.	11d.	1/-	1/3 ea.
Do. do. do. Plated	1/1	1/1	1/2	1/4	1/6 ,,
Do. do. Coachmakers'		1/5	1/6	1/9	,,
Bst. Boxwd. Spokeshaves	1/1	1/1	1/2	1/4	1/6 ,,
Ct. Stl. Spokeshave Irons					,,
Ditto Brush do.					
Ditto Coopers'					
Ditto Coach					

11

BRACES AND BITS.

Plated Beech Braces ... 3/- 3/9 5/- and 11/- each.
Scotch Iron Braces ... 4/6 5/- 6/- 7/6 & 10/- ,,
German Braces .... 1/3 1/6 2/- and 2/9 ,,
Iron Wagon Braces, $6\frac{1}{2}$ & 7 inch sweep, 5/6 each.
Best Plain Brace, 36 Black Bits 20/-
,, Plated ,, ,, Bright ,, ... 25/-
,, ,, ,, ,, Straw Coloured Bits......... 32/-
Patent Metalic Ebony Framed Brace, with 36 Bright Bits, 32/-; with Straw Coloured ditto 35/-
Scotch Iron Brace, 36 Black Bits 22/-
,, ,, ,, ,, Bright ,, ... 24/-
,, ,, ,, ,, ,, ,, Brass Neck 28/-
Long Screw Wagon Bits $\frac{7}{16}$ $\frac{9}{16}$ $\frac{11}{16}$ $\frac{13}{16}$ $\frac{15}{16}$ $\frac{17}{16}$ in.
Leadbeater's Pattern...... 1/3 1/6 1/6 1/9 2/- 2/3 ea.
Gilpin's Pattern .... 2/- 2/3 2/6 2/9 3/- 3/3 ea.

Gilpin's Patent Brace Bits.

$\frac{3}{8}$	$\frac{1}{2}$	$\frac{5}{8}$	$\frac{3}{4}$	$\frac{7}{8}$	1	$1\frac{1}{4}$	$1\frac{1}{2}$	$1\frac{3}{4}$	2 in.
1/4	1/6	1/8	1/10	2/1	2/4	3/-	3/6	4/6	5/6 ea.

Cast Steel Centre Bits,

-/4 -/4 -/$4\frac{1}{2}$ -/5 -/$5\frac{1}{2}$ -/6 -/8 -/10 1/- 1/2 ea.
Screw Nose Centre Bits 1/3 1/4 1/6 1/9 2/ ea.
To $\frac{1}{4}$ $\frac{5}{16}$ $\frac{3}{8}$ $\frac{7}{16}$ $\frac{1}{2}$ inch.
Black Shell & Nose Bits -/4 -/$4\frac{1}{2}$ -/5 -/6 -/7 each.
Boat Builders' Bits...... -/$4\frac{1}{2}$ -/5 -/6 -/8 -/10 ,,
Set of 36 Cast Steel Black Bits assorted........... 11/6
Set of 36 ,, ,, Bright Bits ,, ... 13/-
Best Shell Gimlet Bits......................... -/4 each.
,, Twist Gimlet Bits .... -/5 ,,
German Gimlet Bits .... -/$3\frac{1}{2}$,,
Patent American Spoke or Dowel Rounders & Bits,

$\frac{3}{4}$	$\frac{7}{8}$	1	$1\frac{1}{8}$
6/-	7/-	8/-	9/- each.

AUGERS.

Shell Augers, Tang'd

$\frac{3}{8}$	$\frac{1}{2}$	$\frac{5}{8}$	$\frac{3}{4}$	$\frac{7}{8}$	1	$1\frac{1}{4}$	$1\frac{1}{2}$	$1\frac{3}{4}$	2 inch.
-/6	-/7	-/8	-/10	1/-	1/2	1/6	1/8	2/-	2/4 each.

Screw Augers, Tanged,

-/10 -/10 1/- 1/2 1/4 1/6 2/- 2/4 2/9 3/3 ,,

Screw Augers, Eyed,

1/2 1/2 1/4 1/6 1/9 2/- 2/9 3/6 4/- 4/6 ,,

*Gilpin's Pattern Augers,

1/8 1/8 1/10 2/1 2/3 2/8 3/4 3/10 4/9 6/- ,,

12

SUNDRIES.

A great varity of Addis' Carving Tools.
Cumberland Pencils, Round or Oval... 8d. per doz.
Steel Name Punches, $2\frac{1}{2}$d. pr. letter, EX. J. SMITH 1/3
Figure Punches......................... from 2/- per set.
Letter Punches .... from 5/6 ,,
Glass Paper and Emery Cloth, Oakey's.
Vices, Plyers, and Cutting Nippers.
Bell Hangers' Plyers and Long Gimlets.
Tinmen's Hand Shears and Bench Shears.
Glue Pots, Pruning Saws, Oil Cans.
Bill Hooks, Choppers and Hatchets,
Plumbers' Mallets, Chase Wedges, Dressers, Turnpins, Shave Hooks, and Knives.
Gauges for Wire and Metal, &c.
Amateurs' Tool Chests.................. 3/6 to £5 each.
Carpenters' Tool Baskets............... 1/6 & 1/9 each.
Carpenters' Lined ,, ... 2/6 & 3/- ,,
Grinding Iron Stones in Frames, from 6 to 22 inches.
All kinds of Coopers' Tools kept in stock.
Gun Files and Rasps.
Cabinet Rifflers.
Saw Files.
Mill ditto ditto.
Gun Tools of every description.

Every Article Warranted.

Carriage Paid on all amounts above 20/-

☞ *Post Office Orders to be made payable at Head Office, to*

HENRY PRESTON,

LICHFIELD STREET, BIRMINGHAM.

	REF	DATING	NOTES
E.PRESTON	A	1825 —	This is the earliest Preston mark and is not common
E.PRESTON 77 LICHFIELD ST BIRM	B	— 1855	Use of this mark presumed to cease in 1855 as the Lichfield St. premises were renumbered (97)
E.PRESTON	C	Uncertain	Likely a mark of E.P. Senior
E.PRESTON	D	Uncertain	Likely a mark of E.P. Senior
E·PRESTON	E		Likely a mark of E.P. Junior
E·PRESTON	F		Likely a mark of E.P. Junior
H.PRESTON 4 ASTON ST LATE OF LICHFIELD ST BIRM	G	1874 - 1883	This is a rare mark. Henry Preston
E.PRESTON TRADE MARK	H	— 1876 - 1889	

E. PRESTON & SONS EP TRADE MARK	I	1889 —	
TRADE MARK EP	J	1880's - 1900's	Used on planes sold to dealers who were also expected to mark the item
EDWD PRESTON & SONS TRADE EP MARK WARRANTED	K	1920's	
TRADE EP MARK	L		Rare mark. Probably intended for use on items also to be marked by the vendor
EDWD PRESTON & SONS TRADE EP MARK WARRANTED B' HAM. ENG	M	1920's-30's	This mark exists in 2 sizes. The larger size is usually found on bench planes but has been recorded on a moulding plane also
EDWD PRESTON & SONS TRADE EP MARK WARRANTED B' HAM. ENG	N		

NOTES:

1. The marks are drawn actual size but have been drawn by eye and may, therefore, vary somewhat from the original.

2. They are listed in what I believe to be chronological order.

3. If anybody has planes bearing marks other than these, would you please let me know.

WHITTALL WORKS,

BIRMINGHAM, ENG.

May, 1909.

We have pleasure in submitting this edition (No. 18) of catalogue of goods of our manufacture.

In doing so it is a gratification to us to state that our aim in placing upon the market a reliable article and introducing improvements from time to time, has resulted in an increased demand for our manufactures.

The catalogue has undergone entire revision, many new articles being added.

Our Specialities are:

<u>RULES, LEVELS, PLUMBS and LEVELS, PLANES,</u>

and various

<u>PATENTED IMPROVED HAND TOOLS,</u>

including

<u>Iron Planes, Iron Spokeshaves, Chamfer Shaves,</u>

<u>Reeding Tools, Saw Sets, etc.</u>

These have met with considerable favor and may be recommended with confidence by Dealers to all users of Tools.

Our goods may be known by the colour of our packing, all the articles being packed in *yellow* coloured boxes, similar to the cover of this catalogue.

We give below copies of our registered Trade Marks, and take this opportunity of thanking our numerous Customers for their support in the past, and hope this edition of our catalogue may be the means of increasing our business relations.

EDWARD PRESTON & SONS, LTD.

—— REGISTERED TRADE MARKS. ——

T. BRADBURN & SONS

INDEX.

INDEX.—*Continued.*

EDWARD PRESTON & SONS, L^{TD.}

The Rules catalogued in the following pages comprise a very large range of patterns in common use. They are made of well seasoned material and may confidently be accepted as "British Standard Measures."

ONE FOOT FOUR-FOLD BOXWOOD RULES.

French Polished.   Packed in Dozens in Cardboard Boxes.

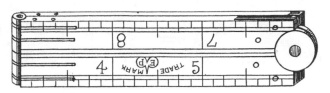

No 3232.   Round Joint, marked 8ths, ⅝-inch wide   ...   .   4/4 per dozen.
" 3132.   "   "   as 3232 mounted 6 Rules on a card   ...   ...   4/10   "

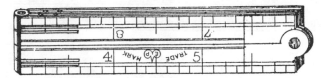

No. 3032.   Square Joint, marked 8ths and 16ths, ⅝-inch wide   ...   .   6/3 per dozen.

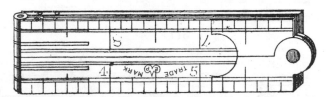

No. 3112.   Arch Joint, marked 8ths and 16ths, ⅞-inch wide   ...   .   8/9 per dozen.

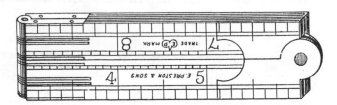

No. 3212.   Arch Joint, Edge plates. marked 8ths and 16ths. ⅞-inch wide   ...   .   11/9 per dozen.

GENT'S THIN ONE FOOT FOUR-FOLD BOXWOOD RULES.

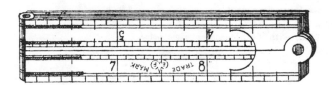

No. 3230.   Arch Joint, Brass Mounts, marked 8ths. 16ths, 10ths, 12ths, ⅝-inch wide; thin   ...   12/- per dozen.
" N3230.   "   G.S   "   "   "   "   "   ..   18/-   "

Any of the above No's if marked Two Measures, 6d. per dozen extra.

Drawings are full size.

EDWARD PRESTON & SONS, L^{TD}.

TWO FEET FOUR-FOLD BOXWOOD RULES
AND PRICES OF
TWO FEET and THREE FEET FOUR-FOLD BOXWOOD RULES.

Packed in Dozens in Cardboard Boxes.

Inches marked in 8ths and 16ths.

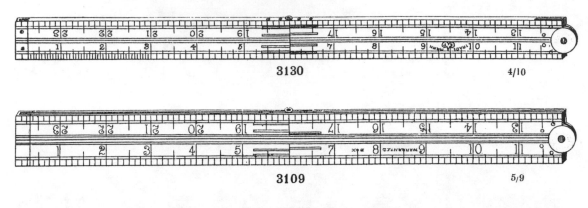

3130   4/10

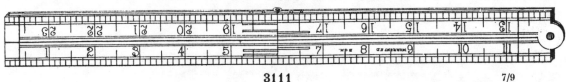

3109   5/9

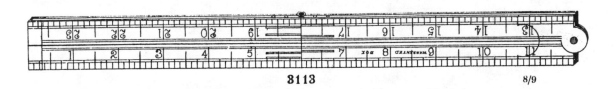

3111   7/9

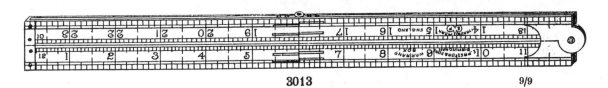

3113   8/9

3013   9/9

							2-ft.	3-ft.	
No. 3128.	Round Joint, thick, English Measure only,		⅝-inch wide	...	...	...	4/4	—	per dozen.
,, 3129.	As 3128, but mounted Six Rules on a card	...	⅝-inch ,,	...	...	...	4/10	—	,,
,, 3130.	Round Joint, extra thick	...	⅝-inch ,,	...	...	...	4/10	6/9	,,
	3130, with Two Measures, same price.								
,, 3109.	Round Joint, French Polished	...	1-inch ,,	...	...	...	5/9	7/3	,,
,, 3111.	Square Joint ,, ,,	...	1-inch ,,	...	...	...	7/9	9/3	,,
,, 3112.	Arch Joint ,, ,,	...	⅝-inch ,,	...	...	...	8/9	—	,,
,, 3113.	,, ,, ,, ,,	...	1-inch ,,	...	...	...	8/9	10/3	,,
,, 3013.	,, ,, inches in 8ths, 16ths, 10ths and 12ths, French Polished 1-inch ,,	...		...	...		9/9	11/9	,,

If marked Two Measures 6d. per dozen extra.

Drawings are Half Size.

EDWARD PRESTON & SONS, LTD.

TRADE EP MARK.

TWO FEET FOUR-FOLD BOXWOOD RULES
AND PRICES OF
TWO FEET and THREE FEET FOUR-FOLD BOXWOOD RULES.

Packed in Half-dozens in Cardboard Boxes.

Inches marked in 8ths and 16ths.   French Polished.

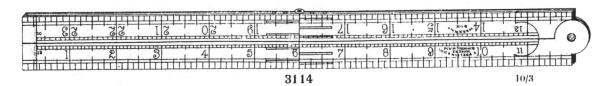

3114   10/3

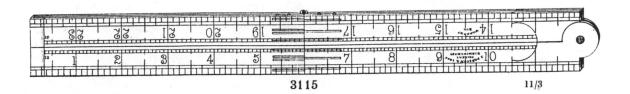

3115   11/3

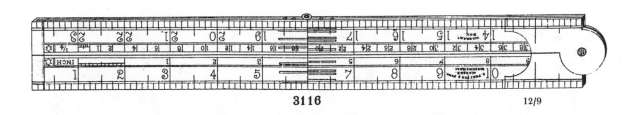

3116   12/9

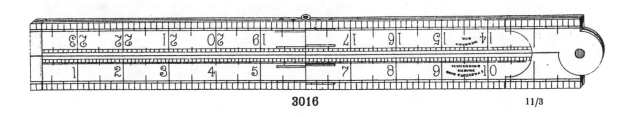

3016   11/3

				2-ft.	3-ft.
No 3114.	Arch Joint, inches in 8ths, 16ths, 10ths and 12ths, 1⅜-inch wide			10/3	12/3 per dozen.
,, 3115.	,, ,, ,, ,, 1⅝-inch ,, ...			11/3	13/6 ,,
,, 3116.	,, 8ths, 16ths and Scales ... 1½ inch ,, ...			12/9	15/6 ,,
. 3016.	,, 8ths, 16ths, 10ths and 12ths, English Measure only, 1⅛ inch wide			11/3	13/6 ,,

If marked Two Measures, 6d. per dozen extra.

Drawings are Half Size.

TRADE (E P) MARK.

TWO FEET FOUR-FOLD BOXWOOD RULES
AND PRICES OF
TWO FEET and THREE FEET FOUR-FOLD BOXWOOD RULES.
WITH EXTRA STRONG SMALL JOINTS.
Packed in Half-dozens in Cardboard Boxes.

Inches marked in 8ths and 16ths.   French Polished.

Rules Nos. 3054, 3057, 3071 and 3075 have one outside edge Bevelled.

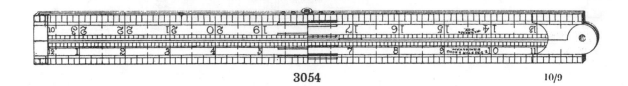

3054   10/9

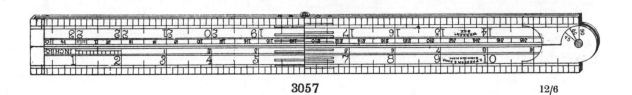

3057   12/6

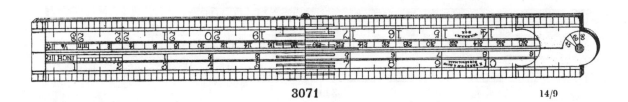

3071   14/9

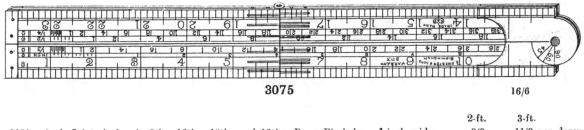

3075   16/6

				2-ft.	3-ft.	
No. 3050.	Arch Joint, inches in 8ths, 16ths, 10ths and 12ths, Brass Pin-holes	¾-inch wide		9/9	11/9	per dozen.
,, 3054.	,, ,, ,, ,, ,, ,, ,,	1-inch ,,		10/9	12/9	,,
,, 3057.	,, inches in 8ths, 16ths and Scales, Angles on Joint	1¼-inch ,,		12/6	15/6	,,
,, 3071.	,, ,, ,, ,, ,, ,,	1⅜-inch ,,		14/9	17/6	,,
,, 3075.	,, ,, ,, ,, ,, ,,	1½-inch ,,		16/6	19/6	,,

Above Pattern Rules may be had with Iron Tips, but without Angles on Joints, at List Prices. When so required please order them under Nos 3150, 3154, 3157, 3171, and 3175.

If marked Two Measures, 1/- per dozen extra.

Drawings are Half Size.

EDWARD PRESTON & SONS, L<u>TD.</u>

TWO FEET FOUR-FOLD BOXWOOD RULES
AND PRICES OF
TWO FEET and THREE FEET FOUR-FOLD BOXWOOD RULES.

THE SMALL JOINTS OF THESE RULES HAVE OUTSIDE EDGE PLATES WHICH FORM PART OF THE JOINT.
THUS GIVING STRENGTH AND DURABILITY.

Packed in Half-dozens in Cardboard Boxes

Inches marked in 8ths and 16ths.   French Polished.

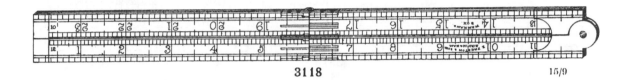

3118   15/9

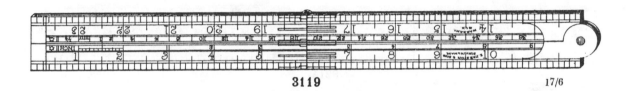

3119   17/6

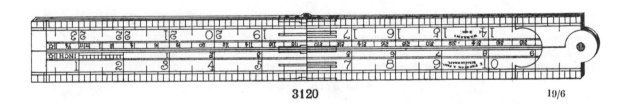

3120   19/6

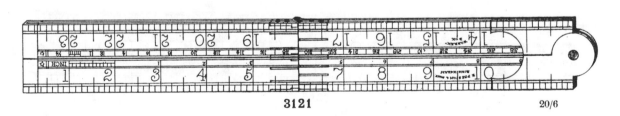

3121   20/6

									2-ft.	3-ft.	
No. 3117.	Arch Joint, edge plates, inches in 8ths, 16ths, 10ths and 12ths						$\frac{3}{4}$-inch wide	...	15/9	18/6	per dozen.
,, 3118.	,,	,,	,,	,,	,,	,,	1-inch ,,	..	15/9	18/6	,,
,, 3119.	,,	,,	,, inches in 8ths, 16ths and Scales				$1\frac{1}{8}$-inch ,,	...	17/6	20/6	,,
,, 3120.	,,	,,	,,	,,	,,	,,	$1\frac{3}{8}$-inch ,,	...	19/6	22/6	,,
,, 3121.	,,	,,	,,	,,	,,	,,	$1\frac{1}{2}$-inch ,,	...	20/6	23/6	,,

If marked Two Measures, 1/- per dozen extra.

Drawings are Half Size.

EDWARD PRESTON & SONS, L^{TD.}

TWO FEET FOUR-FOLD BOXWOOD RULES

AND PRICES OF

TWO FEET and THREE FEET FOUR-FOLD BOXWOOD RULES.

WITH THREE ARCH JOINTS.

Packed in Half-dozens in Cardboard Boxes.

Inches marked in 8ths and 16ths.   French Polished.

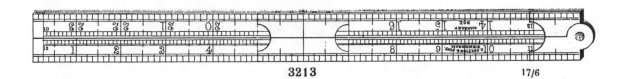

3213   17/6

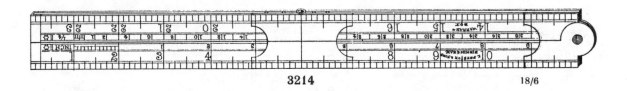

3214   18/6

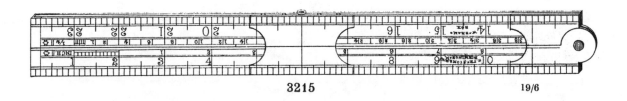

3215   19/6

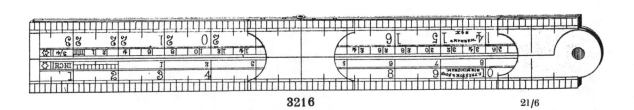

3216   21/6

			2-ft.	3-ft.
No. 3213.	Three Arch Joints, inches in 8ths, 16ths, 10ths and 12ths, Brass Pin-holes, 1-inch wide		17/6	20/6 per dozen.
„ 3214.	„ „ „ inches in 8ths, 16ths and Scales „ 1½-inch „		18/6	21/6 „
„ 3215.	„ „ „ „ „ „ „ „ 1⅜-inch „		19/6	22/6 „
„ 3216.	„ „ „ „ „ „ „ „ 1½-inch „		21/6	24/6 „

If marked Two Measures, 1/- per dozen extra.

Drawings are Half Size.

EDWARD PRESTON & SONS, L^{TD.}

TWO FEET FOUR-FOLD BOXWOOD RULES

AND PRICES OF

TWO FEET and THREE FEET FOUR-FOLD BOXWOOD RULES.

WITH BRASS BOUND EDGES.

Packed in Half-dozens in Cardboard Boxes.

Inches marked in 8ths and 16ths.   French Polished.

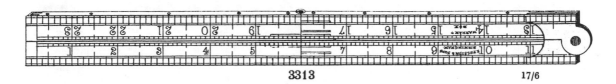

3313   **17/6**

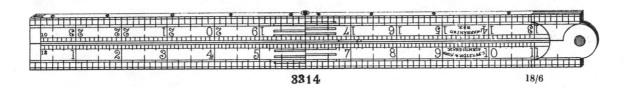

3314   **18/6**

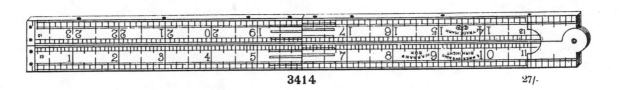

3315   **21/6**

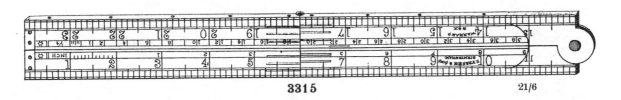

3414   **27/-**

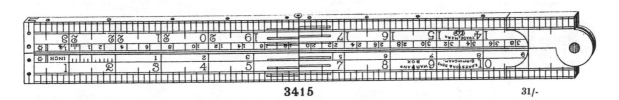

3415   **31/-**

									2 feet	3 feet	
No. 3313.	Arch Joint, Brass bound outside edges, inches in 8ths, 16ths, 10ths and 12ths,							1-in. wide	17/6	23/9 per doz.	
,, 3314.	,,	,,	,,	,,	,,	,,	,,	1¼-in. ,,	18/6	24/9 ,,	
,, 3315.	,,	,,	,,	,,	inches in 8ths, 16ths and Scales			1⅜-in. ,,	21/6	32/- ,,	
,, 3316.	,,	,,	,,	,,	,,	,,	,,	1½-in. ,,	25/-	35/- ,,	
,, 3414.	,, Brass bound inside and outside edges, inches in 8ths, 16ths, 10ths &							1⅛-in. ,,	27/-	39/- ,,	
,, 3415.	,,	,,	,,	,,	inches in 8ths, 16ths and Scales			1⅜-in. ,,	31/-	44/- ,,	
,, 3416.	,,	,,	,,	,,	,,	,,	,,	1½-in. ,,	35/-	49/- ,,	

If marked Two Measures, 1/- per dozen extra.

Drawings are Half Size.

EDWARD PRESTON & SONS, L^{TD.}

TWO FEET FOUR-FOLD BOXWOOD RULES

AND PRICES OF

TWO FEET and THREE FEET FOUR-FOLD BOXWOOD RULES.

Packed in Half-dozens in Cardboard Boxes.

TRADE  MARK.

ARCHITECTS' RULES with BEVELLED INSIDE EDGES.

These Rules have the inside Edges Bevelled and marked with various Drawing Scales.
Inches marked in 8ths, 16ths, 10ths and 12ths.   French Polished.

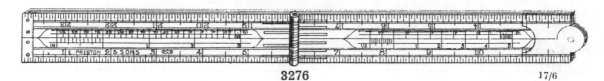

3276   17/6

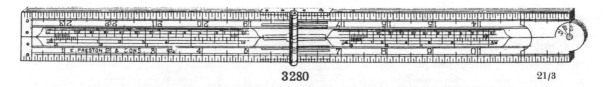

3280   21/3

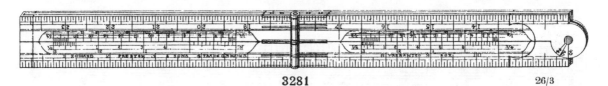

3281   26/3

								2 ft.	3-ft.
No. 3276.	Arch Joint, Bevelled Edges, with 4 Scales	...	1-inch wide	...	...	17/6	— per dozen.
„ 3280.	„	Brass Edge Plates „ 8 „	...	1-inch „	...	...	21/3	29/3 „
„ 3281.	„	„ „ „ 8 „	...	1⅛-inch „	...	..	26/3	35/- „
„ 3285.	„	„ „ „ 8 „	...	1½-inch „	...	...	29/3	— „

If marked London and Metre, 3/- per dozen extra.

EXTRA BEST ARCHITECTS' RULES.

These Rules are not French Polished, but have Special Finish.

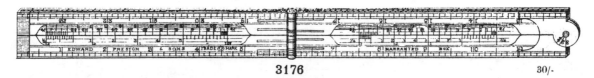

3176   30/-

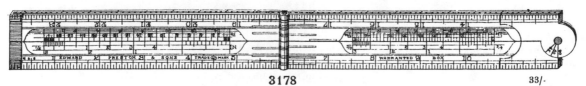

3178   33/-

							2-ft.	3-ft.
No. 3176.	Arch Joint, Bevelled Edges, 8 Scales	...	1-inch wide	...	...	...	30/-	38/- per dozen.
„ 3178.	„	„	„	...	1⅛-inch „	...	...	...	33/-	42/- „
„ 3278.	„	„	„	...	1⅜-inch „	...	...	...	36/-	46/- „

If marked London and Metre, 3/- per dozen extra.

Drawings are Half Size.

EDWARD PRESTON & SONS, L^{TD.}

TWO FEET FOUR-FOLD BOXWOOD RULES
AND PRICES OF
TWO FEET and THREE FEET FOUR-FOLD BOXWOOD RULES.
Packed in Half-dozens in Cardboard Boxes.

ARCHITECTS' RULES, with GERMAN SILVER MOUNTS.
French Polished.

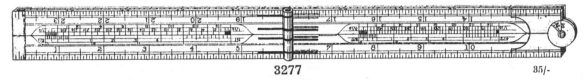

3277   35/-

	2-ft.	3-ft.

No. 3277. Arch Joint, G.S. Mounts, Bevelled Edges, 8 Scales, 1-inch wide ... ... 35/- 44/- per dozen.

EXTRA BEST ARCHITECTS' RULES, with GERMAN SILVER MOUNTS.
These Rules are not French Polished, but have Special Finish.

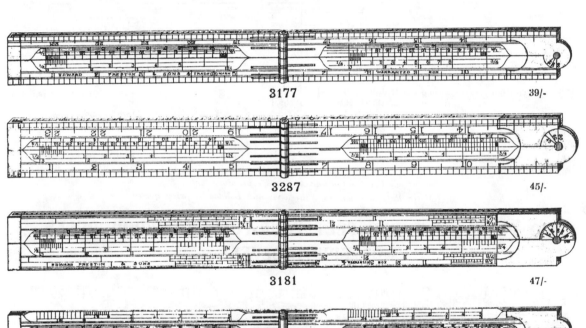

3177   39/-

3287   45/-

3181   47/-

3180B   53/-

						2-ft.	3-ft.	
No. 3177.	Arch Joint,	G.S. Mounts,	Bevelled Edges, with 8 Scales, 1-inch wide	...	..	39/-	50/-	per dozen.
,, 3287.	,,	G.S.	,,	,,	,, 1¼-inch ,,	...	...	45/-	56/-	,,
,, 3181	,,	G.S.	,,	,,	16 ,, 1⅜-inch ,,	...	...	47/-	58/-	,,
,, 3282.	,,	G.S.	,, and Edge Plates, with 16 Scales 1¼-inch ,,	...	...	60/-	72/-	,,
,, 3283.	,,	G.S.	,, ,, ,, ,, 16 ,, 1⅜-inch ,,	...	...	64/-	76/-	,,
,, 3180B.	,,	G.S.	,, 8 Bevels, 8 Drawing Scales, 4 Chain Scales 1-inch wide	...	53/-	—	,,
,, 3181B.	,,	G.S.	,, ,, ,, ,, 1⅛-inch ,,	...	64/-	—	,,
,, 3288	,,	G.S.	,, Bevelled Edges, with 16 Scales and Slide 1⅜-inch ,,	...	6/9	—	each.
,, 3289	,,	G.S.	,, ,, ,, and Calliper gauge 1⅜ inch ,,	...	6/9	—	each.

If marked London and Metre, 3/- per dozen extra.

Drawings are Half Size.

EDWARD PRESTON & SONS, L^{TD.}

EXTRA BEST TWO FEET, THREE FEET and 1 METRE FOUR-FOLD BOXWOOD RULES.

WITH STEEL TIPS AND STEEL PLATES IN JOINTS.

Packed in Half-dozens in Cardboard Boxes.

These Rules are not French Polished, but have Special Finish.

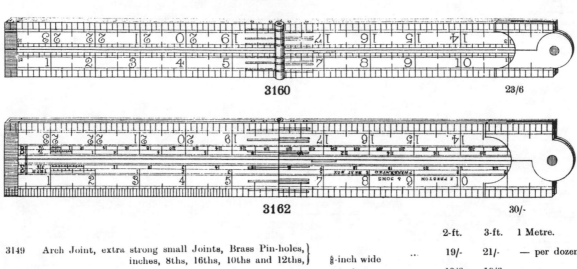

3160   23/6

3162   30/-

							2-ft.	3-ft.	1 Metre.
No 3149	Arch Joint, extra strong small Joints, Brass Pin-holes, inches, 8ths, 16ths, 10ths and 12ths,					⅝-inch wide	...	19/-	21/-	— per dozen.
,, 3148.	,,	,,	,,	,, .	,,	¾-inch ,,	...	18/6	19/6	— ,,
,, 3151.	,,	,,	,,	,,	and Scales	1-inch ,,	...	19/6	21/-	29/- ,,
,, 3160.	,,	,,	,,	,,	,,	1¼-inch ,,	...	23/6	26/-	34/- ,,
,, 3161.	,,	,,	,,	,,	,,	1⅜-inch ,,	...	26/6	28/6	36/6 ,,
,, 3162	,,	,,	,,	,,	,,	1½-inch ,,	...	30/-	32/-	40/- ,,

If marked London and Metre, 2/- per dozen extra.

Metre Rules are marked Millimetres and London at prices quoted.

TWO FEET and THREE FEET FOUR-FOLD BOXWOOD RULES, with SPIRIT LEVELS.

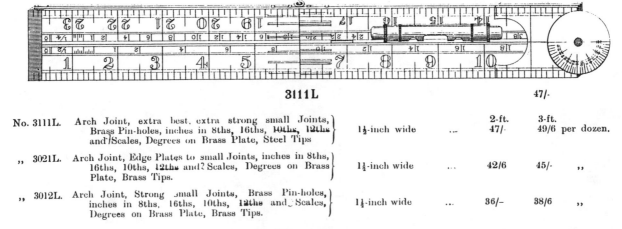

3111L   47/-

			2-ft.	3-ft.
No. 3111L.	Arch Joint, extra best, extra strong small Joints, Brass Pin-holes, inches in 8ths, 16ths, 10ths, 12ths and Scales, Degrees on Brass Plate, Steel Tips	1½-inch wide ...	47/-	49/6 per dozen.
,, 3021L.	Arch Joint, Edge Plates to small Joints, inches in 8ths, 16ths, 10ths, 12ths and Scales, Degrees on Brass Plate, Brass Tips.	1½-inch wide ...	42/6	45/- ,,
,, 3012L.	Arch Joint, Strong small Joints, Brass Pin-holes, inches in 8ths, 16ths, 10ths, 12ths and Scales, Degrees on Brass Plate, Brass Tips.	1¼-inch wide ...	36/-	38/6 ,,

French Polished.

Drawings are Half Size.

EDWARD PRESTON & SONS, L^{TD}.

TWO FEET FOUR-FOLD BOXWOOD RULES

AND PRICES OF

TWO FEET and THREE FEET FOUR-FOLD BOXWOOD RULES, with BRASS SLIDES.

Packed in Half Dozens in Cardboard Boxes.   Inches marked in 8ths and 16ths.

French Polished.

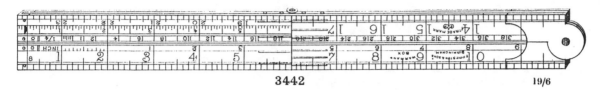

3442   **19/6**

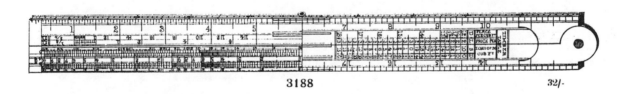

3443   **19/6**

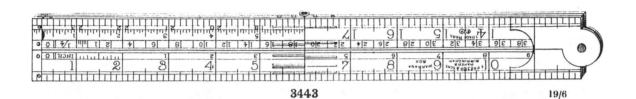

3444   **23/6**

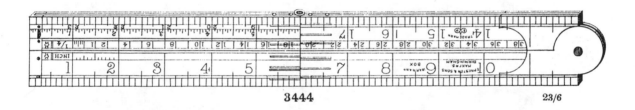

3188   **32/-**

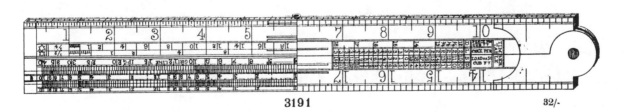

3191   **32/-**

				2 feet.	3 feet.
No. 3442.	Arch Joint, Slide marked inches in 16ths	1⅛ inch wide	19/6	25/6 per dozen.
,, 3443	,, ,, ,, ,, ,, ...	1⅜ ,,	19/6	25/6 ,,
,, 3444	,, ,, ,, ,, ,, ...	1½ ,,	23/6	29/- ,,
,, 3188.	,, ,, Inches in 8ths, 10ths, 12ths, 16ths, Scales and Timber Table ...	1⅛ ,,	32/-	41/6 ,,
,, 3191.	,, ,, ,, ,, ,, ,, ,, ,, ...	1½ ,,	32/-	41/6 ,,

If marked Two Measures, 2/- per dozen extra.   If marked London and Metre 3/- per dozen extra.

Drawings are Half Size.

EDWARD PRESTON & SONS, L<u>TD</u>.

TWO-FEET FOUR-FOLD BOXWOOD RULES WITH BRASS SLIDES AND CALLIPER GAUGES

Packed in Half Dozens in Cardboard Boxes.   Inches marked in 8ths and 16ths.

French Polished.

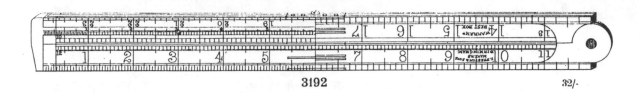

3192   32/-

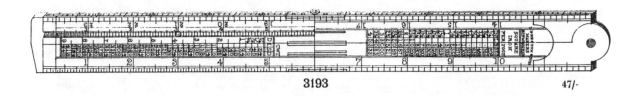

3193   47/-

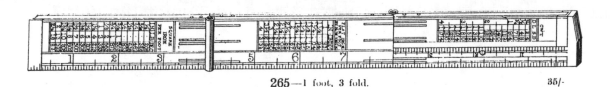

265—1 foot, 3 fold.   35/-

						2-feet.	
No 3192.	Arch Joint, marked inches in 8ths, 16ths, 10ths and 12ths, Calliper Gauge				1½ inch wide	32/- per dozen.	
,, 3196.	,, ,, ,, , ,, ,, ,, ,, Scales, Calliper Gauge				1¼ ,,	35/-	,,
,, 3193.	,, ,, Ironmongers' Rule ...	...	...	...	1⅛ ,,	47/-	,,
,, 265.	One-foot, Three fold Ironmongers' Rule ...	...	...	...	1⅜ ,,	35/-	,,

If marked Two Measures, 2/- per dozen extra.   *If marked London and Metre, 3/- per dozen extra.*

COACHMAKERS' FOUR FEET FOUR-FOLD BOXWOOD RULES.

							4-feet.	
No. 3271.	Arch Joint, inches in 8ths, 16ths, 10ths 12ths and Scales	...	..	...	1⅜-inch wide	29/3 per dozen.		
,, 3275.	,, ,, ,, ,, ,, ...	...	...	1½ ,,	29/3	,,		
,, 3220.	,, ,, ,, ,, ,, Edge plates to small joints			1⅜ ,,	35/-	,,		
,, 3221.	,, ,, ,, ,, ,, ,, ,, ,,			1½ ,,	35/-	,,		
,, 32218.	,, ,, ,, ,, ,, with 12-inch brass slide ...			1½ ,,	58/6	,,		
,, 3261.	,, Extra Best, with Steel Tips, and Steel Plates in joints ...		...	1⅜ ,,	37/-	,,		
,, 3262.	,, ,, ,, ,, ,, ,, ...	...	1½ ,,	42/-	,,			

EDWARD PRESTON & SONS, L^{TD.}

BOXWOOD RULES AND CALLIPER GAUGES.

TRADE E︶P MARK.

French Polished.   Packed in Half Dozens in Cardboard Boxes.

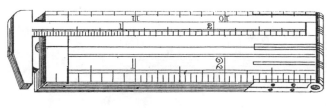

ONE FOOT FOUR-FOLD BOXWOOD RULE, WITH SLIDE AND CALLIPER GAUGE.

No. 3248.   ¾-inch wide   ...   . 24/- per dozen.

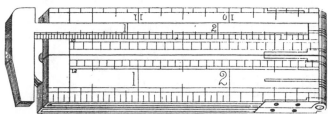

ONE FOOT FOUR-FOLD BOXWOOD RULE, WITH SLIDE AND CALLIPER GAUGE.

No. 3088.   1-inch wide   ...   . 25/- per dozen

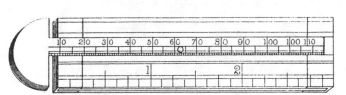

SIX INCH TWO-FOLD BOXWOOD CALLIPER GAUGE.

No. 3046.   1-inch wide   ...   . 14/6 per dozen.

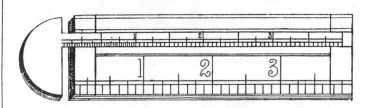

BOXWOOD BUTTON GAUGE.

Slide marked in 40ths.

No. 3045.   3 inches long, ¾ inch wide   ... 13/6 per dozen.

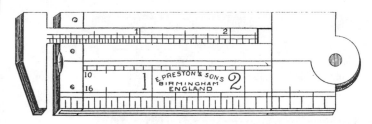

BOXWOOD CALLIPER GAUGE.

No. 3044.   3 inches long, 1 inch wide   ... 13/6 per dozen.
„   3144.   4   „   „   „   ... 17/6   „

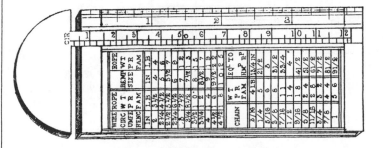

BOXWOOD ROPE AND CHAIN GAUGE.

No. 3776.   4 inches long ...   . 21/6 per dozen.
„   3777.   6   „   ...   . 29/-   „

BOXWOOD HATTERS' RULE.

No. 3676.   Wood Slide, 5 inches long, ¾-inch wide... 13/6 per dozen.
„   3677.   Brass   „   „   „   „   ... 16/6   „
„   3678.   Ivory   „   „   „   „   ... 31/6   „

EDWARD PRESTON & SONS, LᵀᴰP.

TWO-FEET TWO-FOLD BOXWOOD RULES.

Packed in Dozens in Cardboard Boxes.　　　Inches marked in 8ths and 16ths.

French Polished.

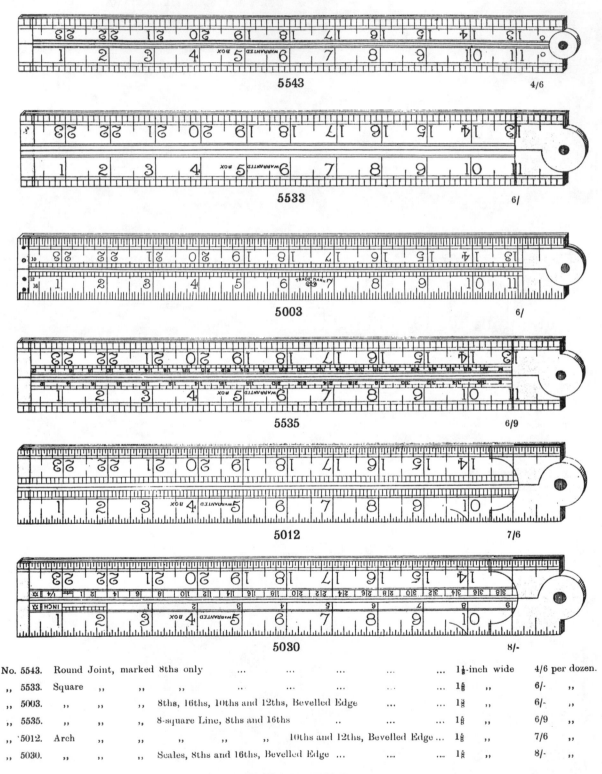

No. 5543.	Round Joint, marked 8ths only						1¼-inch wide	4/6 per dozen.
,, 5533.	Square ,,	,,	,,	..	...	...	..	1⅜ ,,	6/- ,,
,, 5003.	,, ,,	,, 8ths, 16ths, 10ths and 12ths, Bevelled Edge				...	1⅜ ,,	6/- ,,
,, 5535.	,, ,,	,, 8-square Line, 8ths and 16ths		..	...	...	1⅝ ,,	6/9 ,,
,, 5012.	Arch ,,	,, ,, ,, ,, 10ths and 12ths, Bevelled Edge			...	1⅝ ,,	7/6 ,,
,, 5030.	,, ,,	,, Scales, 8ths and 16ths, Bevelled Edge ...		...	...	1⅝ ,,	8/- ,,

Drawings are Half Size.

EDWARD PRESTON & SONS, L^{TD}.

TWO FEET TWO-FOLD BOXWOOD RULES.

Packed in Dozens in Cardboard Boxes

Inches marked in 8ths and 16ths.   French Polished.

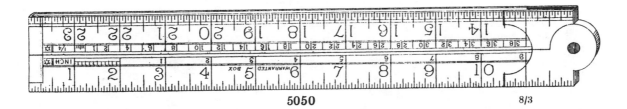

5050   8/3

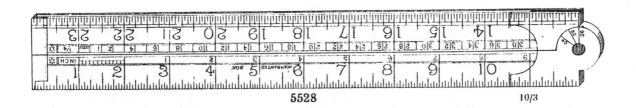

5528   10/3

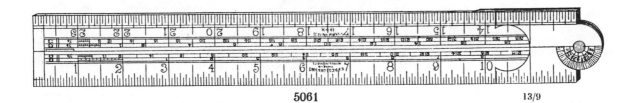

5130   11/9

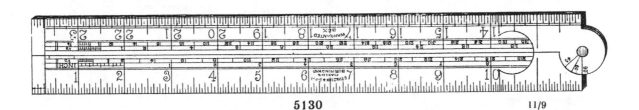

5061   13/9

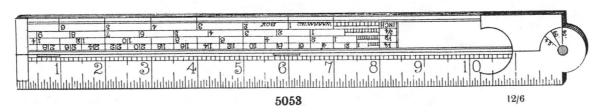

5053   12/6

No. 5050.	Arch Joint, marked 8-Square Lines, Scales, 8ths and 16ths, Bevelled Edge, 1⅝-inch wide ...	8/3 per dozen.
,, 5528. ,,	Brass Pin-holes, marked 8-Square Lines, Scales, 8ths and 16ths, Angles on Joint, Bevelled Edge ,,	10/3 ,,
,, 5130 ,, ,,	4 Scales and 8-Square Line, Bevelled Edge ,,	11/9 ,,
,, 5061 ,, ,,	4 ,, ,, Double Bevelled Edges ,,	13/9 ,,
,, 5053 ,, ,,	4 ,, ,, and 10ths, Bevelled Edge ,,	12/6 ,,

Drawings are Half Size.

EDWARD PRESTON & SONS, L^TD.

TWO FEET TWO-FOLD BOXWOOD RULES.

Packed in Dozens in Cardboard Boxes.

Inches marked in 8ths and 16ths.   French Polished.

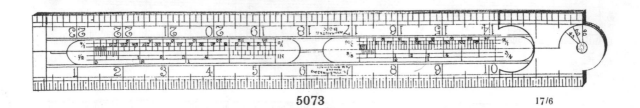

5073   17/6

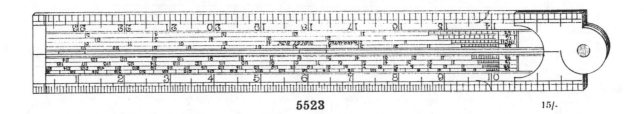

5523   15/-

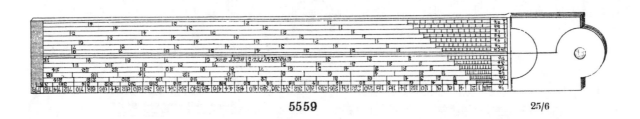

5559   25/6

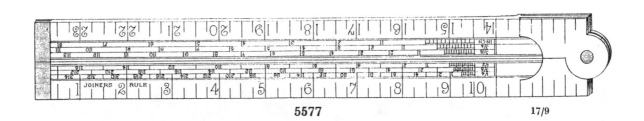

5577   17/9

No. 5073.   Arch Joint, Brass Pin-holes, 8 Scales and 8-Square Lines, 4 Inside Bevelled Edges,   1⅛-inch wide   17/6 per dozen.

  ,, 5065.   ,,   ,,   4   ,,   ,,   4   ,,   ,,   ...   ,,   14/-   ,,

  ,, 5523.   ,,   ,,   8   ,,   ,,   Double   ,,   ...   ,,   15/-   ,,

  ,, 5559.   ,,   ,,   14   ,,   ,,   ,,   ,,   ...   ,,   25/6   ,,

  ,, 5577.   ,,   ,,   6   Scales, inches in 4ths, 8ths, 10ths, 12ths and 16ths }
Double Bevelled Edges }   ,,   17/9   ,,

Drawings are Half Size.

EDWARD PRESTON & SONS, L<u>TD</u>.

TRADE ⒺⓅ MARK.

TWO FEET TWO-FOLD BOXWOOD RULES.

Packed in Dozens in Cardboard Boxes.

Inches marked in 8ths and 16ths.   French Polished.

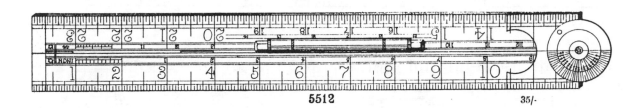

5579   27/-

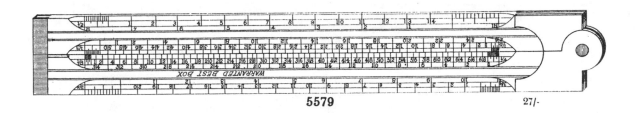

5512   35/-

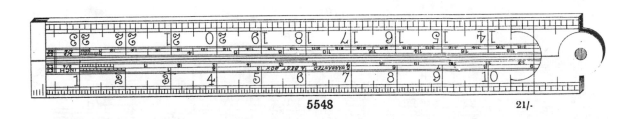

5548   21/-

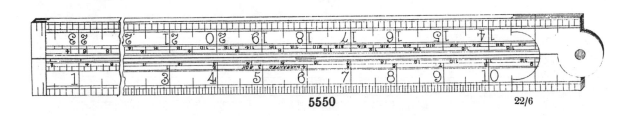

5550   22/6

No. 5579.	Arch Joint, Brass Pin-holes 8 Scales, Inches in 8ths, 10ths, 12ths and 16ths, Four Bevelled Edges	1⅝-inch wide	27/- per dozen.
„ 5512.	Arch Joint, Spirit Level, Brass Pin-holes, Scales and 8-square Line, Degrees on Brass Plate	1⅝ „	35/- „
„ 5513.	Arch Joint, Spirit Level, Brass Pin-holes, Scales and 8-square Line, Degrees on Brass Plate, with Brass Slide	1⅝ „	45/- „
„ 5548.	Arch Joint, Brass Pin-holes, 2 Scales and 8-square Line, Brass-bound Edges ...	1⅝ „	21/- „
„ 5550.	„ „ 4 „ „ „ and Bevelled	1⅝ „	22/6 „

Drawings are Half Size.

EDWARD PRESTON & SONS, L^{TD}.

TWO FEET TWO-FOLD BOXWOOD RULES, with BRASS SLIDES.

Packed in Dozens in Cardboard Boxes.　　French Polished.

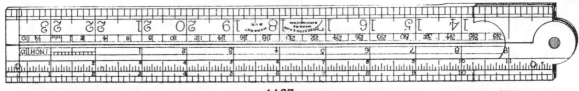

1067　　　　　　　　　　　　　　　　　11/3

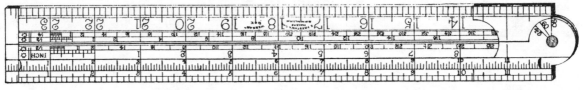

1167　　　　　　　　　　　　　　　　　15/-

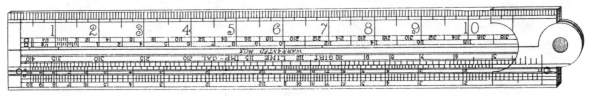

1161　　　　　　　　　　　　　　　　　18/-

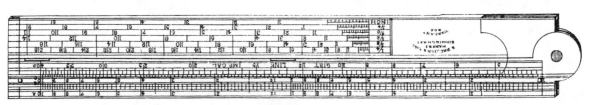

1170　　　　　　　　　　　　　　　　　19/6

1064　　　　　　　　　　　　　　　　　22/6

No. 1067.	Arch Joint, 10ths and 12ths and 8-square Line, Slide marked Inches in 8ths and 16ths, Bevelled Edge　...　...　...　...　...	1⅝-inch wide	11/3 per dozen
,, 1167.	Arch Joint, 2 Scales and 8 square Line, Slide marked Inches in 8ths and 16ths, Bevelled Edge　...　...　...　...　...	1⅝　,,	15/-　,,
,, 1161.	Arch Joint, 4 Scales and 8-square Line, Slide marked inches in 8ths and 16ths, Bevelled Edge and Angles　...　...　...　...	1⅝　,,	18/-　,,
,, 1170.	Arch Joint, Brass Pin-holes, 2 Scales and 8-square Line, Slide marked Inches in 8ths and Gunter's Line, Bevelled Edge...　...　...　...	1⅝　,,	19/6　,,
,, 1064.	Arch Joint, Brass Pin-holes, 6 Scales, 8-square Line and Gunter's Line, Bevelled Edge　..　...　...　...　...　...	1⅝　,,	22/6　,,

Drawings are Half Size.

EDWARD PRESTON & SONS, L^{TD.}

TRADE **EP** MARK.

TWO FEET TWO-FOLD BOXWOOD RULES with BRASS SLIDES.

Packed in Half-dozens in Cardboard Boxes.

Inches marked in 8ths and 16ths.   French Polished.

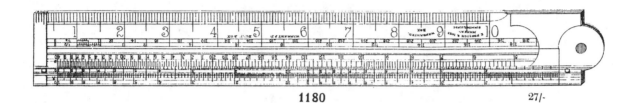

1180   27/-

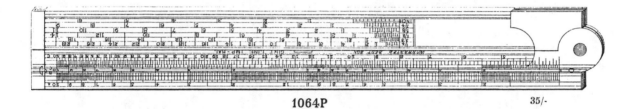

1064P   35/-

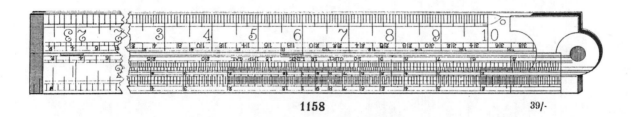

1158   39/-

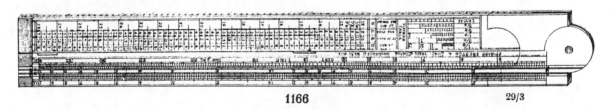

1166   29/3

No. 1180.	Arch Joint, Brass Pin-holes, 2 Scales, 8-square Line and Gunter's Line, Bevelled Edge, 1⅝-inch wide 27/- per dozen.								
,, 1064P.	,,	,,	,,	6	,,	,,	,, Brass-bound Edges	1⅝ ,,	35/- ,,
,, 1158.	,,	,,	,,	2	,,	,,	,, Brass-bound & Bevelled Edge	1⅝ ,,	39/- ,,
,, 1185.	,,	,,	,,	2	,,	,,	,, Bevelled Edge, Ivory Slide	1⅝ ,,	58/- ,,
,, 1166.	. ,,	,,	,,	8-square Line and Gunter's Line, Tables for Timber			Measuring	1⅝ ,,	29/3 ,,
,, 1080.	,,	Brass Slide **Two Feet Three Fold**, Tables for Timber Measuring				...	1⅝ ,,	5/- each	
,, 1081.	,,	Ivory	,,	,,	,,	,,	,,	1⅝ ,,	6/- ,,

**Books of Instructions for " The Slide Rule " published by Edward Preston & Sons,
2/9 per dozen.**

Drawings are Half Size.

EDWARD PRESTON & SONS, LTD.

TRADE  MARK.

ENGINEERS' BOXWOOD RULES with BRASS SLIDES.

Inches marked in 8ths and 16ths.

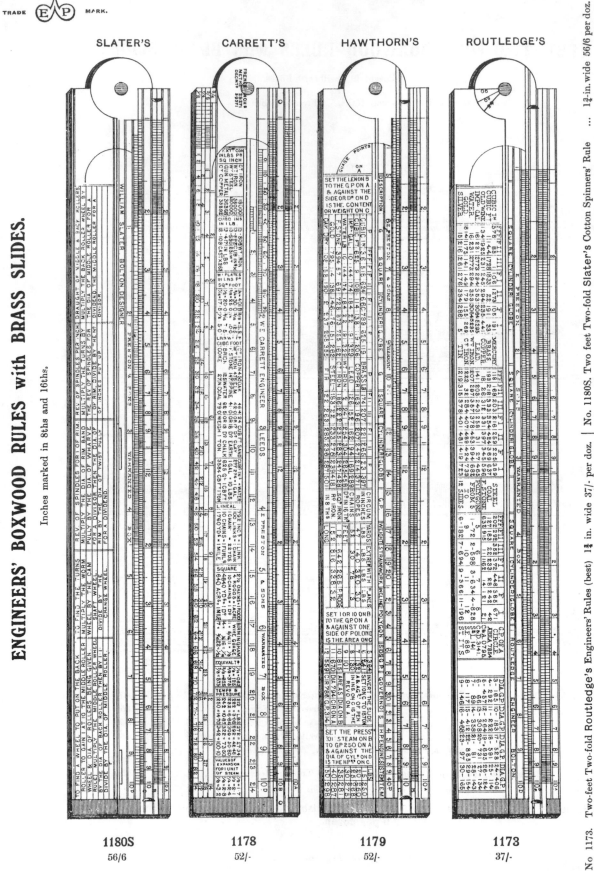

SLATER'S   CARRETT'S   HAWTHORN'S   ROUTLEDGE'S

1180S	1178	1179	1173
56/6	52/-	52/-	37/-

No. 1180S. Two feet Two-fold Slater's Cotton Spinners' Rule ... 1¼-in. wide 56/6 per doz.

"	1171.	" Wilkinson's, Routledge's Engineers' } 1¾	"	44/-
		" Rule }	"	58/-
"	1181.	" brass-bound outside edges } 1¾	"	
"	1182.	" brass-bound inside and outside edges 1¾	"	82/-

Books of Instructions for Wilkinson's Engineers' Rules, 14/- per dozen

No. 1173.   Two-feet Two-fold Routledge's Engineers' Rules (best)   1¼ in. wide   37/- per doz.

"	1174.	"	"	1½	31/-
"	1172.	" brass-bound edges	1¾	"	52/6
"	3105.	" Four-fold	1⅛	"	52/6
"	3015.	" brass-bound edges	1¾	"	70/-
"	1179.	" Two fold Hawthorn's	1¾	"	52/-
"	1178.	" Carrett's	1¾	"	52/-

Books of Instructions for above, 3/- per dozen

EDWARD PRESTON & SONS, L^{TD.}

TRADE 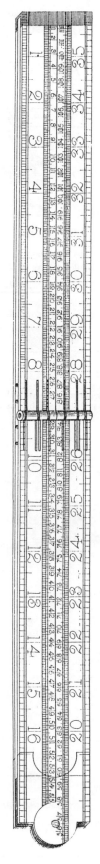 MARK.

EXTRA BEST TWO FEET and THREE FEET FOUR-FOLD BOXWOOD RULES.

Marked with Mechanics' and Circumference Scales.

TWO FEET and THREE FEET FOUR-FOLD BOXWOOD RULES.

Marked with Circumference Scale.

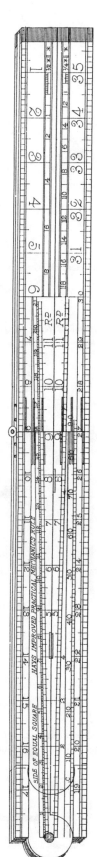

M3562 OUTSIDE VIEW, SHEWING MECHANICS' SCALE.

INSIDE VIEW, SHEWING CIRCUMFERENCE SCALE.

			2-feet.	3-feet.
No. M3561.	Arch Joint, Extra Strong Small Joints, Brass Pin holes inches in 8ths and 16ths, and Mechanics' and Circumference Scales ...	1¾-inch wide	48/6	50/6 per doz.
,, M3562.	,,	,,	52/-	54/- ,,
,, M3567.	Three Arch Joints ,,	,,	56/6	59/9 ,,
,, M3568,	,,	,,	62/6	65/6 ,,

			2-feet.	3-feet.
No. C3571.	Arch Joint, Inches in 8ths, 16ths, Scales, and Circumference Scale (See Inside Drawing of No M3562) ...	1¾-inch wide	24/3	27/- per doz.
,, C3575.	,,	,,	25/6	29/- ,,
,, C3515.	Three Arch Joints ,,	,,	29/-	32/- ,,
,, C3516.	,,	,,	31/-	34/- ,,

Drawn Half Size of Three-feet Four-fold Rule.

Edward Preston & Sons, L^{TD.}

TRADE MARK
REGISTERED.

T. BRADBURN & SONS.

TRADE  MARK.

PROPRIETORS AND SOLE MANUFACTURERS OF

BRADBURN'S

PATENT BOLTED JOINT RULES.

(LION  BRAND.)

THE ILLUSTRATIONS below will show the advantages these Bolted Joint Rules possess.   They enable the user to bolt the Joint at any of 45°, 60°, 90°, and straight open.

They will be found most useful to Gentlemen, Architects, Draughtsmen, Mechanics, Carpenters, &c., being applicable to nearly every kind of *Best* Quality Rule at a small additional cost.

DIRECTIONS FOR USE.—Take one leg of the Rule in each hand, fix the Rule by the mark on the Joint to the Angle required, and with Thumb of the left hand push the bolt firmly in.

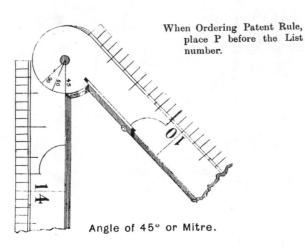

When Ordering Patent Rule, place P before the List number.

Angle of 45° or Mitre.

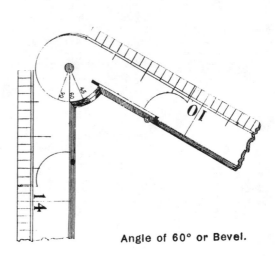

Angle of 60° or Bevel.

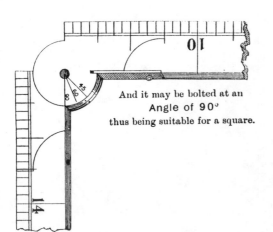

And it may be bolted at an Angle of 90° thus being suitable for a square.

Also it may be bolted **straight open,** making a firm, straight ruler for ruling.

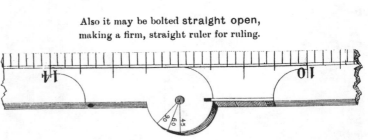

EDWARD PRESTON & SONS, LTD.

TWO FEET and THREE FEET FOUR-FOLD BEST QUALITY (Lion Brand) RULES.

TRADE (E/\P) MARK.

With Steel Tips and Steel Plates in Joints.

(MARK: THOMAS BRADBURN & SONS, MAKERS, BIRMINGHAM. ESTABLISHED 1834.)

The Patent Rules will fix at Mitre, Square and Straight.

Packed in Half-dozens in Cardboard Boxes.

The Tip Legs of the Two-feet Rules have Bevelled Edges; the Three-feet have Square Edges.

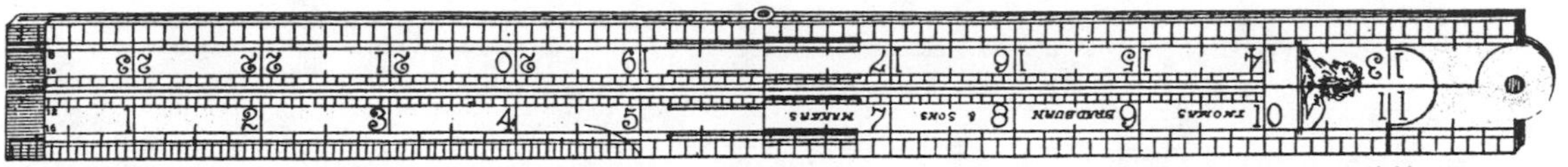

527 17/4

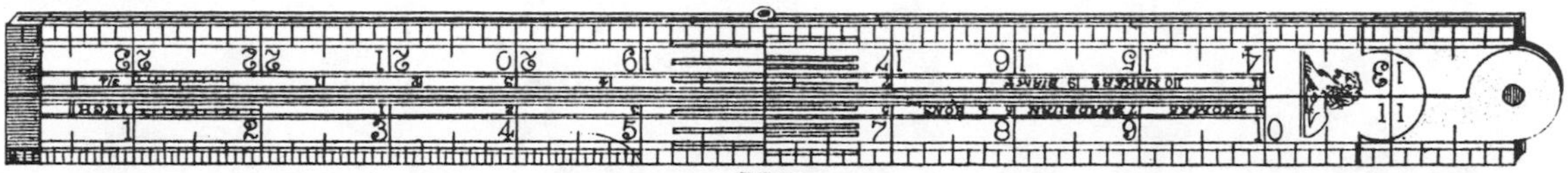

529 20/8

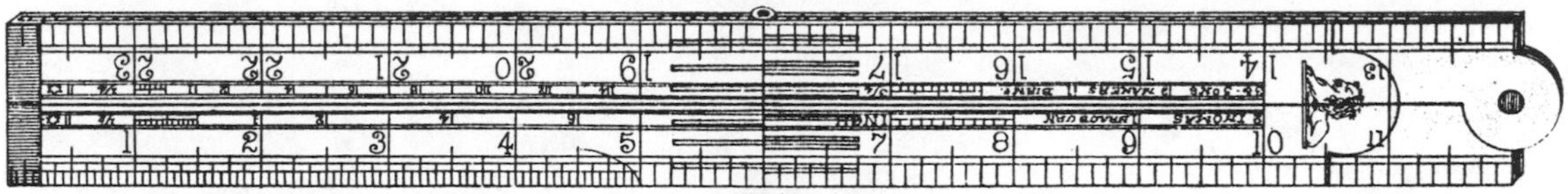

531 23/4

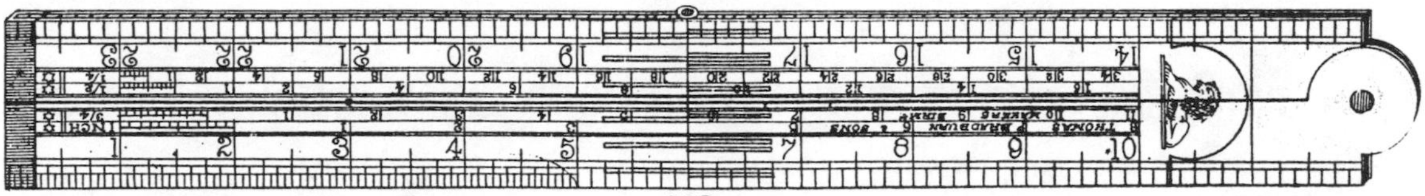

533 26/-

No.	Description		Width	2-feet.	3-feet.	
No. 521.	Brass Arch Joint, marked 8ths, 16ths, 10ths, 12ths	... ...	3/4-inch wide	14/-	15/4	per dozen.
,, 527.	,, ,, ,, ,, ,,	... ...	1 ,,	17/4	18/8	,,
,, 529.	,, ,, ,, ,, ,, and Scales	...	1 1/8 ,,	20/8	22/8	,,
,, 531.	,, ,, ,, ,, ,, ,,	...	1 3/8 ,,	23/4	25/4	,,
,, 533.	,, ,, ,, ,, ,, ,,	...	1 1/2 ,,	26/-	28/-	,,
,, P529.	Patent Brass ,, ,, ,, ,, ,,	...	1 1/8 ,,	24/8	26/8	,,
,, P531.	,, ,, ,, ,, ,, ,,	...	1 3/8 ,,	27/4	29/4	,,
,, P533.	,, ,, ,, ,, ,, ,,	...	1 1/2 ,,	30/-	32/-	,,
,, N521.	Silverine ,, ,, ,, ,,	... ...	3/4 ,,	16/8	17/4	,,
,, N527.	,, ,, ,, ,, ,,	... ...	1 ,,	20/-	21/4	,,
,, N529.	,, ,, ,, ,, ,, and Scales	...	1 1/8 ,,	24/-	26/-	,,
,, N531.	,, ,, ,, ,, ,, ,,	...	1 3/8 ,,	26/8	28/8	,,
,, N533.	,, ,, ,, ,, ,, ,,	...	1 1/2 ,,	31/4	33/4	,,
,, PN529.	Patent Silverine ,, ,, ,, ,, ,,	...	1 1/8 ,,	28/-	30/-	,,
,, PN531.	,, ,, ,, ,, ,, ,,	...	1 3/8 ,,	30/8	32/8	,,
,, PN533.	,, ,, ,, ,, ,, ,,	...	1 1/2 ,,	35/4	37/4	,,

TWO FEET and THREE FEET FOUR-FOLD SECOND QUALITY (Rule and Compass Brand) RULES.

With Steel Tips and Steel Plates in Joints.

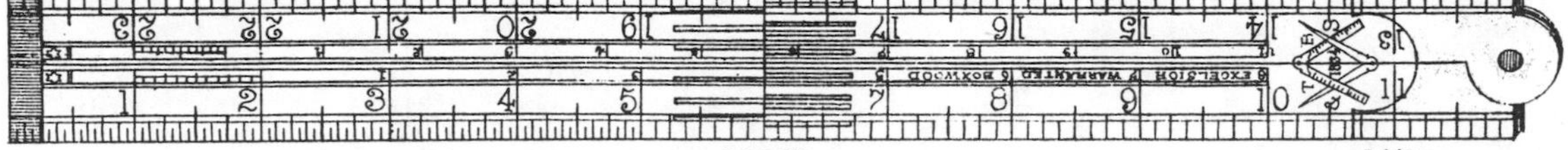

529M 14/8

No.	Description		Width	2-feet.	3-feet.	
No. 527M.	Brass Arch Joint, marked 8ths, 16ths, 10ths and 12ths	... ...	1-inch wide	13/4	14/4	per dozen.
,, 529M.	,, ,, ,, 8ths and 16ths and Scales ...	... ...	1 1/8 ,,	14/8	16/-	,,
,, 531M.	,, ,, ,, ,, ,, ...	... ...	1 3/8 ,,	16/8	18/-	,,
,, 533M.	,, ,, ,, ,, ,, ...	... ...	1 1/2 ,,	18/8	20/-	,,

Drawings are Half Size.

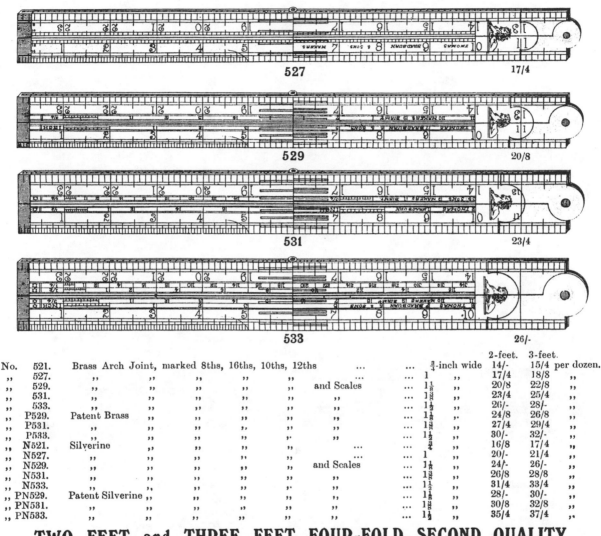

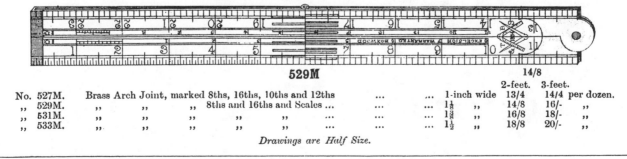

EDWARD PRESTON & SONS, L^{TD.}

TWO FEET and THREE FEET FOUR-FOLD BEST QUALITY (Lion Brand) RULES.

With Steel Tips and Steel Plates in Joints.

(MARK: THOMAS BRADBURN & SONS, MAKERS, BIRMINGHAM.   ESTABLISHED 1834.)

The Patent Rules will fix at Mitre, Square and Straight.

Packed in Half-dozens in Cardboard Boxes.

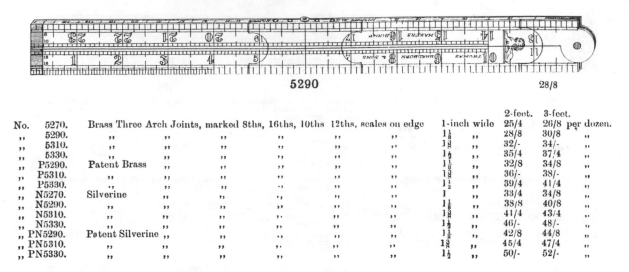

5290   28/8

No.									2-feet.	3-feet.	
5270.	Brass Three Arch Joints, marked 8ths, 16ths, 10ths 12ths, scales on edge						1-inch wide	25/4	26/8	per dozen.
,, 5290.	,,	,,	,,	,,	,,	,,	1⅛ ,,	28/8	30/8	,,
,, 5310.	,,	,,	,,	,,	,,	,,	1¼ ,,	32/-	34/-	,,
,, 5330.	,,	,,	,,	,,	,,	,,	1½ ,,	35/4	37/4	,,
,, P5290.	Patent Brass ,,	,,	,,	,,	,,	,,	1⅛ ,,	32/8	34/8	,,
,, P5310.	,,	,,	,,	,,	,,	,,	1¼ ,,	36/-	38/-	,,
,, P5330.	,,	,,	,,	,,	,,	,,	1½ ,,	39/4	41/4	,,
,, N5270.	Silverine ,,	,,	,,	,,	,,	,,	1 ,,	33/4	34/8	,,
,, N5290.	,,	,,	,,	,,	,,	,,	1⅛ ,,	38/8	40/8	,,
,, N5310.	,,	,,	,,	,,	,,	,,	1¼ ,,	41/4	43/4	,,
,, N5330.	,,	,,	,,	,,	,,	,,	1½ ,,	46/-	48/-	,,
,, PN5290.	Patent Silverine ,,	,,	,,	,,	,,	,,	1⅛ ,,	42/8	44/8	,,
,, PN5310.	,,	,,	,,	,,	,,	,,	1¾ ,,	45/4	47/4	,,
,, PN5330.	,,	,,	,,	,,	,,	,,	1½ ,,	50/-	52/-	,,

TWO FEET and THREE FEET FOUR-FOLD BEST QUALITY RULES.

With Inside Bevelled Edges, Marked Scales, for Architects, Draughtsmen, &c.

Packed in Half-dozens in Cardboard Boxes.

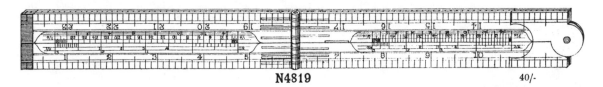

N4819   40/-

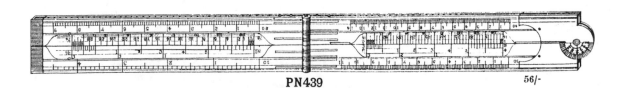

PN439   56/-

No.								2 feet.	3-feet.	
4817.	Brass Arch Joint, Bevelled Edges, 8 Scales			...	...	...	1-inch wide	26/8	—	per dozen.
,, 4819.	,,	,,	,,	,,	...	...	1⅛ ,,	29/4	37/4	,,
,, P4819.	Patent Brass ,,	,,	,,	,,	...	...	1⅛ ,,	33/4	41/4	,,
,, N4817.	Silverine ,,	,,	,,	,,	...	...	1 ,,	36/-	—	,,
,, N4819.	,,	,,	,,	,,	...	...	1⅛ ,,	40/-	50/-	,,
,, PN4819.	Patent Silverine ,,	,,	,,	,,	...	...	1⅛ ,,	44/-	54/-	,,
,, N437.	Silverine ,,	,,	,,	and 4 Chain Scales, fine divided all over			1 ,,	48/-	—	,,
,, N439.	,,	,,	,,	,,	,,		1⅛ ,,	52/-	—	,,
,, PN439.	Patent Silverine ,,	,,	,,	,,	,,		1⅛ ,,	56/-	—	,,
,, N449.	Silverine ,, and Edge Plates	,,	,,	,,	,,		1¼ ,,	64/-	—	,,
,, PN449.	Patent Silverine ,,	,,	,,	,,	,,		1¼ ,,	68/-	—	,,

Drawings are Half Size.

EDWARD PRESTON & SONS, L^{TD}.

TRADE ᴇᴘ MARK.

TWO FEET TWO-FOLD BEST QUALITY (Lion Brand) RULES.

With Steel Tips and Steel Plates in Joints.

(MARK: THOMAS BRADBURN & SONS, MAKERS, BIRMINGHAM.   ESTABLISHED 1834.)

The Patent Rules will fix at Bevel, Mitre, Square and Straight.

Packed in dozens in Cardboard Boxes.

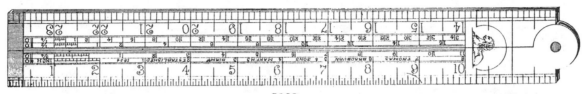

5060   14/-

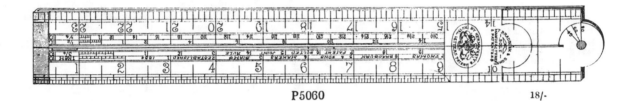

P5060   18/-

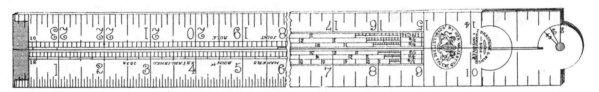

P5060J   SHEWING BOTH SIDES OF RULE.   19/4

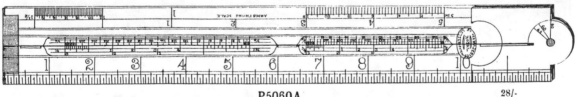

P5060A   28/-

No.											
No. 5060.	Brass Arch Joint, marked 8ths and 16ths, 4 Scales, 8 Square Line, Bevelled Edge							1⅝-inch wide	14/- per dozen.		
„ P5060.	Patent Brass	„	„	„	„	„	„	1⅝ „	18/-	„
„ N5060.	Silverine	„	„	„	„	„	„	1⅝ „	16/8	„
„ PN5060.	Patent Silverine	„	„	„	„	„	„	1⅝ „	20/8	„
„ 5060J.	Brass	„	„ 8ths, 16ths. 10ths, 12ths, and 6 Scales, Double „ THE JOINERS' RULE }					1⅝ „	15/4	„
„ P5060J.	Patent Brass	„	„	„	„	„	„	1⅝ „	19/4	„
„ N5060J.	Silverine	„	„	„	„	„	„	1⅝ „	18/-	„
„ PN5060J.	Patent Silverine	„	„	„	„	„	„	1⅝ „	22/-	„
„ 5060A.	Brass	„	„	„	8 Drawing Scales and Arm- } strong Scale, 6 Bevels }			1⅝ „	24/-	„
„ P5060A.	Patent Brass	„	„	„	„	„	„	1⅝ „	28/-	„
„ N5060A.	Silverine	„	„	„	„	„	„	1⅝ „	26/8	„
„ PN5060A.	Patent Silverine	„	„	„	„	„	„	1⅝ „	30/8	„

Drawings are Half Size.

TRADE EP MARK.

TWO FEET TWO-FOLD BEST QUALITY (Lion Brand) RULES.

With Brass Slides; with Steel Tips and Steel Plates in Joints.

(MARK: THOMAS BRADBURN & SONS, MAKERS, BIRMINGHAM. ESTABLISHED 1834.)

The Patent Rules will fix at Bevel, Mitre, Square and Straight.

Packed in dozens in Cardboard Boxes.

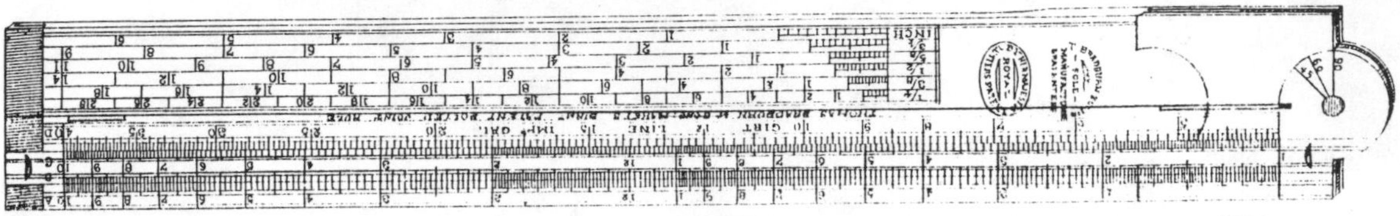

P5120 28/-

No. 5120.	Brass Arch Joint,	marked 8ths, 16ths, 8 Square Line and 6 Scales, Bevelled Edge					1⅝-inch wide	24/-	per dozen.
,, P5120.	Patent Brass	,,	,,	,,	,,	,,	1⅝ ,,	28/-	,,
,, N5120.	Silverine	,,	,,	,,	,,	,,	1⅝ ,,	26/8	,,
,, PN5120.	Patent Silverine	,,	,,	,,	,,	,,	1⅝ ,,	30/8	,,
,, 514.	Brass Arch Joint,	Routledge Engineers', Bevelled Edge	...	...	...		1¾ ,,	40/-	,,
,, P514.	Patent Brass	,,	,,	...	...	...	1¾ ,,	44/-	,,
,, N514.	Silverine	,,	,,	...	...	...	1¾ ,,	50/8	,,
,, PN514.	Patent Silverine	,,	,,	...	...	...	1¾ ,,	54/8	,,

TWO FEET TWO-FOLD SECOND QUALITY (Rule and Compass Brand) RULES.

With Steel Tips and Steel Plates in Joints.

Packed in Dozens in Cardboard Boxes

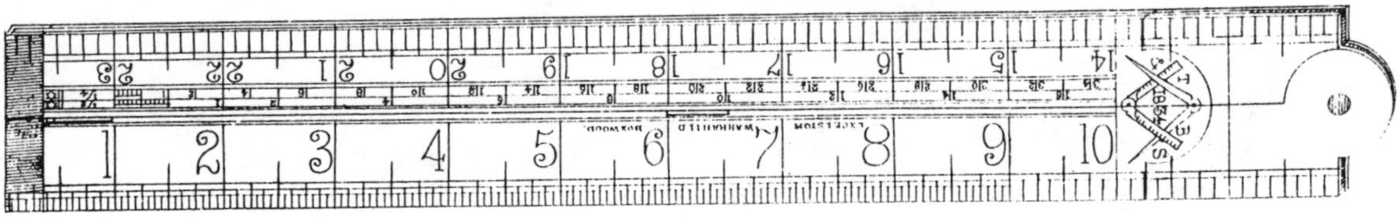

314 10/8

No. 314. Brass Arch Joints, marked 8ths, 16ths, 8 Square Line and 2 Scales, Bevelled Edge 1⅝-inch wide 10/8 per dozen.

COACHMAKERS' FOUR FEET FOUR-FOLD BEST QUALITY RULES.

									4 feet	
No. 531.	Brass Arch Joint,	marked 8ths,	16ths,	10ths,	12ths and Scales	...	...	1⅜-inch wide	36/6	per dozen.
,, 533.	,,	,,	,,	,,	,,	...	...	1½ ,,	38/8	,,
,, N531.	Silverine	,,	,,	,,	,,	...	...	1⅜ ,,	40/-	,,
,, N533.	,,	,,	,,	,,	,,	...	...	1½ ,,	44/-	,,

Drawings are full size..

EDWARD PRESTON & SONS, LTD.

BOXWOOD and IVORY SCALES.

TRADE MARK.

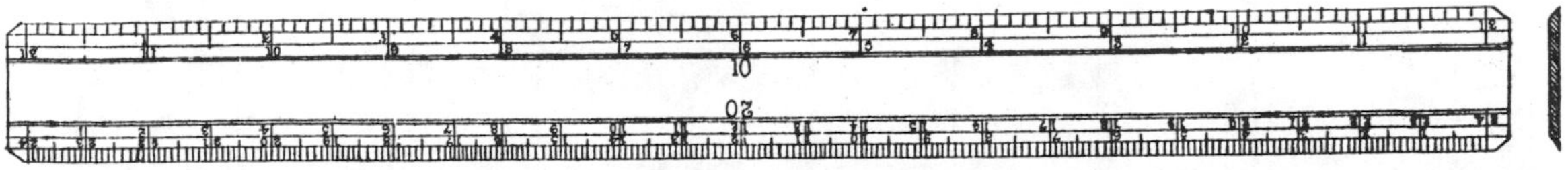

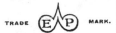

1310. IVORY, **0310.**

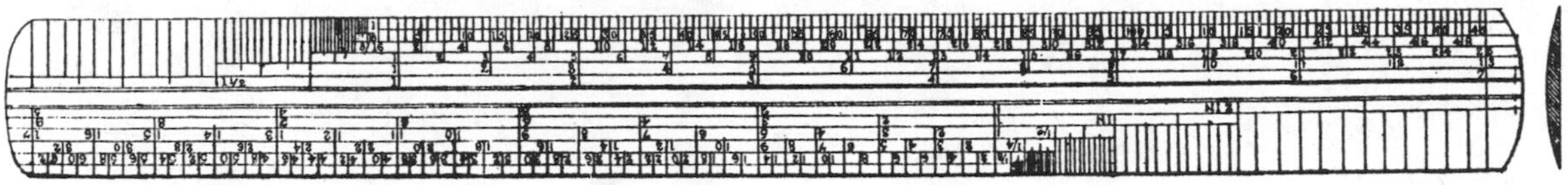

1314 or 1314C. IVORY, **0314.**

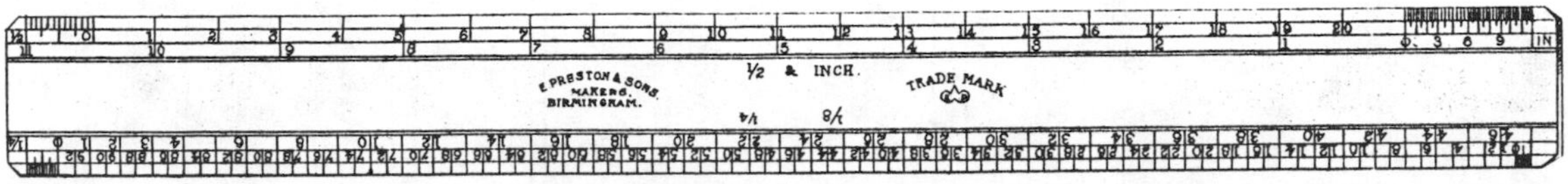

1307 or 1307C. IVORY, **0307.**

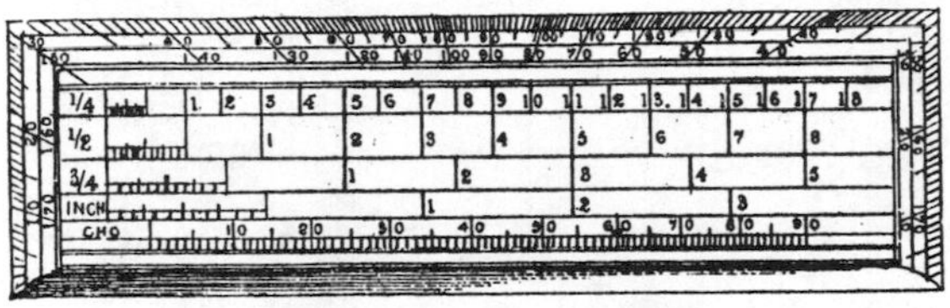

1316. IVORY, **0316.**

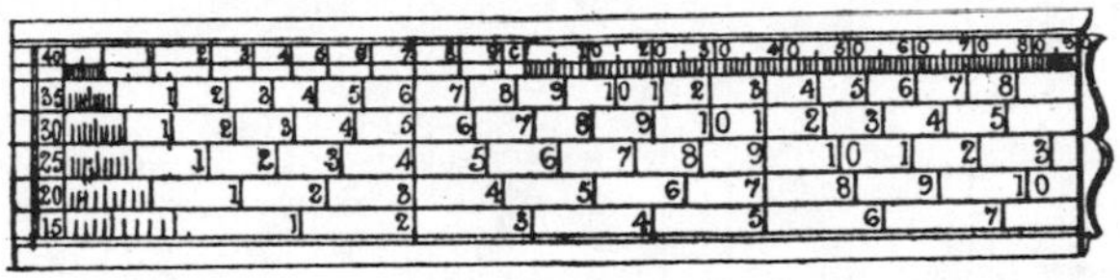

1315. IVORY, **0315.**

	BOXWOOD. No.	BOXWOOD. Per doz.	IVORY. No.	IVORY. Each
12-inch Chain Scale, 10 and 20 to inch	1310	24/-	0310	10/3
,, ,, 20 and 40 ,, ...	1311	24/-	0311	10/3
,, ,, 30 and 60 ,, ...	1312	24/-	0312	10/3
2-inch off set, to match above	1318	7/6	0318	1/9
12-inch Ordnance Scales, 1·500 and feet (or links)	1321	24/-	0321	10/3
,, ,, ,, 1·2500 ,, ,, ...	1322	24/-	0322	10/3
,, ,, ,, 6-inch to a mile, and feet (or links)	1323	24/-	0323	10/3
,, ,, ,, 44 and 88 to inch	1324	24/-	0324	10/3
12-in Half Oval Universal Builder's Scale, 16 Scales, Best Quality	1314	24/-	0314	10/3
,, ,, ,, ,, ,, ,, C ,, ...	1314C	12/-	—	—
,, Oval ,, ,, ,, ,, Best ,, ...	1320	24/-	0320	10/3
,, ,, ,, Armstrong ,, $\frac{1}{8}$ $\frac{1}{4}$ $\frac{3}{8}$ $\frac{1}{2}$ $\frac{3}{4}$ 1 $1\frac{1}{2}$ 3 inch Scales, Best Quality	1307	24/-	0307	10/3
,, ,, ,, ,, ,, ,, ,, ,, C ,,	1307C	12/-	—	—
,, Flat Bevel ,, Architect's ,, 16 Scales, Best Quality	1319	24/-	0319	10/3
,, ,, ,, ,, ,, ,, C ,, ...	1319C	12/-	—	—
,, Open divided on two edges $\frac{1}{8}$ and $\frac{1}{4}$ inch	1300	26/-	0300	10/3
,, ,, ,, ,, $\frac{1}{5}$ and $\frac{1}{10}$,, ...	1308	26/-	0308	10/3
,, ,, ,, ,, $\frac{1}{2}$ and 1 ,, ...	1301	23/-	0301	10/3
,, ,, ,, ,, $\frac{3}{8}$ and $\frac{3}{4}$,, ...	1302	23/-	0302	10/3
,, ,, ,, ,, $1\frac{1}{2}$ and 3 ,, ...	1303	23/-	0303	10/3
,, ,, ,, four edges $\frac{1}{8}$ $\frac{1}{4}$ $\frac{1}{2}$ 1 ,, ...	1304	32/-	0304	10/3
,, ,, ,, $\frac{3}{8}$ $\frac{3}{4}$ $1\frac{1}{2}$ 3 ,, ...	1305	29/-	0305	10/3
6 inch Protractor Scales, 4 Scales, $1\frac{3}{4}$ inch wide	1316	13/6	0316	4/-
,, ,, ,, 8 ,, ,, ...	1306	18/9	0306	5/-
Sectors, Brass Button Joint	1317	16/9	0317	7/6
Plotting Scales	1315	2/-	0315	2/2

EDWARD PRESTON & SONS, LTD.

Full Size Drawings of THREE FEET FOUR-FOLD BOXWOOD RULES.

FOR SCOTCH MARKET.

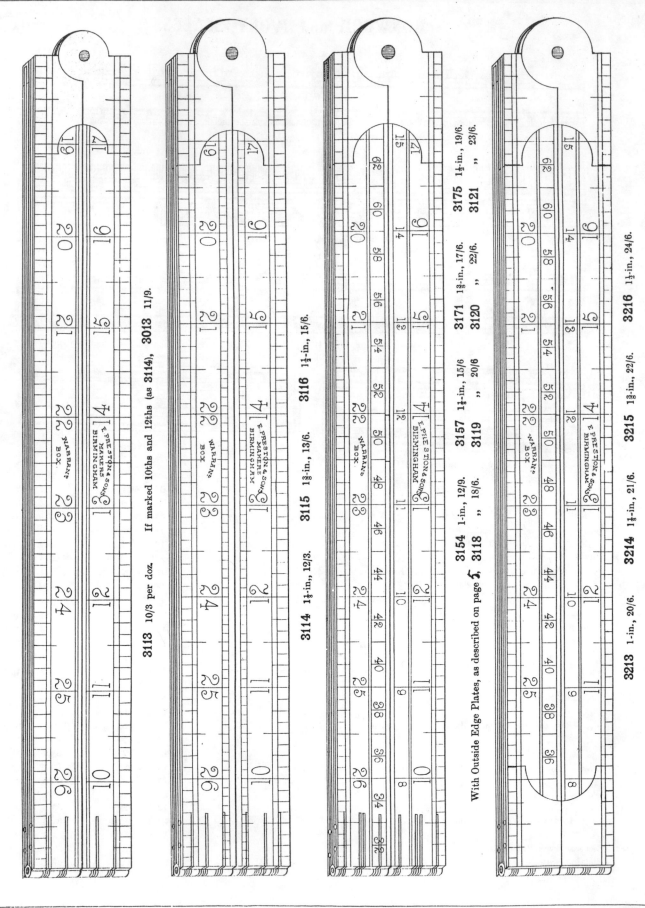

3113 10/3 per doz.   If marked 10ths and 12ths (as 3114), 3013 11/9.

3116 1¼-in. 15/6.

3115 1⅜-in, 13/6.

3114 1½-in., 12/3.

3175 1½-in., 19/6.
3121 ,, 23/6.

3171 1⅜-in, 17/6.
3120 ,, 22/6.

3157 1¼-in, 15/6
3119 ,, 20/6

3154 1-in, 12/9.
3118 ,, 18/6.

With Outside Edge Plates, as described on page 5.

3216 1½-in, 24/6.

3215 1⅜-in, 22/6.

3214 1¼-in, 21/6.

3213 1-in, 20/6.

EDWARD PRESTON & SONS, LTD.

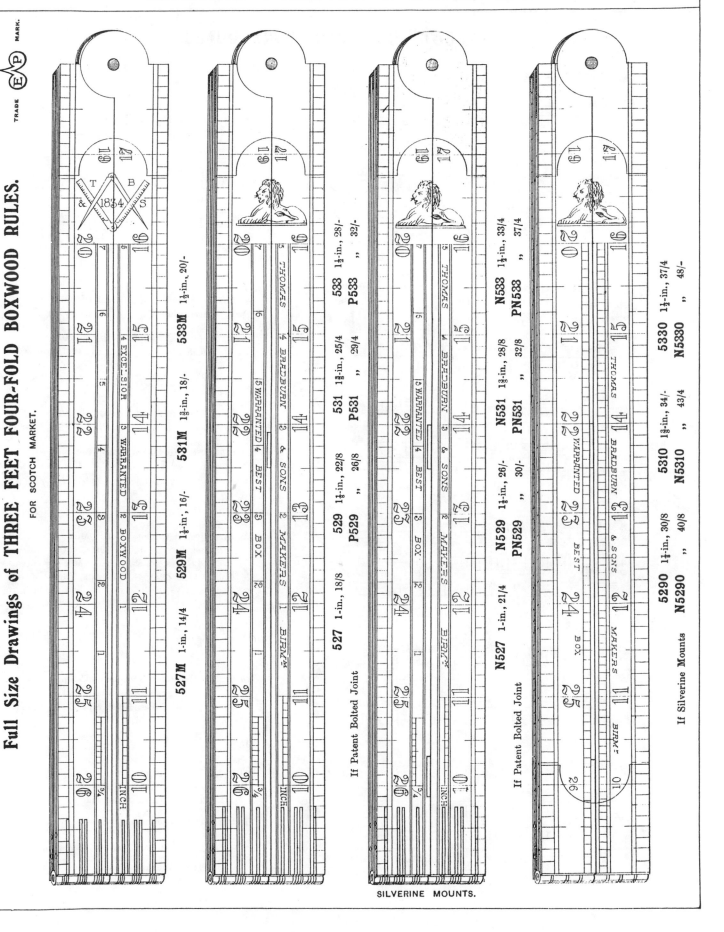

Full Size Drawings of THREE FEET FOUR-FOLD BOXWOOD RULES.

FOR SCOTCH MARKET.

527M 1-in., 14/4
529M 1¼-in., 16/-
531M 1⅜-in., 18/-
533M 1½-in., 20/-

527 1-in., 18/8
529 1¼-in., 22/8   **P529** „ 26/8
531 1⅜-in., 25/4   **P531** „ 29/4
533 1½-in., 28/-   **P533** „ 32/-

If Patent Bolted Joint

N527 1-in., 21/4
N529 1¼-in., 26/-   **PN529** „ 30/-
N531 1⅜-in., 28/8   **PN531** „ 32/8
N533 1½-in., 33/4   **PN533** „ 37/4

If Patent Bolted Joint

5290 1¼-in., 30/8   **N5290** „ 40/8
5310 1⅜-in., 34/-   **N5310** „ 43/4
5330 1½-in., 37/4   **N5330** „ 48/-

If Silverine Mounts

SILVERINE MOUNTS.

EDWARD PRESTON & SONS, L^{TD.}

ONE FOOT FOUR-FOLD IVORY RULES.

Marked inches in 8ths and 16ths.

No. 0156. Round Joint, Brass Mounts,
½-inch wide ... ... 25/6 per dozen.

No. N534. Round Joint, G.S. Mounts,
½-inch wide ... ... 29/6 per dozen.

No. 0157. Round Joint, Brass Mounts,
⅝-inch wide ... ... 29/6 per dozen.

No. N834. Round Joint, G.S. Mounts,
⅝-inch wide ... ... 35/6 per dozen.

No. 0158. Round Joint, Brass Mounts,
¾-inch wide ... .. 40/- per dozen.

No. N535. Round Joint, G S. Mounts,
¾-inch wide ... ... 46/- per dozen.

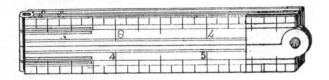

No. 0153. Square Joint, Brass Mounts,
⅝-inch wide ... ... 35/- per dozen.

No. 0154. Square Joint, G.S. Mounts,
⅝-inch wide ... ... 41/- per dozen.

No. 0162. Arch Joint, G.S. Mounts,
marked 8ths, 16ths, 10ths, 12ths
and Scales, ¾-inch wide .. 58/6 per dozen.

No. 0165. Arch Joint, G.S. Mounts, Edge
Plates .. ... 90/- per dozen.

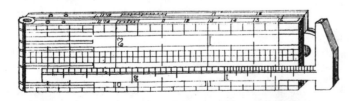

No. 0163. Arch Joint, G.S. Mounts, Calliper
Gauge, marked 8ths, 16ths, 10ths,
12ths and Scales, ¾-inch wide ... 10/3 each.

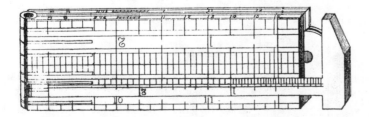

No. 0173. Arch Joint, G.S Mounts, Calliper
Gauge, marked 8ths, 16ths, 10ths,
12ths and Scales, 1-inch wide ... 12/9 each.

If marked with 2 or more measures, a small extra
charge is made.

Nos. 0163 and 0173, if marked London and
Metre, 6d. each extra.
Three Measures, 1/- each extra.

Drawings are full size..

EDWARD PRESTON & SONS, LTD.

TWO FEET FOUR-FOLD IVORY RULES.

Marked Inches in 8ths, 16ths 10ths and 12ths.

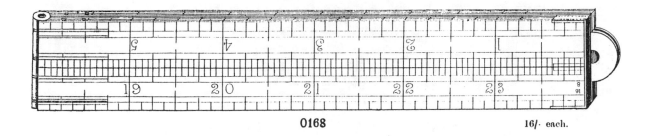

0168

16/- each.

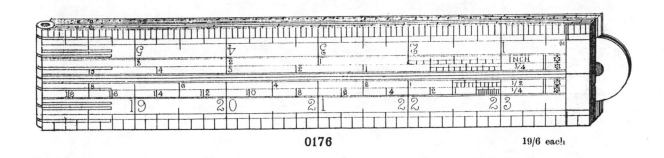

0176

19/6 each

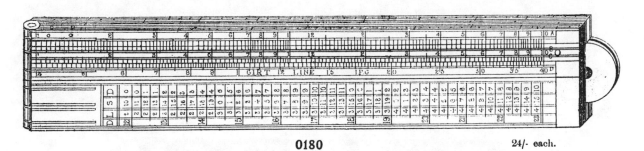

0180

24/- each.

				2-feet.	3-feet.
No. 0162.	Arch Joint, G.S. Mounts ...	... ...	¾-inch wide	13/-	— each.
,, 0165.	,, Edge Plates, G.S. Mounts	... ...	¾ ,,	15/-	— ,,
,, 0168.	,, G.S. Mounts ...	... .	1 ,,	16/-	24/- ,,
,, 0176.	,, G.S. Mounts ...	... .	1⅛ ,,	19/6	28/- ,,
,, 0174.	,, Edge Plates, G.S. Mounts	... ...	1⅛ ,,	21/-	— ,,
,, 0179.	,, G.S. Mounts ...	... ...	1¼ ,,	24/-	— ,,
,, 0188	,, G.S. Mounts ...	... .	1½ ,,	29/-	— ,,

If marked London and Metre, 6d. each extra.

,, 0180.	,, G.S. Mounts and Slide, with Gunter's Line, Inches in 8ths and 16ths	1⅜ ,,	24/-	— ,,

If marked London and Metre, 1/- each extra.

Drawings are full size.

EDWARD PRESTON & SONS, LTD.

TWO FEET FOUR-FOLD IVORY RULES.
With G.S. Slides and Calliper Gauges.

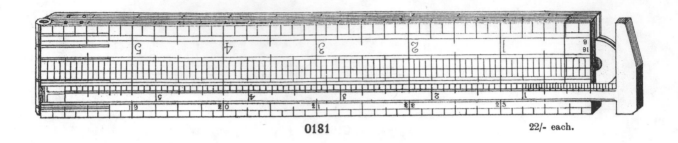

0181   22/- each.

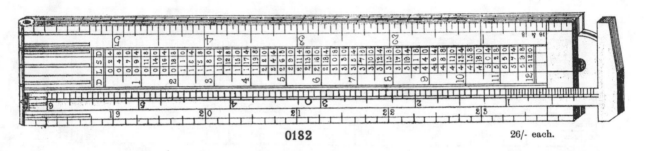

0182   26/- each.

2-feet.

No. 0173.	Arch Joint, Slide, Calliper Gauge, G.S. Mounts	...	...	...	...	1-inch wide	20/- each.
,, 0181.	,, ,, ,, ,,	...	...	...	...	1⅛ ,,	22/- ,,
,, 0182.	,, ,, ,, ,, Ironmongers' Tables	...	...	...	1⅜ ,,	26/- ,,
,, 0184.	,, ,, G.S. Mounts, Routledge's Engineer's Slide Rule	...	...	...	1¾ ,,	38/6 ,,

0173 and 0181, if marked London and Metre, 1/- each extra.

ONE FOOT THREE-FOLD IVORY RULES
With G.S. Slide and Calliper Gauge.

Marked with Ironmongers' Tables.

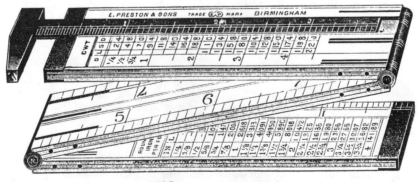

0196   25/6 each.

Drawings are Full Size.

EDWARD PRESTON & SONS, L^TD.

TRADE (E P) MARK.

TWO FEET FOUR-FOLD IVORY RULES with INSIDE BEVELLED EDGES.

Marked Inches in 8ths and 16ths.

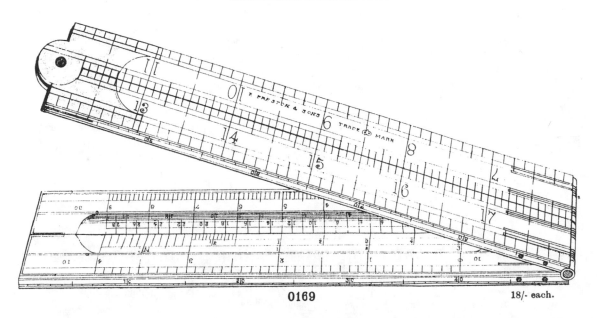

0169   18/- each.

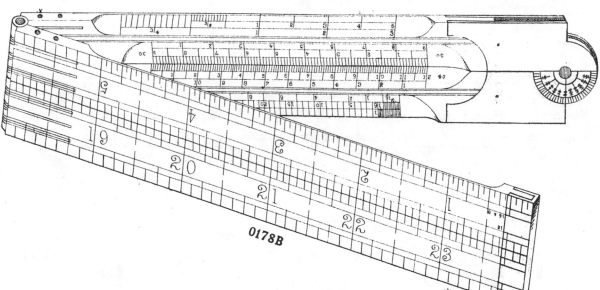

0178B

23/6 each.

					2 feet.	3 feet.	
No. 0169.	Arch Joint, G.S. Mounts, marked Drawing Scales and Chain Scales			... 1-inch wide	18/-	-—	each.
,, 0178.	,,	,,	,, ,, ,, ,, and Degrees	... 1¼ ,,	21/6	30/-	,,
,, 0178B.	,,	,, 8 Bevels ,,	,, , ,, ,,	... 1⅛ ,,	23/6	—	,,

TWO-FEET FOUR-FOLD IVORY RULES,

With Inside Edges Bevelled, and Patent Bolted Joints, as described on Page 22.

					2 feet	3 feet	
No. P0178.	Arch Joint, G.S. Mounts, Drawing and Chain Scales		..	... 1¼ inch wide	22/6	31/-	each.
,, P0178B.	,,	,, 8 Bevels ,,	,,	... 1⅛ ,,	24/6	—	,,

Drawings are Full Size.

EDWARD PRESTON & SONS, L<u>TD</u>.

TRADE Ⓔ⩕Ⓟ MARK.

TWO FEET TWO-FOLD BRASS RULES.

Marked inches in 8ths and 16ths.

Packed in Dozens in Cardboard Boxes.

2009

6/9

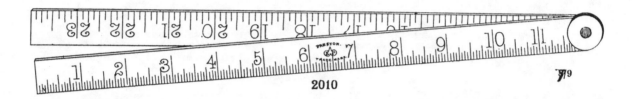

2010

7/9

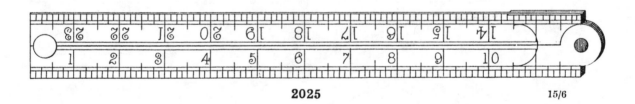

2025

15/6

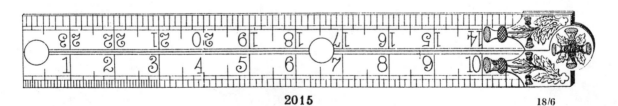

2015

18/6

No. 2009.	Two Feet Two-Fold Flexible Brass Rule, Round Joint	...	...	...	⅝-inch wide	6/9 per dozen.
,, 2010.	,, ,, ,, ,,	,,	...	...	¾ ,,	7/9 ,,
,, 2010S.	,, ,, ,, ,,	as 2010, but with Stop Joint		...	¾ ,,	9/3 ,,
,, 2012	,, ,, ,, ,,	...	...	...	⅞ ,,	9/9 ,,
,, 2012S.	,, ,, ,, ,,	as 2012, but with Stop Joint		...	⅞ ,,	11/9 ,,
,, 2025	,, ,, ,, ,,	Arch Joint	..	...	1⅜ ,,	15/6 ,,
,, 2015.	,, ,, ,, ,,	Engraved Acorn Joint	...	...	1½ ,,	18/6 ,,
,, 2011.	,, Four-Fold ,, ,,	as 2010, but Four-fold	...	...	¾ ,,	17/6 ,,

If marked Two Measures, 3/9 per dozen extra.

Drawings are Half Size.

EDWARD PRESTON & SONS, LTD.

BRASS COUNTER MEASURES.

With Holes for Screwing down on Counters.

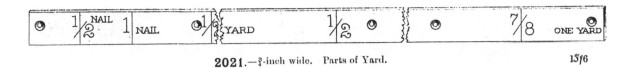

2021.—¾-inch wide.   Parts of Yard.   15/6

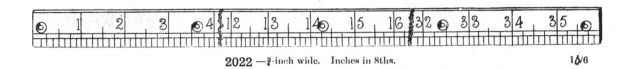

2022—¾-inch wide.   Inches in 8ths.   16/6

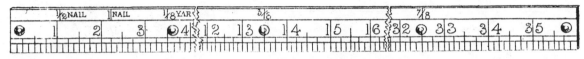

2023.—1-inch wide.   Inches in 8ths and Parts of Yard.   21/6

No. 2021.	Yard Counter Measure, marked parts of Yard	...	...	...	¾-inch wide	15/6 per dozen	Special
,, 2022.	,, ,, ,, inches in 8ths	...	...	...	¾ ,,	16/6 ,,	Quotation
,, 2024.	,, ,, ,, inches and parts of Yard ...	...	...	...	¾ ,,	19/6 ,,	for 3, 6 or 12
,, 2023.	,, ,, ,, ,, ,, ,,	...	...	...	1 ,,	21/6 ,,	dozen lots.

DRAPERS' ROUND AND FLAT YARD MEASURES.

It is required by the Government that all Wood Yard Measures must be Brass Ferruled or Tipped at Ends.

706F.—Draper's Round Yard Measures, with Brass Ferrules at each end.

No 705F.	Common Round Yard Measure, Ferruled at Ends, marked parts of Yard ...		6/- per dozen.
,, 706CF.	,, ,, ,, ,, ,, and inches in 8ths ...		8/3 ,,
,, 706F.	Best ,, ,, ,, ,, ,, ..		9/9 ,,

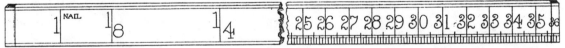

Drapers' Flat Yard Measure, Brass Tipped, showing method of marking each side of 707D, 702D and 705D.

No. 707D.	Boxwood Flat Yard Measure, Brass Tipped, ⅞-inch wide and ⅛-inch thick, marked parts of Yard and inches in 8ths		10/6 per dozen.
No. 702D.	,, ,, ,, ,, 1 ,, 3/16 ,, ,, ,, ,,	11/9 ,,
,, 705D.	,, ,, ,, ,, 1⅛ ,, 3/16 ,, ,, ,, ,,	14/- ,,

Yard Measures may be had Government Stamped. 3/4 per dozen extra.

CLOTH MEASURES.

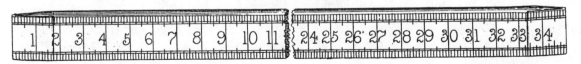

			36	48	54	60 inch.
No. 662.	Boxwood Cloth Measures, with Tapered Tipped Ends, 1¼-inch wide × ¼-inch thick		27/-	34/-	42/-	46/- per dozen.

EDWARD PRESTON & SONS, L^{TD.}

TRADE  MARK.

ENGINE DIVIDED STEEL RULES.

These Rules are made of Best Hardened and Tempered Cast Steel, Straight on the Edges and Divided with the greatest accuracy.

		¾ inch Wide by 21 W.G. Thick.	¾ inch wide by 21 W.G. Thick.	1⅛ inch Wide by 19 W.G. Thick.	
		3 inch.	4 inch.	6 inch.	12 inch.
No. 100.	Marked London on Edge only. Inches divided in 8th, 16ths, 32nds, and 64ths,	...	4/6	6/-	11/-	per dozen.
„ 101.	Marked London on Two Edges. Inches divided in 8ths and 16ths	6/-	6/-	7/-	12/-	„
„ 104.	„ „ 8ths, 16ths, 32nds, and 64ths	7/-	7/-	8/-	15/-	„
„ 105.	„ „ 16ths, 32nds, 64ths and 10ths, 20ths, 50ths ...	...	7/-	8/-	15/-	„
„ 107.	„ „ 16ths, 32nds, 64ths, and 10ths 20ths, 40ths, 50ths, and 100ths ...	...	9/-	10/-	16/-	„
„ 110.	Marked London on Four Edges. Inches divided in 8ths, 16ths, 32nds, and 64ths	...	10/-	12/-	18/-	„
„ 113.	Marked London and Metre on Two Edges Inches divided in 16ths and Millimetres ...	...	7/-	9/-	16/-	„
„ 116.	Inches divided in 16ths, 32nds, and 64ths and Millimetres	...	8/-	10/-	18/-	„
„ 16.	Marked London and Tapping and Spanner Sizes. Inches divided in 8ths, 16ths, 32nds and 64ths and Tapping and Spanner Sizes. ...	Whitworth Pitch.		10/-	16/-	„
„ C16.	„ „ „ „ „	Clyde Pattern.		10/-	16/-	„

NARROW STEEL RULES.

¼ inch wide × 21 W.G. thick.

		3 inch.	4 inch.	6 inch.	12 inch.	
No. 100N.	Marked as 100 above	—	4/6	6/-	—	per dozen.
„ 101N.	„ „ 101 „	6/-	6/-	7/-	12/-	„
„ 104N.	„ „ 104 „ ... — ..	7/-	7/-	8/-	15/-	„
„ 58.	„ London Two Edges, 8ths, 16ths, 32nds	—	12/-	14 -	20/-	„
„ 59.	„ „ 32nd and Millimetres ...	—	14/-	16/-	22/-	„

ENGINE DIVIDED STEEL RULES.

18 to 72 inches long.

		1⅛ inch wide. by 17 W.G. Thick.		1½ inch wide. by 15 W.G. Thick.		2 inch wide. by 12 W.G. Thick.	
		18	24	36	48	60	72 inches.
No 101.	Marked London on Two Edges. Inches divided in 8ths and 16ths	2/-	3/6	12/-	15/-	20/-	28/- each.
„ 104.	„ „ 8ths 16ths 32nds and 64ths ...	2/6	4/-	14/-	17/-	22/-	30/- „
	Marked London and Metre on Two Edges.	24			48	60	inches
		50	100	100			200 Centimetres.
„ 113.	Inches divided in 16ths, and millimetres	3/-	4/-	9/-	15/-	20/-	25/-	36/- each.
„ 116.	„ „ 16ths, 32nds, 64ths, and millimetres.	3/6	4/6	10/-	16/-	—	—	—

1⅛ inch wide by 17 W.G. Thick.	1½ inch wide by 15 W.G. Thick.	2 inch wide by 12 W.G. Thick.

ENGINE DIVIDED STEEL CONTRACTION RULES FOR PATTERN MAKERS.

			12 inches.	24 inches.
No. 11.	Inches into 16ths Standard on one edge Single Contraction for Iron other edge 1⅛ inch wide × 17 W.G.		1/3	4/- each.
„ 12.	„ „ „ „ Double „ „ „ „		1/3	4/- „
„ 13.	„ „ „ „ Single „ „ Brass „ „		1/3	4/- „
„ 14.	Standard, Single and Double Contraction for Iron and Single Contraction for Brass „		2/-	6/6 „

EDWARD PRESTON & SONS, LTD.

ENGINE DIVIDED STEEL RULES.

TRADE **EP** MARK.

LONDON 1 2 3 4 5 6 7 8 9 10 11 12

100 12 inch. 11/-

LONDON 1 2 3 4 5 6 7 8 9 10 11 12

101 12 inch. 12/-

LONDON 1 2 3 4 5 6 7 8 9 10 11 12

104 12 inch 15/-

LONDON 1 2 3 4 5 6 7 8 9 10 N⁰105 11 12

105 12 inch. 15/-

LONDON 1 2 3 4 5 6 7 8 9 10 N⁰107 11 12

107 12 inch. 16/-

LONDON 1 2 3 4 5 6 7 8 9 10 N⁰110 11 12

LONDON 1 2 3 4 5 6 7 8 9 10 11 12

110 12 inch. 18/-

Shewing both sides of Rule.

METRE 1 2 3 4 5 6 7 8 9 10 11 12 13 14 15 16 17 18 19 20 21 22 23 24 25 26 27 28 29 30
LONDON 1 2 3 4 5 6 7 8 9 10 N⁰113 11 12

113 12 inch. 16/-

METRE 1 2 3 4 5 6 7 8 9 10 11 12 13 14 15 16 17 18 19 20 21 22 23 24 25 26 27 28 29 30
LONDON 1 2 3 4 5 6 7 8 9 10 11 12

116 12 inch. 18/-

SPANNER TAPPING THREADS PER INCH.
LONDON 1 2 3 4 5 6 7 8 9 10 11 12

C 16 12 inch. 16/-

LONDON 1 2 3 4 5 N⁰58 6

58 6 inch 14/-

LONDON 1 2 3 4 5 6 7 8 9 10 11 12 13 14 15 N⁰59

59 6 inch. 16/-

Drawings are Half Size.

EDWARD PRESTON & SONS, L^TD.

ENGINE DIVIDED STEEL RULES.

These Rules have Square Ends, are Standard Length, straight on edges, and made of Best Hardened and Tempered Cast Steel.

		3 × ½ 21 W.G.	4 × ½ 21 W.G.	6 × ¾ 21 W.G.	12 × 1 inch. 19 W.G
No. 01.	Marked London on Two Edges. 1st Edge marked inches in 32nds, one inch of 64ths at end 2nd ,, ,, ,, ,, 20ths ,, ,, 50ths ,,	9/6	10/6	13/	24/- per dozen.
,, 02	Marked London on Four Edges 1st Edge marked inches in 8ths ... ... 2nd ,, ,, ,, ,, 16ths ... ... 3rd ,, ,, ,, ,, 32nds one inch of 64ths at end 4th ,, ,, ,, ,, 20ths ,, ,, 50ths ,,	11/-	12/-	16/-	30/- ,,
,, 03.	1st Edge marked inches in 8ths ... ... 2nd ,, ,, ,, ,, 16ths ... ... 3rd ,, ,, ,, ,, 32nds ... ... 4th ,, ,, ,, ,, 64ths	11/-	12/-	16/-	30/- ,,
,, 06.	Marked London and Metre on Four Edges. 1st Edge marked inches in 8ths ... ... 2nd ,, ,, ,, ,, 16ths, one inch of 64ths at end 3rd ,, ,, ,, ,, 16ths ... ... 4th ,, ,, Millimetres.	—	12/-	16/-	30/- ,,

NARROW STEEL RULES.

				6 inch.	12 inch.
,, 04.	Marked exactly as No. 03 above, but ½ inch wide only × 21 W.G.	—	—	16/-	30/- per dozen.

		3 inch.	4 inch.	6 inch.	12 inch.
,, 05.	Flexible Steel Rule ¼ inch wide × 28 W.G. ... ... Marked Two Edges of one side in 32nds and 64ths ...	9/6	10/6	13/-	24/- per dozen.

EXTRA NARROW STEEL RULES.

³⁄₁₆ inch wide × 21 W.G.

		6 inch.
	Marked London on One Edge.	
,, 60.	Marked inches in 16ths	10/6 per dozen,
,, 61.	,, ,, 32nds	14/6 ,,
	Marked London and Metre on Two Edges.	
,, 62.	One Edge marked inches in 32nds, Other ,, Millimetres ...	... ... 22/6 ,,
	Marked London on Two Edges.	
,, 63.	One Edge marked inches in 10ths Other ,, ,, ,, 20ths	... ... 22/6 ,,

EDWARD PRESTON & SONS, L^{TD.}

ENGINE DIVIDED STEEL RULES.

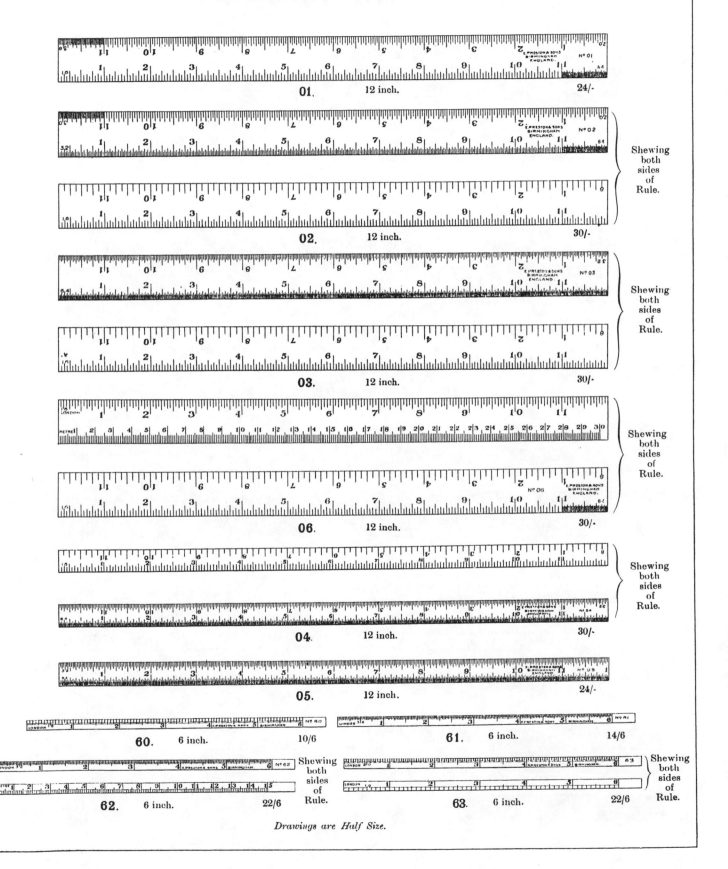

01. 12 inch. 24/-

02. 12 inch. 30/-
Shewing both sides of Rule.

03. 12 inch. 30/-
Shewing both sides of Rule.

06. 12 inch. 30/-
Shewing both sides of Rule.

04. 12 inch. 30/-
Shewing both sides of Rule.

05. 12 inch. 24/-

60. 6 inch. 10/6

61. 6 inch. 14/6

62. 6 inch. 22/6
Shewing both sides of Rule.

63. 6 inch. 22/6
Shewing both sides of Rule.

Drawings are Half Size.

EDWARD PRESTON & SONS, L<u>TD</u>.

FLEXIBLE JOINTED STEEL RULES.

WITH BRIGHT RAISED FIGURES.

5010

15/-

No. 5010.   Two feet, Two fold, inches marked in 8ths and 16ths Stop Joint and Brass Bitted Ends... ¾ inch wide, 15/- per dozen.
,, 5010C.   ,,   ,,   ,,   ,,   as 5010, without Stop or Brass Ends   ¾   ,,   12/-   ,,
,, 5006.   ,,   Four fold, one Stop Joint, two Button Joints, and Brass Bitted Ends   ...   ...   ¾   ,,   18/-   ,,
,, 5008.   Three feet, Three fold, inches in 8ths and 16ths, Two Stop Joints   ...   .   ¾   ,,   20/-   ,,

WITH SUNK FIGURES.

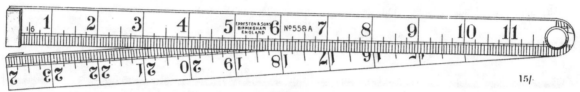

558A

15/-

No. 558A.   Two feet, Two fold, inches marked in 8ths and 16ths, Stop Joint and Brass Bitted Ends ¾ inch wide, 15/- per dozen.
,, 560A.   ,,   ,,   ,,   8ths, 16ths, 32nds and 64ths.   ,,   ¾   ,,   16/-   ,,
,, 558C.   ,,   ,,   ,,   marked 8ths and 16ths without Stop or Brass Bitted Ends   ¾   ,,   14/-   ,,
,, 558B.   Three feet, Three fold, inches marked in 8ths and 16ths, Two Stop Joints   ...   ...   ¾   ,,   33/-   ,,

THIN FLEXIBLE JOINTED STEEL RULES.

WITH BRIGHT RAISED FIGURES.

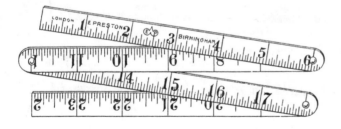

No. 505 Folding to 6 inches, ½ inch wide.

2 feet	3 feet	...	½ Metre.	1 Metre.
9/-	14/-	...	7/6	15/- per dozen.

No. 506 Folding to 4 inches.

1 foot.	2 feet.	3 feet.	½ Metre.	1 Metre.
5/-	9/6	14/-	7/6	15/- per dozen.

No. 504 Folding to 3 inches.

1 foot.	2 feet.	3 feet.	¼ Metre.	1 Metre.
5/-	10/-	15/-	8/-	16/- per dozen.

LEATHER CASES WITH N.P. STEEL RIMS.

Suitable for Rules Nos. 504 to 506.

1 foot.	2 feet.	3 feet.	½ Metre.	1 Metre.
2/-	2/6	3/-	2/6	3/- per dozen.

Drawings are Half Size.

EDWARD PRESTON & SONS, LTD.

TRADE MARK.

ENGINE DIVIDED JOINTED STEEL RULES, TWO FEET TWO-FOLD WITH BRASS BITTED ENDS.

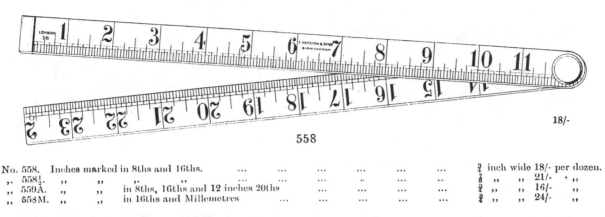

18/-

558

No. 558.	Inches marked in 8ths and 16ths.							$\frac{3}{4}$ inch wide 18/- per dozen.
,, 558½.	,,	,,	,,					$\frac{7}{8}$,, ,, 21/- ,,
,, 559A.	,,	,,	in 8ths, 16ths and 12 inches 20ths					$\frac{3}{4}$,, ,, 16/- ,,
,, 558M.	,,	,,	in 16ths and Millemetres					$\frac{3}{4}$,, ,, 24/- ,,

560

20/-

No 560.	Inches marked in 8ths, 16ths, 32nds and 64ths						$\frac{7}{8}$ inch wide 20/- per dozen.
,, 560½	,,	,,	,,	,,			$\frac{7}{8}$,, ,, 24/- ,,
,, 561	,,	,,	,,	,, 10ths and 20ths			$\frac{3}{4}$,, ,, 21/- ,,

FLEXIBLE ENGINE DIVIDED JOINTED STEEL RULES.

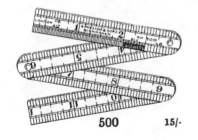

500   15/-

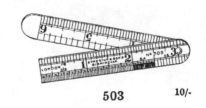

503   10/-

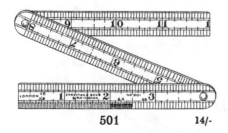

501   14/-

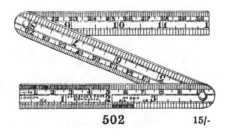

502   15/-

No. 500.	1 Foot Four-fold, inches marked in 16ths, 32nds, and 64ths					15/- per dozen.
,, 501.	,, Three-fold ,, ,, ,, ,,					14/- ,,
,, 502.	,, ,, ,, ,, ,, and Millemetres					15/- ,,
,, 503.	6 inch inches marked in 16ths, 32nds, and 64ths					10/- ,,

LEATHER CASES WITH N.P. STEEL RIMS.

Suitable for Rules Nos. 500 to 503 ... ... 2/6 per dozen.

Drawings are Half Size.

EDWARD PRESTON & SONS, L^{TD}.

ENGINE DIVIDED JOINTED STEEL RULES.

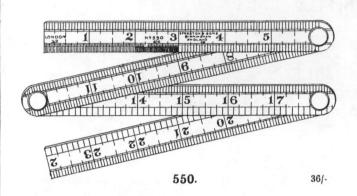

550.　　　36/-

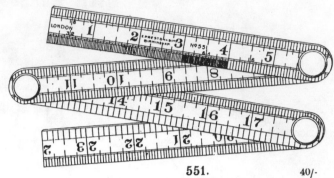

551.　　　40/-

No. 550.　Two Feet Four-fold, Button Joint, inches marked 8ths, 16ths, 32nds, 64ths, on Two Edges of one side, ⅝ inch wide,　36/- per dozen.
　,,　551.　　,,　　,,　　,,　　Stop Joints　　,,　　,,　　,,　　,,　　,,　　,,　　,,　　¾　,,　　40/-　　,,
　,,　552.　　,,　　,,　　,,　　inches in 16ths on one edge of one side　　...　　,,　　...　　...　　...　　28/-　　,,
Leather Cases with N.P. Steel Rims suitable for Rules.　Nos. 551 to 552　　...　　...　　...　　...　　...　　4/-　　,,

ENGINE DIVIDED JOINTED STEEL RULES.

These Rules open and form a Square, as well as opening straight.

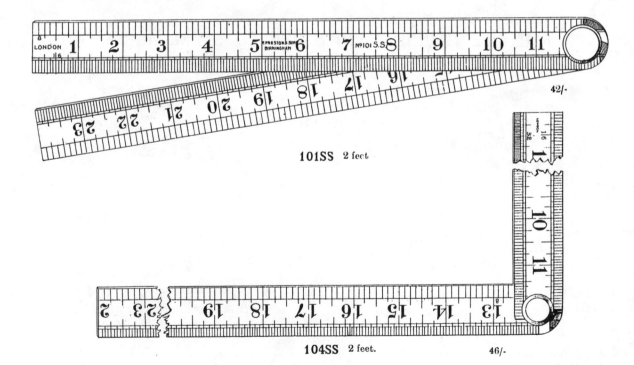

101SS　2 feet

42/-

104SS　2 feet.　　　46/-

			1 ft. × ⅞ × 20 W.G.	2 ft. 1⅛ × 19 W.G.
No. 101SS.	Two-fold, inches marked on two edges in 8ths and 16ths		—	42/- per dozen.
,, 104SS.	,, ,, ,,	8ths, 16ths, 32nds and 64ths	33/-	46/- ,,
,, 110SS.	,, ,, ,, four edges ,, ,, ,,		39/-	54/- ,,
,, 116SS.	,, ,, ,, two edges ,, ,, ,, and millimetres		36/-	50/- ,,
,, 16SS.	,, ,, ,, four edges in 8ths, 16ths 32nds, 64ths, and Tapping and Spanner sizes		39/-	54/- ,,

Drawings are Half Size.

EDWARD PRESTON & SONS, L^{TD.}

DRAUGHTSMENS' BRIGHT STEEL STRAIGHT EDGES.

TRADE EP MARK.

One Bevelled Edge and hole at one end for hanging up.

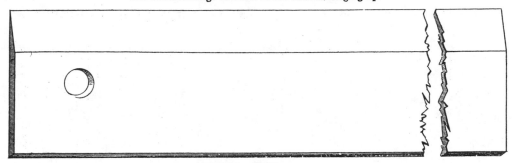

2028 to 2031

						12	18	24	30	36	42	48	54	60	72	Inches.
No. 2028.	1½ inch wide × 14 W.G. thick	...	...	...	2/-	3/-	4/-	5/6	—	—	—	—	—	—	each.
„ 2029.	1¾ „ × 13 W.G. „	...	...	...	—	—	—	—	6/9	8/-	—	—	—	—	„
„ 2030.	2 „ × 12 W.G. „	...	...	...	—	—	—	—	—	—	10/3	11/3	12/6	—	„
„ 2031.	2½ „ × 12 W.G. „	...	...	...	—	—	—	—	—	—	—	—	—	18/-	„

DRAUGHTSMENS' ENGINE DIVIDED STEEL STRAIGHT EDGES.

With one Bevelled Edge.

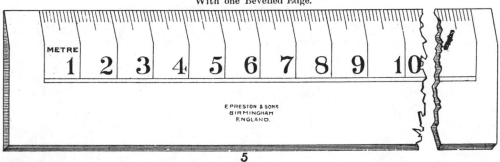

E PRESTON & SONS
BIRMINGHAM
ENGLAND.

5

	Marked inches on Bevelled Edge	1½ inch Wide by 15 W.G. Thick.			1¾ inch Wide by 14 W.G. Thick.	2 inch Wide by 13 W.G. Thick.		2½ inch Wide by 12 W.G. Thick.
		12 inch.	18 inch.	24 inch.	36 inch.	48 inch.	60 inch.	72 inches.
No. 4.	Inches Divided into 16ths.	3/-	4/6	6/6	10/-	15/-	19/-	25/- each.

	Metre on Bevelled Edge.	1½ inch Wide by 15 W.G. Thick.		1¾ inch Wide by 13 W.G. Thick.	2 inch Wide by 13 W.G. Thick.	2½ inch Wide by 12 W.G. Thick.
		50	75	100	150	200 Centimetres.
No. 5.	Marked in Millimetres	5/6	9/-	12/-	20/-	30/- each.

ENGINEERS' STRONG STEEL STRAIGHT EDGES.

ONE EDGE BEVELLED. No. 548.

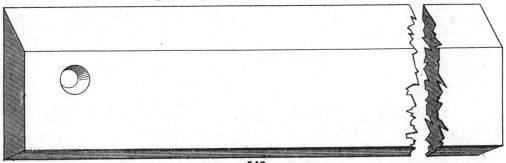

548

Width and Thickness	1¾ × ³⁄₁₆			2½ × ¼		3 × ⁵⁄₁₆		3½ × ⅜ inch.		
Length in Inches	12	18	24	30	36	42	48	54	60	66	72
Price each	5/6	8/-	11/-	16/-	19/-	25/-	30/-	34/-	40/-	44/-	50/-

TRADE EP MARK.

ENGINEERS' STEEL STRAIGHT EDGES.

Marked Inches in 16ths on one Edge. These Straight Edges have Square Edges and Ends.

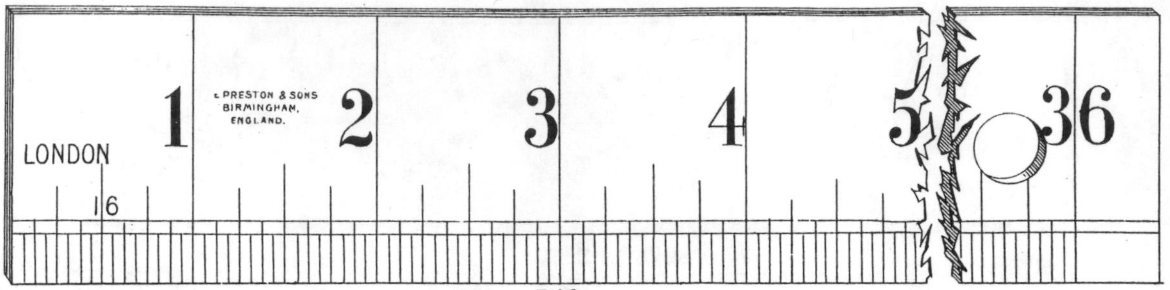

549

Width and Thickness...	1¾ × ⅛	2 × 3/16		2½ × ¼ inch.	
Length in Inches ...	24	30	36	48	60
Price each ...	9/-	12/-	15/-	24/-	30/-

MOUNT CUTTERS' STEEL STRAIGHT EDGES.

One Edge Bevelled to Angle of 40°

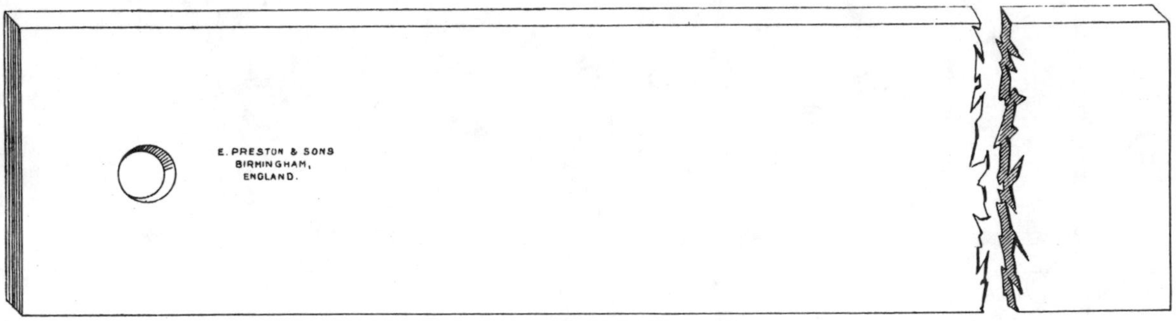

6

Width and Thickness ...	1¼ × ⅛	1½ × ⅛	1¾ × ⅛	2 × ⅛ inch.
Length in Inches ..	24	30	36	48
Price each ...	2/6	4/-	6/-	9/-

Drawings and Prices of Mount Cutter Handles and Knives, See page 105.

MASONS' AND SMITHS' IRON AND STEEL SQUARES.

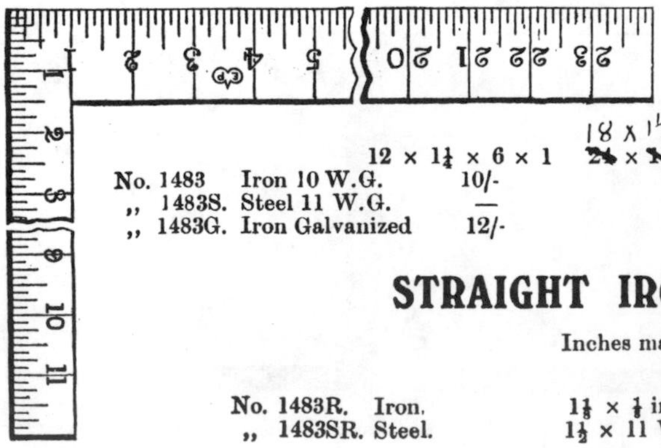

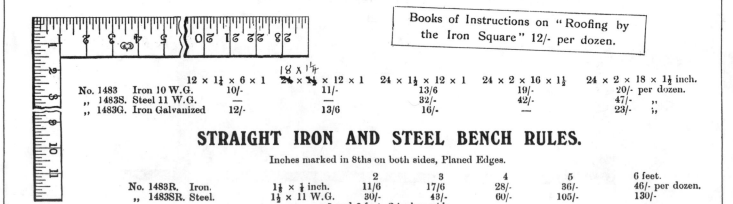

Books of Instructions on "Roofing by the Iron Square" 12/- per dozen.

		12 × 1¼ × 6 × 1	~~24 × 1¼~~ (18 × 1¼ handwritten) × 12 × 1	24 × 1½ × 12 × 1	24 × 2 × 16 × 1½	24 × 2 × 18 × 1½ inch.
No. 1483	Iron 10 W.G.	10/-	11/-	13/6	19/-	20/- per dozen.
,, 1483S.	Steel 11 W.G.	—	—	32/-	42/-	47/- ,,
,, 1483G.	Iron Galvanized	12/-	13/6	16/-	—	23/- ,,

STRAIGHT IRON AND STEEL BENCH RULES.

Inches marked in 8ths on both sides, Planed Edges.

			2	3	4	5	6 feet.
No. 1483R.	Iron.	1⅛ × ¼ inch.	11/6	17/6	28/-	36/-	46/- per dozen.
,, 1483SR.	Steel.	1½ × 11 W.G.	30/-	43/-	60/-	105/-	130/-

5 and 6 feet, 2 inches wide.

EDWARD PRESTON & SONS, L^TD.

TAILORS' SQUARES AND MEASURES.

TRADE E P MARK.

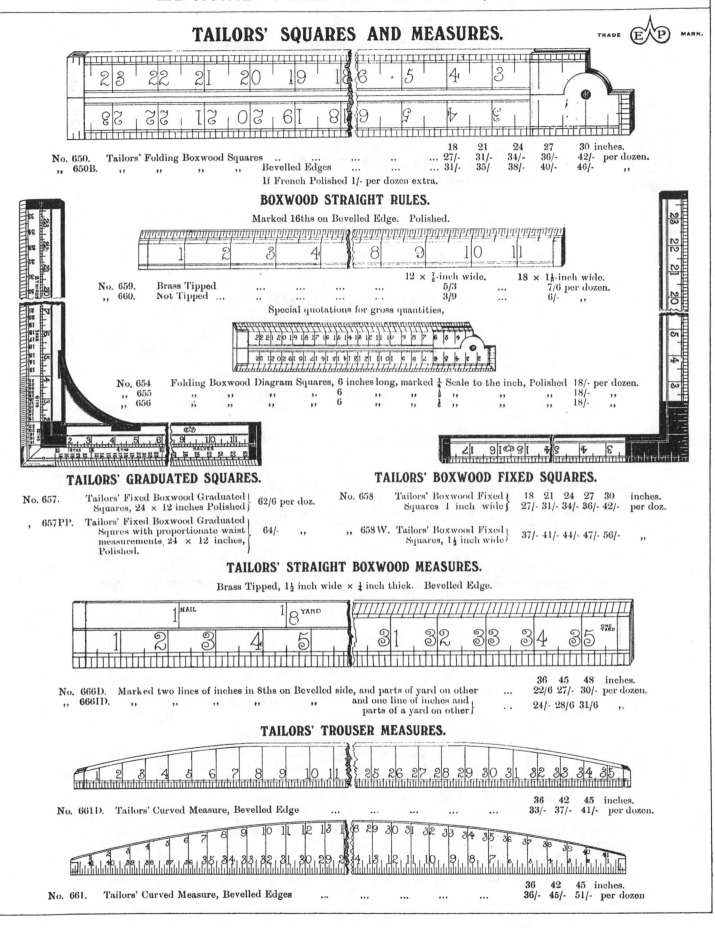

					18	21	24	27	30 inches.
No. 650.	Tailors' Folding Boxwood Squares	..	...	...	27/-	31/-	34/-	36/-	42/- per dozen.
„ 650B.	„ „ „ „ „ Bevelled Edges	...	...	...	31/-	35/	38/-	40/-	46/- „

If French Polished 1/- per dozen extra.

BOXWOOD STRAIGHT RULES.

Marked 16ths on Bevelled Edge. Polished.

					12 × ⅞-inch wide.		18 × 1¼-inch wide.
No. 659.	Brass Tipped	...	...	...	...	5/3	...	7/6 per dozen.
„ 660.	Not Tipped ...	...	...	...	3/9	...	6/- „

Special quotations for gross quantities,

No. 654.	Folding Boxwood Diagram Squares, 6 inches long, marked ⅛ Scale to the inch, Polished 18/- per dozen.
„ 655	„ „ „ „ „ 6 „ „ „ ⅛ „ „ „ 18/- „
„ 656	„ „ „ „ „ 6 „ „ „ ⅛ „ „ „ 18/- „

TAILORS' GRADUATED SQUARES.

| No. 657. | Tailors' Fixed Boxwood Graduated Squares, 24 × 12 inches Polished | 62/6 per doz. |
| 657PP. | Tailors' Fixed Boxwood Graduated Squres with proportionate waist measurements, 24 × 12 inches, Polished. | 64/- „ |

TAILORS' BOXWOOD FIXED SQUARES.

No. 658	Tailors' Boxwood Fixed Squares 1 inch wide	18	21	24	27	30	inches.
		27/-	31/-	34/-	36/-	42/-	per doz.
„ 658W.	Tailors' Boxwood Fixed Squares, 1½ inch wide	37/-	41/-	44/-	47/-	56/-	„

TAILORS' STRAIGHT BOXWOOD MEASURES.

Brass Tipped, 1½ inch wide × ¼ inch thick. Bevelled Edge.

							36	45	48	inches.
No. 666D.	Marked two lines of inches in 8ths on Bevelled side, and parts of yard on other	...	22/6	27/-	30/-	per dozen.
„ 666ID.	„ „ „ „ „ and one line of inches and parts of a yard on other	..	24/-	28/6	31/6	„

TAILORS' TROUSER MEASURES.

							36	42	45	inches.
No. 661D.	Tailors' Curved Measure, Bevelled Edge	...	...	...	...	...	33/-	37/-	41/-	per dozen.

							36	42	45	inches.
No. 661.	Tailors' Curved Measure, Bevelled Edges	...	...	...	...	...	36/-	45/-	51/-	per dozen

Edward Preston & Sons, Ltd.

TRADE (E P) MARK.

GLAZIERS' T SQUARES AND LATHS.

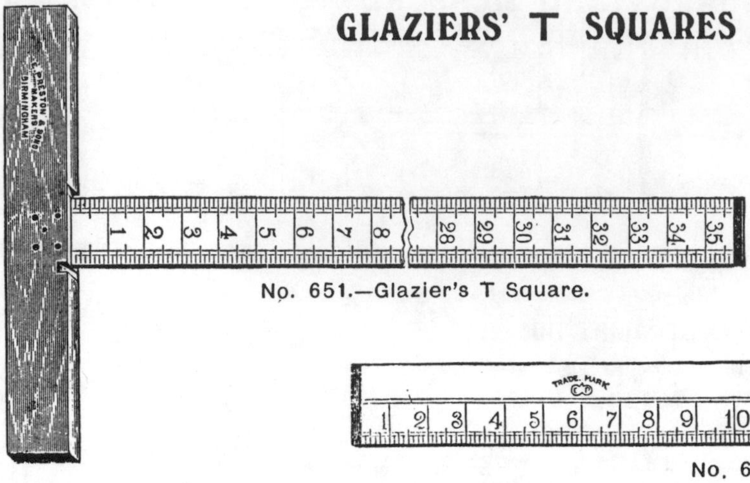

No. 651.—Glazier's T Square.

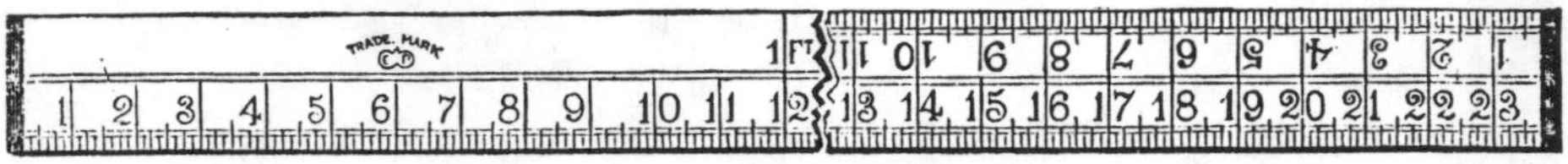

No. 652.—Glaziers' Lath.

BEST GLAZIERS' T SQUARES, BRASS TIPPED.

		24	30	36	42	48	60 inches.
No. 651.	Marked inches in 8ths	20/6	23/6	26/6	32/-	36/-	52/6 per dozen.
,, 651P.	Glaziers' T Squares with Brass-Plated Head	...	...	...	...	...	14/- per dozen extra.

BEST GLAZIERS' THIN LATHS, BRASS TIPPED,

		24	30	36	42	48	60	72 inches.
No. 652.	Marked inches in 8ths, ⅛ inch thick	11/6	16/6	20/6	23/6	27/6	41/-	58/- per dozen.

BOXWOOD BENCH RULES, BRASS TIPPED.

Marked inches in 8ths, Brass Tipped.

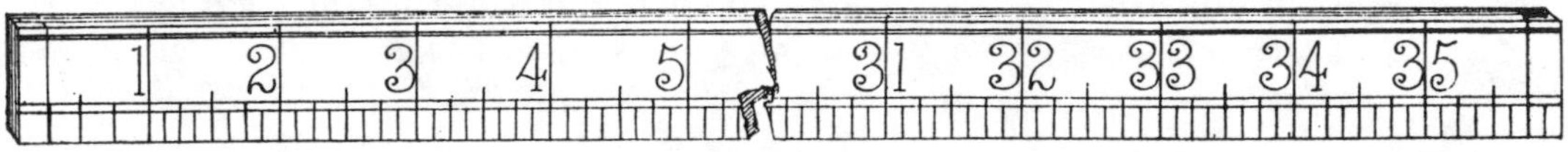

No 702.

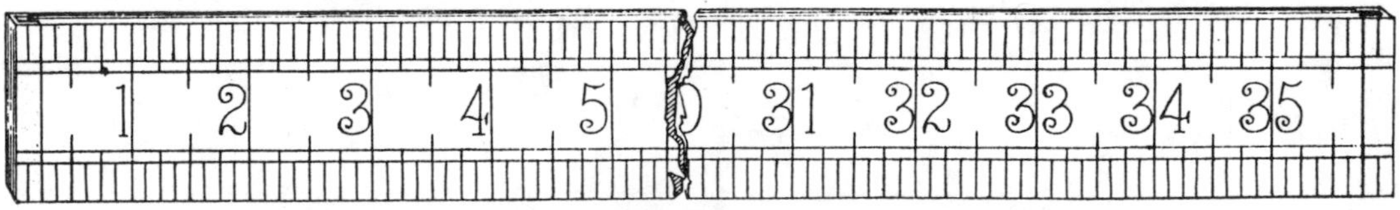

No. 704.

			2	3	4	5	6 feet.
No. 702.	Marked inches in 8ths, 1 inch wide $\frac{3}{16}$ inch thick	... ...	9/9	11/9	—	—	— per dozen.
,, 704.	,, ,, ,, 1¼ ,, ¼ ,,	... ...	14/6	17/6	26/6	39/-	58/6 ,,
,, 708.	,, ,, ,, 1¼ ,, ¼ ,,	... ...	12/6	15/6	23/6	36/-	56/6 ,,

BOXWOOD SADDLERS' RULES, BRASS TIPPED.

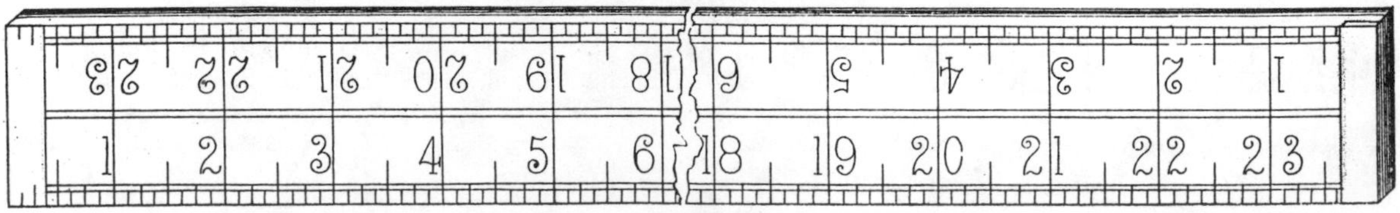

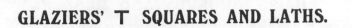

No. 701.

			2	3	4	5	6 feet.
No. 701.	Marked inches in 8ths, 1¾ inch wide × ⅜ inch thick	... ...	19/-	26/-	41/-	52/6	70/- per dozen.

EDWARD PRESTON & SONS, LTD.

SHOEMAKERS' FOLDING SIZE STICKS.

French Polished.   Marked inches in 8ths and Shoe Sizes.
Packed in Dozens in Cardboard Boxes.

712   9/- per dozen.

715   11/3 per dozen.

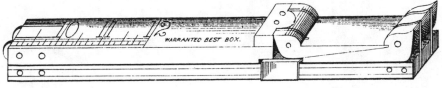

716   14/3 per dozen.

No. 710.	Folding Size Sticks, Brass Feet	...	...	...	...	...	...	...	⅜-inch wide 6/9 per dozen.
,, 711.	,,	,,	,,	,, ...	...	...	...	...	½-inch ,, 8/- ,,
,, 712.	,,	,,	,,	,, ...	...	...	...	...	9⁄16-inch ,, 9/- ,,
,, 713.	,,	,,	,,	,, ...	..	...	...	...	⅝-inch ,, 10/6 ,,
,, 714.	,,	,,	,, ,, Ivory Tip	...	...	...	...	...	¾-inch ,, 11/3 ,,
,, 715.	,,	,,	Wood ,, ...	...	...	...	...	..	⅝-inch ,, 11/3 ,,
,, 716.	,,	,,	,, ,, ...	...	...	...	...	...	⅞-inch ,, 14/3 ,,

Size Sticks may be had marked Foreign Measures to order.

PRESTON'S PATENT COUNTER SIZE STICK.

French Polished.   Packed in Half Dozens in Cardboard Boxes.

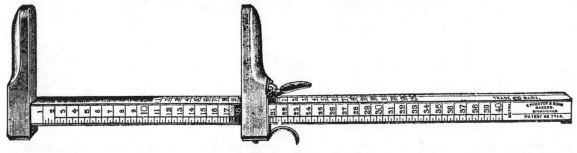

This is the most accurate and best Size Stick in the market, French polished and highly finished.

It is Supplied with a novel Automatic Attachment to the sliding foot. which fixes itself. and is held perfectly upright and rigid at all times. Mistakes in measurement will be avoided by its use, as the sliding foot cannot become loose as in the ordinary Size Sticks.

The Patent attachment consists of a brass thumb piece on the top, and a brass hook-shaped finger-plate underneath the Stick. By pressing on the thumb piece and pulling the hook with the fore-finger the foot is released, and slides smoothly along. Instantly the pressure on the thumb piece is removed, the foot becomes firm and rigid and allows the stick to be drawn from the foot or last, without moving its position.

Marked with English and French Sizes, and inches in 8ths and Millimetres.

No. 760, 6/- EACH.

EDWARD PRESTON & SONS, L^{TD.}

COUNTER SIZE STICKS.

Marked inches in 8ths, and Shoe Sizes.

French Polished.

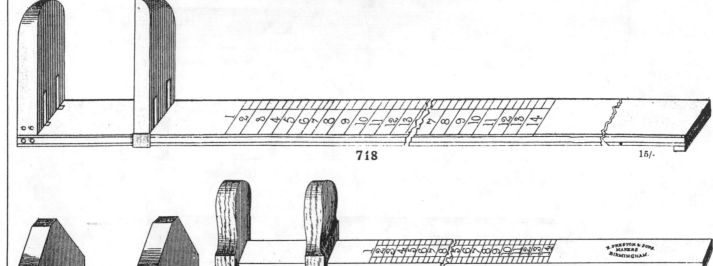

718   15/-

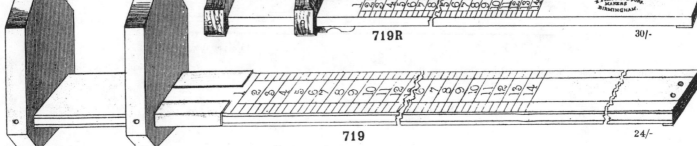

719R   30/-

719   24/-

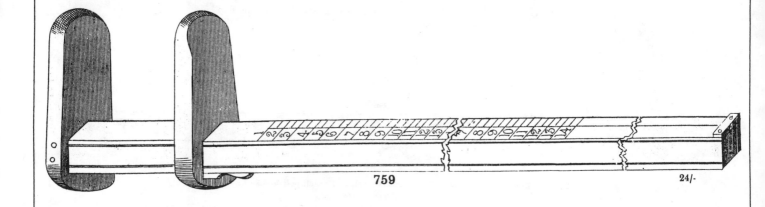

759   24/-

No. 718.	Straight Counter Size Stick	...	...	...	...	...	...	...	...	...	¾-inch wide	15/- per dozen.
,, 719.	,,	,,	,,	,,	...	...	...	...	...	...	1-inch ,,	24/- ,,
,, 719S.	,,	,,	,,	,,	Extra strong	...	...	...	...	...	1-inch ,,	33/- ,,
,, 719R.	,,	,,	,,	,,	with shaped Rosewood Feet	...	...	...	...	...	1-inch ,,	30/- ,,
,, 759.	,,	,,	,,	,,	...	...	...	...	...	...	¾-inch square	24/- ,,

EDWARD PRESTON & SONS, LTD.

PATTERN MAKERS' TWO FEET CONTRACTION LATHS.

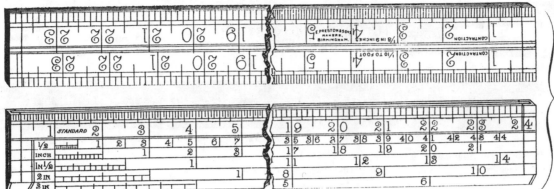

View of both sides of Pattern Makers' Contraction Lath —No. 739.

Step Pattern Contraction Lath.—No. 740.

These Contraction or Shrinkage Laths are made with Contraction graduations marked on two edges of one side and Standard measure and Drawing Scales on the other side.

They may be had with the following Contractions to the foot, viz $\frac{1}{8}$, $\frac{1}{16}$, $\frac{1}{12}$, $\frac{3}{16}$, $\frac{1}{4}$, $\frac{3}{8}$ inch Contraction in 9 inches or $\frac{1}{3}$ inch Contraction in 10 inches at the prices given below.

No. 736. Lath marked any one of the above contractions to the foot on two edges of one side, Standard and Scales on other side.   29/3 per dozen.

No. 739. Lath marked combination of any two of the above Contractions on two edges of one side and Standard and Scales on other side   35/- per dozen.

No. 740. Lath marked combination of any two of above Contractions on one edge of each side.   18/- per doz.

Contraction Laths 60 c/m long, may be had marked in the Metric System equivalent to any of the above English Contractions and Standard Metre at 12/- per dozen or 1/3 each extra.

IMPORTANT.— When ordering please state No. of Lath and Contraction required.

HORSE GAUGES, TIMBER AND BALE CALLIPERS.

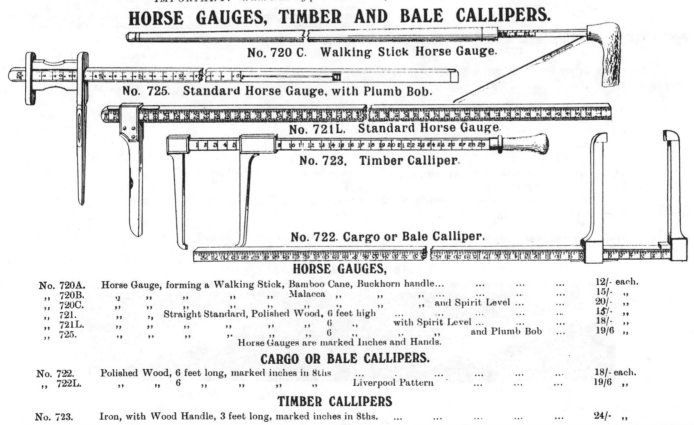

No. 720 C. Walking Stick Horse Gauge.

No. 725. Standard Horse Gauge, with Plumb Bob.

No. 721L. Standard Horse Gauge.

No. 723. Timber Calliper.

No. 722. Cargo or Bale Calliper.

HORSE GAUGES,

No. 720A.	Horse Gauge, forming a Walking Stick, Bamboo Cane, Buckhorn handle...	...	...	...	12/- each.
,, 720B.	,, ,, ,, ,, ,, Malacca ,, ,, ,, ...	...	...	...	15/- ,,
,, 720C.	,, ,, ,, ,, ,, ,, ,, ,, and Spirit Level ...	...	...	20/- ,,
,, 721.	,, ,, Straight Standard, Polished Wood, 6 feet high ...	...	...	...	15/- ,,
,, 721L.	,, ,, ,, ,, ,, ,, 6 ,, with Spirit Level ...	...	...	18/- ,,
,, 725.	,, ,, ,, ,, ,, ,, 6 ,, ,, ,, and Plumb Bob ...	19/6 ,,

Horse Gauges are marked Inches and Hands.

CARGO OR BALE CALLIPERS.

No. 722.	Polished Wood, 6 feet long, marked inches in 8ths	...	...	...	18/- each.
,, 722L.	,, ,, 6 ,, ,, ,, ,, Liverpool Pattern	...	...	...	19/6 ,,

TIMBER CALLIPERS

No. 723.	Iron, with Wood Handle, 3 feet long, marked inches in 8ths.	...	...	...	...	24/- ,,

EDWARD PRESTON & SONS, L™·

BUILDERS' AND SURVEYORS' FOLDING LATHS.

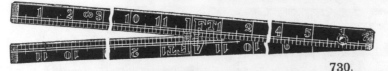

These Laths are graduated inches in 8ths throughout, and each foot is plainly indicated in large figures.

730.

731.

		5 feet.	6 feet.
No. 728.	Boxwood Folding, with Spring Stop Joint, $\frac{7}{8}$ inch wide	3/6	4/6 each.
,, 730.	Black with White Figures, with Spring Stop Joint, $\frac{7}{8}$ inch wide	3/6	4/6 ,,

STRAIGHT, WITHOUT JOINT.

		5 feet.
No. 729.	Boxwood, 1 inch wide × $\frac{1}{8}$ inch thick	3/- each.
,, 731.	Black with White Figures, 1 inch wide × $\frac{1}{8}$ inch thick	3/6 ,,

BREWERS' GAUGING AND DIP RODS.

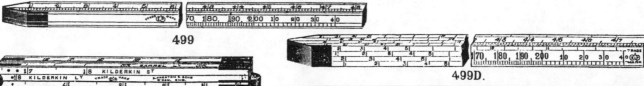

499.

499D.

418.

417D.

496A.

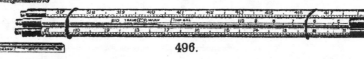

496.

479.

		4 feet.	5 feet.
No. 499.	Square Boxwood Gauging Rods, Brass Tipped, marked inches in 10ths, and Imperial gallons	32/-	42/- per doz.
,, 499D.	,, ,, ,, ,, ,, ,, ,, ,, ,, and Dips for Beer }	44/-	54/- ,,
,, 417D.	Square Boxwood Folding Gauging Rods, Brass Tipped, marked inches in 10ths, and Imperial gallons, and Dips for Beer, 4-feet 4-fold, 5/-		5-feet 6-fold, 6/6 each.
,, 418.	Two-feet four-fold Square Boxwood Beer Dip Rod		2/6 ,,
,, 496.	Round Screw Jointed Gauging Rod, marked inches and Imperial gallons, 4-feet 4-joints, 3/9		5-feet 5-joints, 4/6 ,,
,, 496A.	Round Screw Jointed Gauging Rod, marked with Dips for 9, 18, 36, 54 gallons, 33-inches long, 3 joints		3/3 ,,
,, 479.	Boxwood Square Spile Rods, marked with Dips for 9, 18, 36, 54 gallons, 33-inches by $\frac{3}{16}$-in. square		10/9 per doz.
,, 479S.	Steel ,, ,, ,, ,, ,, ,, ,, ,, ,, ,, ,, Nickel Plated }		27/- ,,
,, 479R.	Boxwood Round Spile Rods, marked with Dips for 9, 18 36, 54, gallons, 33-inches by $\frac{1}{4}$-in. dia.		19/- ,,
,, 480.	,, ,, ,, ,, ,, ,, ,, ,, ,, ,, ,, 33-inches by $\frac{1}{4}$-in. dia., Brass Point End }		27/- ,,

EBONY PARALLEL RULES.

		6	9	12	15	18	21	24 inch.
No. 508.	Brass Mounts, Best	6/-	15/-	20/-	25/-	30/-	35/-	48/- per dozen.

EDWARD PRESTON & SONS, L^TD.

TRADE EP MARK.

The following pages show a very complete range of Spirit Levels suitable for all Markets. They are fitted with Best Proved Tubes and may be relied upon as to accuracy and quality of material.

SPIRIT LEVELS, WARRANTED.

French Polished.   With Best Proved Tubes.   Packed in Half-dozens in Cardboard Boxes.

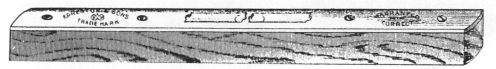

No. 1012.

LIGHT BRASS-PLATED LEVEL.

			4	6	8	9	10	12	inch.
No. 1012.	Brass-Plated Top	... ...	5/3	7/-	9/-	10/-	11/6	13/9	per dozen.
„ 1013.	„ „ „ and Tipped Bottom	—	10/6	12/6	13/6	15/-	16/-	„

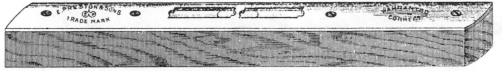

No. 1014.

BRASS-PLATED LEVEL.

			6	8	9	10	12	14	inch.
No. 1014.	Brass-Plated Top	... ...	8/-	10/-	11/6	12/9	15/-	18/6	per dozen.

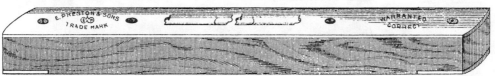

No. 1015.

BRASS-PLATED LEVEL.

			6	8	9	10	12	14	inch
No. 1015.	Brass-Plated Top and Tipped Bottom	... ...	11/6	14/-	15/9	17/6	19/6	22/6	per dozen.

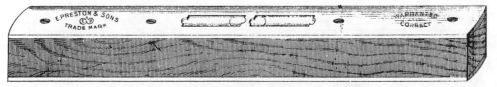

No. 1018.

BRASS-PLATED LEVEL.

			6	8	9	10	12	14	inch.
No. 1018.	Brass-Plated Top and Bottom	... ...	16/-	18/6	20/-	25/6	32/-	37/6	per dozen.

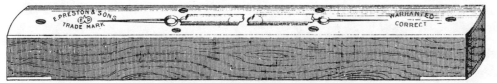

No. 1223.

STRONG BRASS-PLATED LEVEL.

			8	9	10	12	14	18	inch.
No. 1222.	Strong Brass-Plated Top	... ...	16/-	17/6	19/6	24/-	27/6	—	per dozen.
„ 1223.	Strong Brass-Plated Top and Tipped Bottom ...	19/6	21/-	23/-	26/-	32/-	50/-	„

No. 1224.

STRONG BRASS-PLATED LEVEL.

			8	9	10	12	14	18	inch.
No. 1224.	Strong Brass-Plated Top and Bottom	... ...	24/6	28/6	32/-	37/-	44/-	70/-	per dozen.

Drawings are Half Size.

SPIRIT LEVELS, WARRANTED.

French Polished. With Best Proved Tubes. Packed in Half-dozens in Cardboard Boxes.

TRADE **E◡P** MARK.

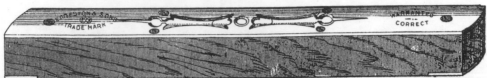

No. 1226.

FANCY BRASS-PLATED LEVEL.

		8	9	10	12	14	16	18	24	inch.
No. 1226.	Strong Fancy Brass-Plated Top and Tipped Bottom	23/-	24/6	26/6	32/-	35/6	44/-	54/-	88/6	per dozen.
,, 1227.	,, ,, ,, ,, ,, Bottom	29/-	32/-	35/6	40/6	48/6	60/-	74/-	120/-	,,

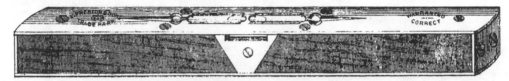

No. 1232.

STRONG BRASS-PLATED ROSEWOOD LEVEL.

		8	9	10	12	14	inch.
No. 1232.	Strong Brass-Plated Top and Bottom, Brass Side Views and Ends	34/-	37/-	40/-	46/-	54/-	per dozen.

No. 1237.

BROAD ROSEWOOD LEVEL.

		8	9	10	12	14	16	18	inch.
No. 1240.	Extra Strong Brass-Plated Top and Tipped Bottom	28/-	30/6	33/-	36/-	48/-	54/-	60/-	per dozen.
,, 1237.	,, ,, ,, ,, Bottom ...	35/6	39/-	42/6	49/6	60/-	72/-	88/6	,,
,, 1220.	,, ,, ,, ,, Steel Bottom	44/-	48/-	56/-	68/-	80/-	—	—	,,

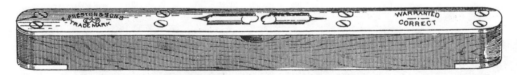

No. 1207.

NARROW ROSEWOOD LEVEL.

		6	8	9	10	12	inch.
No. 1207.	Brass-Plated Top and Tipped Bottom	16/-	20/-	24/-	26/-	32/-	per dozen.

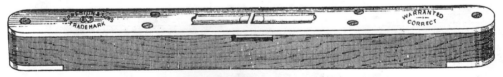

No. 1241.

NARROW ROSEWOOD LEVEL.

		8	9	10	12	inch.
No. 1241.	Extra Strong Brass-Plated Top and Tipped Bottom	21/-	25/-	28/-	34/-	per dozen.

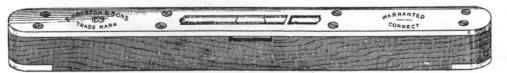

No. 1242.

NARROW ROSEWOOD LEVEL.

		8	9	10	12	inch.
No. 1242.	Extra Strong Brass-Plated Top and Tipped Bottom, with Slide to protect glass	26/6	30/-	33/6	39/-	per dozen.

Drawings are Half Size.

Edward Preston & Sons, L<u>TD</u>.

SPIRIT LEVELS, WARRANTED.

French Polished.   With Best Proved Tubes.   Packed in Half-dozens in Cardboard Boxes.

No. 1209.

NARROW EBONY LEVEL.

No. 1209.	Brass-Plated Top and Tipped Bottom			6	8	9	10	12 inch.
				16/6	17/9	19/-	20/3	24/- per dozen.

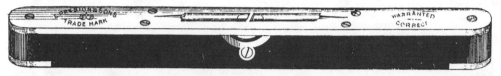

No. 1243.

NARROW EBONY LEVEL.

No. 1243.	Extra Strong Brass-Plated Top and Tipped Bottom, with Brass Side Views	8	9	10	12 inch.
		24/-	28/-	32/-	38/- per dozen.

No. 95.

ADJUSTING EBONY LEVEL.

No. 95.	Strong Brass-Plated Top and Tipped Bottom				8	9	10 inch.
					33/-	36/-	40/- per dozen.

No. 1244.

ORNAMENTAL EBONY LEVEL.

No. 1244.	Brass-Plated Top and Tipped Bottom, with Brass Side Views		8	9	10	12 inch.
			30/-	35/-	40/-	50/- per dozen.

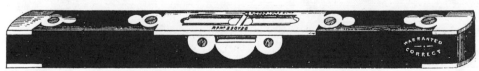

No. 1248.

ORNAMENTAL EBONY LEVEL.

No. 1248.	Brass-Plated, Tips and Side Views				8	9	10	12 inch.
					37/-	39/-	42/6	48/- per dozen.

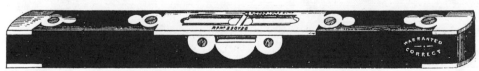

REGISTERED (No. 390723).   ORNAMENTAL EBONY LEVEL.

No. 1010.	Brass-Plated, Tips and Side Views, fitted with Mirror Tubes				10 inch.
					36/- per dozen.

Drawings are Half Size.

EDWARD PRESTON & SONS, L^TD.

PLUMB AND SPIRIT LEVELS, WARRANTED.

French Polished.   With Best Proved Tubes.   Packed in Half-dozens in Cardboard Boxes.

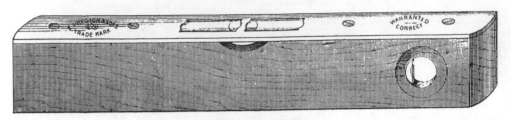

PLUMB AND LEVEL.

No. 1052.

					8	9	10	12	14	inch.
No. 1052.	Brass-Plated Top	...	...	...	17/9	20/3	22/-	26/6	31/-	per dozen

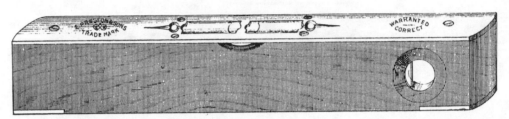

BEST PLUMB AND LEVEL.

No. 1053.

				8	9	10	12	14	inch.
No. 1053.	Best Brass-Plated Top and Tipped Bottom..	..	...	25/6	28/6	31/-	37/-	42/6	per dozen.

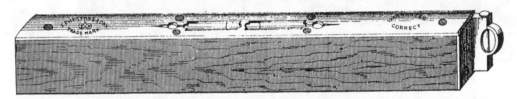

BEST PLUMB AND LEVEL, WITH FIELD SIGHT.

No. 1256.

					8	9	10	12	14	inch.
No. 1255.	Brass-Plated Top and Ends	...	...	...	33/-	36/-	39/-	45/-	51/-	per dozen.
,, 1256.	Best Brass-Plated Top and Ends	...	...	...	39/6	43/6	47/6	55/6	63/6	,,

BEST PLUMB AND LEVEL, WITH SCREW SLIDE TO SHEW FALL PER FOOT.

No. 1258.

							12	inch.
No. 1258.	Best Brass-Plated Top and Ends	...	...	...	...	...	84/-	per dozen.
,, 1258S.	,, ,, ,, ,, with Field Sight through, as 1256	...	...	...	91/-	,,
,, 1258FS.	,, ,, ,, ,, ,, Hinged Field Sight	...	...	...	114/-	,,

The Screw Slide may be marked with any Foreign Measure

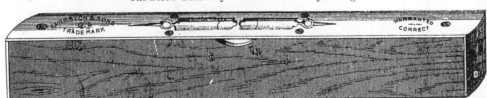

FIELD SIGHT LEVEL.

No. 1251.

					8	9	10	12	14	inch.
No. 1250.	Brass-Plated Top and Ends	...	...	...	24/-	27/-	30/-	36/-	42/-	,,
,, 1251.	Best Brass-Plated Top and Ends ...	...	...	...	32/-	36/-	42/-	48/-	56/-	,,

Drawings are Half Size.

EDWARD PRESTON & SONS, L<u>TD.</u>

SPIRIT LEVELS, WARRANTED.

French Polished.   With Best Proved Tubes.   Packed in Half-dozens in Cardboard Boxes.

No. 1261.

ROSEWOOD LEVEL, TAPERED ENDS.

				6	9	12	inch.
No. 1261.	Ornamental Brass Plating and Tipped Bottom	...	...	15/-	20/-	23/-	per dozen.

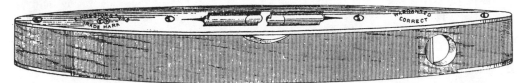

No. 1062.

ROSEWOOD PLUMB AND LEVEL, TAPERED ENDS.

					6	9	10	12	inch.
No. 1062.	Brass Plated Top and Tipped Bottom	...	...	...	17/-	20/-	22/-	26/-	per dozen.
,, 1065.	Level as 1062 but not Tapered Ends	...	...	...	17/-	20/-	22/-	26/-	,,

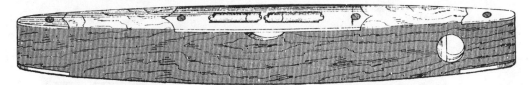

No. 1262.

ROSEWOOD PLUMB AND LEVEL, TAPERED ENDS.

				6	9	10	12	inch.
No. 1262.	Ornamental Brass Plating and Tipped Bottom	...	...	19/-	22/-	24/-	28/-	per dozen.
,, 1066.	Level as 1262 but not Tapered Ends	...	...	19/-	22/-	24/-	28/-	,,

May be had in Ebony at 4/- per dozen extra.

Drawings are Half Size.

No. 1267.
10 in. Level, 14/- each.
12 in.   ,,   16/-   ,,

Best Field Sight
Surveying Level,
Mounted on
Wood Staff.

No. 1268.
10 in. Level, 28/- each.
12 in.   ,,   30/-   ,,

Best Field Sight
Surveying Level,
Mounted on
Tripod Stand.

EDWARD PRESTON & SONS, L^{TD}.

SPIRIT LEVELS, WARRANTED.

French Polished. With Best Proved Tubes. Packed in Half-dozens in Cardboard Boxes.

These Boxwood Levels may be had marked with Two Measures at List Prices. State Measures required.

No. 1263.

MASONS' BOXWOOD LEVEL.

		6	9	12 inch.
No. 1263.	Brass Fittings and Tipped Bottom and Ends	15/-	18/-	22/- per dozen.

No. 1264.

MASONS' BOXWOOD PLUMB AND LEVEL.

		6	8	9	10	12 inch.
No. 1264.	Brass Fittings and Tipped Bottom and Ends	15/6	17/-	18/6	20/-	22/- per dozen.

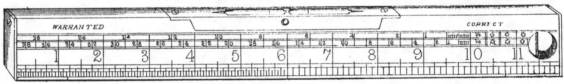

No. 1265.

MASONS' BEST BOXWOOD PLUMB AND LEVEL.

		6	8	9	10	12	18	24 inch.
No. 1265.	Brass Fittings and Tipped Bottom and Ends ...	19/6	20/6	22/-	23/-	25/-	~~30/6~~	~~40/~~ per dozen.

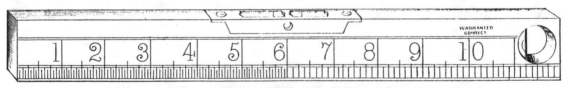

No. 1064.

MASONS' PLUMB AND LEVEL.

		12 inch.
No. 1064.	Brass Fitting and Tipped Bottom	~~10/6~~ per dozen.

Drawings are Half Size.

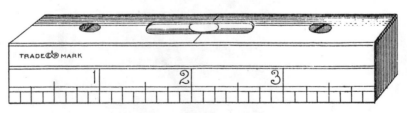

No. 1211.

BOXWOOD POCKET LEVEL.

		4	6	8 inch.
No. 1211.	Brass Plated Top	5/6	8/6	11/6 per dozen.
„ 1011.	„ „ „ and Tipped Bottom	9/6	12/6	15/6 „

Drawing is Full Size.

EDWARD PRESTON & SONS, LTD.

ENGINEERS' SPIRIT LEVELS, WARRANTED.

With Best Proved Tubes. Packed in Half-dozens in Cardboard Boxes.

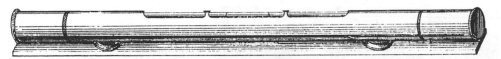

No. 1271.

BRASS LEVEL, IN CASE.

			4	5	6	7	8	9	10	12	inch.
No. 1271.	Brass Level in Case	... ...	16/-	20/-	24/-	28/-	32/-	36/-	40/-	48/-	per dozen.

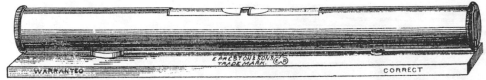

No. 1600.

BRASS ADJUSTING LEVEL, IN CASE.

			4	5	6	7	8	9	10	12	14	inch.
No. 1600.	Brass Adjusting Level in Case	...	16/6	20/6	24/9	29/3	33/3	37/3	47/-	55/-	—	per dozen.
,, 1601.	Best Brass ,, ,, ,,	...	—	—	31/-	36/3	40/9	46/-	51/6	62/-	72/6	,,

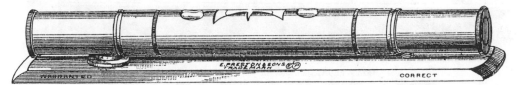

No. 1602.

BRASS ADJUSTING LEVEL, IN CASE.

			6	7	8	9	10	12	14	inch.
No. 1602.	Brass Adjusting Level, with Revolving Tube Protector, in Case		31/-	36/3	40/9	46/3	51/3	61/-	—	per dozen.
,, 1604.	Best Brass ,, ,, ,, ,, ,, ,,		35/3	41/6	47/9	58/6	63/9	79/6	95/6	,,

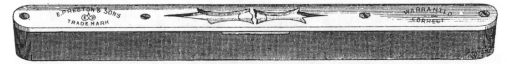

No. 1287.

BRIGHT IRON LEVEL.

			4	5	6	7	8	9	10	12	inch.
No. 1287.	Brass-Plated Top	... ...	10/-	11/-	12/-	13/-	14/-	16/-	21/-	26/-	per dozen.

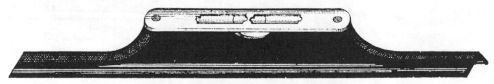

No. 1288.

IRON SHAFTING LEVEL, WITH V BASE.

			6	8	9	10	12	inch.
No. 1288.	Brass-Plated Top, Japanned Iron	... ...	15/-	18/-	20/-	22/-	26/-	per dozen.

No. 1270.

BUILDERS' AND ROAD MAKERS' LEVEL.

			7½	9½	11½	inch.
No. 1270.	Fitment for Mounting in Wood Stock	... ...	17/-	21/-	26/-	per dozen.

Drawings are Half Size.

EDWARD PRESTON & SONS, LTD.

SPIRIT LEVELS, WARRANTED.

French Polished.   With Best Proved Tubes.   Packed in Half-dozens in Cardboard Boxes.

TRADE **EP** MARK.

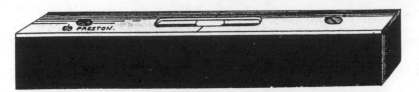

No. 1211E.—SMALL EBONY LEVEL.

Brass-Plated Top, 4-inch   ...   5/6 per dozen.

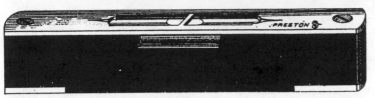

No. 1206.—SMALL EBONY LEVEL.

Brass-Plated Top and Tipped Bottom, 4-inch ~~4/4~~ per dozen.

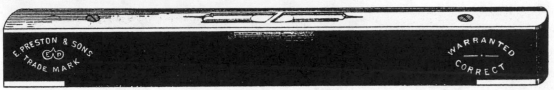

No. 1208.

SMALL EBONY LEVEL.

No. 1208. Brass-Plated Top and Tipped Bottom, 6-inch   ...   .   ~~4/4~~ per dozen.

Drawings are full size.

SPIRIT LEVEL TUBES.

Packed in Dozens in Cardboard Boxes.

Best Proved Spirit Level Tube.

		$1\frac{1}{2}$	$1\frac{3}{4}$	2	$2\frac{1}{2}$	3	$3\frac{1}{2}$	4	$4\frac{1}{2}$	5	6 inch.
No. 1293.	Spirit Level Tubes	~~1/3~~	1/3	1/6	1/9	2/-	2/6	2/9	3/6	4/6	— per doz.
,, 1294.	Best Fine Proved Spirit Level Tubes	1/6	1/9	2/-	2/6	3/-	3/6	4/-	4/6	5/-	6/- ,,
,, 1295.	,, ,, ,, ,, ,, ,, Assorted 2 to 4in.	—	—	—	—	—	—	~~8/-~~	—	—	— ,,
,, 1296.	,, ,, ,, ,, ,, ,, ,, 2 ,, 4½in.	—	—	—	—	—	—	—	3/6	—	— ,,

These Tubes have a proof mark at one end which should always be placed upwards when setting in Level Stock.

. . . PATENT . . .
"CAT'S EYE" SPIRIT LEVEL TUBES.

This is a new and novel form of Level Tube, the Air Bubble being made to resemble a Cat's Eye, which is very easily distinguished under the average conditions of light and shade, and ensures Quick and Accurate Readings.

These Tubes can be Fitted (with one or two exceptions) to Any No. of Level in our Catalogue at a charge of 3/3 per dozen extra, Plumb and Levels, 5/- per dozen extra to List Prices.

When "Cat's Eye" Tubes are required, please add "W" to List No.

Prices of "Cat's Eye" Tubes only, asstd. 2½ to 3½ in., 5/9 per dozen.

1 to 1¼	1½	2	2½	3	3½	4 inch
2/9	3/3	4/9	5/9	6/3	6/9	7/6 per dozen.

SPIRIT LEVELS, WARRANTED.

With Best Proved Tubes.   Packed in Half-dozens in Cardboard Boxes.

TRADE 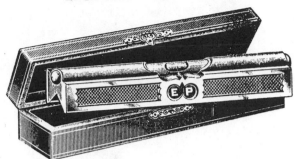 MARK.

BRASS POCKET LEVEL.

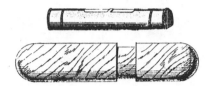

No. 1278.   In Boxwood Case   2¾ inch, 10/- per dozen.
,, 1279   ,,   ,,   ... 4   ,,   17/6   ,,
,, 1280.   ,,   ,,   ... 5   ,,   20/-   ,,

BRASS POCKET LEVEL.

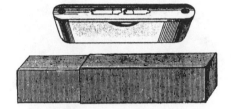

No. 1281.   In Cloth Covered Case ... 3 inch, 11/6 per dozen.

BRASS POCKET LEVEL
ON STAND.

No. 1285.   In Velvet Lined Case   3 4 5 6 inch 15/- 20/- 25/- 30/- per doz.

JAPANNED IRON POCKET LEVEL.

No. 1283.   To screw on square or straight edge   3 in. 6/- per doz.

BRASS POCKET LEVEL.

No. 1282.   To screw on square or straight edge   3 in 12/- per doz.

ENGINEERS' SPIRIT LEVEL.

This is a very handy form of iron level.

The V shaped base for standing on shafting and other round surfaces is very desirable for Engineers' and Machinists' use

It is accurately machined and highly finished, nickel plated and each one is packed in a velvet lined case.

May be fitted with "Preston's Best Proved" or "The Patent Cat's Eye Tubes."

No. 1088C.   With Preston's Best Proved Tubes   4 6 in. 33/- 42/- doz. 66/-
,, 1088CW.   ,, Patent Cat's Eye Tubes ...   36/3 45/3 ,, 69/3

No. 1087.   Nickel Plated Iron Level   4 inch, 18/- per dozen.

HEXAGON POCKET LEVELS.

No. 1286.   Nickel-Plated   ...   2½ 3 4 inch. 12/- 16/- 22/- per doz.
Round Cloth Covered Cases for above   ..   2/-   ,,

ENGINEERS' BRIGHT SQUARE IRON LEVEL.

No. 1291.   ...   3 4 5 6 inch. 15/- 20/- 25/- 30/- per dozen.

BRIGHT IRON POCKET LEVEL.
WITH BRASS TOP PLATE.

No. 1284.   To screw on square or straight edge   3 inch. 8/- per doz.

EDWARD PRESTON & SONS, L^TD.

SPIRIT LEVELS, WARRANTED.

With Best Proved Tubes.   French Polished.   Packed in Cardboard Boxes.

	12	15	18 inch.
No. 504. Brass Centre Plate, Side Views	15/-	17/6	22/- per dozen.

PLUMB AND SPIRIT LEVELS.

With Best Proved Tubes.   Varnished.

This Plumb and Level is Varnished and the top plate is not flush with the Wood Stock.

	24	27	30 inch.
No. 506C. Brass Arch Top Plate, Side Views	~~42/6~~	~~45/-~~	~~48/-~~ per dozen.

THE IMPROVED PLUMB AND SPIRIT LEVELS.

With Best Proved Tubes.   French Polished.

	24	27	30 inch.
No. 506. Brass Arch Top Plate, Side Views	~~35/6~~	~~38/-~~	~~41/-~~ per dozen.
„ 508. „ „ „ „ Half Brass Tipped	~~42/6~~	~~45/-~~	~~48/-~~ „

For Drawings see opposite page.

. . . PRESTON'S . . .

IMPROVED REGISTERED PLUMB AND LEVEL.

(Registered No. 269393.)

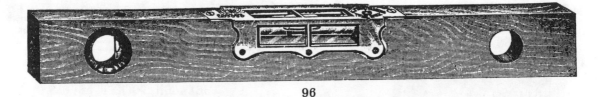

96

98

The Bubble Tube is set in the centre of a Brass Frame, which has Glass at the top and sides, with very large openings for the top and side views, thus enabling the user to see the bubble very plainly, and from a distance.

The large side views are especially useful when testing overhead work.

The Level is Proved or Tested on the top as well as on the base, so that it can be used for testing overhead work from the top of the level in places where it is not possible to place the Level on its base.

It can also be used as a Plumb Level.   Builders, Plasterers, Carpenters, Joiners, Engineers, &c., will find this Level of very great service.

The Brass Frame covering the centre tube is raised above the wood stock on the sides of the Level and forms a side grip.

There is a hole in one end for hanging the Level up.

		15 or 18 inch.
No. 96. Mahogany, French Polished ..		72/- per dozen.
„ 98. „ „ „ and Tipped Top and Bottom Corners		80/- „
„ 99. Rosewood „ „ „ „ „ Triple Stock		104/- „
„ 100. Ebony „ „ „ „ „		112/- „
Leather Cases for holding above Levels		45/- „

EDWARD PRESTON & SONS, L^{TD.}

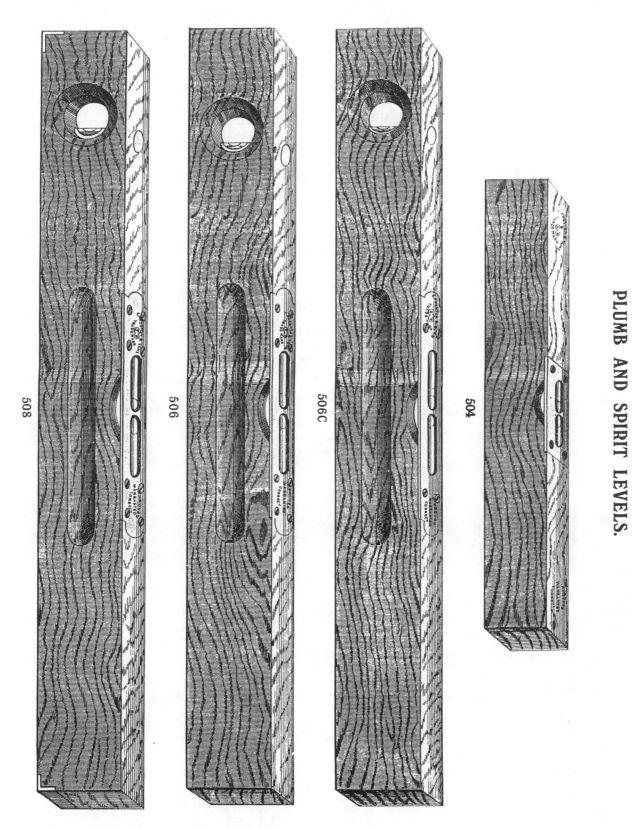

For Prices and Description see opposite page.

508

506

506C

504

PLUMB AND SPIRIT LEVELS.

EDWARD PRESTON & SONS, L^{TD.}

The following Range of Plumb and Levels are of Superior Quality and fitted with Best Proved Tubes. The Brass Fittings are dressed off flush with the wood, which gives them a high-grade style and finish. They are made with the "IMPROVED CONCAVE SIDE GRIP" which gives a feeling of security from dropping the Level to the workman when carrying.

THE PATENT IMPROVED ADJUSTABLE PLUMB AND SPIRIT LEVELS.

INVENTED AND MANUFACTURED BY EDWARD PRESTON & SONS.

With Best Proved Tubes.　French Polished.　Packed in Cardboard Boxes.

		24	27	30	inch.
No. 507.	Brass Arch Top Plate, Side Views	48/-	52/-	56/-	per dozen.
„ 509.	„ „ „ „ „ „ Half Brass Tipped	52/-	56/-	60/-	„
„ 511.	„ „ „ „ „ „ Full .. „	56/-	59/6	63/-	„
„ 513.	„ „ „ „ „ Brass Lipped Side Views, Full Brass Tipped ...	63/-	66/6	70/-	„
„ 517.	Mahogany Stock, Brass Arch Top Plate, Side Views, Full Brass Tipped ...	63/-	66/6	70/-	„
„ 519.	Mahogany Stock, Brass Arch Top Plate. Brass Lipped Side Views, Full Brass Tipped	74/-	77/-	81/-	„
„ 520.	Rosewood and Mahogany Triple Stock, Brass Arch Top Plate, Brass Lipped Side Views, Full Brass Tipped	88/-	99/6	100/-	„

All Levels above are fitted with Edward Preston & Sons Improved Adjustment, as described below.

(See Section on opposite page.)

The Spirit Glass, or Bubble Tube, is set in a Metallic Case, which is attached to the Brass Top Plate of the Level— at one end by a hinged joint, and at the other by an Adjusting Screw, which passes through a shoulder at the end of the Metallic Case. Upon the Adjusting Screw and between the Top Plate and the shoulder is placed a strong Spiral Spring, and by simply tightening or loosening the Adjusting Screw, the Spirit Glass can be instantly adjusted to a position parallel with the bottom of the Level. The Spirit Glass in the Plumb is also set in a Metallic Case, and is instantly adjusted to a position at right angles with the bottom of the Level, by means of the Adjusting Screw.

Should either of the Spirit Glasses be broken it can be easily replaced and adjusted by means of the Adjusting Screw. This easy method of adjusting the Spirit Glasses will commend itself to every mechanic.

For Drawings see opposite page.

PRESTON'S ADJUSTABLE PLUMB LEVEL.

No. 545.　Mahogany Stock, Full Brass Tipped, 30-inches long ... ... 13/- each.

This Plumb Level will be found useful to Electrical Contractors and all who have Tapering Poles to fix perpendicularly. A Milled Wheel operating upon a Graduated Gauge indicates by means of the Level Tube, the adjustment which the Pole requires.

They are made with the "Improved Concave Side Grip."

Edward Preston & Sons, Ltd.

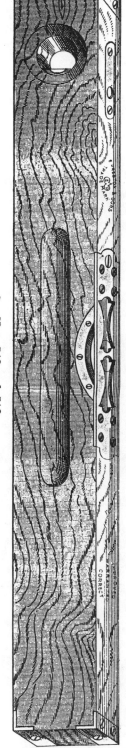

See Nos **513** and **519**.

For Prices and Description see opposite page.

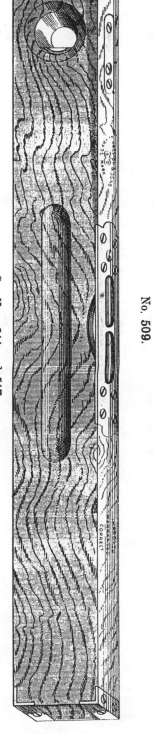

See Nos. **511** and **517**.

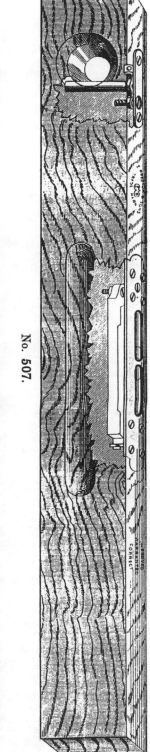

No. **509**.

No. **507**.

IMPROVED ADJUSTABLE PLUMB AND SPIRIT LEVELS.

THE PATENT

INVENTED AND MANUFACTURED BY EDWARD PRESTON & SONS.

EDWARD PRESTON & SONS, LTD.

THERMOMETERS, WARRANTED.

French Polished.   For indoor or outdoor use.   Packed in Half-dozens in Cardboard Boxes.

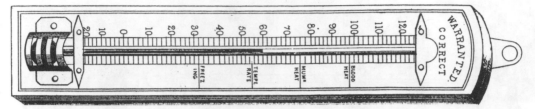

No. 1312.

BOXWOOD THERMOMETER.

						8 × 1½	10 × 1½ inch.
No. 1312. Square Edges, Plain Tube, Spirit						7/6	10/- per dozen.
„ 1312M. „ „ „ „ Mercury						9/-	11/6 „

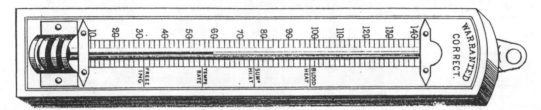

No. 1313.

BOXWOOD THERMOMETER.

					8 × 1¾	10 × 1¾ inch.
No. 1313. Bevelled Edges, Plain Tube, Spirit					9/6	14/6 per dozen.
„ 1313M. „ „ „ „ Mercury					11/-	16/- „

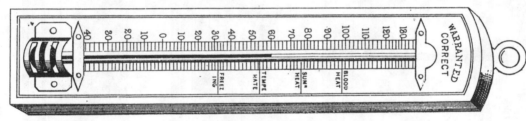

BEST BOXWOOD THERMOMETER.

				8 × 1¾	10 × 1¾ inch.
No. 1314. Bevelled Edges, Enamelled Tube, Mercury				11/6	18/- per dozen.

No. 1314.

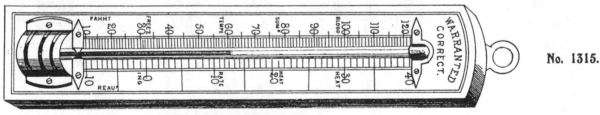

BEST BOXWOOD THERMOMETER.

			8 × 1¾	10 × 1¾ inch.
No. 1315 Bevelled Edges, Half Sunk and Enamelled Tube, Spirit			16/-	22/- per dozen.

No. 1315.

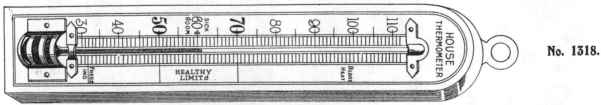

BEST BOXWOOD HOUSE THERMOMETER.

			8 × 1¾	10 × 1¾ inch.
No. 1318. Bevelled Edges, Half Sunk and Enamelled Tube, Mercury			18/-	24/- per dozen.

No. 1318.

(50° and 70° are figured in Red.)

Drawings are Half Size.

EDWARD PRESTON & SONS, L^{TD.}

THERMOMETERS, WARRANTED.

French Polished.   Packed in Half dozens in Cardboard Boxes.

TRADE (E⋀P) MARK.

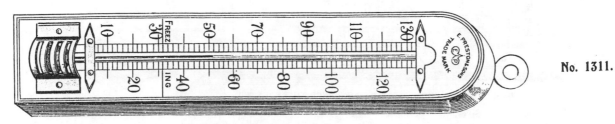

No. 1311.

BEST BOXWOOD THERMOMETER.

	8 × 1¾	10 × 1¾ inch.
No. 1311. Square Edges, Bold Figures, Enamelled Tube, Mercury	20/-	26/- per dozen.

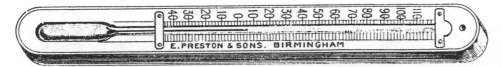

No. 1309.

BOXWOOOD COLD STORAGE THERMOMETER.

	10 × 1 1/16 inch.
No. 1309. Square Edges, Spirit	15/- per dozen.

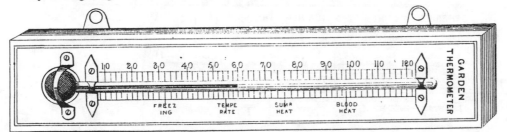

No. 1306.

BOXWOOD GARDEN THERMOMETER.

	8 × 1½ inch.
No. 1306. Square Edges, Self-Registering Plain Tube, Minimum	10/- per dozen.

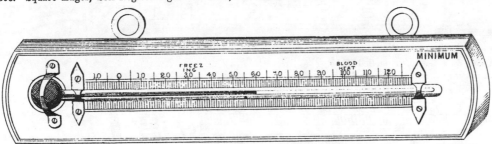

No. 1316.

BEST BOXWOOD GARDEN THERMOMETER.

	8 × 1¾	10 × 1¾ inch.
No. 1316. Bevelled Edges, Self-Registering Enamelled Tube, Minimum	15/-	20/- per dozen.

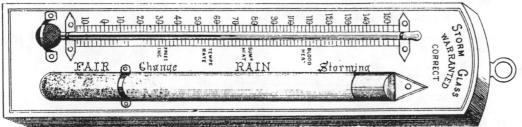

No. 1328.

BOXWOOD THERMOMETER AND STORM GLASS.

	8 × 2¼	10 × 2¼ inch.
No. 1328. Best, Bevelled Edges, Enamelled Tube, Spirit	30/-	40/- per dozen.
	8 × 1¾	10 × 1¾ inch
No. 1329. Square Edges, Plain Tube, Spirit	16/-	22/- per dozen.

Drawings are Half Size.

EDWARD PRESTON & SONS, L^{TD.}

THERMOMETERS, WARRANTED.

Packed in Cardboard Boxes.

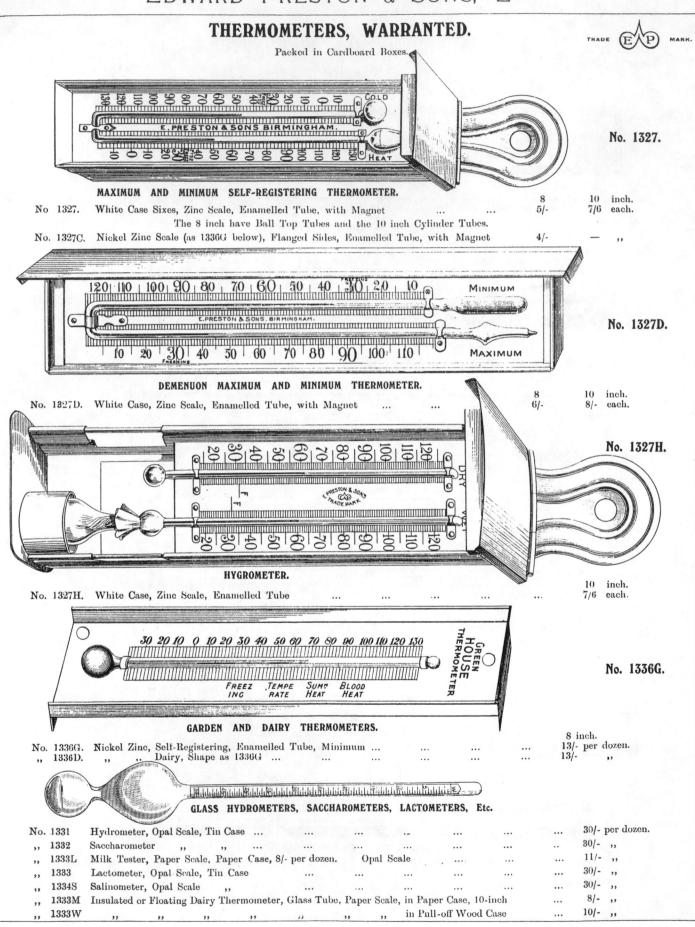

No. 1327.

MAXIMUM AND MINIMUM SELF-REGISTERING THERMOMETER.

			8	10	inch.
No 1327.	White Case Sixes, Zinc Scale, Enamelled Tube, with Magnet		5/-	7/6	each.

The 8 inch have Ball Top Tubes and the 10 inch Cylinder Tubes.

No. 1327C.	Nickel Zinc Scale (as 1336G below), Flanged Sides, Enamelled Tube, with Magnet	4/-	—	,,

No. 1327D.

DEMENUON MAXIMUM AND MINIMUM THERMOMETER.

			8	10	inch.
No. 1327D.	White Case, Zinc Scale, Enamelled Tube, with Magnet		6/-	8/-	each.

No. 1327H.

HYGROMETER.

			10	inch.
No. 1327H.	White Case, Zinc Scale, Enamelled Tube		7/6	each.

No. 1336G.

GARDEN AND DAIRY THERMOMETERS.

			8 inch.
No. 1336G.	Nickel Zinc, Self-Registering, Enamelled Tube, Minimum	13/- per dozen.
,, 1336D.	,, ,, Dairy, Shape as 1336G	13/- ,,

GLASS HYDROMETERS, SACCHAROMETERS, LACTOMETERS, Etc.

No. 1331	Hydrometer, Opal Scale, Tin Case	30/- per dozen.
,, 1332	Saccharometer ,, ,, ...	30/- ,,
,, 1333L	Milk Tester, Paper Scale, Paper Case, 8/- per dozen. Opal Scale	11/- ,,
,, 1333	Lactometer, Opal Scale, Tin Case	30/- ,,
,, 1334S	Salinometer, Opal Scale ,, ...	30/- ,,
,, 1333M	Insulated or Floating Dairy Thermometer, Glass Tube, Paper Scale, in Paper Case, 10-inch ...	8/- ,,
,, 1333W	,, ,, ,, ,, ,, ,, ,, in Pull-off Wood Case ...	10/- ,,

EDWARD PRESTON & SONS, L^TD.

THERMOMETERS, WARRANTED.

Packed in Half-dozens in Cardboard boxes.

BREWERS' THERMOMETER.

No. 1321.

		8	10	12	14	inch.
No. 1321.	Japanned Case, Plain Tube, Mercury	14/-	17/-	21/-	24/-	per dozen.
„ 1322.	„ „ Enamelled Tube, Mercury	18/-	22/-	27/-	33/-	„

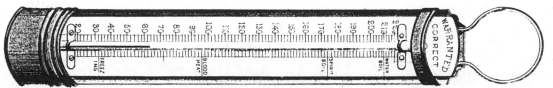

BREWERS' THERMOMETER.

No. 1323.

	8	10	12	14	inch.
No. 1323. Copper Case, Best Enamelled Tube, Mercury	24/-	30/-	36/-	43/-	per dozen.

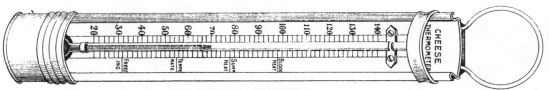

DAIRY THERMOMETER.

No. 1324.

	8	10	12	inch.
No. 1324. White Case, Enamelled Tube, Spirit	18/-	22/-	27/-	per dozen.

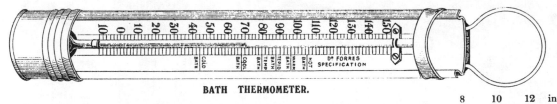

BATH THERMOMETER.

No. 1325.

	8	10	12	inch.
No. 1325. White Case, Enamelled Tube, Mercury, Dr. Forbe's Specification	18/-	22/-	27/-	per dozen.

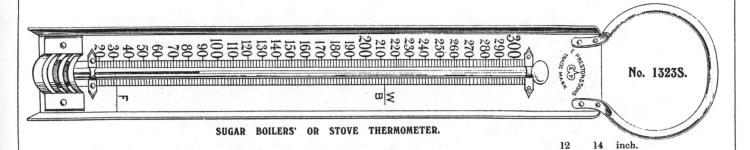

SUGAR BOILERS' OR STOVE THERMOMETER.

No. 1323S.

	12	14	inch.
No. 1323S. Brass Scale, Flanged Sides, Enamelled Tube, Mercury	60/-	69/-	per dozen.

EDWARD PRESTON & SONS, L^TD.

THERMOMETERS.

No. 2350.

HOT BED THERMOMETER.

			15	18 inch.
No. 2350. Polished Oak Frame, Brass Points, Spirit			4/6	5/- each.

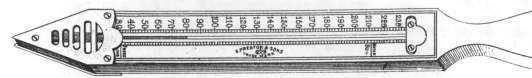

No. 2351.

MALT KILN THERMOMETER.

No. 2351. Boxwood, 18 inch long ... ... 8/6 each.

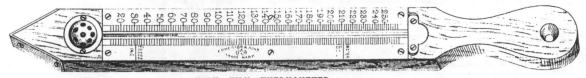

No. 2352.

MALT KILN THERMOMETER.

No. 2352. Oak, with Silvered Scale, 18 inch long ... ... 8/6 each.

No. 2353.

OVEN THERMOMETER.

Silvered Scale, with Bent Enamelled Tube, Japanned Iron Frame, and Iron Tube Casing.

No. 2353. 14½ × 3⅜ inch Front, with 24 inch Bend 32/- each.
,, 2354. ,, ,, ,, ,, 36 ,, 34/- ,,
,, 2355. ,, ,, ,, ,, 48 ,, 36/- ,,

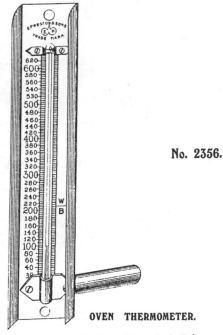

No. 2356.

OVEN THERMOMETER.

Brass Flanged Scale, with Bent Enamelled Tube, and Brass Tube Casing.

No. 2356   10 × 1¾ inch, with 3 inch Bend ... 10/6 each.

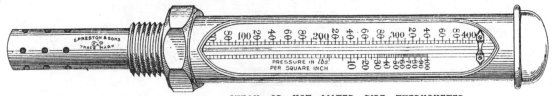

No. 2357.

STEAM OR HOT WATER PIPE THERMOMETER.

This Thermometer is indicated Fahrenheit degrees, and relative lbs. pressure per square inch. It is made with Revolving Brass Tube Protector. May be had screwed, either ¾ or 1 inch Gas Thread.

No. 2357. 14 inch long over all ... ... 23/- each.

EDWARD PRESTON & SONS, LTD.

WIND-UP MEASURING TAPES.

TRADE [EP] MARK.

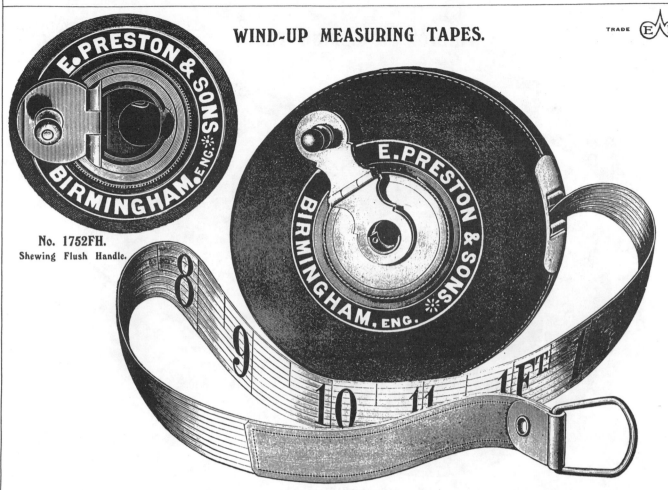

No. 1752FH.
Shewing Flush Handle.

No. 1752.

BEST METALLIC WIRED TAPE.

Marked feet and inches one side, and Links on other.
(Charged as if marked one side only.)

	MARKING.	DESCRIPTION.	24	33 10	40	50 15	66 20	75	25	100 feet. 30 Metres.
No. 1752.	One side	⅝ in. Tape in Best Solid Leather Case Folding Handle	4/3	5/-	5/6	6/2	7/-	7/9	8/3	9/9 each.
,, 1752B.	Two sides	,,　,,　,,　,,　,,　,,	4/6	5/3	5/9	6/6	7/6	8/3	8/10	10/6 ,,
,, 1752FH.	One side	⅝ in. Tape in Solid Leather Case Flush Handle ...	4/9	5/6	6/-	6/8	7/9	8/6	9/-	10/9 ,,
,, 1752BFH.	Two sides	,,　,,　,,　,,　,, ...	5/-	5/9	6/3	7/-	8/3	9/-	9/8	11/6 ,,
,, 1752T.	One side	Tapes only for above, without Cases	1/10	2/6	3/-	3/4	4/-	4/6	5/-	6/6 ,,
,, 1752TB.	Two sides	,,　,,　,,　,,　,, ...	2/2	2/9	3/3	3/9	4/6	5/-	5/6	7/3 ,,

SECOND QUALITY METALLIC TAPE.

Marked feet and inches one side, and Links on other.
(Charged as if marked one side only.)

	MARKING.	DESCRIPTION	24	33 10	40	50 15	66 20	75	25	100 feet. 30 Metres.
No. 1894.	One side	⅝ in. Tape in Good Solid Leather Case Folding Handle	3/3	3/6	4/2	4/9	5/9	6/5	7/-	8/- each.
,, 1894B.	Two sides	,,　,,　,,　,,　,,　,,	3/6	4/-	4/6	5/2	6/3	7/-	7/6	8/6 ,,
,, 1894T.	One side	Tapes only for above, without Cases	1/5	1/10	2/4	2/9	3/6	3/11	4/5	5/3 ,,
,, 1894TB.	Two sides	,,　,,　,,　,,　,, ...	1/7	2/-	2/6	3/-	3/9	4/3	4/9	5/9 ,,

Metallic, Linen and Steel Tapes marked **feet and inches** one side, and **Links and Poles** on the other side, are charged
as if marked one side only.

Foreign Measures to Order.

EDWARD PRESTON & SONS, L^{TD.}

WIND-UP MEASURING TAPES.

Nos. 2100 and 2101.

BEST LINEN TAPE.
Marked feet and inches one side, and Links on the other.
(Charged as if marked one side only.)

No.	MARKING.	DESCRIPTION.	24	33	40	50	66	75		100 feet.
				10		15	20		25	30 Metres.
No. 1762.	One side	½ in. Tape in Best Solid Leather Case Folding Handle	2/10	3/2	3/10	4/3	4/8	5/2	5/6	6/3 each.
,, 1762B.	Two sides	,, ,, ,, ,, ,, ,,	3/-	3/4	4/-	4/6	5/-	5/6	6/-	6/9 ,,
,, 1762FH.	One side	½ in. ,, ,, ,, ,, Flush Handle	3/4	3/8	4/4	4/9	5/4	5/9	6/4	7/3 ,,
,, 1762BFH.	Two sides	,, ,, ,, ,, ,, ...	3/6	3/10	4/6	5/-	5/9	6/3	6/9	7/9 ,.
,, 1762T.	One side	Tapes only for above, without Cases	1/-	1/4	1/7	2/-	2/9	3/-	3/4	3/9 ,,
,, 1759.	One side	⅝ in. Tape in Best Solid Leather Case Folding Handle	3/3	3/9	4/3	4/10	5/6	6/-	6/4	7/3 ,,
,, 1759B.	Two sides	,, ,, ,, ,, ,, ...	3/6	4/-	4/6	5/3	6/-	6/6	6/9	8/- ,,
,, 1759FH.	One side	⅝ in. ,, ,, ,, ,, Flush Handle	3/9	4/3	4/9	5/4	6/-	6/9	7/2	8/3 ,,
,, 1759BFH.	Two sides	,, ,, ,, ,, ,, ...	4/-	4/6	5/-	5/9	6/6	7/3	7/9	9/- ,,
,, 1759T.	One side	Tapes only for above, without Cases	1/2	1/6	1/11	2/4	3/-	3/4	3/8	4/6 ,,

LINEN TAPE.
Marked feet and inches one side, and Links on the other.
(Charged as if marked one side only.)

No.	MARKING.	DESCRIPTION.	24	33	50	66	75		100 feet.
				10	15	20		25	30 Metres.
No. 2100.	One side	⅝ in. Tape, Red Painted Leather Case Folding Handle	...	2/2	2/4	2/10	3/3	4/-	4/1	4/8 each.
,, 2101.	One side	⅝ in. Tape, Self Color Leather Case Folding Handle	...	2/2	2/4	2/10	3/3	4/-	4/1	4/8 ,,

Foreign Measures to Order.

EDWARD PRESTON & SONS, L^{TD}

WIND-UP MEASURING TAPES.

No. 1756. ETCHED STEEL TAPES.

DESCRIPTION:— Solid Leather Cases, Flush Handles.		MARKING:— Feet and Inches in 8ths, one side only.						MARKING:— Feet and Inches in 8ths one side and Links on other.						
Tape	No.	25	33	50	66	75	100 feet.	No.	25	33	50	66	75	100 feet.
¾ inch	1756	9/-	10/-	14/6	17/-	19/-	23/6 each.	1756B	9,3	10/6	15/-	18/-	20/-	25/- each.
½ „	1757	11/-	12/6	17/6	22/-	24/-	30/- „	1757B	12/-	14/-	19/-	25/-	27/6	35/- „

		Millimetres one side only.						London one side, Millimetres other side.						
Tape	No.	5	10	15	20	25	30 metres	No.	5	25 / 10	33 / 15	50 / 20	66 / 25	75	100 feet. 30 metres.
¾ inch	1756M	8/6	10/6	15/-	18/-	21/6	25/- each.	1756BM	9/6	10/3	12/-	17/-	21/-	23/- 25/-	30/- each.
½ „	1757M	10/-	14/-	19/-	25/-	30/-	35/- „	1757BM	11/-	14/-	17/-	23/-	31/-	33/- 36/-	42/- „

SURVEYORS' LAND CHAINS.

				33 / 2	66 / 4	100 feet. — poles.
No. 0756.	Best No 8 Bright Iron Wire, with Strong Brass Handles and Marks, and Two Sawn Oval Rings			5/-	8/-	— each.
„ 0757.	Best No. 8, Bright Iron Wire, with Best Swivel Handles and Strong Marks, and Three Sawn Oval Rings			—	10/6	13/6 „
„ 0758.	Best No. 12, Japanned, Hardened and Tempered Steel Wire, with Best Swivel Handles, and Three Sawn Oval Rings			—	11/6	14/6 „

LAND CHAIN ARROWS.

In Sets of Ten.

No. 0759.	Best Bright No. 7 Iron Wire	...	...	...	...	...	...	...	1/- per set.
„ 0760.	„ Japanned No. 8 Steel Wire	...	...	...	...	...	...	...	1/3 „

EDWARD PRESTON & SONS, L^{TD.}

WIND-UP MEASURING TAPES.

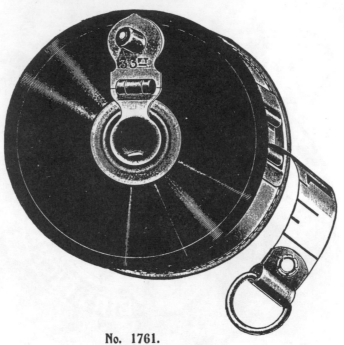

No. 1761.

MARKED ONE SIDE ONLY.	20 5	33 10	50 15	66 20	80 25	100 feet. 30 metres.
No. 1761. Japanned Leather Case, Folding Handle, ½ in Best Cotton Tape	18/-	20/-	25/-	31/-	35/-	42/- per doz.
,, 1774. Brass Rim Case, Cloth Sides, ½ in. Best Cotton Tape	13/-	14/-	17/-	21/-	26/-	30/- ,,

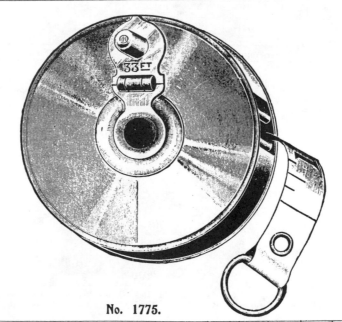

No. 1775.

MARKED ONE SIDE ONLY.	20 5	33 10	50 15	66 20	80 25	100 feet. 30 metres.
No. 1775. Ass Skin Case, Folding Handle, with ½ in. Oiled Cotton Tape	9/-	9/6	12/-	13/-	18/-	21/- per doz.

MARKED ONE SIDE ONLY.				25	33	50 66 feet.
,, 1761C. Japanned Leather Case, ½ in. Cotton Tape				16/-	16.6	19/6 21/- per doz.
,, 1775C. Ass Skin ,, ½ in. ,, ,, ...				8/-	8/6	10/- 10/9 ,,

Foreign Measures to Order.

EDWARD PRESTON & SONS, LTD.

SPRING MEASURING TAPES.

TRADE (E P) MARK.

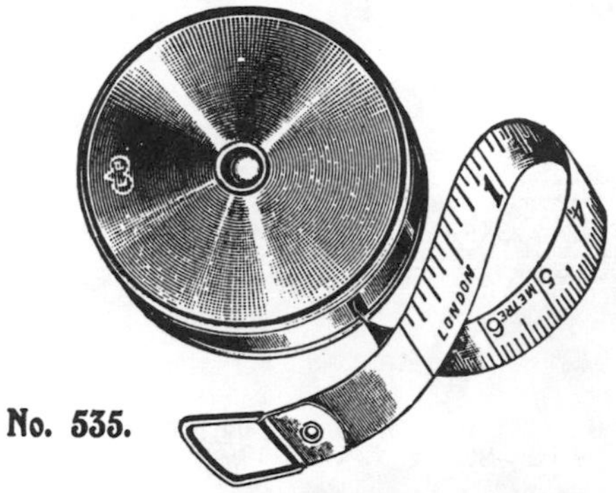

No. 535.

No. 2000.

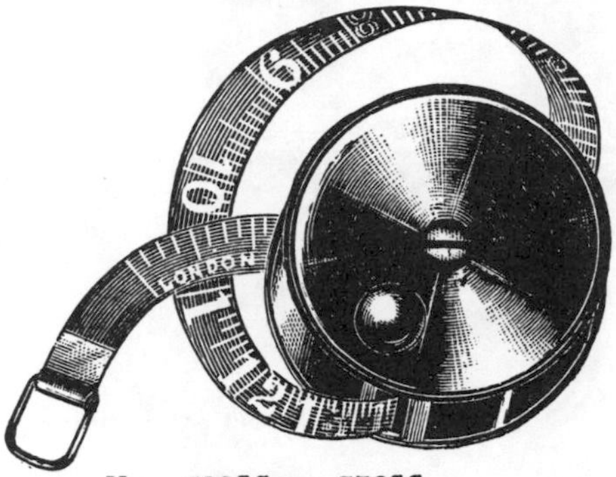

Nos. 598SS or 536SS.

No. 581SS.

Marked one side English, other side Metre.

		3	6	12 feet.
No. 535.	Nickel Plated Case, Centre Spring Stop, Steel Tape, $\frac{1}{4}$ inch	21/-	36/-	— per doz.
,, 521.	Brass Case, Best Linen Tape, $\frac{1}{4}$ inch wide	16/-	22/-	38/- ,,
,, 521SS.	,, ,, with Spring Stop, Best Linen Tape, $\frac{1}{4}$ inch wide	20/-	26/-	42/- ,,
,, 598.	,, ,, Steel Tape, $\frac{1}{4}$ inch	26/-	40/-	68/- ,,
,, 598SS.	,, ,, with Spring Stop, Steel Tape, $\frac{1}{4}$ inch	30/-	46/-	72/- ,,
,, 524SS.	German Silver Case ,, ,, Linen ,, $\frac{1}{4}$,, ...	26/-	36/-	60/- ,,
,, 536.	,, ,, ,, Best Steel Tape, $\frac{1}{4}$ inch wide	32/-	50/-	84/- ,,
,, 536SS.	,, ,, ,, with Spring Stop, Best Steel Tape, $\frac{1}{4}$ inch wide	36/-	54/-	88/- ,,
,, 581SS.	,, ,, ,, ,, Round Edges, Spring Stop, Best Steel Tape, $\frac{1}{4}$ inch wide ...	40/-	58/-	94/- ,,
			18	36 inch.
,, 2000.	,, ,, ,, Steel Tape, "Small Charm Tape"		15/-	17/- per doz.

GIRTHING TAPE FOR MEASURING TIMBER.

		3	6	9	12 feet.
No. 55G.	$\frac{5}{8}$ inch Metallic Tape marked Girth both sides	3/-	5/-	7/6	10/- per doz.
,, 56G.	$\frac{5}{8}$ inch ,, ,, ,, ,, one side, feet, inches and halves the other				
,, 57G.	The improved Girthing Tape, $\frac{5}{8}$ inch Metallic ... — This Tape is so arranged as to give the girth of a tree, both over and under the bark at one measurement, according to the proportions usually followed	4/-	6/-	8/6	11/- ,,

DRESSMAKERS' TAPE.

60 Inches Long.

No. 083.	$\frac{5}{8}$ inch Linen Tape, marked London and Metre, for Dresscutting	15/6 per gross.

EDWARD PRESTON & SONS, L^TD.

BOAT BUILDERS' BEVELS.

French Polished.   Packed in Cardboard Boxes.

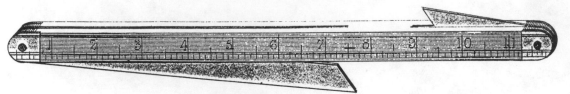

No. 1204.

BOAT BEVEL.

No. 1104. Boat Builders' Bevel, Boxwood, Two Brass Tongues, Marked inches in 8ths   ...   12 inch, 9/6 per dozen.
 „   1204.   „   „   „   „   „   „   „   „   „   Extra Strong 12 inch, 13/-   „

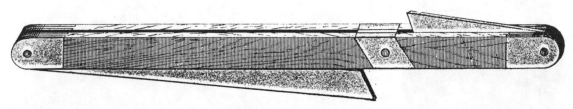

No. 1205.

BOAT BEVEL.

No. 1105. Boat Builders' Bevel, Rosewood, Two Brass Tongues   ...   .   12 inch, 9/6 per dozen.
 „   1205.   „   „   „   „   „   „   Extra Strong   ...   ...   12 inch, 13/-   „

TRAMMEL HEADS.

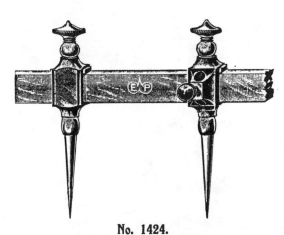

No. 1424.

Drawing shews Trammel Head
with Pencil Holder.

These Tools are of Best Quality and Finish, and are useful to Carpenters, Millwrights, Mechanics, and all others who have occasion to strike circles larger than can be done by ordinary compasses.

They are made of Brass with Hardened Steel Points and are supplied with and without Pencil Holders.

Sizes of Bar they will take.	No.	Without Pencil Holder.	No.	With Pencil Holder.
$\frac{9}{16} \times \frac{1}{4}$ inch ...	1422	... 16/6 ...	1422½	19/6 per dozen pairs.
$\frac{11}{16} \times \frac{5}{16}$ „	1423	... 19/- ...	1424	22/- „ „
$\frac{13}{16} \times \frac{7}{16}$ „	1425	... 23/- ...	1426	26/- „ „
$1 \times \frac{1}{2}$ „	1427	... 28/- ...	1428	31/- „ „
$1\frac{3}{8} \times \frac{5}{8}$ „	1429	... 45/- ...	1430	49/- „ „
$1\frac{1}{4} \times \frac{7}{16}$ „	—	... — ...	1431	60/- „ „

EXTRA LARGE TRAMMEL HEADS, without Pencil Holder, can be supplied as follows :—

Sizes of Bar ...	$1\frac{5}{8} \times 1\frac{3}{8}$	$2 \times \frac{3}{4}$	$2 \times 1\frac{1}{4}$	2×2	$2\frac{1}{4} \times 1\frac{1}{2}$	$2\frac{1}{2} \times \frac{5}{8}$	$2\frac{1}{2} \times \frac{3}{4}$	$2\frac{1}{2} \times \frac{7}{8}$	$2\frac{1}{2} \times 1\frac{1}{2}$ inch.
Per Pair ...	8/6	8/6	9/-	10/6	10/6	13/-	13/-	13/-	15/- „

They may be had with Pencil Holders at 2/6 per pair extra.

Drawings are Half Size.

EDWARD PRESTON & SONS, L^{TD.}

BRASS PLUMB BOBS.

BEST QUALITY.

These Plumb Bobs are made with removable screwed tops for inserting the line. They are accurately turned and have steel points.

The weights given are approximate.

	1½oz.	2½oz.	3½oz.	4½oz.	6oz.	8oz.	10oz.	13oz.
No. 1403.	00	0	1	2	3	4	5	6
	6/6	8/-	10/-	12/-	14/-	16/-	20/-	25/- per dozen.

	1lb.	1¼lbs.	1½lbs.	2lb.	2½lb.	3lb.	4lb.
	6½	7	8	9	10	11	12
	29/-	34/-	44/-	56/-	70/-	85/-	104/- per dozen.

Larger sizes can be supplied to order.

BRASS PLUMB BOBS.

SECOND QUALITY.

These Plumb Bobs differ slightly from our well-known No. 1403 Best Quality Pattern above, and are introduced as a cheaper article. While not being quite so well finished as our No. 1403, they may be accepted as reliable tools

The weights given are approximate.

	1½oz.	2½oz.	3oz.	4½oz.	6oz.	8oz.	10oz.	13oz.
No. 1405.	00	0	01	2	3	4	5	6
	4/9	6/-	7/6	9/-	11/3	14/-	16/9	21/- per dozen.

	1lb.	1¼lbs.	1½lbs.	2lbs.	2½lbs.	3lbs.
	6½	7	8	9	10	11
	26/-	32/-	40/-	52/-	64/-	76/- per dozen.

IRON PLUMB BOBS.

These Plumb Bobs are Japanned, with removable screwed tops for inserting the line, and have turned centre bands and points.

The weights given are approximate.

	¼lb.	½lb.	¾lb.	1lb.	1¼lb.	1½lb.	1¾lb.	2lb.
No. 1402.	5/6	6/3	7/-	7/9	8/6	9/3	10/-	10/9 per dozen.

IRON AND LEAD PLUMB BOBS.

No. 1420.　Egg Shape Japanned Iron
　　　　　Plumb Bobs ... 6d. per lb.

,, 1421.　Egg Shape Turned Lead
　　　　　Plumb Bobs ... 6d ,,

No. 1400.

STONEMASONS' BRASS SHIFT STOCKS OR BEVELS.

These Shift Stocks being made of Brass are entirely free from liability to rust owing to damp usage. They have wing nuts and set screws, and are so made that the user may, by setting the square end of the tongue to the back edge of the stock, and tightening the thumb screw, form a square.

They are also marked with the angles of 45°, 60°, and at square, 90°.

	6	7½	9	10½	12 inch.
No. 1400	16/6	20/-	23/-	25/-	28/- per dozen.

STONEMASONS' IRON SHIFT STOCKS OR BEVELS.

These Iron Shift Stocks are coated with a covering of Aluminium Paint, which prevents liability to rust. They may be used in the form of a square as described above, but are not marked with the angles.

	6	7½	9	10½	12 inch.
No. 1401.	10/-	11/-	12/-	13/-	14/- per dozen.

EDWARD PRESTON & SONS, L^{TD}.

IRON PLANES.

PACKED ONE IN A BOX.

The following Planes are well made and highly finished tools. They are constructed for very fine work, and will be found most useful to Cabinet Makers, Coach Builders, Carpenters and Wood Workers generally where great accuracy is required.

The sides and bottom being square with each other, the Planes will lie perfectly flat on either side and may be used either right or left hand.

They are supplied with PRESTON'S PATENT ADJUSTMENT to the Cutting Iron. This easy manner of adjusting the Cutting Iron has great advantages and effects a saving in fixing and setting the irons for work.

The Cutting Irons are of Best Cast Steel, hardened and tempered, and are sharpened ready for use, and each Plane is subjected to a working test before leaving our factory.

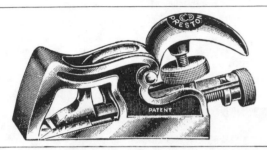

PRESTON'S PATENT ADJUSTABLE BULL NOSE RABBET PLANE.

NICKEL PLATED.

| No. 1355A. | 4 inches long, ⅞ inch Cutting Iron | ... | ... | .. | 4/6 each |
| ,, 1355. | 4 ,, ,, 1⅛ ,, ,, ,, | ... | ... | ... | 5/6 ,, |

PRESTON'S
PATENT ADJUSTABLE SHOULDER RABBET PLANE.

NICKEL PLATED.

| No 1368. | 5 inches long, ⅝ inch Cutting Iron | ... | 6/6 each |

,, 1368A.	8 inches long, ¾ inch Cutting Iron	...	12/- ,,
,, 1368B.	8 inches long, 1 inch Cutting Iron	...	13/- ,,
,, 1368C.	8¼ inches long, 1¼ inch Cutting Iron	...	14/- ,,
,, 1368D.	8¼ inches long, 1½ inch Cutting Iron	...	15/- ,,

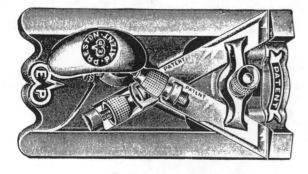

PRESTON'S
PATENT ADJUSTABLE SIDE RABBET PLANE.

NICKEL PLATED.

This is a Combined Right and Left Hand Side Rabbet Plane, and will be found a most useful tool for side rabbeting, clearing grooves and such like.

The nose of the plane can be removed for working close up into corners.

| No. 1369 | ... | 7/6 each. |

PLANE IRONS.

For Nos. 1355A,	1355,	1368	..	.	...	...	10/- per dozen.
,, ,, 1368A,	1368B,	1368C,	1368D,		..	...	12/- ,,
,, ,, 1369 Pairs ...		...	...	.	...	12/- ,,

EDWARD PRESTON & SONS, L^{TD.}

TRADE E&P MARK.

IRON PLANES.

PACKED ONE IN A BOX.

These Planes are similar in description to those on the preceding page, but without the Patent Adjustment to the cutting iron.

PRESTON'S PATTERN BULL NOSE RABBET PLANE.

No. 1347.   Japanned Bull Nose Rabbet Plane, 3¾ inch long, 1⅛ inch Cutting Iron   ...   .   3/- each.

No. 1347 N.P.   Nickel Plated Bull Nose Rabbet Plane, 3¾ inch long, 1⅛ inch Cutting Iron   ...   ...   3/6 each.

These Planes have Brass Set Screw to the Lever.

PRESTON'S REGISTERED BULL NOSE RABBET PLANE.

No. 1363A.   Japanned Bull Nose Rabbet Plane, 3¾ inch long, ⅝ inch Cutting Iron   ...   .   2/9 each.

No. 1363.   Japanned Bull Nose Rabbet Plane, 3¾ inch long, 1⅛ inch Cutting Iron   ...   .   3/6 each.

No. 1363 N.P.   Nickel Plated Bull Nose Rabbet Plane, 3¾ inch long, 1⅛ Inch Cutting Iron   ...   .   4/- each.

These Planes have Set Screw underneath the Lever.

PRESTON'S REGISTERED BULL NOSE RABBET PLANE.

No. 1366.   A Small Bull Nose Rabbet Plane, Nickel Plated with Rosewood Wedge, 3 inches long, ⅝ inch Cutting Iron   2/6 each.

PRESTON'S REGISTERED SHOULDER RABBET PLANE.

No. 1367.   Nickel Plated, with Rosewood Wedge, 5 inches long, ⅝ inch Cutting Iron   ...   .   5/6 each.

PLANE IRONS.

For Nos. 1347,   1347 N.P.,   1363,   1363 N.P.   ...   ...   8/- per dozen.

No. 1366.   ...   .   6/-   ,,

No. 1367.   ...   .   7/6   ,,

EDWARD PRESTON & SONS, LTD.

MALLEABLE IRON AND GUN METAL PLANES.

TRADE (EP) MARK.

PACKED ONE IN A BOX.

These Planes are made of Malleable Iron, and Gun Metal, and in place of the lever and screw for holding the cutting iron are fitted the Iron with Rosewood, and the Gun Metal with Ebony Wedges

They are of substantial and superior make and finish, the Bull Nose are supplied with concave side grip.

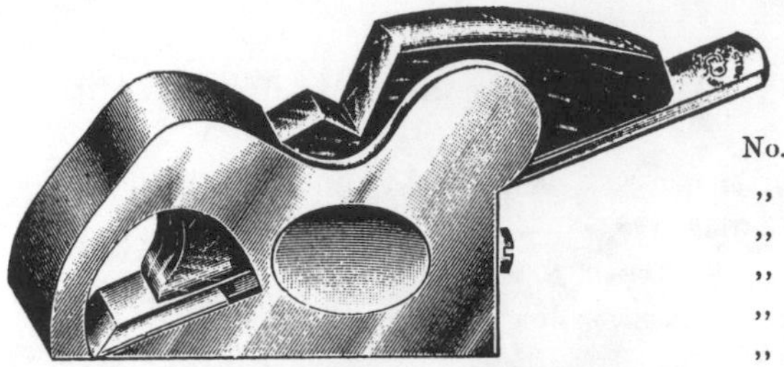

1344 or 1345.

MALLEABLE IRON BULL NOSE RABBET PLANES.

No. 1344.	Round Nose,	$3\frac{1}{2}$ inches long,	1 inch Cutting Iron	...	6/6 each.
,, 1344.	Round Nose,	$3\frac{3}{4}$,, ,,	$1\frac{1}{8}$,, ,, ,,	...	7/- ,,
,, 1344.	Round Nose,	$3\frac{3}{4}$,, ,,	$1\frac{1}{4}$,, ,, ,,	...	7/6 ,,
,, 1344L.	Square Nose,	$3\frac{1}{2}$,, ,,	1 ,, ,, ,,	...	6/6 ,,
,, 1344L.	Square Nose,	$3\frac{3}{4}$,, ,,	$1\frac{1}{8}$,, ,, ,,	...	7/- ,,
,, 1344L.	Square Nose,	$3\frac{3}{4}$,, ,,	$1\frac{1}{4}$,, ,, ,,	...	7/6 ,,

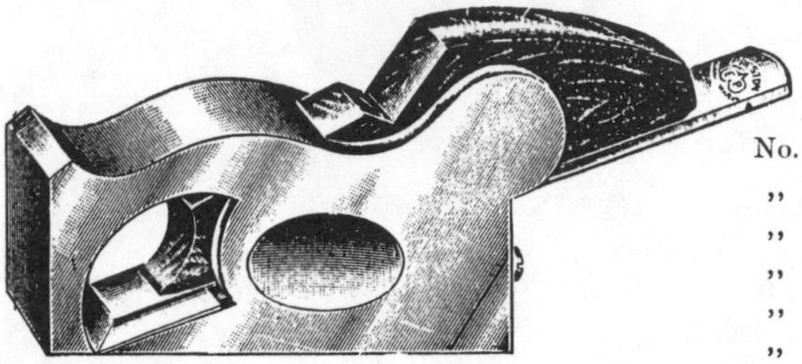

1344L or 1345L.

GUN METAL BULL NOSE RABBET PLANES.

No. 1345	Round Nose,	$3\frac{1}{2}$ inches long,	1 inch Cutting Iron	...	8/- each.
,, 1345.	Round Nose,	$3\frac{3}{4}$,, ,,	$1\frac{1}{8}$,, ,, ,,	...	8/6 ,,
,, 1345.	Round Nose,	$3\frac{3}{4}$,, ,,	$1\frac{1}{4}$,, ,, ,,	...	9/- ,,
,, 1345L.	Square Nose,	$3\frac{1}{2}$,, ,,	1 ,, ,, ,,	...	8/- ,,
,, 1345L	Square Nose,	$3\frac{3}{4}$,, ,,	$1\frac{1}{8}$,, ,, ,,	...	8/6 ,,
,, 1345L.	Square Nose,	$3\frac{3}{4}$,, ,,	$1\frac{1}{4}$,, ,, ,,	...	9/- ,,

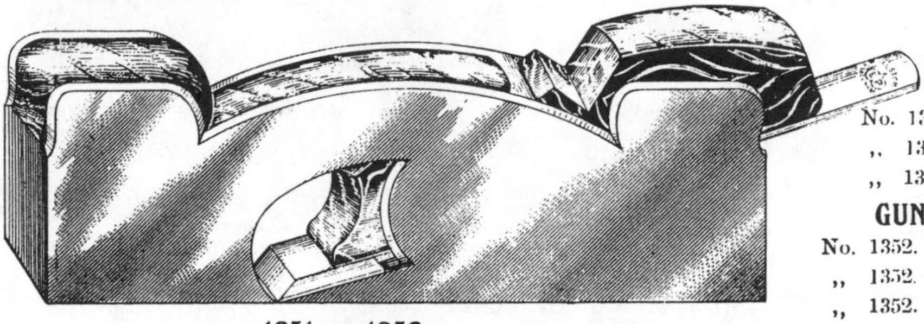

1351 or 1352.

MALLEABLE IRON SHOULDER RABBET PLANES.

No. 1351.	8 inches long,	1 inch Cutting Iron	...	13/6 each
,, 1351.	8 ,, ,,	$1\frac{1}{4}$,, ,, ,,	...	14/6 ,,
,, 1351.	8 ,, ,,	$1\frac{1}{2}$,, ,, ,,	...	15/6 ,,

GUN METAL SHOULDER RABBET PLANES.

No. 1352.	8 inches long,	1 inch cutting Iron	...	16/- each
,, 1352.	8 ,, ,,	$1\frac{1}{4}$,, ,, ,,	...	17/- ,,
,, 1352.	8 ,, ,,	$1\frac{1}{2}$,, ,, ,,	...	18/- ,,

CHARIOT PLANES.

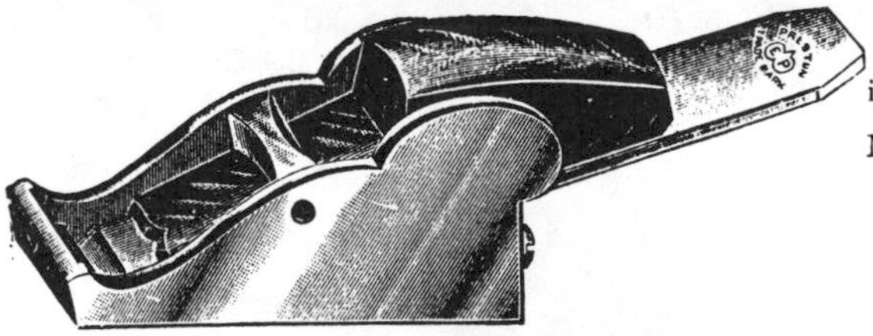

These are well-made Tools the mouth being formed by a separate piece let in the face of the plane, thus ensuring a fine mouth.

No. 1348. $3\frac{1}{4}$ inches long, Malleable Iron, Rosewood Wedge, $1\frac{1}{8}$ inch Cutting Iron ... ... 8/- each.

,, 1349. $3\frac{1}{4}$ inches long Gun Metal, Ebony Wedge, $1\frac{1}{8}$ inch Cutting Iron ... ... 9/- ,,

IRISH PATTERN CHARIOT PLANES.

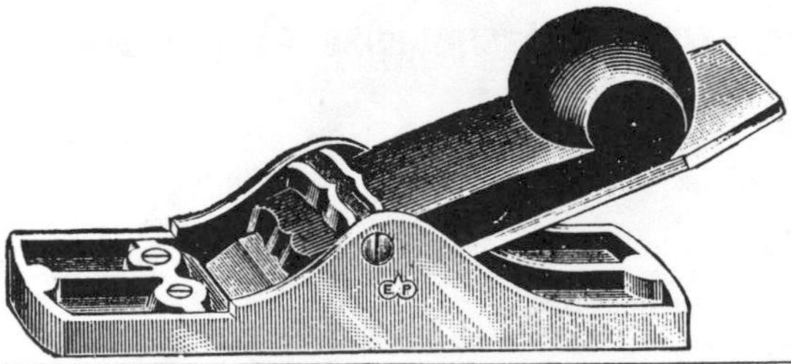

No. 1364. $7\frac{1}{2}$ inches long, Malleable Iron, Rosewood Wedge, $1\frac{3}{4}$ inch Cutting Iron .. .. 10/- each.

,, 1365. $7\frac{1}{2}$ inches long, Gun Metal, Ebony Wedge, $1\frac{3}{4}$ inch Cutting Iron ... ... 14/- ,,

PLANE IRONS.

For No. 1344,	1344L,	1345,	1345L	...	...	...	...	8/- per dozen.
,, 1351,	1352,	...	...	...	to $1\frac{1}{4}$ inch, 9/-		$1\frac{1}{2}$ inch, 10/-	,,
,, 1348,	1349,	...	...	...	...	...	...	10/6 ,,
,, 1364,	1365,	...	...	...	...	...	...	12/- ,,

EDWARD PRESTON & SONS, L^{TD.}

STEEL PLANES.
PACKED ONE IN A BOX.

TRADE E P MARK.

These Planes are made of Steel, dovetailed together and are of substantial and superior make and finish. To Cabinet Makers, Joiners, and all workers in hardwoods, they are indispensable tools, and should find a place in every workmans kit. The first cost will be saved many times over.

They have a strong Gun Metal Lever and Screw for holding down the cutting iron, which is of Best Cast Steel, bright and parallel.

The Handle and Wood Fitments are of Rosewood, and each Plane is subjected to a working test before leaving our factory.

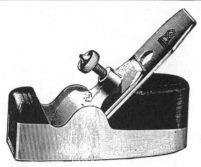

STEEL
SMOOTH PLANE.
SHAPED PATTERN.
No. 1370.

			$2\frac{1}{8}$	$2\frac{1}{4}$ inch Iron.
No. 1370	...	...	19/-	19/6 each.

STEEL
SMOOTH PLANE
WITH
HANDLE.
SHAPED PATTERN.
No. 1371.

			$2\frac{1}{8}$	$2\frac{1}{4}$ inch Iron.
No. 1371	...	...	21/-	21/6 each.

STEEL
SMOOTH PLANE
WITH
HANDLE.
PARALLEL SIDES.
No. 1372.

			$2\frac{1}{8}$	$2\frac{1}{4}$ inch Iron.
No. 1372	...	..	21/-	21/6 each.

STEEL
SMOOTH PLANE
WITH CLOSE
HANDLE.
PARALLEL SIDES.
No. 1372A.

			$2\frac{1}{8}$	$2\frac{1}{4}$ inch Iron.
No. 1372A	...	...	23/-	23/6 each.

			$2\frac{1}{8}$	$2\frac{1}{4}$ inch Iron.
No. 1341. MALLEABLE IRON Smooth Plane, shape as No. 1372			19/6	20/6 each.

STEEL PANEL PLANE
WITH
CLOSE HANDLE.

			$13\frac{1}{2}$	$15\frac{1}{2}$ inches long.
No. 1398. $2\frac{1}{2}$ inch Iron	...		30/-	32/- each.

PLANE IRONS.

					$2\frac{1}{8}$	$2\frac{1}{4}$ inch.
For No. 1370, 1371, 1372, 1372A, 1341—Bright Parallel Cut Irons only		...	...	...	1/-	1/2 each.
Double Irons	...	...	...	...	1/6	1/8 ,,

,, ,, 1398. $2\frac{1}{2}$ inch Bright Parallel Cut Irons only, 1/6, Double Irons, 2/- each.

EDWARD PRESTON & SONS, L^{TD}.

BLOCK PLANES.

These Planes are made of Cast Iron, Japanned, and are well made and finished; special attention being given to the fineness of the mouths. The Irons are of Best Cast Steel, and ready for work.

1343.

PRESTON'S PATENT ADJUSTABLE BLOCK PLANE.

This Plane is made with Preston's Patent Adjustment to the Cutting Iron

No. 1343.   7 inches long, 1⅝ inch Cutting Iron   ...   4/6 each.

„ 1342.   This Plane is same as 1343, but without Patent Adjustment to Cutting Iron   ...   3/6 „

1339.

BLOCK PLANE.

This Plane is made with Lever and under Screw.

No. 1339.   5½ inches long, 1¼ inch Cutting Iron   ...   21/- per dozen.

1356.

BLOCK PLANES.

The following Planes are made with Screw on top of Lever.

No. 1356.   3½ inches long, 1 inch Cutting Iron   ...   ...   8/- per dozen.

„ 1360.   4½ inches long, 1¼ inch Cutting Iron   ...   ...   14/- „

1357.

BULL NOSE BLOCK PLANES.

These Planes are made with the mouths or beds for Cutting Irons close to the front or nose of the Planes.

No. 1357.   3½ inches long, 1 inch Cutting Iron   ...   ...   8/- per dozen.

„ 1361.   4½ inches long, 1¼ inch Cutting Iron   ...   ...   14/- „

1358.

DUPLEX BLOCK PLANES.

These Planes have two mouths and beds for the Cutting Iron, thus forming a combination Block and Bull Nose Plane.

No. 1358.   3½ inches long, 1 inch Cutting Iron   ...   ...   11/- per dozen.

„ 1359.   5½ inches long, 1¼ inch Cutting Iron   ...   ...   18/- „

PLANE IRONS.

For Nos. 1343	...	...	...	...	...	...	...	...	6/- dozen.
„ 1342	...	...	...	...	...	...	...	...	5/- „
„ 1339, 1360, 1361, 1359	...	...	...	...	...	...	...	4/6 „
„ 1356, 1357, 1358	...	...	...	...	...	...	...	3/- „

EDWARD PRESTON & SONS, L^{TD}.

PLANES.

TRADE MARK.

These Planes are made of Best Selected and well Seasoned Steamed Beech, they are fully warranted, and are unsurpassed for quality and finish.

When required oiled, please state so on order, otherwise they will be supplied unoiled.

200.

SMOOTHING PLANES.

Fitted with Double Irons.

			2	2⅛	2¼	2⅜	2½ inch.
No. 200.	Best Quality Cast Steel Irons	... ...	3/9	4/-	4/3	4/9	5/3 each.
,, 200S.	Second Quality G.S. ,,	... ...	3/3	3/6	3/9	4/3	4/9 ,,
,, 200A.	Boxmakers or Floggers low pitch C.S. Irons		4/6	—	—	—	— ,,
,, 200B.	,, ,, ,, G.S. ,,		4/-	—	—	—	— ,,

205.

			2	2⅛	2¼ inch.
No. 205	Movable Iron Front, C.S. Irons	.. ..	8/6	9/-*	9/6 each.

205A.

			2	2⅛	2¼ inch.
No. 205A.	Iron Sole Shoe, C.S. Irons...	... ...	10/6	11/-	11/6 each.
,, 205G.	Plated Face screwed on, C.S. Irons ..	... ...	8/6	9/-	9/6 ,,

222.

COMPASSED SMOOTHING PLANE, SCREW TOP.

			1¾	2	2⅛	2¼ inch.
No. 219.	Compassed Cast Steel Irons	... ...	—	4/3	4/6	4/9 each.
,, 222.	,, ,, ,, with Screw Stop ...		—	8/6	9/-	9/6 ,,
,, 222A.	,, ,, ,, ,, with Boxwood T Stop		—	8/6	9/-	9/6 ,,
,, 225.	Fork Staff to 1¼ inch Hollow	... ...	6/-	—	—	— ,,
,, 342.	Mast Cast Steel Irons,	... ...	—	7/6	7/6	7/6 ,,

223. TOOTHING.

SMOOTHING PLANES.

With Single Irons.

		1	1⅛	1¼	1½	1¾	2	2⅛	2¼ inch.
No. 200G.	Gentlemens	—	—	—	2/4	2/6	2/6	2/8	2/10 each.
,, 200C.	Boxmakers or Floggers	—	—	—	—	—	3/3	—	— ,,
,, 223.	Toothing, Coarse, Medium, or Fine	—	—	—	—	—	3/3	—	— ,,
,, 224.	with two Irons, assorted teeth	--	—	—	—	—	4/6	—	— ,,
,, 369.	Thumb, for length see 369T, Page 90	2/-	2/3	2/3	2/4	—	—	—	— ,,
,, 340.	Spout, shaped half way down ...	—	—	—	—	—	5/6	—	— ,,

OLD WOMAN'S TOOTH PLANE.

230. Without Iron	...	2/3 each.
230I. With Iron	...	2/9 ,,

OLD WOMAN'S TOOTH PLANE, ROUTER PATTERN.

230A. Without Iron	...	2/9 each.
230AI. With Iron	...	3/3 ,,

EDWARD PRESTON & SONS, L^{TD.}

PLANES.

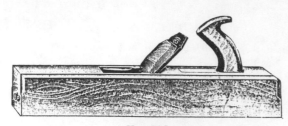

No. 206
JACK PLANE.

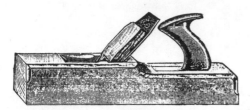

No. 206A
SUNK HANDLE JACK.

JACK PLANES.
Fitted with Double Irons.

	2	2⅛	2¼	2⅜	2½ inch.
	Length 16	17	17	17	18 ,,
No. 206. Best Quality Cast Steel Irons	4/9	5/-	5/3	6/-	6/6 each.
,, 206S. Second ,, G.S ,,	4/3	4/6	4/9	5/6	5/9 ,,
,, 206A. Technical or Sunk Handle, 14 inch, C.S. Irons	5/6	—	—	—	,,
,, 206H. Technical or Sunk Handle and Boxwood Striking Knob, 14 inch C.S. Irons	5/9	—	—	—	,,

BADGER AND PANEL PLANES.
Fitted with Cast Steel Double Irons.

	2¼	2½ inch.
No. 211. Jack Badger Skew, 16 inches long	9/6	— each.
,, 211A. ,, ,, ,, Slipped box, 16 inches long	11/-	— ,,
,, 211B. ,, ,, ,, Shoulder Box ,, ,,	13/-	— ,,
,, 211C. ,, ,, ,, Dovetailed Box ,, ,,	16/-	— ,,
,, 212. Panel, 16 inches long	—	6/6 ,,
,, 213. ,, Slipped, 16 inches long	—	7/6 ,,

JACK PLANES.
With Single Irons.

No. 232. Gentlemen's Jack, 1½ inch Iron	3/4 each
,, 314. Spout Jack, 2 inch Irons	5/6 ,,

GERMAN JACK OR ROUGHING PLANES.

No. 206½
GERMAN JACK, WITH PEG.

8 × 1¼ ... 10 × 1¼ ... 12 × 1½ inch.
3/3   3/3   3/6 each.

No. 207½
GERMAN JACK, WITH HORN.

10 × 1¼ ... 10 × 1½ ... 12 × 1¾ inch.
3/6   3/6   3/9 each.

TRYING PLANES,
FITTED WITH DOUBLE IRONS.

No. 214

TRYING PLANE.

No. 214. Best Quality Cast Steel Irons, 22 inches long, 2½ inch	6/9 each.
,, 215. ,, ,, ,, ,, ,, 24 ,, ,, ,, ...	7/- ,,
,, 216. ,, ,, ,, ,, ,, 26 ,, ,, ,, ...	7/6 ,,
,, 217. ,, ,, ,, ,, ,, 28 ,, ,, ,, ...	8/- ,,
,, 214S. Second Quality G.S. ,, ,, 22 ,, ,, ,, ...	6/3 ,,
,, 228. Coopers Croze ... ... 12 inch 5/6 ... ... 14 inch	6/- ,,
,, 229. ,, Jointers to 6 ft., 3¼ Single Iron. 20/- ; G S Double Iron	25/- ,,
,, 229A. ,, ,, ,, with two mouths and two irons, 3¼ in. Single Irons, 26/- ; G.S. Double Irons	32/- ,,
,, 229B. ,, Sun Planes ... ... —	9/- ,,

STOP CHAMFER PLANES.

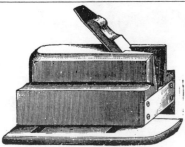

No. 360
STOP CHAMFER PLANE, POLISHED.
6/9 each.

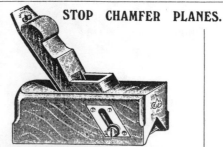

No. 361
STOP CHAMFER PLANE.
6/9 each.

No. 362.
STOP CHAMFER PLANE.
5/- each

EDWARD PRESTON & SONS, L^{TD}

PLANES.

 TRADE MARK.

PLOUGH PLANES.

PLOUGH PLANE, CAPPED STEMS.

PLOUGH PLANE, SCREW STEMS.

HANDLED PLOUGH PLANE, SCREW STEMS.

No. 270	Plough Plane, Double Plate, Eight Black Irons, Screw Stop ...	15/- each
,, 271	Plough Plane, Double Plate, Eight Black Irons, Screw Stop and Capped Stems ...	16/6 ,,
,, 272	Plough Plane, Double Plate, with Eight Bright Irons and Capped Stems ...	17/6 ,,
,, 273	Best Plough Plane, Double Plate, with Eight Bright Irons, extra work on Fence ...	19/6 ,,
,, 274	Best Plough Plane, Double Plate, with Eight Bright Irons, Improved Stop, extra work on Fence ..	21/- ,,
,, 275	Best Plough Plane, Double Plate, with Eight Bright Irons, Screw Stems, extra work on Fence ...	23/- ,,
,, 276	Best Plough Plane, Double Plate, with Eight Bright Irons, Box Screw Stems ...	27/- ,,
,, 278	Best Plough Plane, Double Plate, with Eight Bright Irons, Improved Stop, with Handles ...	27/- ,,
,, 279	Best Plough Plane, Double Plate, with Eight Bright Irons, Improved Stop, with Handles and Beech Screw Stems ...	29/- ,,
,, 280	Best Plough Plane, Improved Stop, Double Plate, Eight Bright Irons, Handles and Box Screw Stems ...	33/- ,,
,, 280½	Best Handled Plough Plane, Improved Stop, Double Plate, Eight Bright Irons, Box Screw Stems and Skate End Plates ...	34/- ,,
,, 281	Best Plough Plane, to work straight or circular ...	40/- ,,

With Dovetail T Box or Solid Box Fence, 2/- extra
If Skate End Plates ... 1/- ,,
If with Rivetted Plates ... 2/- ,,

MOVING FILLISTER PLANES.

MOVING FILLISTER PLANE, SHOULDER BOXED.

No. 240	Moving Fillister, Slipped Boxed, Brass Slip Stop and Tooth ...	6/6 each.
,, 241	Moving Fillister, Brass Screw Stop and Forked Tooth, Shoulder Boxed ...	10/- ,,
,, 242	Moving Fillister ditto, with Improved Fence ...	10/9 ,,
,, 243	Moving Fillister, with Improved Fence, Dovetail Boxed ...	14/6 ,,
,, 243A	Moving Fillister ditto, with Improved Fence, T Box Face ...	15/6 ,,

SASH FILLISTER PLANES.

SASH FILLISTER, SHOULDER BOXED.

No. 244	Sash Fillister, Wood Stop ..	6/6 each.
,, 245	,, ,, Screw Stop	9/6 ,,
,, 246	,, ,, ditto and Capped Stems, Slipped Boxed	12/- ,,
,, 246A	Sash Fillister, Left Hand and Improved Stop, Slipped Boxed ...	16/- ,,
,, 247	Sash Fillister, Left Hand Shoulder Boxed, Forked Tooth and Improved Stop ...	18/- ,,
,, 248	Sash Fillister, Left Hand, Dovetailed Boxed on Face...	21/- ,,
,, 249	Sash Fillister, Left Hand, T Box Face and ditto Fence	22/- ,,

Sash Fillisters, Solid Box Fence ... 2/- extra.

PLANES.

TRADE (E P) MARK.

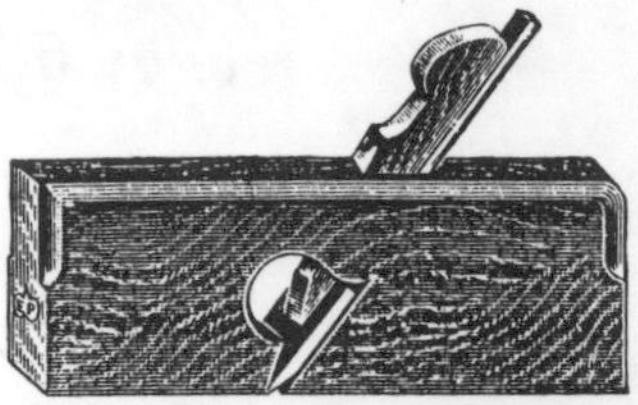

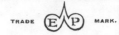

285.—SKEW RABBET PLANE.

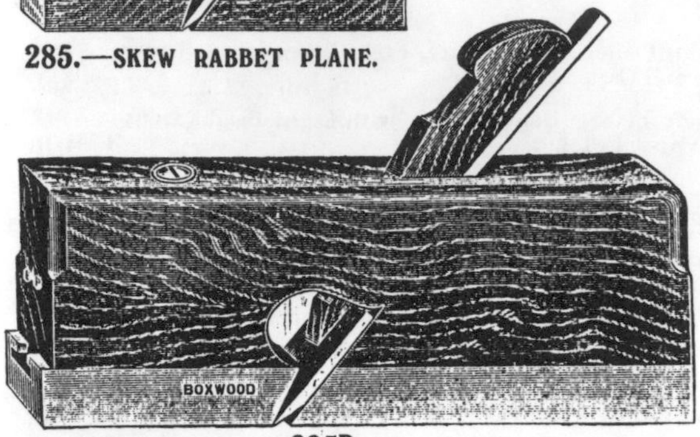

285B.

RABBET PLANES.

No. 284. Square Rabbets, to $1\frac{1}{4}$ inch ... ... 2/6 each.
,, 285. Skew ,, $1\frac{1}{4}$,, ... 2/6 ,,
$1\frac{3}{8}$ in., 2/9 ; $1\frac{1}{2}$ in., 3/- Every $\frac{1}{8}$ in. above, 3d. extra.
Boxed Edges, Skew or Square, double price.

,, 285B. Skew Rabbets, T Boxed, Moveable Face, $1\frac{1}{4}$ inch 5/6 ,,
,, 285B. ,, ,, ,, ,, ,, $1\frac{1}{2}$,, 6/- ,,

,, 282. Side Rabbets ... ... 5/6 per pair.
,, 283. Side Rounds ... ... 4/8 ,,

SNIPE BILLS.

No. 286. Snipe Bills ... ... 5/6 per pair.
,, 287. ,, ,, Shoulder Boxed ... ... 8/- ,,
,, 288. Side Snipe ... ... 7/6 ,,
,, 289. ,, ,, Shoulder Boxed ... ... 10/- ,,

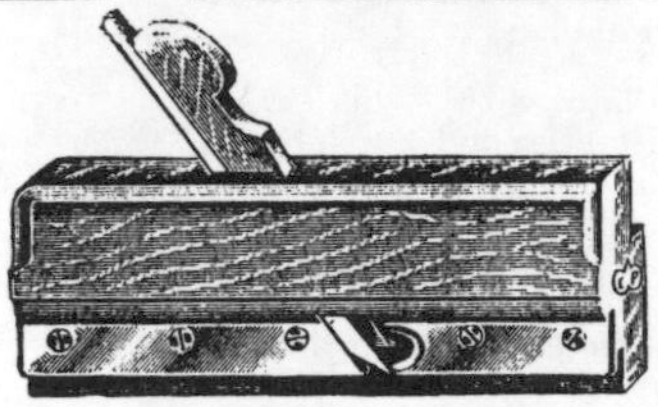

PAIR OF GROOVING PLANES. 253.

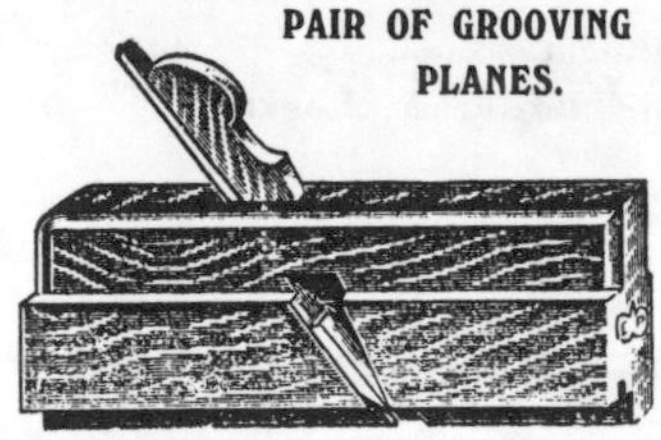

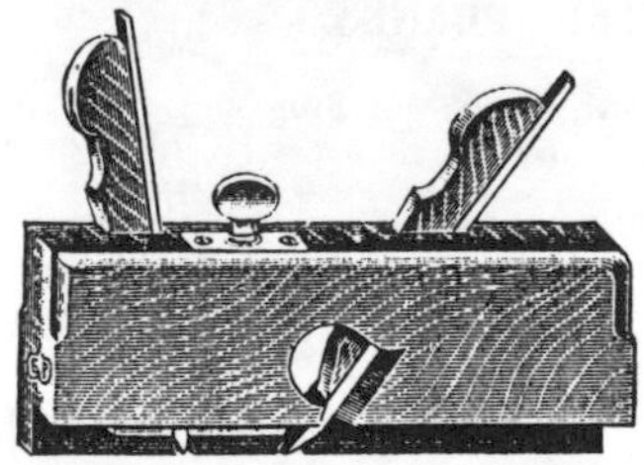

257.—DADO GROOVE PLANE, SCREW STOP

GROOVING OR MATCH PLANES.

		$\frac{1}{4}$	$\frac{3}{8}$	$\frac{1}{2}$	$\frac{5}{8}$	$\frac{3}{4}$	$\frac{7}{8}$	1 inch.
No. 253.	Grooving or Match Planes	6/-	5/6	5/6	5/6	5/6	5/10	6/- per pair.

Every $\frac{1}{8}$ inch 6d. per pair extra.

		$\frac{1}{4}$	$\frac{3}{8}$	$\frac{1}{2}$	$\frac{5}{8}$	$\frac{3}{4}$	$\frac{7}{8}$	1 inch.
,, 254.	Grooving in one Plane	6/-	5/6	5/6	5/6	5/6	5/10	6/- each.

Every $\frac{1}{8}$ inch 6d. extra.

,, 254H. Grooving with Solid Handle to $\frac{3}{4}$ inch ... 12/- each.
,, 255. Long Grooving with Handles, $1\frac{1}{4}$ and $1\frac{1}{2}$ inch 10/- per pair.
Every $\frac{1}{8}$ inch 1/- per pair extra.

,, 256. Dado Grooving or Trenching, wood stop ... 4/6 each.
,, 257. ,, ,, ,, screw ,, ... 6/6 ,,
,, 258. Grooving for Draw Bottoms .. .. 3/6 ,,
,, 257A. He Grooving with Plate right hand .. ... 3/- ,,
,, 257B. ,, ,, ,, left ,, ... 3/3 ,,
Every $\frac{1}{8}$ in 3d. extra.

,, 259. Moving Grooving, with three pair irons ... 13/- ,,
,, 259A. ,, ,, with Handles ... ... 16/- ,,

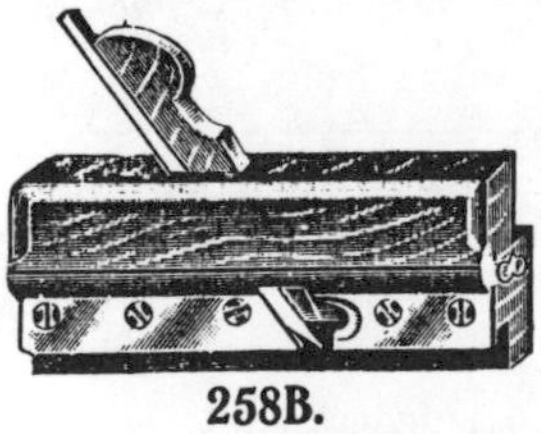

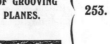

258B.

DRAWER BOTTOM GROOVING PLANES.

WITH STEEL PLATES.

No. 258B. $7\frac{1}{2}$ inches long, to groove $\frac{3}{16}$ inch ... ... 3/6 each.

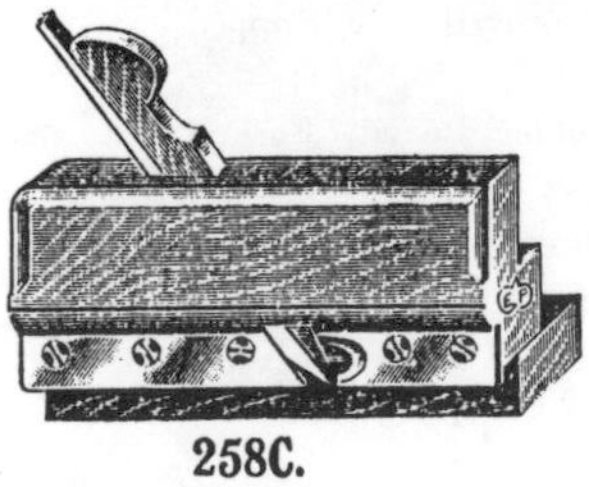

258C.

WITH MOVEABLE FENCE.

No. 258C. $7\frac{1}{2}$ inches long, to groove $\frac{3}{16}$ inch ... ... 4/6 each.

EDWARD PRESTON & SONS, L^{TD.}

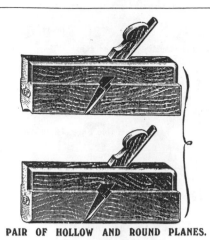

PAIR OF HOLLOW AND ROUND PLANES.

BEAD PLANE.

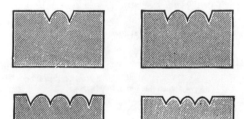

SINGLE REED, SHEWING SQUARE QUIRK.

REEDS, SHEWING BEVELLED QUIRKS.

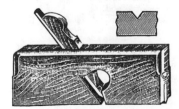

V PLANE.

PLANES.

TRADE **E P** MARK.

HOLLOW AND ROUND PLANES.

No. 260 Hollows and Rounds, Square Mouthed, per pair to 1⅛ or
No. 15 ... ... 4/4
Every ⅛ inch 4d. extra.

,, 261 Half Set Hollows and Rounds, of 9 pairs 40/-

,, 262 Full Set ,, ,, of 18 pairs 80/-

,, 263 Hollows and Rounds, Skew Mouthed, per pair to
1⅛ or No 15 ... ... 4/10
Every ⅛ inch 4d. extra.

,, 264 Half Set Hollows and Rounds, of 9 pairs 44/6

,, 265 Full Set ,, ,, of 18 pairs 89/-

,, 266 Table Planes, per pair 5/-
Gauges for ditto 6d. each.

BEAD PLANES.

No. 322 Bead Planes, Boxed to ⅝ inch ... ... 2/6 each.
,, ,, ¾ in. 2/9 ; ⅞ in. 3/- ; 1 in. ... ... 3/3 ,,

,, 323 ,, ,, Slipped to ⅝ inch ... ... 3/- ,,
,, ,, ¾ in. 3.3 ; ⅞ in. 3/6 ; 1 in. ... ... 3/9 ,,

,, 324 Bead and Torus, to ⅝ inch ... ... 3/6 ,,
,, ,, ¾ in. 3/10 ; ⅞ in. 4/2 ; 1 in.... ... 4/6 ,,

,, 324A ,, ,, Slipped, ⅝ in. 4/- ; ¾ in. 4/4 ; ⅞ in.
4/8 ; 1 in. ... ... 5/- ,,

,, 325 Beads Double Boxed, to ⅝ in. ... ... 3/- ,,
,, ,, ¾ in. 3/3 ⅞-in. 3/6 ; 1 in. ... 3/9 ,,
All above 1 inch wide 4d. per ⅛ in. extra.

,, 326 Centre Beads to ⅜ inch ... ... 3/4 ,,
,, ,, ½ in. 3/7 ; ⅝ in. 3/10 ; ¾ in. 4/1 ;
⅞ in. 4/4 ; 1 in. ... ... 4/7 ,,

,, 327 Cock Beads, to ⅜ inch ... ... 2/6 ,,

,, 328 Double Cock Beads .. .. 4/- ,,

BEAD PLANES IN SETS.

No. 329 Bead Planes, to 1 in., 10 to the set ... ... 27/6 per set.

,, 330 ,, ,, ,, ,, ,, Slipped to ½ in. 32/- ,,

,, 331 Bead Planes, to ⅞ in., 9 to the set ... ... 24/6 ,,

,, 332 assorted ,, ⅞ in. ,, ,, ,, Slipped to ½ in.
... ... 27/6 ,,

,, 333 Bead Planes, to ¾ in., 8 to the set ... ... 21/- ,,

,, 334 ,, ,, ,, ,, ,, Slipped to ½ in. 24/6 ,,

,, 334A Bead Planes, to 1 in. 8 to the set ... ... 22/6 ,,

,, 334B ,, ,, ,, ,, ,, Slipped to ½ in. 24/6 ,,

,, 324B Bead and Torus, 9 to set (6 Slipped Beads to
½ inch, and 3 Slipped Torus to ⅞ in.) ... ... 32/- ,,

,, 325A Beads Double Boxed to 1 in., 10 to set ... ... 33/- ,,

,, 325B Beads Double Boxed to ⅞ in., 9 to set ... ... 29/- ,,

,, 324C Bead and Torus, 9 to set (6 Double Boxed Slipped
Beads to ½ inch, and 3 Slipped Torus, not Double
Boxed ... ... 35/- ,,

REED OR CENTRE BEAD PLANES.
BOXWOOD QUIRKS.

No. 354 Reed Plane, Fenced, to work more Reeds ... 5/6 each.

,, 355 Single Reed, with Square Quirks, any size to ⅜ in. 3/4 ,,

,, 356 Two ,, ,, ,, ,, ¼ in. 3/10 ,,

,, 357 Three ,, ,, ,, ,, ,, 4/6 ,,

,, 358 Four ,, ,, ,, ,, ,, 6/- ,,

,, 355B Single ,, Bevelled ,, ,, ,, 3/7 ,,

,, 356B Two ,, ,, ,, ,, ,, 4/1 ,,

,, 357B Three ,, ,, ,, ,, ,, 4/9 ,,

,, 358B Four ,, ,, ,, ,, ,, 6/3 ,,

V PLANES.

No. 359 V Plane, Boxed ... ... 3/4 each.

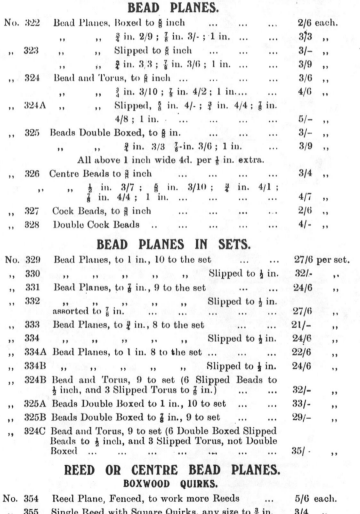

EDWARD PRESTON & SONS, LTD.

MOULDING PLANES.

TRADE (E)(P) MARK.

The sizes given of Moulding Planes are for the thickness of wood upon which the Moulding is to be run.

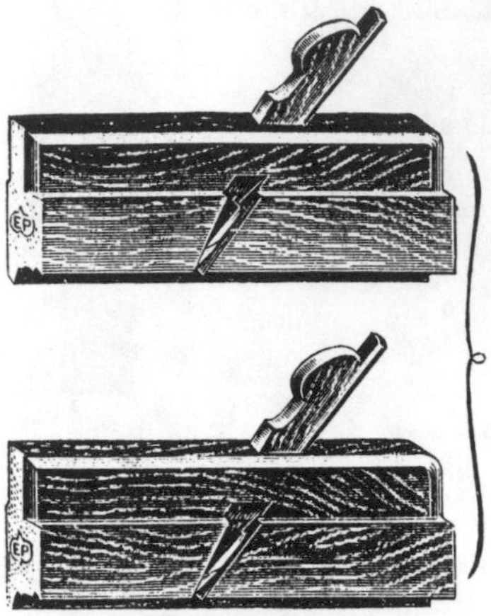

PAIR OF SASH PLANES.

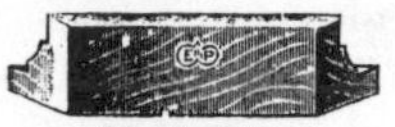

Single Side.

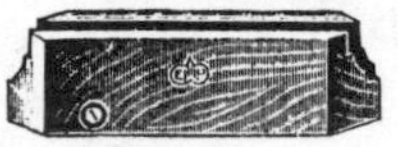

Double or Saddle.

PAIR OF TEMPLETS.

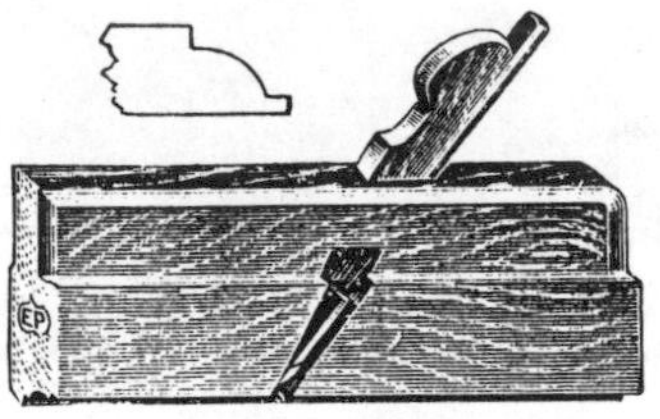

No. 335
COMMON OVELOE.

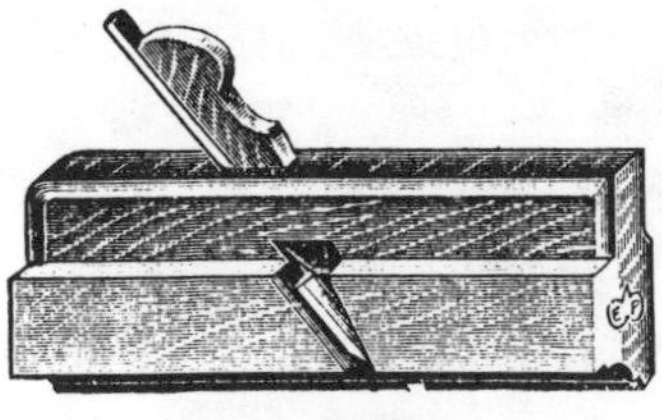

No. 335S
SQUARE OR EQUAL OVELOE.

For Sections of Moulding Planes,
see opposite page.

SASH PLANES.

No. 290 Rustic Sash and Templets to 5/8 inch ... ... 7/- per pair.

Size	1/2	9/16	5/8	5/8	3/4	inch.
For Bar	1 1/2	1 1/2	1 1/2	1 3/4	1 3/4	inch.

,, 294 Oveloe Sash and Templets to 5/8 inch ... ... 7/- ,,

Size	1/2	9/16	5/8	5/8	3/4	inch.
For Bar	1 1/2	1 1/2	1 1/2	1 3/4	1 3/4	inch.

,, 294A Oveloe Sash and Brass ended Scribing Templets to 5/8 inch ... ... 12/- ,,

Size	1/2	9/16	5/8	5/8	3/4	inch.
For Bar ...	1 1/2	1 1/2	1 1/2	1 3/4	1 3/4	inch

,, 294B Oveloe Sash and Brass ended Scribing Templets, with 2 Gouges one with adjustable Brass Stop to 5/8 inch ... . 14/6 ,,

Size	1/2	9/16	5/8	5/8	3/4	inch.
For Bar	1 1/2	1 1/2	1 1/2	1 3/4	1 3/4	inch.

,, 296 Gothic Sash and Templets to 5/8 inch ... . 8/- ,,

Size	1/2	9/16	5/8	5/8	3/4	inch.
For Bar	1 1/2	1 1/2	1 3/4	2	2	inch.

,, 300 Lambtongue Sash and Templets to 5/8 in. ... ... 8/- ,,

Size ...	1/2	9/16	5/8	5/8	3/4	inch.
For Bar	1 1/2	1 1/2	1 3/4	2	2	inch.

,, 306 Astragal and Hollow and Templets to 5/8 inch ... ... 8/- ,,

Size	1/2	9/16	5/8	3/4	inch.
For Bar	1 1/2	1 1/2	1 3/4	2	inch.

,, 310 Oveloe Sash to Stick and Rabbet, with two Irons to 5/8 inch ... ... 6/- each.
,, 311 Oveloe Sash to Stick and Rabbet, with two Irons and Templets to 5/8 in. 7/6 ,,
Sizes same as Oveloe above.
,, 312 Gothic Sash to Stick and Rabbet, with two Irons to 5/8 inch ... ... 8/- ,,
,, 313 Gothic Sash to Stick and Rabbet, with two Irons and Templets, to 5/8 in. 9/6 ,,
Sizes same as Gothic above.
,, 314 Lambtongue Sash to Stick and Rabbet, with two Irons to 5/8 inch ... 8/- ,,
,, 315 Lambtongue Sash to Stick and Rabbet, two Irons with Templets to 5/8 in. 9/6 ,,
Sizes same as Lambtongue above.
,, 316 Astragal and Hollow to Stick and Rabbet, with two Irons to 5/8 in. .. 8/- ,,
,, 317 Astragal and Hollow to Stick and Rabbet, 2 Irons with Templets to 5/8 in. 9/6 ,,
Sizes same as Astragals and Hollows above.
NOTE.--All above advance 6d. per pair per 1/8 inch above 5/8 inch.

TEMPLETS { Templets, Single or Side, 8d. each; Double or Saddle Screwed, 1/1 each. Single and Double, 1/9 per pair; Brass Ended Scribing Oveloe, 6/9 per pair.

,, 297 Scribing Planes ... ... 2/6 ,,
,, 298 ,, ,, Boxed ... ... 3/3 ,,
,, 318 Gothic Sash Routers, 5/8 in. 10/6 per pair; 3/4 in. ... ... 11/- per pair.
,, 319 Oveloe ,, ,, 5/8 in. 10/6 ,, 3/4 in. ... ... 11/- ,,
,, 320 Lambtongue Sash Routers, 5/8 in. 10/6 per pair; 3/4 in. ... ... 11/- ,,
For price of Preston's Improved Iron Sash Routers, see page 99.

ASTRAGAL PLANES.

No. 321 Astragal, to 5/8 in. ... ... 2/4 each.
Every 1/8 inch 3d. to 1 inch. Above 1 inch 4d. per 1/8 inch extra.

OVELOE AND OGEE PLANES.

No. 335 Common Oveloes to 5/8 in. 2/4 each.
,, 335S Square or Equal Oveloes to 5/8 in. ... . 2/6 ,,
,, 336 Common Ogees to 5/8 in. ... 2/4 ,,
Every 1/8 inch 3d. extra, up to 1 inch, above 1d. per 1/8 inch extra.
,, 337 Quirk Ogees, to stick on to 1 inch ... ... 3/6 ,,

Thickness of Wood	3/8	1/2	5/8	3/4	7/8	1	in.
To Stick on ...	5/8	3/4	7/8	1	1 1/8	1 1/4	in.

No. 338 Quirk Oveloes to stick on to 1 in. ... ... 3/6 each

Thickness of Wood	3/8	1/2	5/8	3/4	7/8	1	in.
To Stick on ...	3/4	1	1 1/8	1 1/4	1 3/8	1 1/2	in.

No. 344 Quirk Oveloes and Beads to Stick on to 1 in. ... 4/- each.

Thickness of Wood	3/8	1/2	5/8	3/4	7/8	1	in.
To Stick on ...	5/8	3/4	1	1 1/8	1 1/4	1 3/8	in.

No. 345 Quirk Oveloes and Astragals to 1 inch ... 4/- each.

Thickness of Wood	3/8	1/2	5/8	3/4	7/8	1	in.
To Stick on ...	3/4	1	1 1/8	1 1/4	1 3/8	1 1/2	in.

No. 346 Coves to 5/8 in ... 2/6 each.
Every 1/8 inch 3d. extra.
,, 347 Coves and Beads to 1 in. 3/3 ,,

Thickness of Wood	3/8	1/2	5/8	3/4	7/8	1	in.
To Stick on ...	5/8	3/4	7/8	1 1/8	1 1/4	1 3/8	in.

No. 348 Quirk Ogees and Beads to 1 in. ... ... 4/- each.

Thickness of Wood	3/8	1/2	5/8	3/4	7/8	1	in
To Stick on .	1	1 1/4	1 3/8	1 1/2	1 3/4	1 7/8	in.

No. 349 Grecian Oveloes to 1 in. .. 4/- each.

Thickness of Wood	3/8	1/2	5/8	3/4	7/8	1	in.
To Stick on ...	1	1 1/4	1 3/8	1 1/2	1 3/4	1 7/8	in.

Grecian Overloes, Double Boxed, 4d. extra

No. 350 Grecian Ogees to Stick on to 1 inch .. 4/– each.

Thickness of Wood	3/8	1/2	5/8	3/4	7/8	1	in.
To Stick on ...	1	1 1/4	1 3/8	1 1/2	1 3/4	1 7/8	in.

No. 351 Grecian Ogees and Quirk Beads to 1 in. ... ... 5/- each.

Thickness of Wood	3/8	1/2	5/8	3/4	7/8	1	in.
To Stick on ...	1	1 1/4	1 1/2	1 5/8	1 3/4	1 7/8	in.

Every 1/8 inch to 2 inch 4d. extra; all above, 6d. per 1/8 inch extra.

No. 359 Necking and Nosing to Stick on to 1 in. .. .. 4/- each.

Thickness of Wood	3/8	1/2	5/8	3/4	7/8	1	in.
To Stick on ...	3/4	7/8	1	1 1/8	1 1/4	1 3/8	in.

No. 352 Necking or Scotia to 5/8 in. 2/6 each.
,, 353 Nosing to 1 in. ... ... 3/4 ,,
Every 1/8 inch 4d. extra.
,, 362 Scotia Planes to 5/8 in. ... 2/6 ,,

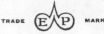

SECTIONS OF MOULDING PLANES.

TRADE (EP) MARK.

290

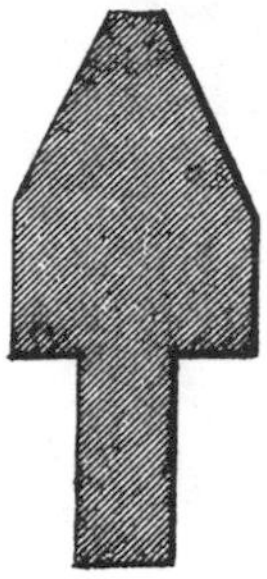

⅝ in. Rustic.

294

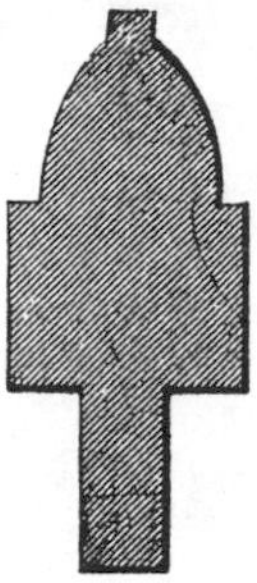

⅝ in. Oveloe
for 1½ in. Bar.

296

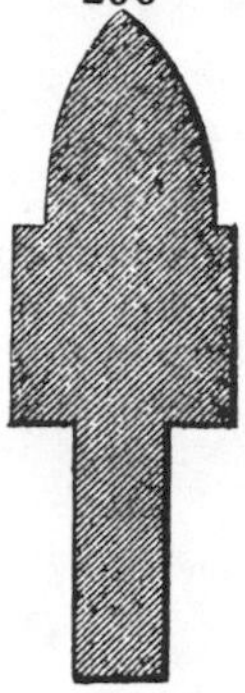

⅝ in. Gothic
for 2 in. Bar.

300

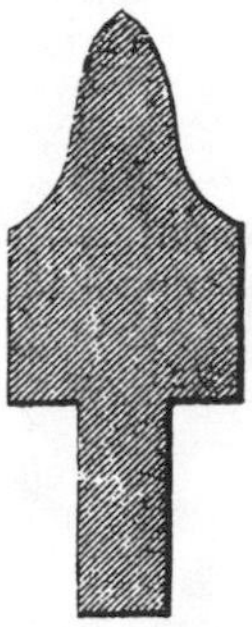

⅝ in. Lambtongue
for 1¾ in. Bar.

306

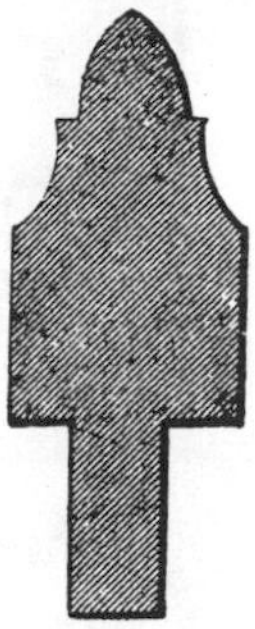

⅝ in. Astragal and Hollow
for 1¾ in. Bar.

321

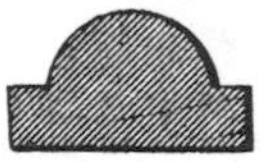

⅝ in. Astragal.

322

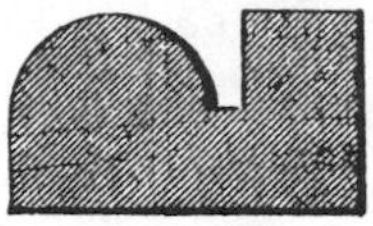

⅝ in. Bead.

324

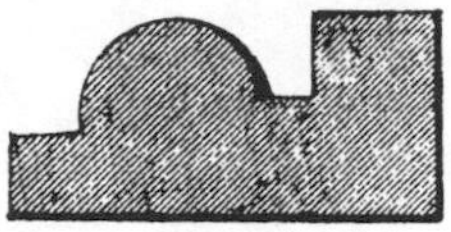

⅝ in. Torus Bead.

335

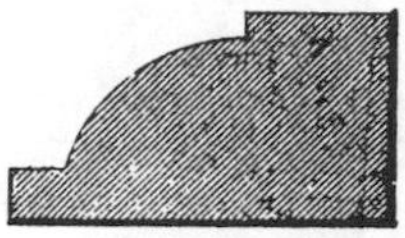

⅝ in. Oveloe

336

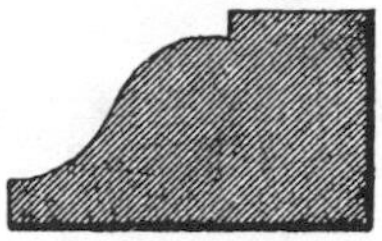

⅝ in. Ogee

337

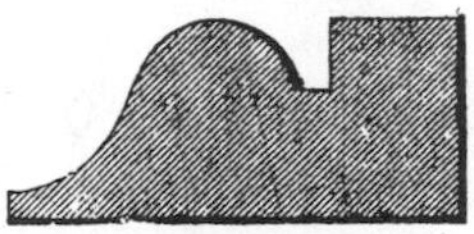

⅝ in. Quirk Ogee
to stick on ⅞ in.

338

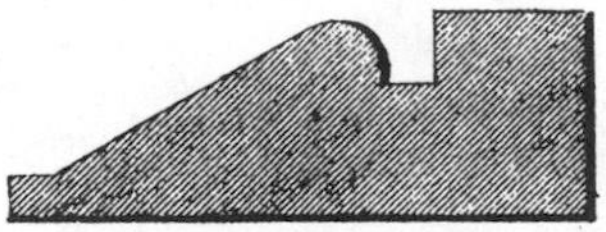

⅝ in. Quirk Oveloe
to stick on 1⅛ in.

344

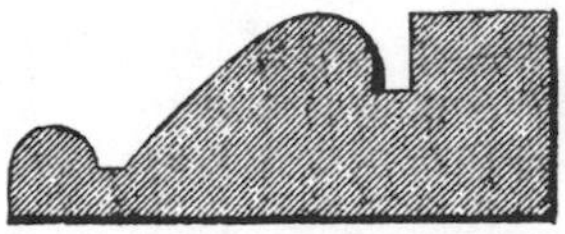

⅝ in Quirk Oveloe and Bead
to stick on 1⅛ in.

345

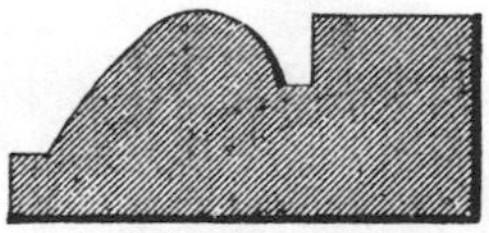

⅝ in. Quirk Oveloe and Astragal
to stick on ⅞ in.

346

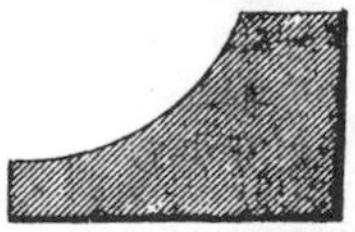

⅝ in. Cove.

347

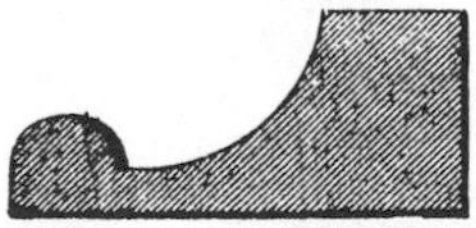

⅝ in. Cove and Bead
to stick on ⅞ in

348

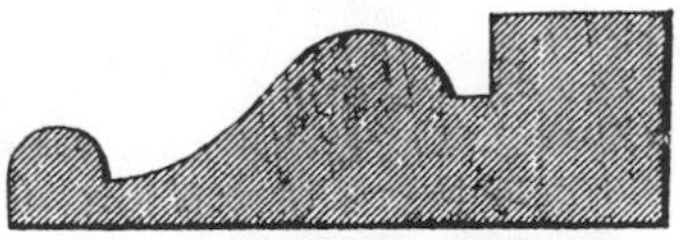

⅝ in Quirk Ogee and Bead
to stick on 1⅜ in.

349

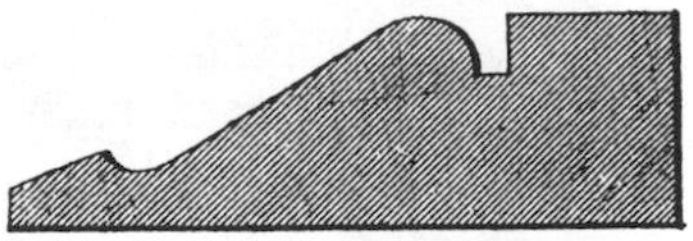

⅝ in. Grecian Oveloe
to stick on 1⅜ in.

350

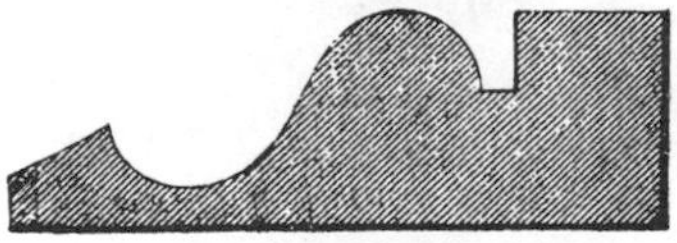

⅝ in. Grecian Ogee
to stick on 1⅜ in.

351

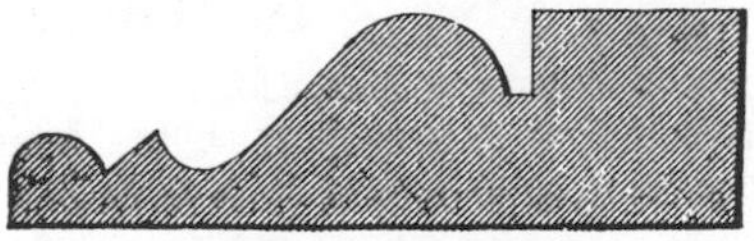

⅝ in. Grecian Ogee and Quirk Bead
to stick on 1½ in.

359

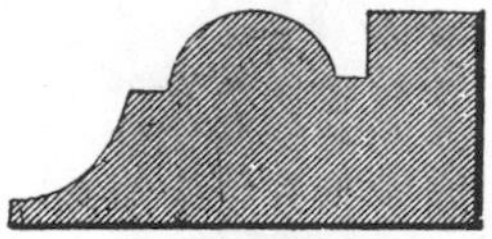

⅝ in. Necking and Nosing
to stick on 1 in.

For Prices of Moulding Planes, see opposite page.

EDWARD PRESTON & SONS, L^{TD}.

COACHMAKERS' PLANES.

T RABBET PLANE.

T RABBET PLANES.

Straight to 1½ in. ... .. 4/- each.	Compassed to 1½ in. ... ... 4/6 each.
Straight, Dovetail Boxed Face 6/- ,,	,, Dovetail Boxed Face 6/6 ,,
Every ⅛ inch 3d. extra.			
Coach Door Rabbet Planes, Square Mouth ... ... 3/- .
,, ,, ,, Skew Mouth... ... ... 3/3 ,,

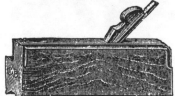

COACH DOOR SMOOTH PLANE.

SMOOTHING PLANES.

Smoothing Planes to 1¾ inch ... ... 3/9 each.
Compass ,, ,, ... 4/3 ,
, ,, ,, Set of Six ... . 25/6 per set.
Concave ,, ,, ... 4/6 each.
Coach Door, Smooth ,, ...,. ... 4/9 ,,
,, , ,, ,, Plated at mouth ... ... 6/9 ;,

COACH DOOR JACK PLANE.

JACK PLANES.

Coach Door Jack Planes to 2 in. ... ... 6/6 each.
,, ,, ,, ,, ,, Plated at mouth .. .. 8/6 ,,

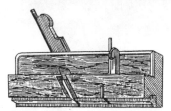

COACH SIDE CHAMFER PLANE.

SIDE CHAMFERING OR BEVELING PLANES.

Coach Side Chamfer or Beveling Planes (¼, ⅜, ⁷⁄₁₆ or ½ in.) ... 2/9 ,,
,, ,, ,, ,, ,, ,, Boxed ,, ,, ... 3/3 ,,
,, ,, ,, ,, ,, ,, with Tooth ... ... 4/6 ,,
,, ,, ,, ,, ,, ,, ,, Boxed ... 5/- ,,

COACH SIDE CHAMFER PLANE,
BOXED, WITH TOOTH.

TONGUEING, ROUNDING AND BEAD PLANES.

Tongueing Planes ... ... 5/6 per pair.
Coach Rounding Planes to ⅝ inch, Square Mouth ... ... 2/6 each.
,, ,, ,, ,, ,, ,, Skew Mouth ... 3/- ,,
,, Bead Planes to ⅝ inch ... ... 2/9 ,,
Every ⅛ inch 3d. extra.

No. 1488
HORIZONTAL SQUARE.

No. 1489   T BEVEL.

COACHMAKERS' SQUARES AND BEVELS.

No. 1488 Coachmakers' Horizontal Steel Squares, Gun Metal
Handles ... ... 46/- per doz.
,, 1489 Coachmakers' T Bevels ... ... 25/9 ,,
,, 1490 ,, Spider Mortice Bevels ... ... 30/- ,,
,, 1491 ,, Mortice Bevels ... ... 21/6 ,,

No. 1490
SPIDER MORTICE BEVEL.

No. 1491
MORTICE BEVEL.

EDWARD PRESTON & SONS, L^{TD.}

COACHMAKERS' ROUTERS AND ROUTER IRONS.

TRADE  MARK.

No. 600

BEADING ROUTER.

With One Pair Irons ... ... 8/- each.

No. 600R

ROUNDING TOOL.

With One Pair Irons ... ... 7/6 each.

 **BEADING ROUTER IRONS.** 1/3 per pair.  **LISTING IRONS.** 1/3 per pair. 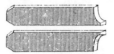 **ROUNDING IRONS.** 1/3 per pair.

No. 601

BOXING ROUTER.

No. 601 With Iron ... ... 3/6 each.
„ 601E „ „ and Eyehole ... ... 4/- „

| | $\frac{1}{2}$ | $\frac{5}{8}$ | $\frac{3}{4}$ | inch. |

Boxing Router Irons ... ... 7d. 7d. 7d. each.
„ „ „ Hooked Pattern 9d. 9d. 10d. „

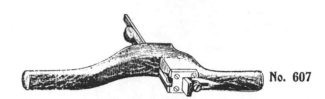

No. 607

PISTOL ROUTER.

16/- per pair.

No. 602

JIGGER OR SIDE ROUTER.

12/- each.

No. 603

LONDON PATTERN JIGGER, OR SIDE ROUTER.

With Gun Metal Fittings ... . 12/- each.

No. 605

FENCE OR GROOVING ROUTER.

With Improved Fence ... ... 16/- per pair.

No. 606

FENCE OR GROOVING ROUTER, LONDON PATTERN.

With Thumb Screw to adjust Fence .. 16/- per pair

 **FENCE ROUTER IRONS.** 1/- per pair.

No. 610

NELSON ROUTER.

With Iron Face .. .. 9/- each.

Nc 611

SIDE CUTTING ROUTER.

6/- each.

No. 608

WHEELERS' JARVIS.

With Iron Face .. .. 11/- each.

WHEELERS' ROUNDERS.

| Tapering | $\frac{7}{8}\times\frac{5}{8}$ | $1\times\frac{3}{4}$ | $1\frac{1}{8}\times\frac{7}{8}$ | $1\frac{1}{4}\times1$ | $1\frac{3}{8}\times1\frac{1}{8}$ | $1\frac{1}{2}\times1\frac{1}{4}$ | $1\frac{5}{8}\times1\frac{3}{8}$ | $1\frac{3}{4}\times1\frac{1}{2}$ in. |
| | 5/3 | 5/9 | 6/3 | 6/9 | 7/6 | 8/3 | 8/9 | 9/3 each. |

Prices quoted refer to small end of hole.

EDWARD PRESTON & SONS, LTD.

BOXWOOD THUMB PLANES.

THESE PLANES ARE 3½ INCHES LONG.

TRADE  MARK.

362T
SINGLE IRON SMOOTH.

Irons	1	1⅛	1¼	1½ inch.
Length	4	4½	4¾	5¾ ,,
	2/8	3/-	3/4	4/- each.

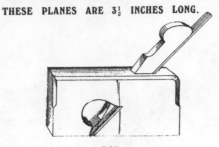

363
SQUARE RABBET.

½	⅝	¾	⅞	1 inch.
2/10	2/10	2/10	2/10	2/10 each.

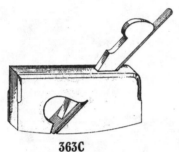

363C
SQUARE RABBET.
Compassed Face.

½	⅝	¾	⅞	1 inch.
3/3	3/3	3/3	3/3	3/3 each.

365
SQUARE RABBET.
Circular on both sides to 1 inch, 4/3 each.

366
HOLLOWS AND ROUNDS.
Square Mouth to No. 12, 5/3 per pair

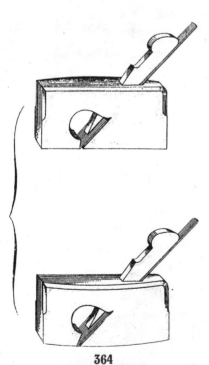

364
SQUARE RABBET.
Circular on one side, right and left to 1 inch,
7/- per pair.

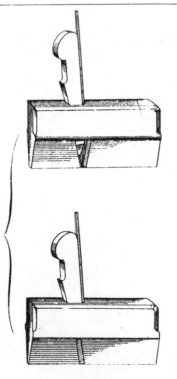

365S
SIDE RABBET.
6/6 per pair.

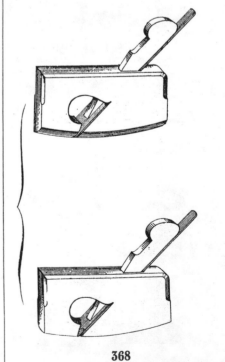

368

No. 367	Side Rounds	...	...	6/6 per pair.
,, 368	,,		compassed	7/6 ,,

EDWARD PRESTON & SONS, L^TD.

PLANES.

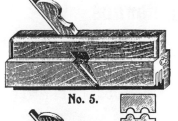

No. 5.

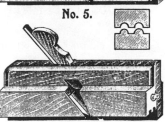

No. 6.

AIR-TIGHT CASE MAKERS' PLANES.

No. 5.	Air-tight Case Planes, Double Round ...	...	...	7/9 each	} 15/ per pair.
,, 6.	,, ,, ,, ,, Hollow	...	...	7/6 ,,	
,, 2.	,, ,, ,, Single Round ...	...	...	6/9 ,,	} 13/3 ,,
,, 3.	,, ,, ,, ,, Hollow ...	...	...	6/6 ,,	

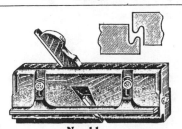

No. 11.

HOOK JOINT PLANES.

No. 11. Hook Joint Case Plane, with Adjustable Fence ... ... 10/- each.

SHUTEING PLANES.

No. 380 to 383.

No. 386 to 387.

SHUTEING PLANES, WITH THUMB PIECE.

No. 380.	22 inch long, 2¾ inch Single Iron, Square Mouth	...	...	...	...	...	...	11/6 each.
,, 381.	22 inch long, 3 inch Single Iron, Square Mouth	..	...	...	...	...	.	13/6 ,,
,, 382.	22 inch long, 2¾ inch Single Iron, Skew Mouth	..	...	...	...	...	..	12/6 ,,
,, 383.	22 inch long, 3 inch Single Iron, Skew Mouth	...	...	...	...	...	...	15/6 ,,

PLATED ON FACE AT MOUTH ONLY.

| No. 384 | 22 inch long, 3 inch Single Iron, Square Mouth | ... | ... | ... | .. | ... | ... | 16/- each. |
| ,, 385 | 22 inch long, 3 inch Single Iron, Skew Mouth | ... | .. | ... | ... | ... | ... | 18/- ,, |

Nos. 386 and 387.—PLATED ALL ALONG THE FACE.

| No. 386. | 22 inch long, 3 inch Single Iron, Square Mouth | ... | ... | ... | ... | ... | ... | 21/- each. |
| ,, 387. | 22 inch long, 3 inch Single Iron, Skew Mouth | ... | ... | ... | ... | ... | ... | 24/- ,, |

PLATED ON FACE AND SIDE.

| ,, 388. | 22 inch long, 3 inch Single Iron, Square Mouth | ... | ... | ... | ... | ... | ... | 25/6 ,, |
| ,, 389. | 22 inch long, 3 inch Single Iron, Skew Mouth | ... | ... | ... | ... | ... | ... | 28/6 ,, |

BEECH MITRE BOXES AND SHUTEING BOARDS.

 TRADE MARK.

Full size drawing of Patent Saw Guide.

PRESTON'S PATENT ADJUSTABLE MITRE BOX.

This Mitre Box is made of well seasoned Beechwood. The Iron Guides may be adjusted to the varying thicknesses of Saw Blades.

For Amateurs, Picture Framing and Mitreing generally it is indispensible.

No. 566. For Mouldings up to 3 inches wide ... 30/- per dozen

,, 568. ,, ,, ,, 4 ,, ... 36/- ,,

,, 567. Pattern as 566. For Mouldings up to 3 inches wide, but without Patent Guides 18/- ,,

---

MITRE BOXES.

BEECH MITRE BOXES.

No. 396.	10	12	14 inch.
	2/9	3/6	5/- each.

SHUTEING BOARDS.

BEECH SHUTEING BOARD.

No. 391D. 16 inches long ... ... 3/3 each.

---

394 S.

394.

BEECH MITRE BLOCKS.

No. 394S. Single, Solid, 9 inch ... 10/- per dozen.

,, 394. ,, Screwed, 9 inch ... 16/6 ,,

BEECH SHUTEING BOARD.
With Mitre Saw Cuts at back.

No. 391B. 18 inches long ... ... 4/- each.

BEECH MITRE TEMPLETS.

No. 395. ... ... 6/- per dozen.

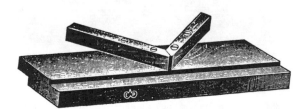

BEECH SHUTEING BOARD.
With Solid Mitre Piece and Saw Cuts at back.

No. 391C. 18 inches long ... ... 4/- each.

EDWARD PRESTON & SONS, L^{TD.}

PLANE FITTINGS.

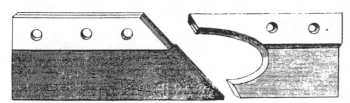

PAIR OF PLOUGH PLATES.

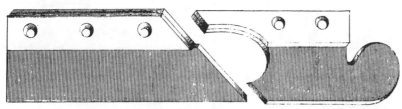

PAIR OF SKATE END PLOUGH PLATES.

PLOUGH PLATES.

No. 440	Iron	6/8	per doz. pairs.
,, 441	Steel	8/-	,,
,, 442	Steel, Long Fore End	11/4	,,
,, 443	Steel, Long Fore and Back End for Handled Ploughs	14/8	,,
,, 444	Steel, Skate Fore End	11/4	,,
,, 445	Steel, Large Skate Fore End	13/4	,,
,, 446	Set of 3 Pairs, Steel Plough Plates for Circular Plough Planes	35/-	per doz. sets.
,, 428	Iron Grooving Plates	26/9	per gross pairs.
,, 429	Jack ,, ,,	40/-	,,

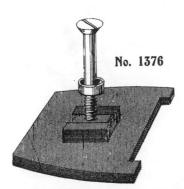

No. 1376

SMOOTHING PLANE FRONTS,
WITH SCREW AND CUP.

	2⅛	2¼	2⅜	2½ inch.
No. 1375 Cast Iron ...	14/3	14/3	14/3	14/3 per doz.
,, 1376 Malleable Iron...	17/-	17/-	17/-	17/- ,,

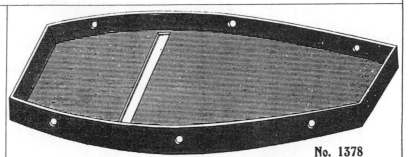

No. 1378

IRON SMOOTHING PLANE SOLES.

These are machined on face.

		2 and 2¼ in.	2⅜ and 2½ in.
No. 1378	English Pattern	17/- ...	18/3 per dozen.
,, 1378S	Scotch ,, ...	17/- ...	18/3 ,,

MALLEABLE IRON SMOOTHING PLANE FACES.

Not machined on face, but holes drilled and countersunk.

	1½	1⅝	1¾	2	2⅛	2¼ inch.
No 1378F	10/-	10/-	10/-	11/-	12/-	13/- per doz.

No. 435

No. 435	Screws, Cups and Diamonds, 2¾ inch ...	3/6	per doz.
,, 430	Short Plough Rivets	3/-	per gross.
,, 431	Long ,, ,, ...	5/-	,,
,, 432	Small Fillister Screws	4/3	,,
,, 433	Large ,, ,, ...	5/9	,,
,, 434	Top Irons Screws	5/-	,,
Plough Ferrules, Diamonds, etc., Castings	...	per lb.	

PLANE LEVERS.

No. 436 Brass, with Screws at side, Bright Polished—

2	2⅛	2¼	2⅜	2½	2⅝	2¾ inch.
15/4	16/-	16/8	17/4	18/-	18/8	19/4 per doz.

,, 438 Gun Metal, with Screws at side, Bright Polished—

2	2⅛	2¼	2⅜	2½	2⅝	2¾ inch.
24/-	25/4	26/8	28/-	29/4	30/8	32/- per doz.

Above may be had with Pins right through (instead of screws at side) at same prices. When so required, please add " P " to number.

EDWARD PRESTON & SONS, LTD.

PLANE STOPS.

TRADE 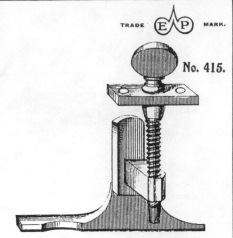 MARK.

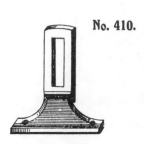

No. 410.

SLIP STOP.

No. 410. Small ... ... 4/8 per dozen
,, 411. Large ... ... 7/4 ,,

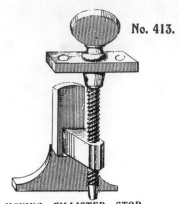

No. 413.

MOVING FILLISTER STOP.

No. 412. ... ... 11/6 per dozen
,, 413. Best ... ... 15/- ,,

No. 415.

BEST LEFT HAND SASH FILLISTER STOP.

No. 414. ... ... 15/9 per dozen
,, 415. Best ... ... 17/4 ,,

No. 416.

RIGHT HAND FILLISTER STOP.
No. 416. Straight Feet ... 11/6 per dozen

No. 418.

COMPASS SMOOTHING STOP.
12/- per dozen.

No. 417.

DADO GROOVE STOP.
12/- per dozen.

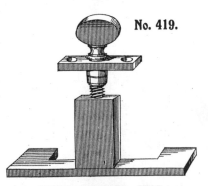

No. 419.

COMMON PLOUGH STOP.
9/4 per dozen.

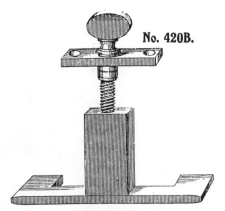

No. 420B.

SOLID PLOUGH STOP.

No. 420. ... ... 14/- per dozen
,, 420B. Best ... ... 16/8 ,,

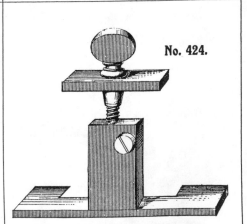

No. 424.

BEST IMPROVED PLOUGH STOP.

No. 423. Screw at side ... 14/8 per dozen
,, 424. Best, Screw at side 17/4 ,,
,, 427. Plough Stops, 1 Straight and
1 Circular, for Circular
Plough Planes, 37/- per doz. pairs

EDWARD PRESTON & SONS, L<u>TD.</u>

IRON SPOKESHAVES.

TRADE MARK.

These Spokeshaves are unsurpassed for style, finish and fineness of the mouths.   The Cutting Irons are of Best Cast Steel, set and sharpened, and are ready for use when sent from our factory.   They are Japanned, and have holes in handles for hanging up.

No. 1380   Double Iron, Straight Handles, 10 inches, 2⅛ inch Cutter   ...   11/- per dozen.

No. 1380½ Double Iron, Raised Handles, 10 inches, 2⅛ inch Cutter   ...   11/- per dozen.

No. 1381   Double Iron, Straight Handles, 10 inches, 2⅛ inch Cutter   ...   11/6 per dozen.

No. 1381½ Double Iron, Raised Handles, 10 inches, 2⅛ inch Cutter   ...   11/6 per dozen.

No. 1382   Adjustable Mouth, Straight Handles, 10 inches, 2⅛ inch Cutter   19/- per dozen.

No. 1382½ Adjustable Mouth, Raised Handles, 10 inches, 2⅛ inch Cutter   19/- per dozen.

No. 1383   Double Iron, Raised Handles, 10 inches Concave Face,
2⅛ inch Cutter ...   .   15/- per dozen.

No. 1383½ Double Iron, Raised Handles, 10 inches, Convex Face, 2⅛ inch
Cutter   ...   .   15/- per dozen.

No. 1384 Double Cutter, Hollow and Straight, 12 inches, 1½ inch Cutters   20/- per dozen.

No. 1379   Double Iron, Straight Handles, 8½ inches, 1¾ inch Cutter   ...   9/- per dozen.

Nos. 1380½, 1381½ may be had with Round Faces at List Prices ; when so desired, please add R.F. to No.

SPOKESHAVE IRONS.

For Nos 1380, 1380½, 1381, 1381½, 1382, 1382½	4/- per dozen.	
,, 1383, 1383½	5/-	,,
,, 1384 ... ... Straight, 4/- per dozen ... | ... 1384 ... ... Hollow	5/-	,,
,, 1379	3/-	,,

EDWARD PRESTON & SONS, LTD.

PATENT IRON SPOKESHAVES.

TRADE MARK.

PACKED IN ¼ DOZENS IN CARDBOARD BOX.

These Spokeshaves are made of Malleable Iron and have "PRESTON'S PATENT ADJUSTMENT" to the Cutting Iron, which is of Best Cast Steel, and each shave is subjected to a working test before leaving our factory. They are supplied either with Flat or Round Faces, and for quality and finish we confidently recommend them as being the "Best Spokeshaves in the Market."

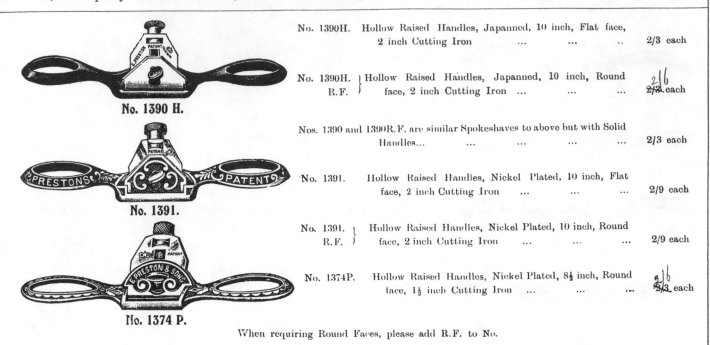

No. 1390 H.

No. 1391.

No. 1374 P.

No. 1390H. Hollow Raised Handles, Japanned, 10 inch, Flat face, 2 inch Cutting Iron ... . 2/3 each

No. 1390H. R.F. } Hollow Raised Handles, Japanned, 10 inch, Round face, 2 inch Cutting Iron ... ... 2/3 each

Nos. 1390 and 1390 R.F. are similar Spokeshaves to above but with Solid Handles... ... ... 2/3 each

No. 1391. Hollow Raised Handles, Nickel Plated, 10 inch, Flat face, 2 inch Cutting Iron ... ... 2/9 each

No. 1391 R.F. } Hollow Raised Handles, Nickel Plated, 10 inch, Round face, 2 inch Cutting Iron ... ... 2/9 each

No. 1374P. Hollow Raised Handles, Nickel Plated, 8½ inch, Round face, 1½ inch Cutting Iron ... ... 2/3 each

When requiring Round Faces, please add R.F. to No.

REGISTERED IRON SPOKESHAVES.

No. 1373. Hollow Raised Handles, Malleable Iron, Nickel Plated, 6 inch, Round face, 1 inch Cutting Iron ... ... 11/6 per dozen

No. 1374. Hollow Raised Handles, Malleable Iron, Nickel Plated, 7 inch, Round face, 1¼ inch Cutting Iron... ... 16/- per dozen

No. 1377.

No. 1377. Solid Straight Handles, Cast Iron, Nickel Plated, 7 inch, Round face, 1¼ inch Cutting Iron... ... 11/6 per dozen

No. 1377T. As above, but with Thumbscrew to top plate ... 14/- per dozen

SPOKESHAVE IRONS.

For No. 1390H. 1390H. R.F. 1391. 1391 R.F. 1374P. ... ... 6/- per dozen
" 1374. 1377. 1377T. ... ... 4/- "
" 1373. ... ... 3/- "

EDWARD PRESTON & SONS, LTD.

PATENT MOULDING TOOLS.

PACKED ONE IN A BOX.

TRADE **EP** MARK.

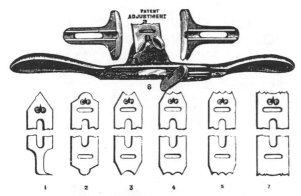

PRESTON'S PATENT ADJUSTABLE HAND REEDER AND MOULDING TOOL.

Will be found of great service for Reeding, Beading and Moulding straight or circular work. Also for light routering.

Seven double ended cutting Irons and three fences, one straight and one each for outside and inside circular work, are supplied with each tool.

No. 1 Iron is for cutting V and Routering.
,, 2 ,, will form $\frac{5}{16}$ inch and $\frac{3}{8}$ inch Hollows
,, 3 ,, ,, $\frac{5}{16}$ inch and $\frac{3}{8}$ inch Rounds.
,, 4 ,, ,, $\frac{1}{8}$ inch and $\frac{1}{4}$ inch double Reeds.
,, 5 ,, ,, treble Reeds.
,, 6 and 7 Irons will form $\frac{3}{4}$ inch and $1\frac{1}{4}$ inch Mouldings.

The easy method of adjusting the Irons will commend itself to all users.

No. 1393P ... . 5/6 each.

Cutting Irons, 6d. each.

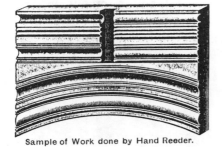

Sample of Work done by Hand Reeder.

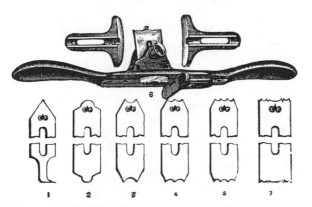

PRESTON'S PATENT HAND REEDER AND MOULDING TOOL.

This is a similar Tool to the above, but without the Patent Adjustment to the Cutting Irons.

No. 1393 ... ... 4/6 each

Cutting Irons, 5d. each.

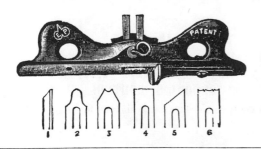

PRESTON'S PATENT REEDING, RABBETING AND MOULDING TOOL.

This will be found a most useful small hand tool for reeding and moulding work. Six different Cutters as per drawing are sent out with each tool. Fretworkers will find it indispensable for giving a finished appearance to their work. No. 1 Cutter is a cutting gauge and grooving tool, No. 2 round, No. 3 hollow. Nos. 4 and 5 Cutters are adapted for taking out the rabbet of picture frames hand mirrors, &c. No. 5 is also useful for Chamfering purposes, and No. 6 is for forming mouldings.

Packed in $\frac{1}{4}$ dozens in Cardboard Boxes.

No. 1393S ... ... 2/- each.

PRESTON'S PATENT LINING OR STRINGING ROUTER.

This will be found a very useful tool to Cabinet Makers, Pianoforte Makers, Fret Workers and other Wood Workers, for inlaying "Strings" and "Bands."

The tool is sent out with six cutters varying in width from $\frac{1}{16}$ inch to $\frac{3}{8}$ inch. These are adjusted to the desired depth of cut by means of "Preston's Patent Adjustment"; it has one fence which is movable and reversible to suit different sweeps of wood.

On very cross grained wood it will be preferable to gauge lines the width of the "band" before using the broad irons.

No. 1396 ... ... 3/- each.

Cutting Irons 4d. each.

EDWARD PRESTON & SONS, LTD.

PATENT ROUTERING TOOLS.

PACKED ONE IN A BOX.

PRESTON'S PATENT ADJUSTABLE CIRCULAR QUIRK OR GROOVING ROUTER.

This tool has one each $\frac{3}{32}$ inch, $\frac{1}{8}$ inch, and $\frac{1}{16}$ inch interchangeable cutting irons. These are fixed in position by means of a clip and thumb screw. The irons are easily adjusted by means of the milled nut, which also acts as a stop, and prevents the cutting irons from being forced back when in use.

Two cutting teeth work in front of the cutter which is slightly narrower than the teeth, so that a clear quirk or groove is formed of one uniform size.

Three fences accompany the tool, one for straight and one each for outside and inside circular work.

No. 1388P ... ... 4/6 each.

PRESTON'S IMPROVED CIRCULAR QUIRK OR GROOVING ROUTER.

This is a similar tool to the above, but without the Patent Adjustment to the cutting irons.

No. 1388 ... ... 3/6 each.

PRESTON'S PATENT ADJUSTABLE CIRCULAR QUIRK OR GROOVING ROUTER.

This tool is held in an upright position when working and has Adjustable Irons exactly as No. 1388P.

No. 1395 ... ... 4/6 each.

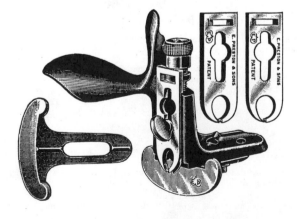

PRESTON'S PATENT ADJUSTABLE CIRCULAR QUIRK OR GROOVING ROUTER.

This will work exactly as No. 1395 but is different in design.

No. 1394 ... ... 4/6 each.

CUTTING IRONS.

For No. 1388 P, 1395, 1394 ... ... 10d. each.
,, 1388 ... ... 8d. ,,

EDWARD PRESTON & SONS, LTD.

CHAMFER SHAVES AND ROUTERING TOOLS.

TRADE (E P) MARK.

PACKED IN CARDBOARD BOXES.

These Tools are all made on the Spokeshave principle, in Iron, Japanned, with best Cast Steel Cutting Irons. They are made to work Right and Left, and are in perfect working order when sent from the factory.

PRESTON'S PATENT ADJUSTABLE STOP CHAMFER SHAVE.

Stop Chamfer, so called inasmuch that the Shave cuts the "Stop" as well as the "Chamfer."

The fences are adjustable up to 1 inch and the tool is fitted with "PRESTON'S PATENT ADJUSTMENT" to the cutting iron

No. 1392 ... . 3/3 each.

Cutting Irons, 6d. each.

PRESTON'S IMPROVED CHAMFER SHAVE.

No. 1385 The fences are adjustable up to $1\frac{1}{8}$ inch ... 2/- each.

Cutting Irons, 4d. each.

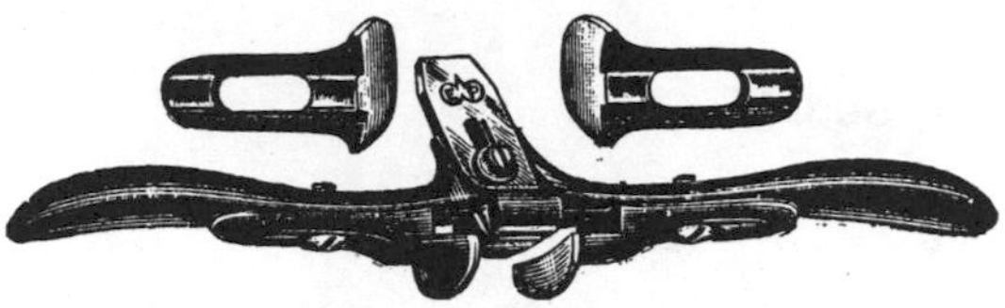

PRESTON'S IMPROVED CIRCULAR RABBETING AND FILLISTER ROUTER.

Is an accompanying tool to the Sash Router (1387), and has one Cutting Iron and two pairs of Adjustable Fences which enables it to be used either as a Rabbeting or Moving Fillister Router, these fences slide along a groove and are adjustable for working out the Rabbet on various thicknesses of bar. The Shouldered or Fillister Fences are adjustable from $\frac{1}{8}$ to $\frac{3}{4}$ inch.

No. 1386 ... . 2/9 each.

Cutting Irons, 5d. each.

PRESTON'S IMPROVED CIRCULAR SASH ROUTER.

No. 1387A Oveloe; No. 1387B Lamb-Tongue.; No. 1387C Gothic.

Has two Cutting Irons and will work right or left (this is a great advantage over the old style made in beechwood, which works only one way, and necessitates having two shaves). It is made in the following sizes, viz.:—$\frac{1}{2}$, $\frac{9}{16}$, $\frac{5}{8}$, and $\frac{3}{4}$ inch, to work either Oveloe, Lamb-tongue, or Gothic Sashes, and can be made to work with any Plane Makers' Pattern Mouldings

3/6 each.

Routers to special pattern or to order charged from 6d. to 1/- each extra.

When ordering, please give the Letter after Number, to insure the correct pattern moulding being sent

PRESTON'S IMPROVED CIRCULAR BEAD ROUTER.

Has two Cutting Irons, and is made in twelve sizes, varying in sixteenths from $\frac{1}{8}$ to $\frac{5}{16}$ inch, and in eighths from $\frac{3}{8}$ to 1 inch, the whole forming a complete set of beads.

	$\frac{1}{8}$	$\frac{3}{16}$	$\frac{1}{4}$	$\frac{5}{16}$	$\frac{3}{8}$	$\frac{7}{16}$	$\frac{1}{2}$	$\frac{9}{16}$	$\frac{5}{8}$	$\frac{3}{4}$	$\frac{7}{8}$	1 inch.
No. 1389	3/-	3/-	3/-	3/3	3/3	3/6	3/6	3/9	3/9	4/-	4/3	4/6 each

PRESTON'S IMPROVED CIRCULAR COMMON OVELOE ROUTER.

Has two Cutting Irons as described above.

	$\frac{1}{4}$	$\frac{3}{8}$	$\frac{1}{2}$	$\frac{5}{8}$	$\frac{3}{4}$ inch.
No. 1387D	3/-	3/3	3/6	3/9	4/3 each.

PRESTON'S IMPROVED CIRCULAR EQUAL OR SQUARE OVELOE ROUTER.

	$\frac{1}{4} \times \frac{1}{4}$	$\frac{3}{8} \times \frac{3}{8}$	$\frac{1}{2} \times \frac{1}{2}$	$\frac{5}{8} \times \frac{5}{8}$	$\frac{3}{4} \times \frac{3}{4}$ inch.
No. 1387E	3/9	4/-	4/3	4/6	4/9 each.

HOLLOW HANDLE TOOL PADS.

 TRADE MARK.

These Tool Pads are of superior quality and finish, with warranted tools to hold the tools.   The Handles are made of Boxwood and are hollow   The tool holder or pad is made of brass.

PACKED IN HALF DOZENS IN CARDBOARD BOXES.

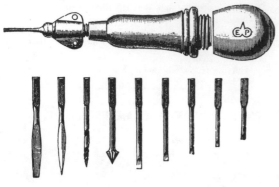

No. 1450   Improved Hollow Boxwood Handle Tool Pads, containing 6 Awls 13/- doz.
,,   1451   ,,   ,,   ,,   ,,   ,,   ,,   8 Tools 16/-   ,,
,,   1452   ,,   ,,   ,,   ,,   ,,   ,,   10   ,,   19/-   ,,
,,   1453   ,,   ,,   ,,   ,,   ,,   ,,   12   ,,   25/-   ,,
,,   1454   ,,   ,,   ,,   ,,   ,,   ,,   15   ,,   42/-   ,,
,,   1455   ,,   ,,   ,,   ,,   ,,   ,,   18   ,,   60/-   ,,

Sets of Tools for No.   1450   1451   1452   1453   1454   1455
6/-   7/6   9/-   13/6   21/-   28/- per doz. sets.

We supply a second grade of the above as follows—
No.   1451S   1452S   1453S   1454S
15/-   17/-   22/-   30/-

SOLID HANDLE TOOL PADS.

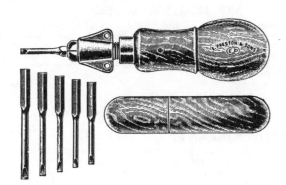

These are made either with Beech or Boxwood Handles and being solid, may be struck with mallet.

No. 1456   Beechwood Handle, Iron Pad, with 6 Awls in wood case, 12/- per doz.
,,   1456B   Boxwood   ,,   ,,   ,,   ,,   ,,   14/-   ,,

Sets of Awls only, 4/6 per dozen sets.

Packed in Half dozens.

PEGGING AWL HAFTS.

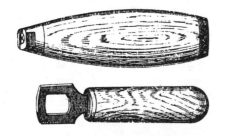

No. 1480   Polished and Pinned Handles, Leather Tops, Steel Screw
with Wrench   ..   ..   80/- per gross.
,,   1478   Common, Leather Tops, not Polished or Pinned   ...   60/-   ,,

Packed in Dozens.

SADDLERS' AND SHOEMAKERS' AWL HANDLES.

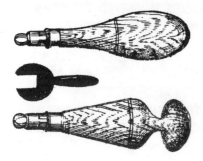

No. 1476   Saddlers' Boxwood Handle, with Improved Brass Pad
and 6 awls   ...   .   10/6 per doz.
,,   1477   Shoemakers'   ditto   ditto   ditto   10/6   ,,

Above are supplied with Iron Key for tightening the Awl in the Pad.

Packed in dozens.

EDWARD PRESTON & SONS, LTD.

TRADE MARK.

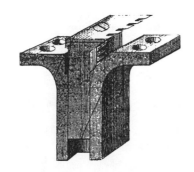

PRESTON'S IMPROVED BENCH STOPS.

These are made of Malleable Iron, with Wrought Iron Screw
and Steel Spring for Regulating.

No. 1463 Small .. .. 10/- per dozen.
,, 1464 Large ... ... 21/6 ,,

Packed in Half dozens.

CARPENTERS' IMPROVED BENCH STOP.

No. 1465 ... ... 22/- per dozen.

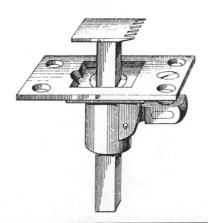

CARPENTERS' BENCH STOP
(MORRELL'S PATTERN).

No. 1565 ... ... 24/- per dozen.

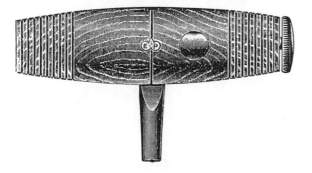

PRESTON'S IMPROVED
UNIVERSAL BRACE BIT HOLDER.

This is a very useful Boxwood Tool Handle, for holding all kinds of
Brace Bits.

The Bit is inserted in the hole, and the tightening screw bearing against
the shank secures it firmly in the handle. Simple and effective.

No. 1445 ... ... 9/6 per dozen.

Packed in Half dozens.

UNIVERSAL AUGER HANDLES.

These are made in Beechwood, polished, and are adjustable to
hold all sizes of augers.

No. 1481 12½ inches long ... ... 18/- per dozen.
,, 1482 14 ,, ,, ... 24/- ,,

EDWARD PRESTON & SONS, L^{TD.}

SAW SETS.

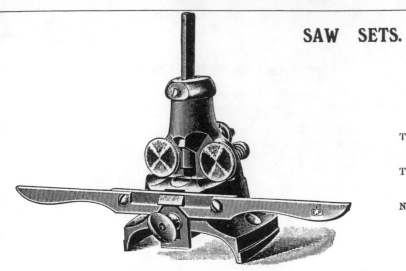

PRESTON'S PATENT PUNCH SAW SET.

This Saw Set is made of Iron, Bronzed, with Adjustable Fences for size and set of saw teeth.

The action of setting the teeth resembles that of setting saws by hammer and steel bed.

No. 1460 ... ... 4/6 each.

Packed one in a box.

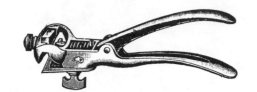

MORRELL'S PATTERN SAW SETS.

| No. 1853 | Bright | ... | ... | ... | 32/- per dozen. |
| ,, 1853NP | Nickel Plated | .. | ... | 40/- | ,, |

IMPROVED BEECH HANDLED PLIER SAW SET.

No. 1462 ... . 5/6 each.

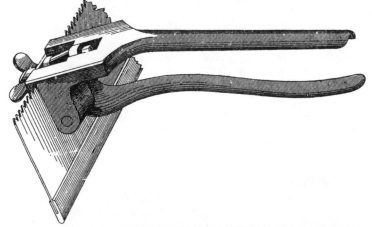

TRICKET'S PATTERN SAW SET.

No. 1854 ... ... 3/3 each.

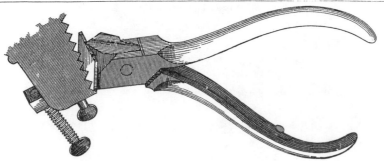

BRIGHT PLYER SAW SET

No. 1852 ... ... 3/- each.

EDWARD PRESTON & SONS, L^{TD.}

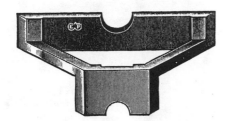

BRASS MITRE TEMPLETS.

These Mitre Templets are accurately made and of superior finish.

They are very useful Tools for all kinds of Mitreing purposes.

No. 920 ... ... $3\frac{1}{4}$ $4\frac{1}{4}$ $5\frac{3}{4}$ inch.

                      11/4   15/4   21/- per dozen.

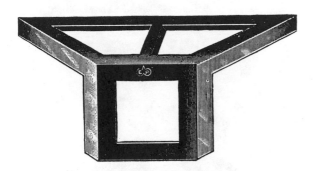

IRON MITRE TEMPLET.

No. $1474\frac{1}{2}$ Nickel Plated, $6\frac{1}{4}$ inch ... ... 12/- per dozen.

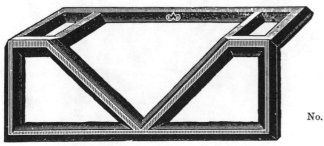

IMPROVED SQUARE AND MITRE TEMPLET.

For Mitreing and Squaring up the Ends of Wood.

No. 1475 Nickel Plated, 6 inch ... ... 15/- per dozen.

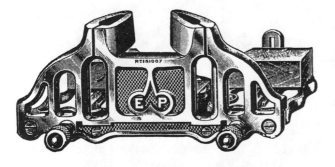

PRESTON'S REGISTERED
ADJUSTABLE IRON MITRE BOX.

This Mitre Box is made of Iron and has two saw guides and two grips for holding the moulding while sawing.

These advantages will appeal to all users of Mitre Boxes.

The Saw Guides adjust themselves to the varying thicknesses of saw blades.

The Grips for holding the moulding firmly while sawing are tightened by means of the milled nuts. Will take 3 inch Moulding.

When fixing the Mitre Box to the work bench, care should be taken to place the front of the box level with the edge of the bench, so as to allow freedom for tightening the adjusting milled nuts. Never attempt to use the Mitre Box until it is firmly screwed to the bench.

No. 569 ... ... 7/6 each.

Packed One in a Box.

EDWARD PRESTON & SONS, LTD.

PICTURE FRAMING OR CORNER CRAMPS.

These Cramps consist of Four Corner Cramps, which have lugs projecting from them, with holes through which the Chain passes and surrounds the entire frame. This Chain is operated upon by means of a hooked screw and fly nut. When the Chain is passed round the Frame, the hook is inserted in any convenient link, and then screwed up tightly by means of the hooked screw and fly nut.

No. 0144 is supplied with Top Corner Pressure Grips; these are useful for pressing down the pieces of the frame when nailing, and being fitted with rubber underneath will not damage the moulding. The Cramps may be had either with or without the top pressure grips. They are accurately made and attractive in appearance, being nickel plated. They will cramp from 9 inches upwards, and take in mouldings up to 3¼ inches. The Cramps are supplied with 10 feet of Chain.

Packed One in Box.

No. 0143
7/6 per set

No. 0144
10/6 per set.

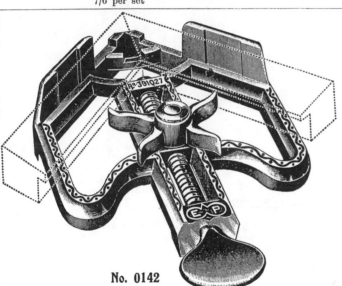

No. 0142

PRESTON'S REGISTERED IMPROVED GRIP CORNER CRAMP.

Will take 2¼ inch Moulding ... 2/3 each.

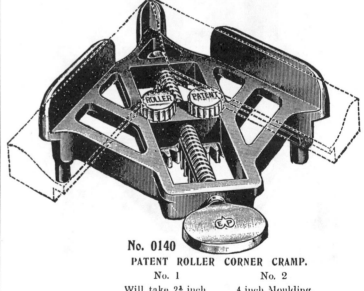

No. 0140

PATENT ROLLER CORNER CRAMP.

No. 1	No. 2
Will take 2¼ inch	4 inch Moulding.
40/-	51/- per dozen

No. 0137

IMPROVED CORNER CRAMP.

	No. 1	2	3
Will take	... 1¼	2¼	4 inch Moulding.
		10/- 15/-	23/6 per dozen.

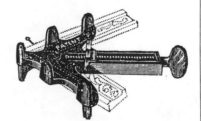

No. 0138

PATENT CORNER CRAMP.

	No. 1	2	3
Will take	1¼	2¼	4 inch Moulding.
	15/- 20/-	28/- per dozen.
	13/6	17/6	25/6 " "

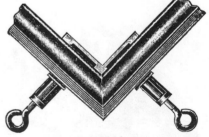

No. 0141

EUREKA PATTERN NICKEL PLATED CORNER CRAMPS.

Will take in 2¼ inch Moulding.
10/6 per dozen.

EDWARD PRESTON & SONS, LTD.

TRADE MARK.

MOUNT CUTTER HANDLES AND KNIVES.
Rosewood, Brass Ferrule at each end.

No. 160 Rosewood Mount Cutters' Handles only 13/- per dozen.

,, 161 Knives for ditto. Spear Pointed ... 5/- ,,

,, 160 C Handles and Knives complete ... 18/- ,,

Brass Framed and Ebony Fitted

No. 162 Ebony, London Pattern Mount
Cutters' Handles only ... 20/- per dozen.

,, 163 Knives for ditto, Spear Pointed 6/- ,,

,, 162C Handles and Knives complete ... 26/- ,,

IMPROVED
MALLEABLE IRON JOINERS' DOGS, OR JOINT CRAMPS.
FULL SIZE DRAWINGS.

No. 100
8/-

No. 101
12/-

No. 102
16/-

No. 103, size 2½ inch.
24/-

Per Gross.

FORGED STEEL DOGS.
No. 110

2	2½	3	3½ inch.
16/-	18/-	20/-	22/- per gross.

BRICKLAYERS' LINE PINS.

No. 1550 Malleable Iron Small Black Line Pins, 5 in. long, Round Heads ... ... 1/2 per doz.

,, 1550B Malleable Iron Small Bright Line Pins, 5 inches long, Round Heads ... ... 1/9 ,,

,, 1552 Malleable Iron, Medium Black Line Pins, 6 inches long, Round Heads ... ... 1/8 ,,

,, 1552B Malleable Iron, Medium Bright Line Pins, 6 inches long Round Heads ... ... 2/4 ,,

,, 1552S Cast Steel Medium Black Pins, 6 inches long, Round Heads 3/4 ,,

,, 1552SB ,, ,, Bright ,, ,, ,, ,, 4/- ,,

BRICK JOINTERS.
Polished Bright, with Beech Handles.
No. 1555A

	3½ × 3/16	4½ × 3/16	5 × ¼ inch.
No. 1555A Flat Face ...	8/6	9/6	11/- per dozen.
,, 1555G Grooved Face ...	11/-	12/-	13/6 ,,

CHALK LINE REELS.

No. 20 Brass, 2½ inches in diam. ... ... 5/4 per dozen.

,, 21 Leather, 2½ ,, ,, ... 5/4 ,,

,, 22 Compo, 2½ inches ,, ... 5/4 ,,

EDWARD PRESTON & SONS, L^{TD}.

DOWELLING TOOLS.

1444P.

1444B.

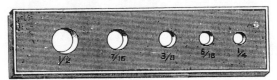

1444A.

DOWEL PLATES.

No. 1444B. Best Dowel Plates—
4 holes, $\frac{1}{4}$, $\frac{5}{16}$. $\frac{3}{8}$, $\frac{1}{2}$ inch.
5 ,, $\frac{1}{4}$, $\frac{5}{16}$, $\frac{3}{8}$, $\frac{7}{16}$, $\frac{1}{2}$ inch.
5 ,, $\frac{1}{4}$, $\frac{5}{16}$, $\frac{3}{8}$, $\frac{1}{2}$ $\frac{5}{8}$ inch.
6 ,, $\frac{1}{4}$, $\frac{5}{16}$, $\frac{3}{8}$, $\frac{7}{16}$, $\frac{1}{2}$, $\frac{5}{8}$ inch.

4	5	5	6 holes.
24/-	28/-	28/-	36/- per doz.

No 1444P. Preston's Patent Dowel Plates, sizes as 1444B ... ...

36/-	40/-	40/-	50/- ,,

1444P.—These Dowel Plates are of superior manufacture, and have a Steel V Tooth inside each hole for grooving the Dowel Peg, which allows the air and superfluous glue to get away, thus avoiding burst holes in the work.

No. 1444B. 5-hole Plate, if fitted with one Jenning's Pattern Bit to each hole   ...   . 8/6 each.

,, 1444P. 5-hole ,,   ,,   ,,   ,,   ,,   ,,   ... 9/6 ,,

,, 1444A. Dowel Plates—
3 holes, $\frac{1}{4}$, $\frac{3}{8}$ $\frac{1}{2}$ inch.
4 ,, $\frac{1}{4}$, $\frac{5}{16}$, $\frac{3}{8}$, $\frac{1}{2}$ inch.
5 ,, $\frac{1}{4}$, $\frac{5}{16}$, $\frac{3}{8}$, $\frac{7}{16}$, $\frac{1}{2}$ inch.
6 ,, $\frac{1}{4}$, $\frac{5}{16}$, $\frac{3}{8}$, $\frac{7}{16}$, $\frac{1}{2}$, $\frac{5}{8}$ inch.

3	4	5	6 holes.
10/6	14/-	18/-	22/- per doz.

FULL SIZE OF $\frac{7}{16}$ IN.

DOWEL ROUNDERS.

These are made of Steel, Nickel Plated, and will work perfectly Round Ends to Dowel Pegs.   They are supplied in the following sizes to cut Dowels $\frac{5}{16}$, $\frac{3}{8}$, $\frac{7}{16}$, $\frac{1}{2}$ and $\frac{9}{16}$ inch.

No 1443   ...   12/- per dozen.

Packed in Half Dozens in Cardboard Boxes.

DOWEL SHAVERS OR TRIMMERS.

Nickel Plated, and will shave or trim rapidly the ends of Dowel Pegs. They are supplied in two sizes to trim $\frac{7}{16}$ and $\frac{3}{4}$ inch pegs.

No. 1441   ...   12/- per dozen.

Packed in Half Dozens in Cardboard Boxes.

DOWEL CENTRES.

1440.   **1440½.**

	$\frac{5}{16}$ and $\frac{3}{8}$ in.	$\frac{7}{16}$ and $\frac{1}{2}$ in.
No. 1440. Brass Dowel Centres, 2 sizes on each	4/-	4/6 per doz.
,, 1440½. ,, ,, ,, single sizes	3/6	4/- ,,

EDWARD PRESTON & SONS, L^{TD.}

ENGINEERS' TOOLS.

TRADE E P MARK.

STEEL SQUARES.

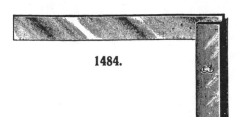

1484.

These Squares are made with Solid Steel Stocks and Hardened and Tempered Steel Blades.

Sizes are measured from inside of Stock.

	2	2½	3	3½	4	4½	5	5½	6	7
No. 1484.	10/-	10/8	11/4	12/-	12/8	13/-	13/8	14/8	15/8	17/4

	8	9	10	12 inch.
	20/-	23/-	26/-	30/- per dozen.

No. 1484S Scotch Pattern, Light. Prices as No. 1484.

STEEL SQUARES.

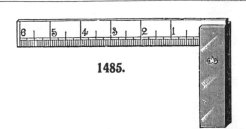

1485.

The Blades of these Squares are fine divided into 16ths of inches.

	2	3	4	5	6	7	8	9	10	12 inch.
No. 1485.	11/8	13/4	15/-	16/8	18/-	21/-	24/-	28/-	32/-	36/- per doz.

STEEL SQUARES.

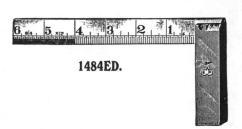

1484ED.

The Blades of these Squares are machine divided into 16ths, 32nds and 64ths.

	2	3	4	5	6 inch.
No. 1484ED.	13/6	16/-	19/-	22/-	25/- per dozen.

STEEL T SQUARES.

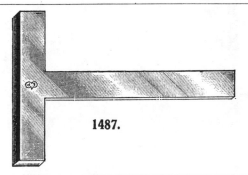

1487.

Hardened and Tempered Steel Blades.

	3	4	5	6	8	9	10	12 inch.
No. 1487.	11/8	15/-	18/-	21/4	28/4	30/-	32/-	38/8 per dozen.

FLAT STEEL L SQUARES.

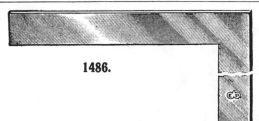

1486.

Hardened and Tempered.

	2	3	4	5	6	8	9	10	12 inch.
No. 1486.	11/-	13/-	15/-	17/-	19/6	23/6	26/-	28/6	32/- per dozen.

BOX OR KEYWAY SQUARES.

55.

These are machined inside and outside with Bevelled Edges for marking Keyways on Shafting, &c.

				4	5	6	8 inch.
No. 55.				4/-	5/-	6/-	8/- each.
„ 55M. Edges marked inches in 16ths and 32nds ...				5/4	6/8	8/-	10/8 „

Edward Preston & Sons, L^{TD}.

PRESTON'S REGISTERED DEPTHING GAUGE HEADS.

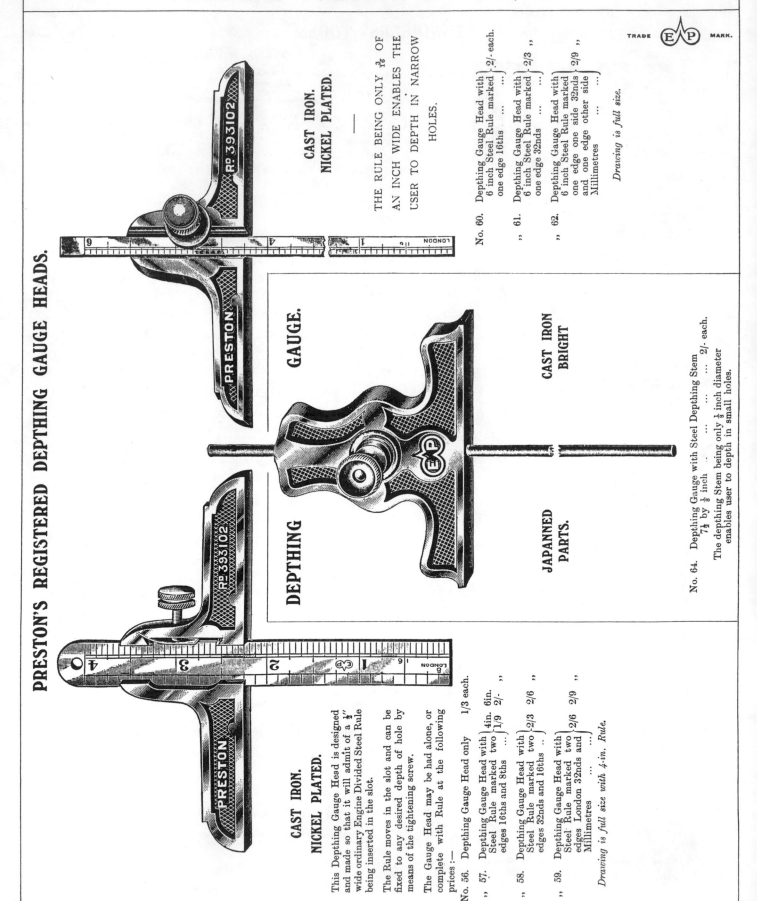

CAST IRON. NICKEL PLATED.

THE RULE BEING ONLY $\frac{1}{16}$ OF AN INCH WIDE ENABLES THE USER TO DEPTH IN NARROW HOLES.

Drawing is full size.

No. 60.	Depthing Gauge Head with 6 inch Steel Rule marked one edge 16ths	2/- each.
" 61.	Depthing Gauge Head with 6 inch Steel Rule marked one edge 32nds ...	2/3 "
" 62.	Depthing Gauge Head with 6 inch Steel Rule marked one edge one side 32nds and one edge other side Millimetres	2/9 "

DEPTHING GAUGE.

CAST IRON BRIGHT

JAPANNED PARTS.

No. 64. Depthing Gauge with Steel Depthing Stem 7½ by ⅛ inch ... ... 2/- each.

The depthing Stem being only ⅛ inch diameter enables user to depth in small holes.

CAST IRON. NICKEL PLATED.

This Depthing Gauge Head is designed and made so that it will admit of a ½" wide ordinary Engine Divided Steel Rule being inserted in the slot.

The Rule moves in the slot and can be fixed to any desired depth of hole by means of the tightening screw.

The Gauge Head may be had alone, or complete with Rule at the following prices :—

No. 56.	Depthing Gauge Head only	1/3 each.
" 57.	Depthing Gauge Head with Steel Rule marked two edges 16ths and 8ths	4in. 6in. 1/9 2/- "
" 58.	Depthing Gauge Head with Steel Rule marked two edges 32nds and 16ths ..	2/3 2/6 "
" 59.	Depthing Gauge Head with Steel Rule marked two edges London 32nds and Millimetres	2/6 2/9 "

Drawing is full size with 4-in. Rule.

EDWARD PRESTON & SONS, LTD.

MASONS' AND ENGRAVERS' SQUARES.

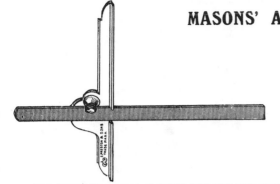

STONEMASONS' DEPTHING SQUARES OR GAUGES.

WITH BRASS HEADS.

These Squares or Gauges are of Superior Make and Finish and have Hardened and Tempered Steel Blades.

	6	8	10	12 inch
No. 1496. Steel Blade let in on side	22/-	26/-	35/-	45/- per dozen.

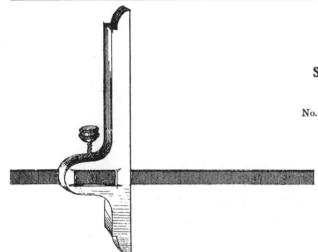

STONEMASONS' DEPTHING SQUARES OR GAUGES.

WITH GUN METAL HEADS,

	6	8	10	12 inch.
No. 1495. Steel Blade mortised through head ...	28/-	36/-	44/-	57/- per dozen.

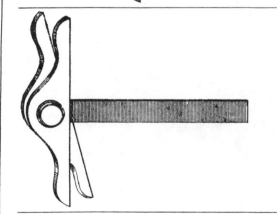

ENGRAVERS' SQUARES.

These Squares have Moveable Brass T Heads and Hardened and Tempered Steel Blades

	4	6	8	10	12 inch.
No. 1493 ...	23/6	31/-	39/-	44/-	51/- per dozen.

ENGRAVERS' SQUARES.

These Squares have Brass Heads and Hardened and Tempered Steel Blades.

	4	6	8	10	12 inch.
No. 1492. ...	16/6	23/6	31/-	35/-	42/- per dozen.

EDWARD PRESTON & SONS, L^{TD.}

ENGINEERS' TOOLS.

TRADE **E P** MARK.

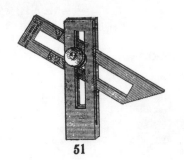

51

STEEL SLIDING BEVELS.

These are marked with the angles of 45°, 60°, and square.

No. 51.   4 inches long × 19 w.g. thick   ...   . 2/6 each.

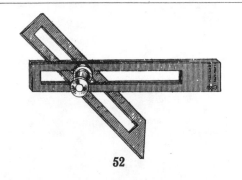

52

STEEL SLIDING BEVELS.

	5½	6½	7½ inch.
No. 52. Not marked with angles, 16 w.g. thick ...	2/-	2/6	3/- each.

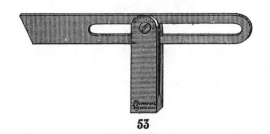

53

STEEL SLIDING BEVELS.
WITH SOLID HANDLES.

	6	7½	9	10½	12 inch.
No. 53.	3/-	3/6	4/-	4/6	5/6 each.

B1500

B1501

B1502

1504

CENTRE PUNCHES.

These Punches are made of Best Cast Steel and are guaranteed.
Each pattern is made in two sizes.

		Size	1	2
No. B1500.	Octagon, Black		3/9	4/9 per dozen
,, B1503.	Octagon, pattern as B1500 but bright		4/6	5/6 ,,
,, B1501.	Octagon Centre, Bright		5/-	6/- ,,
,, B1502.	Heavily Milled Centre		5/-	6/- ,,
,, 1504.	Lightly ,, one size only ...		4/-	— ,,

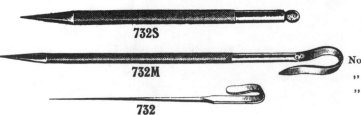

732S

732M

732

ENGINEERS' SCRIBERS.

These are made of Best Cast Steel with Milled Grip.

No. 732S.   Milled, 4 inch long, $\frac{3}{16}$ inch dia. . .   .. 3/6 per dozen.
,, 732M.   ,,   7   ,,   ,,   ,, Hooked End   5/-   ,,
,, 732.   Plain, 7   ,,   ,,   .,   ,,   ,, 5/-   ,,

EDWARD PRESTON & SONS, L^{TD.}

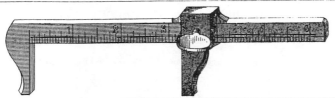

TRADE **E P** MARK.

STEEL SLIDING CALLIPER GAUGE.

| | 3 | 4 inch. |
No. 1097. Inches marked in 32nds and half Millimetres. 4/6 5/- each

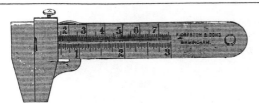

IRON SLIDING CALLIPER GAUGE.

6 inch.
No 1497. Inches marked in 16ths ... ... 2/6 each.

SURFACE GAUGE.

This is a very handy tool, the spindle is of steel and the base heavy and ground true on face. The Scriber is of best drill steel.

No. 2420. Japanned Base—
6 9 12 inch high.
3/4 4/4 5/- each.

No. 2421. Nickel Plated Base—
6 9 12 inch high.
3/8 4/8 5/4 each.

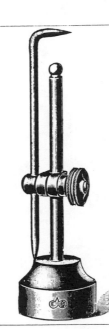

SURFACE GAUGE.

This is a superior and fine finished tool. The base is turned bright and true all over. The Scriber is of best drill steel.

6 9 12 inch high.
No. 2422. ... 5/- 7/- 10/6 each.

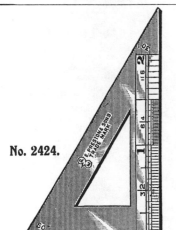

No. 2424.

STEEL SET SQUARES.

These are made of hardened and tempered steel and are machine divided, inches in 16ths, 32nds and 64ths.

2½ 3½ inch.
No 2424. 60° ... 2/6 3/6 each.
„ 2425. 45° ... 2/6 3/6 „

STEEL SET SQUARES.

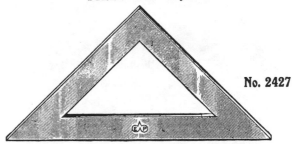

No. 2427

These are plain and made of hardened and tempered steel.

	3	4	6	9	12 inch.
No. 2426. 60° ...	2/3	3/-	4/6	6/6	8/6 each.
„ 2427. 45° ...	2/3	3/-	4/6	6/6	8/6 „

CAST STEEL OCTAGON COLD CHISELS.

No. 600.

3½ 4 4½ 5 × ⁵⁄₁₆ 6 × ⁷⁄₁₆ inch.
No. 600. ... 4/3 5/- 5/9 7/6 9/- per dozen.
„ 601. Assorted to 5 inch × ⁵⁄₁₆ inch Steel 5/9 „

FANCY PLUGGING CHISELS.

No. 602.

No. 602. Assorted shapes, to 5 inch × ⁵⁄₁₆ inch ... 5/9 per dozen.

COLD CHISELS.

No. 603

No. 603 Cast Steel Octagon Cold Chisels up to } 10/- per dozen.
6 × ½ in. }
8 × ⁵⁄₈ 8 × ¾ 9 × ¾ 9 × ⁷⁄₈ 10 × ⁷⁄₈ 10 × 1 in. ... 10d per lb.

PLUGGING CHISELS.

No. 604

No. 604 Joiners' C.S. Plugging Chisels—
⅝ in. Octagon Steel. ¾ in. Octagon Steel.
10/- 11/6 per dozen.

EDWARD PRESTON & SONS, LTD.

ENGINEERS' GAUGES.
INVALUABLE TO ENGINEERS, MACHINISTS AND OTHERS.

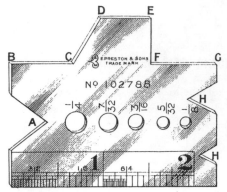

THE "JOHN BULL" POCKET GAUGE.
No. 2407   3/- each.

The "JOHN BULL" has been introduced to meet a demand for a neat and handy Pocket Gauge.

It can be used as a Rule ; a Straight-edge ; a Centre Gauge, A ; 2 Hexagons (inside and Outside). B C D E ; 2 Squares (inside and outside), D E F G ; 2 Screw-cutting Tool Gauges, H H ; 1 Angle Gauge for grinding the points of Drills, B C D ; 5 Drill and Wire Gauges. It can also be used for Setting Tools for Screw Cutting.

These Gauges are made of Fine Steel, are light, small, strong and durable.

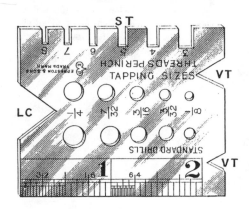

THE ENGINEERS' "UNIVERSAL" POCKET GAUGE.
No. 2406   4/- each.

The Engineers' "Universal" Pocket Gauge serves twenty-two purposes. It contains the best and latest improvements, and is equally useful to the amateur and practical mechanic.

It consists of a Rule and Straight Edge on its bottom side ; the angle L C is 75°, being the most suitable angle for Lathe Centres : those marked V T are 55°, being the proper angle for cutting V thread screws ; the six gauges on the top side, marked S T, are the proper widths for making tools for cutting square threads of the various sizes, the figures will show the number of threads per inch ; the holes down the centre are 5 standard drill sizes and 5 tapping drill sizes, which will be found most useful to all engaged in mechanical pursuits.

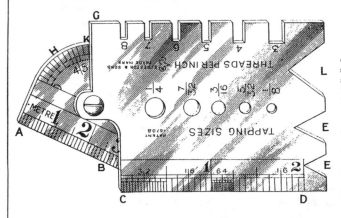

THE ENGINEERS' "VERY" GAUGE.
No. 2408   6/- each.

This Gauge consists of two unequal size plates, one of which serves as an ordinary sector combined with a Metre Rule. The larger plate, as may be seen by reference to the drawing, contains on the top side six openings, of the several widths suitable for making tools for cutting SQUARE THREADS, the number of threads per inch being marked against each opening. Down the centre of the plate are holes of the sizes required for making drills for Tapping purposes. The V shaped opening on its end marked L is an angle of 75°, and is suitable for turning Lathe Centres; those marked E E are angles of 55°, and are useful for making tools to cut screws with V threads. The two plates are united by a screw, which forms an axis on which the smaller one can be made to turn, and can be used to tighten the plates as required, the smaller plate can be used as an ordinary sector for setting out angles of any number of degrees ; also for obtaining the rake of the tool when screw cutting. When the two lines marked H G are together, the two straight edges, A B, C D, are at right angles with each other, then when turned to the angle required (as shewn in drawing), the sector will register the number of degrees by the lines K.

AMATEURS' POCKET GAUGES.

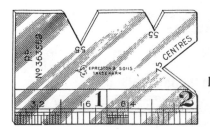

No. 2417 ... 2/- each.

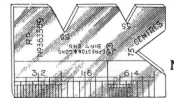

No. 2417S ... 1/6 each.

DRAWINGS ARE FULL SIZE.

EDWARD PRESTON & SONS, LTD.

ENGINEERS' GAUGES.

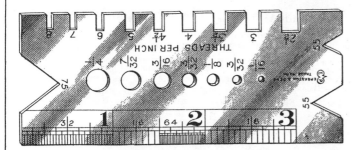

The "HANDY" POCKET SCREW-CUTTING GAUGE.

The advantages of the "Handy" over others are that it has a Longer Rule and Straight-edge, Finer Holes for Drill and Wire Gauges, More Sizes for the Width of Square Thread Tools, and the Angles are marked with the number of degrees they represent, 75° for the Lathe Centres, and 55° for Screw Threads.

No. 2409   5/- each.

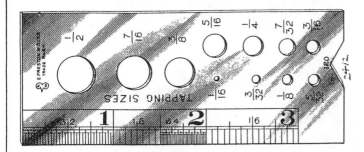

ENGINEERS' IMPROVED TAPPING AND STANDARD DRILL GAUGES.

These Gauges have, in addition to the drill sizes, a Rule and Straight Edge, also an Angle Gauge 120°, which will always be useful when grinding the points of Drills. When this angle is maintained, the Drills cut better and last longer.

No. 2411   Standard Drill Sizes   ...   .   2/3 each.

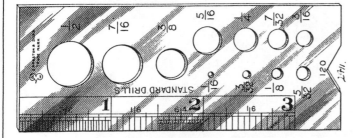

No. 2412   Tapping Drill Sizes   ...   .   2/3 each.

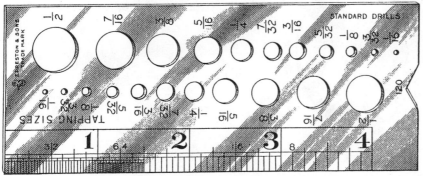

No. 2410   Combined Standard and Tapping Drill Sizes   ...   .   4/- each.

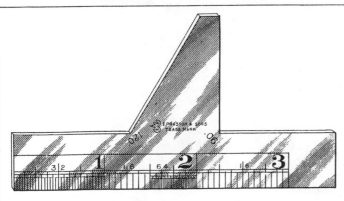

ANGLE POCKET GAUGE.

Graduated in 16ths, 32nds and 64ths of Inch.

	2	3 inch.
No. 2416	2/-	3/- each.

DRAWINGS ARE FULL SIZE.

EDWARD PRESTON & SONS, L^{TD.}

ENGINEERS' GAUGES.

STANDARD AND TAPPING GAUGES.

These Gauges are intended to economise time in the making and selection of Drills, and to facilitate accurate and systematic work.

By drilling holes intended to be tapped to these sizes a proper thread will always be secured, and many taps will be saved from being broken; also the annoyance of having a poor thread when the hole has been too large is dispensed with.

No. 2400   Standard Gauge ... ... 1/6 each.

No. 2401   Tapping Gauge ... ... 1/6 each.

No. 2402   Combined Standard and Tapping Gauge ... ... 3/- each.

No. 2403   Circular Standard Gauge ... 2/- each.

No. 2404   Circular Tapping Gauge ... 2/- each.

No. 2405   Combined Circular Standard and Tapping Gauge ... ... 4/- each.

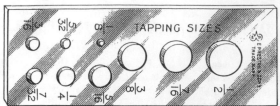

No. 2401

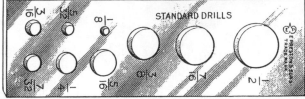

No. 2400

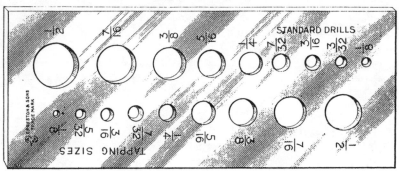

No. 2402

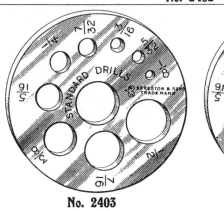

No. 2403

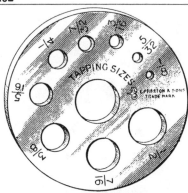

No. 2404

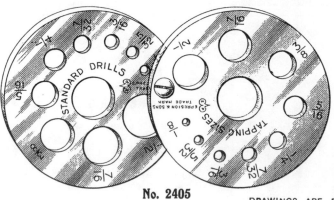

No. 2405

DRAWINGS ARE FULL SIZE.

EDWARD PRESTON & SONS, LTD.

GAUGES.

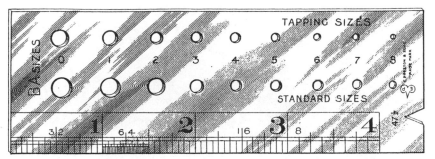

THE STANDARD AND TAPPING GAUGE, B.A. SIZES.

This Gauge is intended for the use of those who are engaged in Electrical Engineering and kindred trades where the B.A. sizes are adopted. The angle for the V thread is $47\frac{1}{2}°$, which is the angle for B.A. Screws, and will be found invaluable to those engaged in Electrical Work for Screw Cutting and Tap Making. It is also rule marked to 4 inches, in 32nds, 64ths, 16ths and 8ths; thus forming a 4-inch Rule and Straight Edge.

No. 2413 .. ... 6/6 each.

FULL SIZE DRAWING.

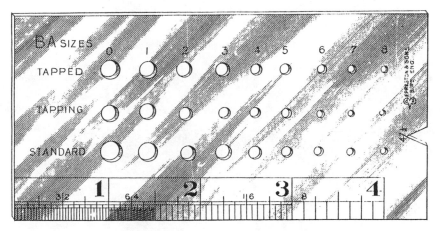

This Gauge is same as No. 2413, but in addition has B.A. Tapped Sizes.

No. 2419 ... ... 10/6 each.

FULL SIZE DRAWING.

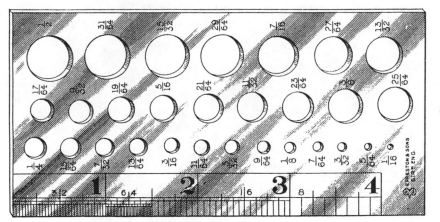

ENGINEERS' STANDARD DRILL GAUGE.

Containing 29 Standard Drill Sizes, from $\frac{1}{16}$th to $\frac{1}{2}$ inch × 64ths of an inch.

No. 2420 ... ... 6/6 each.

FULL SIZE DRAWING.

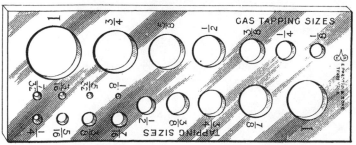

ENGINEERS' TAPPING GAUGE.

No. 2414 Combined Gas Tapping and Whitworth Tapping Gauge ... . 9/- each.

„ 2415 Combined Standard ... ... 9/- „

HALF SIZE DRAWING.

EDWARD PRESTON & SONS, L^{TD}.

GAUGES.

These Wire Gauges may be had with either B.W.G. or Imperial Standard Sizes.

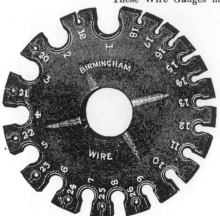

No. 1861   Standard Circular Wire Gauge, 3 inch diam.

Sizes 1 to 26   1 to 30   1 to 36
4/-   5/-   6/- each.

No. 1861B B.W.G. Circular Wire Gauge 3 inch diam.

Sizes, 1 to 26   1 to 30   1 to 36
4/-   5/-   6/- each.

Leather Cases for above, 8/- per doz.

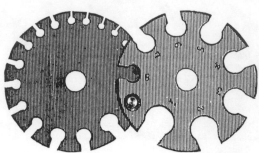

No. 1862S Extra Small Standard Double Circular Wire Gauge, 1¼ in. diam., 1 to 26, 3/6 each.

No. 1862SB Extra Small B.W.G. Double Circular Wire Gauge, 3/6 each.

,,   1862   Standard Double Circular Wire Gauge, 2 inch diam.
Sizes, 1 to 26   1 to 30   1 to 36
3/9   4/6   5/6 each.

,,   1862B B.W.G. Double Circular Wire Gauge, 2 inch diam.
Sizes, 1 to 26   1 to 30   1 to 36
3/9   4/6   5/6 each.

Leather Cases for above, 5/4 per doz.

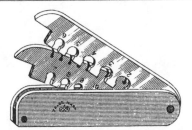

No. 1864   Folding Pocket Standard Wire Gauge, in Brass Case, 3½ in. long, sizes 1 to 26   ...   6/- each.

,,   1864B Folding Pocket B.W.G. Wire Gauge, in Brass Case, 3½ in. long, sizes 1 to 26   ...   6/- ,,

The Cases of these may be graduated in 16ths and 8ths of an inch on one side at 8d. each extra.

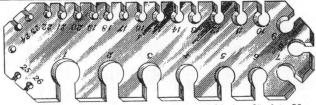

Sizes 1 to 26   1 to 30   1 to 36

No. 1860   Standard Oblong Wire Gauge   4/-   5/-   6/- each.

,,   1860B B.W.G.   ,,   ,,   4/-   5/-   6/- ,,

,,   1860S Extra Small Standard Oblong Wire Gauge, 2⅝ in. long, in Leather Case ...   .   Sizes 4 to 26   3/4 ,,

,,   1860SB B.W.G. Extra Small Standard Oblong Wire Gauge, 2⅝ in. long, in Leather Case   ...   ,,   ,,   3/4 ,,

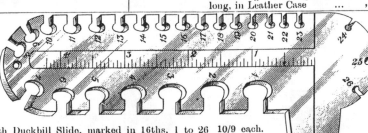

No. 1865   Standard Wire Gauge, with Duckbill Slide, marked in 16ths, 1 to 26 10/9 each.

,,   1865B B.W.G. Wire Gauge, with Duckbill Slide, marked in 16ths, 1 to 26,   10/9 each.

No. 1867
Circular Lead Gauge,
1 to 14.
2/6 each.

No. 1866
Circular Zinc Gauge,
5 to 18,
2/6 each.

Combined Double Circular Lead and Zinc Gauge   ...   .   3/9 each.

EDWARD PRESTON & SONS, L^TD.

ENGINEERS' FEELER (OR THICKNESS) GAUGES.

TRADE MARK.

These Gauges are comprised of Tempered Steel Blades of varying thicknesses, folding into a Steel Case, similar to a pocket knife. They are riveted together, and the figures engraved on the Blades, represent the thickness in 1000ths of an inch.

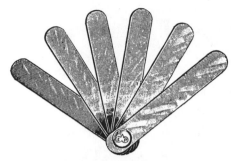

No. 367   Without Steel Case, Six Blades, not Engraved, 2⅞ inches long   ...   12/- per doz.

No. 367

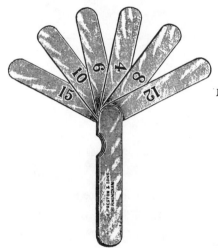

No. 367A   As 367B, but Blades not Engraved   ...   .   18/- per doz.

,,   367B   Six Engraved Blades, 2⅞ inches long, as drawing   ...   .   24/-   ,,

,,   367BE   As 367B, but with two extra Blades, 2 and 3/1000ths of an inch   ...   30/-   ,,

,,   367BE3 With 10 Blades, 12, 4, 2, 8, 2, 6, 3, 10, 2, 15   ...   .   36/-   ,,

No. 367B

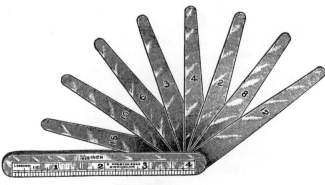

No. ~~367~~ 376 D   As 376DE, but Engraved Blades, 4 inches long 33/- per doz.

,,   367DE   Eight Engraved Blades, 4 inches long, case
marked with 16ths one side and millimeters
on other side, as drawing   ...   .   42/-   ,,

No. 367DE

EDWARD PRESTON & SONS, L^{TD.}

ENGINEERS' FEELER (OR THICKNESS) GAUGES.

TRADE MARK.

These Gauges are similar to those on preceeding page, but are fitted with Nut and Bolt (in place of rivet) so that broken blades may readily be replaced.

No. 321

No. 321　Six Engraved Blades, 2⅞ inches long, as drawing　...　...　...　21/6 per dozen.

,,　322　As 321, but with Two Extra Blades (8), 2 and 3/1000ths of an inch　24/6　,,

,,　3122　As 322, but with Two Extra Blades (10), 1½ and 25/1000ths of an inch ...　31/-　,,

,,　326　10 Blades, 3 No. 2, see 367BE3 for numbers of Blades　...　...　...　32/-　,,

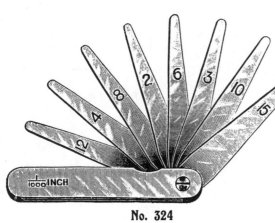

No. 324

No. 323　As 324, but Six Engraved and Tapered Blades, 2⅞ inches long　25/- per doz.

,,　324　Eight Engraved and Tapered Blades, as drawing ...　...　31/-　,,

,,　3124　As 324, but with Two Extra Blades (10), 1½ and 25/1000ths of an inch　...　...　...　...　...　...　...　37/-　,,

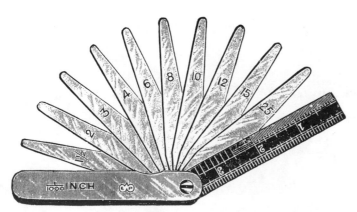

No. 3133

No. 331　Six Engraved and Tapered Blades, 4 inches long　...　...　...　28/- per doz.

,,　332　As 331, but Two Extra Blades (8) 2 and 3/1000ths of an inch ...　35/-　,,

,,　3132　As 332, but Two Extra Blades (10) 1½ and 25/1000ths of an inch ...　43/-　,,

,,　3133　As 332, but with 4 inch Flexible Steel Rule in addition, as drawing　51/　,,

EDWARD PRESTON & SONS, L^{TD.}

CALLIPERS AND SPRING DIVIDERS.

BRIGHT INSIDE CALLIPERS, LANCASHIRE PATTERN.

		3	3½	4	4½	5	6	7	8	9	10	12 in.
1038	Best quality	12/6	14/6	16/6	18/6	20/6	24/6	28/6	32/6	36/6	40/6	48/6 doz.
*2249	Cheaper ,,	6/-	6/-	6/6	6/6	7/-	8/-	12/-	14/-	19/-	—	— ,,

BRIGHT JENNY CALLIPERS, LANCASHIRE PATTERN.

		3	3½	4	4½	5	6	7	8	9	10	12 in.
1039	Best quality	12/6	14/6	16/6	18/6	20/6	24/6	28/6	32/6	36/6	40/6	48/6 doz.
*2247	Cheaper ,,	7/6	7/6	8/-	8/:	9/-	10/-	—	—	—	—	— ,,

BRIGHT OUTSIDE CALLIPERS, LANCASHIRE PATTERN.

		3	3½	4	4½	5	6	7	8	9	10	12 in.
1040	Best quality	12/6	14/6	16/6	18/6	20/6	24/6	28/6	32/6	36/6	40/6	48/6 doz.
*2248	Cheaper ,,	6/-	6/-	6/6	6/6	7/-	8/-	12/-	14/-	19/-	—	— ,,

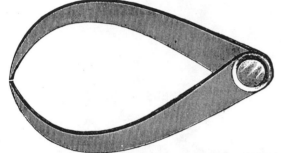

BRIGHT INSIDE AND OUTSIDE CALLIPERS, LANCASHIRE PATTERN.

		3	4	5	6	7	8 in.
1051	Best quality ..	32/-	32/-	38/-	44/-	62/-	80/- doz.
*2250	Cheaper ,, ...	16/-	16/-	16/-	—	—	— ,,

BRIGHT INSIDE AND OUTSIDE CALLIPERS, LANCASHIRE PATTERN

(WITH WING).

			3	4	5	6	7	8 in.
1052	...	...	35/-	38/-	44/-	50/-	68/-	86/- doz.

*IMPORTED.

BRIGHT INSIDE SPRING CALLIPERS, AMERICAN PATTERN.

				4	5	6 in.
1053	...	...	...	35/-	37/-	39/- doz.

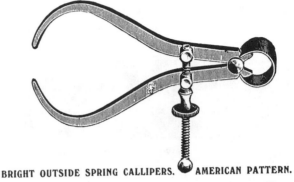

BRIGHT OUTSIDE SPRING CALLIPERS, AMERICAN PATTERN.

				4	5	6 in.
1054	...	...	...	35/-	37/-	39/- doz.

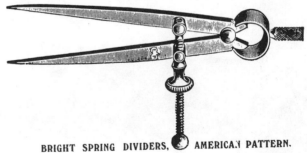

BRIGHT SPRING DIVIDERS, AMERICAN PATTERN.

				4	5	6 in.
1055	...	...	...	35/-	37/-	39/- doz.

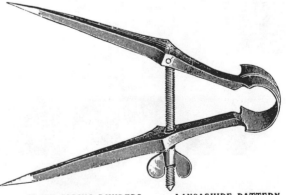

BLACK SPRING DIVIDERS, LANCASHIRE PATTERN.

			3	3½	4	4½	5	6 in
1056	Best quality	...	26/-	26/-	26/-	26/-	26/-	26/- doz.
*2252	Cheaper ,,	...	16/-	16/-	16/-	16/-	16/-	16/-

EDWARD PRESTON & SONS, L^{TD.}

JOINERS' TOOLS.

TRADE  MARK.

JOINERS' SQUARES.

	3	4½	6	7½	9	10½	12	15	18	21	24 inch.
No. 0702 Diamond Plated Squares ... Rosewood	17/-	19/6	23/6	28/6	33/6	39/-	44/-	58/-	74/-	96/-	120/- per dozen.

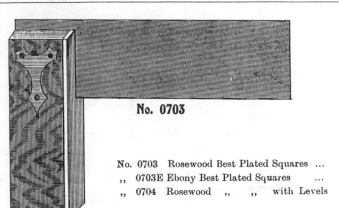

No. 0703

BEST JOINERS' SQUARES.

	3	4½	6	7½	9	10½	12	15	18	21	24 inch.
No. 0703 Rosewood Best Plated Squares	20/6	22/6	26/-	32/-	38/-	43/-	50/-	68/-	84/-	108/-	132/- per dozen.
,, 0703E Ebony Best Plated Squares	22/-	24/-	28/-	34/-	40/-	46/-	54/-	74/-	90/-	—	— ,,
,, 0704 Rosewood ,, ,, with Levels ...	—	—	—	—	78/-	84/-	90/-	108/-	126/-	140/-	160/- ,,

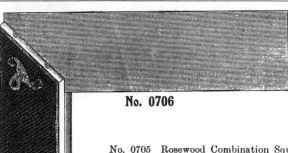

No. 0706

COMBINATION SQUARES.

	4½	6	7½	9	10½	12 inch.
No. 0705 Rosewood Combination Squares	30/-	35/-	40/-	48/-	54/-	60/- per dozen.
,, 0706 Ebony ,, ,, ...	32/-	38/-	44/-	52/-	58/-	64/- ,,

No. 0709

MITRE SQUARES.

		8	10	12	14	16 inch.
No. 0708	Rosewood Plated Mitre Squares ...	34/	40/-	46/-	55/-	64/- per dozen.
,, 0709	Rosewood Best Plated Mitre Squares	50/-	58/-	66/-	77/-	88/- ,,
,, 0709E	Ebony ,, ,,	52/-	60/-	70/-	80/-	92/- ,,

EDWARD PRESTON & SONS, L^{TD}.

JOINERS' TOOLS.

TRADE **E P** MARK.

BEVELS.

	7½	9	10½	12	15 inch.
No. 0712 Rosewood Improved Sliding Bevels	32/-	36/-	40/-	44/-	56/- per dozen.
,, 0712E Ebony ,, ,, ,, ...	33/-	37/-	41/-	45/-	57/- ,,

SPOKESHAVES.

All Sizes up to 2	2¼	2½	2¾	3	3½	4	4½	5 inch.
No. 0719 Beechwood Spokeshaves	12/-	12/-	12/-	13/-	14/-	16/-	18/-	24/- 30/- per dozen.
,, 0728 Boxwood Spokeshaves	18/-	18/-	18/-	19/-	20/-	24/-	28/-	36/- -- ,,
,, 0728RF ,, ,, Rd. Face ... 4⅝ in. long × 1 in. Iron, 18/- 6½ in. × 1¼ in., 18/- 7½ in. × 1½ in., 18/- per dozen.

	2	2¼	2½	3	3½	4	4½	5 inch.
No. 0720 Beechwood Spokeshaves, Plated	16/-	16/-	16/-	18/-	21/-	25/-	30/-	35/- per dozen.
,, 0729 Boxwood ,, ,, ...	23/-	23/-	23/-	26/-	28/-	33/-	43/-	— ,,

	2½	3	3½	4	4½	5 inch.
No. 0720S Beechwood Spokeshaves, Plated, with Screw Irons	34/-	38/-	42/-	48/-	54/-	62/- per dozen.
,, 0729S Boxwood Spokeshaves, Plated, with Screw Irons	45/-	50/-	56/-	70/-	—	— ,,

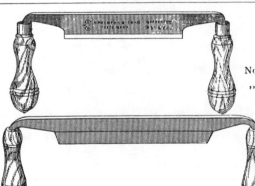

GENTS' C.S. DRAWING KNIVES.

	4	4½	5	5½	6	6½	7 inch.
No. 1906 Beechwood Handles	25/-	27/-	29/-	30/6	33/-	34/-	37/- per dozen.
,, 1907 Boxwood ,, ...	27/-	29/-	31/-	32/6	35/-	37/-	40/- ,,

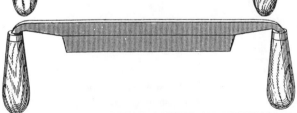

CARPENTERS' DRAWING KNIVES.

	8	9	10	11	12	13	14 inch.
No. 1909 Carpenters' Common	24/-	25/3	27/-	29/-	31/3	34/9	38/6 per doz.
,, 1908 ,, Cast Steel	34/3	36/-	38/6	42/-	46/-	50/-	54/- ,,

C.S. LONDON PATTERN DRAWING KNIVES.

	8	9	10	11	12	13	14 inch.
No 1911 London Pattern Cast Steel	34/3	36/-	38/6	42/-	46/-	50/-	54/- per doz.

CAST STEEL SPOKESHAVE IRONS.

All sizes up to	2½	3	3½	4	4½	5	5½	6 inch.
No. 0737 Cast Steel Joiners' Spokeshave Irons	5/3	5/9	6/6	7/6	9/-	10/6	12/-	15/- per dozen.

SCRAPER BLADES.

	4	4½	5	5½	6 inch.
No. 0789 Cast Steel Scraper Blades	4/-	4/6	5/-	5/6	6/- per dozen.

EDWARD PRESTON & SONS, L^TD.

JOINERS' TOOLS.

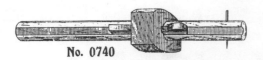

No. 0740

No. 0741

MARKING GAUGES.

No. 0740   Small Beechwood Round Stem Marking Gauge, with Wedge   ...   5/6 per dozen.

No. 0741   Common Beechwood Marking Gauges   ...   .   8/-   ,,
,,   0742   Best   ,,   ,,   ,, ...   10/-   ,,
,,   0743   ,,   ,,   Plated   ,,   ,, ...   13/-   ,,
,,   0744   Hardwood Marking Gauges   ...   .   19/-   ,,

No. 0747

CUTTING GAUGES.

No. 0747   Best Beechwood Cutting Gauges   ...   .   13/- per dozen.
,,   0748   ,,   ,,   Plated Cutting Gauges   ...   ...   16/-   ,,
,,   0749   ,,   Hardwood Cutting Gauges   ...   .   22/-   ,,

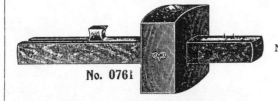

No. 0761

MORTICE GAUGES.

No. 0761   Rosewood Mortice Gauge, Brass Slide   ...   .   28/- per dozen.

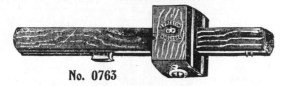

No. 0763

No. 0763   Rosewood Plated Head, Brass Slide   ...   .   40/- per dozen.

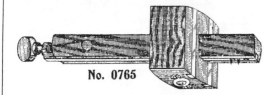

No. 0765

No. 0765   Rosewood Screw Slide, Thumb Screw End ...   .   56/- per dozen.
,,   0766   Ebony   ,,   ,,   ,,   ,, ...   60/-   ,,
,,   0767   Rosewood   ,,   ,,   Head Faced with Brass   ...   .   68/-   ,,
,,   0768   Ebony   ,,   ,,   ,,   ,,   ,, ...   72/-   ,,

No. 0765A

No. 0765A Rosewood, Screw Slide, Turnscrew End   ...   .   56/- per dozen.
,,   0766A Ebony   ,,   ,,   ,,   ,, ...   60/-   ,,
,,   0767A Rosewood   ,,   ,,   ,,   ,,   Head Faced with Brass 68/-   ,,
,,   0768A Ebony   ,,   ,,   ,,   ,,   ,,   ,,   ,,   72/   ,,

No. 0769

No. 0769   Ebony, Oval Head, Faced with Brass, with Round Brass Stem... 76/-   ,,

EDWARD PRESTON & SONS, L^TD.

TURNSCREWS.

TRADE MARK.

No. B774. CABINET TURNSCREWS.

No. B774.	Cast Steel, London Pattern, with Oval Boxwood Handles and Capped Ferrules	1½ to 3	4	5	6	7	8	9	10	12 inch.
		6/-	8/-	10 -	12/-	14/-	16 -	18/-	20/-	24/- per dozen.

No. 0772. LONDON PATTERN TURNSCREWS.

No. 0772 Cast Steel Bright London Pattern Turnscrews, with Beechwood Handles, let in Strong Brass Ferrules—

3	4	5	6	7	8	9	10	11	12	14	15	16	18 inch.
8/-	9/6	11/-	13/-	16/-	18/6	21/-	25/6	29/-	33/-	41/-	45/-	49/-	58/- per dozen.

,, 0773 Cast Steel Bright London Pattern Turnscrews, with Worked Oval Beech Handles—

3	4	5	6	7	8	9	10	11	12 inch.
11/-	13/-	14/6	17/-	21/-	24/6	28/-	33/3	37/-	41/- per dozen.

No. 0773½. CABINET TURNSCREWS.

No. 0773½ Cast Steel Round Blade London Pattern Cabinet Turnscrews, with Beechwood Handles—

3	4	5	6	7	8	9	10	11	12 inch.
9/6	11/-	13/-	16/-	18/6	21/-	25/6	29/-	33/-	38/- per dozen.

,, 0771 Cast Steel Round Blade London Pattern Cabinet Turnscrews, with Worked Oval Beech Handles—

3	4	5	6	7	8	9	10	11	12 inch.
12/6	14/6	16/6	20/-	23/6	27/-	32/6	36/9	41/-	46/- per dozen.

,, 0774 Cast Steel London Pattern Cabinet Turnscrews, with Worked Oval Boxwood Handles—

3	4	5	6	7	8	9	10	12 inch.
16/6	20/-	23/6	28/-	31/6	36/6	43/6	48/-	59/- per dozen.

CAST STEEL ROUND BLADE TURNSCREWS,
WITH ROUND GROOVED HANDLES.

No. 0776 Cast Steel Round Blade Turnscrews, with Round Grooved Handles—

3	4	5	6	7	8	9	10	12 inch.
9/-	10/6	13/-	16/-	19/6	23/-	27/-	31/-	38/- per dozen.

No. 0774A. SPINDLE TURNSCREWS.

			4	6	8	10	12 inch.
No. 0774A	Spindle Turnscrews, Flat Beechwood Handles Cast Brass Ferrules		6/-	6/6	8/-	10/-	11/- per dozen.
,, 0774B	,, ,, Oval ,, ,, Capped Iron ,,		6/6	7 6	10/6	13/-	15/- ,,

GENT'S TURNSCREWS.

No. 0775 Cast Steel Bright London Pattern Gentlemen's Fancy Turnscrews, in Hardwood Handles, assorted, 2½ to 4 inch, 7/- ; all 4 inch, 9/- per dozen.

MOTOR TURNSCREWS.

No. B776	Cast Steel, London Pattern, Oval Boxwood Handle, 16/- per dozen.	No. B777	Cast Steel, Cabinet Pattern, Oval Boxwood Handle, 17/- per dozen.

EDWARD PRESTON & SONS, L^{TD.}

SAW SETS.

TRADE MARK.

No. 0793   Beech Handled Saw Set plain end   ...   12/- per dozen.
,, 0794 Boxwood   ,,   ,,   ,,   ,,   ...   14/- ,,   ,,

No. 0795   Beech Handled Saw Set, turnscrew end ...   13/- per dozen.
,, 0795A Boxwood   ,,   ,,   ,,   ,,   ,, ...   15/- ,,   ,,

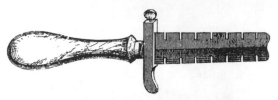

No. 0797   Beech Handled Saw Set, Slide Guard, single edge 22/- per dozen.
,, 0796   ,,   ,,   ,,   ,,   ,,   double ,, 28/- ,,   ,,

No. 0798   Iron Handle Black Pit Saw Set, 5-gate ...   16/- per dozen.
,, 0798A ,,   ,,   ,,   ,,   ,, 6-gate ...   18/- ,,   ,,

SAW PADS AND SAW BLADES.

No. 0784C Saw Pads, Small Beech   ...   .   13/- per dozen.
,, 0784   ,,   ,,   Best Small Beech   ...   ...   16/- ,,
,, 0785   ,,   ,,   ,,   Large   ,, ...   18/- ,,
No. 0786 Saw Pads, Best Large Boxwood ..   ...   24/- per dozen.
,, 0786R ,,   ,,   ,,   ,,   Rosewood ...   ...   24/- ,,
,, 0786S ,,   ,,   ,,   Small   ,, ...   18/- ,,
,, 0787   ,,   ,,   Best Large Ebony   ...   ...   30/- ,,

No. 0788   Cast Steel Pad Saw Blades, assorted up to 12-inch   4/6 per dozen.

TURNING SAWS AND FRAMES.

	To 10	12	14	16	18	20	22 inch.
No. 1831 Beech Handled	54/-	60/-	64/-	76/-	88/-	100/-	112/- per dozen.
,, 1832 Boxwood ,,		60/-	66/-	70/-	85/-	97/-	112/- 124/- ,,

,, 1833 London Pattern Octagon Boxwood Handled—

To 10	12	14	16	18	20	22 inch.
64/-	70/-	74/-	90/-	104/-	118/-	130/- per dozen.

,, 1834 Cast Steel Turning Webbs—

8	10	12	14	16	18	20	22	24	26	28	30	36 inch.
5/-	5/-	5/6	7/-	8/6	11/-	14/-	16/-	19/-	21/-	24/-	30/-	44/- per dozen.

TURNING SAW FRAME HANDLES.

	To 12	14	16	18	20	24 inch.
No. 0335 Beech Polished Round Turning Saw Frame Handles	20/-	20/-	20/-	22/-	25/-	29/- doz. pairs.
,, 0336 Boxwood ,, ,, ,, ,, ,,	24/-	24/-	24/-	26/-	30/-	34/- ,,
,, 0337 ,, ,, Octagon ,, ,, ,, ,,	30/-	30/-	30/-	34/-	38/-	— ,,

EDWARD PRESTON & SONS, LTD.

BRACE BITS.

CAST STEEL BITS, IN SETS, ASSORTED. UNFITTED.

		12	18	24	30	36	42	48	54	60 Bits.
No. 0500	Black Bits, Assorted, Sharpened and Bright Insides	4/8	7/-	9/4	11/10	15/3	17/-	20/-	23/-	26/- Set.
,, 0501	Bright Bits, Assorted ,, ,, ,,	5/3	7/11	10/6	13/4	17/-	19/1	22/4	25/8	28/11 ,,
,, 0502	Straw Coloured Bits, Assorted, Sharpened ,,	5/11	8/11	11/10	15/-	19/-	21/6	25/-	28/8	32/3 ,,

No. 0503—C.S. CENTRE BITS.   No. 0522—C.S. SCREW PIN CENTRE BITS.

	To	3/8	7/16	1/2	5/8	3/4	7/8	1	1 1/8	1 1/4	1 3/8	1 1/2	1 5/8	1 3/4	1 7/8	2	2 1/8	2 1/4	2 3/8	2 1/2	2 5/8	2 3/4	2 7/8	3 in.
No. 0503 Black, Sharpened		4/-	4/6	4/6	4/9	5/-	5/6	6/-	7/-	8/-	9/-	10/-	11/-	12/6	14/-	16/-	20/-	23/-	26/-	30/-	35/-	40/-	46/-	52/-doz
,, 0506 Bright ,,		5/-	5/6	5/6	5/9	6/-	6/6	7/-	8/2	9/2	10/2	11/2	12/4	13/10	15/4	17/4 doz.								
,, 0507 Straw Coloured ,,		5/8	6/2	6/2	6/5	6/8	7/2	7/8	8/10	10/-	11/-	12/-	13/4	14/10	16/4	18/4 ,,								

C.S. SCREW PIN CENTRE BITS.

	To	1	1 1/8	1 1/4	1 3/8	1 1/2	1 3/4	2 in.
No. 0522 Black Screw Pin Centre Bits, usual length		16/-	17/6	19/-	20/-	22/-	27/-	32/- doz.

C.S. CENTRE PLUG BITS.

	To	1	1 1/8	1 1/4 in.
No. 0517 Black		14/6	16/-	18/- doz.

C.S. CENTRE COCK BITS.

		5/8 and 3/4	7/8	1 in.
No. 0518 Black		20/-	22/-	24/- doz.

C.S. NOSE BITS.

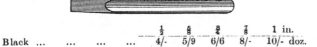

	To	1/4	5/16	3/8	7/16	1/2	5/8	3/4 in.
No. 0508 Black (Bright Insides)		4/8	5/-	5/6	7/-	8/-	12/-	14/6 doz.
,, 0508B Bright		5/3	5/7	6/1	7/7	8/7	13/-	15/6 ,,
,, 0508S Straw Coloured		5/11	6/3	6/9	8/3	9/3	13/8	16/2 ,,

C.S. SHELL BITS.

	To	1/4	5/16	3/8	7/16	1/2	5/8	3/4 in.
No. 0509 Black (Bright Insides)		4/8	5/-	5/6	7/-	8/-	12/-	14/6 doz.
,, 0509B Bright		5/3	5/7	6/1	7/7	8/7	13/-	15/6 ,,
,, 0509S Straw Coloured		5/11	6/3	6/9	8/3	9/3	13/8	16/2 ,,

SPOON BITS.

	To	1/4	5/16	3/8	7/16	1/2	5/8	3/4 in.
No. 0510 Black (Bright Insides)		4/8	5/-	5/6	7/-	8/-	12/-	14/6 doz.
,, 0510B Bright		5/3	5/7	6/1	7/7	8/7	13/-	15/6 ,,
,, 0510S Straw Coloured		5/11	6/3	6/9	8/3	9/3	13/8	16/2 ,,

C.S. SASH BITS.

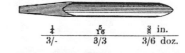

	To	1/4	5/16	3/8 in.
No. 0512 Black (Bright Insides)		5/6	6/-	6/6 doz.
,, 0512B Bright		6/1	6/7	7/1 ,,
,, 0512S Straw Coloured		6/9	7/3	7/9 ,,

C.S. SHELL GIMLET BITS.

	To	1/4	5/16	3/8 in.
No. 0515 Black (Bright Insides)		5/-	6/-	7/- doz.
,, 0515B Bright		5/7	6/7	7/7 ,,
,, 0515S Straw Coloured		6/3	7/3	8/3 ,,

C.S. TAPER BITS.

	To	5/8	3/4	7/8	1 in.
No. 0516 Black (Bright Insides)		7/6	9/6	11/6	13/6 doz.
,, 0516B Bright		8/1	10/2	12/4	14/8 ,,
,, 0516S Straw Coloured		8/9	10/10	13/-	15/6 ,,

No. 0519. C.S. CHAIR BITS.

	1/2	5/8	3/4	7/8	1 in.
Black	4/-	5/9	6/6	8/-	10/- doz.

No. 0521—C.S. COOPERS' DOWLING BITS.

	1/4	5/16	3/8 in.
	3/-	3/3	3/6 doz.

TURNSCREW BITS.

No. 0524 Black.   No. 0524B Bright.   No. 0524S Straw Coloured.

4/-	4/11	5/7 per doz.

FORK END TURNSCREW BITS.

No. 0525 Black.   No. 0525B Bright.   No. 0525S Straw Coloured.

4/6	5/5	6/1 per doz.

No. 1969   No. 1968

COUNTER SINKS.

This is a very handy Countersink to attach with Screw to Shell Bits; it will cut at both ends.

		For 3/16	3/8	1/2 in. Bits.
No. 1968	Without Guard	17/-	27/6	35/- per doz.
,, 1969	With Guard	32/6	45/-	60/- ,,

EDWARD PRESTON & SONS, L^TD.

BRACE BITS.

C.S. SQUARE RIMERS.

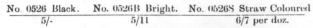

No. 0526 Black.   No. 0526B Bright.   No. 0526S Straw Coloured
5/-   5/11   6/7 per doz.

No. 0531 Bright C.S. Square Rimers, with Boxwood
          Handles ... ... 11/- doz.

C.S. HALF ROUND RIMERS.

No. 0528 Black.   No. 0528B Bright.   No. 0528S Straw Coloured.
5/-   5/11   6/7 per doz.

No. 0532 Bright C.S. Hollow Taper Bits, with
          Boxwood Handles ... ... 13/- doz.

CAST STEEL COUNTERSINK BITS.   Sharpened.

No. 0533

		To ½	9/16	5/8 in.
No. 0533	Flat Heads, Black ...	... 4/6	4/6	5/6 doz.
,, 0534	,, ,, Bright ...	.. 5/5	5/5	6/5 ,,
,, 0535	,, ,, Straw Coloured ...	6/1	6/1	7/1 ,,

		To ½	9/16	5/8 in.
No. 0539	Rose Heads, 8 Cuts, Black ...	... 5/-	6/-	7/- doz.
,, 0540	,, ,, ,, Bright ...	5/11	6/11	7/11 ,,
,, 0541	,, ,, ,, Straw Coloured	6/7	7/7	8/7 ..

		To ½	9/16	5/8	3/4	7/8	1 in.
No. 0542	Rose Heads, 12 Cuts, Black	5/6	6/6	8/-	10/6	14/6	17/- doz.
,, 0543	,, ,, ,, Bright	6/5	7/5	8/11	11/6	15/6	18/- ,,
,, 0544	,, ,, ,, Straw Colored	} 7/1	8/1	9/7	12/3	16/3	18/10 ,,

No. 0536

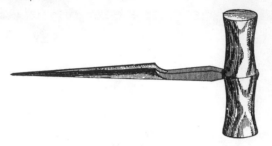

		To ½	9/16	5/8	3/4	7/8	1 inch.
No. 0536	Snail Horns, Black	5/-	5/-	6/-	9/-	13/-	16/ doz.
,. 0537	,, ,, Bright	5/11	5/11	6/11	10/-	14/-	17/10 ,,
,, 0538	,, ,, Straw Col'd	6/7	6/7	7/7	10/8	14/9	17/10 ,,

No. 0539. C.S. ROSEHEAD COUNTERSUNK BIT.

No. 0545—C.S. BRACE DRILL BIT.

				Assorted to ½	9/16	5/8 in.
No. 0545	Black ..	...	... ...	4/-	4/6	5/6 doz
,, 0546	Bright .	...	... ...	4/11	5/5	6/5 ,,
,, 0547	Straw Coloured	...	...	5/7	6/1	7/1 ,,

No. 739—BEST BRIGHT TWIST NOSE BITS.

		1/16	3/32	⅛	5/32	3/16	7/32	¼	5/16	3/8	7/16	½ in.
No. '739	Best Bright	3/-	3/-	3/-	3/-	3/-	3/-	3/-	3/9	4/6	5/3	6/4 doz.
,, '739A	,, ,,	assorted ⅛ to ⅜ in. ... ... 3/3 ,,

*IMPORTED.

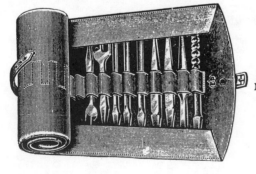

BIT ROLLS.

FOR HOLDING BRACE BITS.

		Bit Roll only.	Fitted with 36 Black Bits.	Fitted with 36 Bright Bits.	Fitted with 36 Straw Col'd Bits.
No. 2430	Leather, to hold 40 Bits ...	4/-	19/3	21/-	23/- each
,, 2131	,, Baize Lined, to hold 40 Bits	5/-	20/3	22/-	24/- ,,
,, 2432	Mole Skin, to hold 40 Bits ...	4/-	19/3	21/-	23/- ,,
,, 2433	Brown Canvas, ,, 36 ,, ...	3/-	18/3	20/-	22/- ,,
,, 2434	,, ,, Baize Lined, to hold 36 Bits	4/-	19/3	21/-	23/- ,,

AUGER BITS AND AUGERS.

TRADE **EP** MARK.

No. 1881—GEDGE'S PATTERN SCREW BIT.

1/4	5/16	3/8	7/16	1/2	9/16	5/8	11/16	3/4	13/16	7/8	15/16	1	1 1/8	1 1/4	1 3/8	1 1/2 inch.
15/6	15/6	15/6	15/6	15/6	17/6	19/-	21/-	21/-	24/-	24/-	27/-	27/-	30/-	34/	39/-	43/- per dozen.

No. 1881D Gedge's Pattern Dowel Bits, same prices as No. 1881.

No. 1882—JENNINGS' PATTERN SCREW BIT.

	1/4	5/16	3/8	7/16	1/2	9/16	5/8	11/16	3/4	13/16	7/8	15/16	1	1 1/8	1 1/4	1 3/8	1 1/2 inch.
No. 1882 ...	18/-	18/-	18/-	18/-	18/-	21/-	23/-	26/-	26/-	29/-	29/-	32/-	32/-	40/-	48/-	56/-	64/- per dozen.

No. 1882D Jennings' Pattern Dowel Bits, same prices as No. 1882.

No. 1877—SOLID NOSE SCREW BIT.

	1/4	5/16	3/8	7/16	1/2	9/16	5/8	11/16	3/4	13/16	7/8	15/16	1	1 1/8	1 1/4	1 3/8	1 1/2 inch.
No. 1877 ...	16/-	16/-	16/-	16/-	16/-	18/-	19/6	22/-	22/-	24/-	24/-	26/6	26/6	30/-	34/-	38/-	42/ per dozen.

No. 1877D Solid Nose Dowel Bits, same prices as No. 1877.

No. 1878—SCOTCH PATTERN SCREW BIT.

	1/4	5/16	3/8	7/16	1/2	9/16	5/8	11/16	3/4	13/16	7/8	15/16	1	1 1/8	1 1/4	1 3/8	1 1/2 inch.
No. 1878 ...	15/6	15/6	15/6	15/6	15/6	17/-	18/-	20/-	20/-	23/-	23/-	26/-	26/-	29/-	33/-	38/-	42/- per dozen.

No. 1878D Scotch Pattern Dowel Bits, same prices as No. 1878.

No. 1883—BRIGHT SCREW WAGON BIT.

	3/8	7/16	1/2	9/16	5/8	11/16	3/4	13/16	7/8	15/16	1	1 1/8	1 1/4	1 3/8	1 1/2 inch.
No. 1883	25/-	26/-	27/-	28/-	29/-	30/-	31/-	35/-	35/-	36/-	38/-	47/-	51/-	55/-	60/- per dozen.

No. 1870—CARPENTERS' SHELL AUGER, Tanged.

	3/8	1/2	5/8	3/4	7/8	1	1 1/8	1 1/4	1 3/8	1 1/2 inch.
No. 1870 Carpenters' Shell Augers, Tanged	9/-	9/-	10/6	13/6	15/-	17/-	18/6	23/-	25/-	30/- per dozen.
,, 1871 ,, ,, ,, Eyed	14/6	14/6	16/-	19/6	21/-	24/-	26/6	32/-	35/-	40/- ,,

No. 1880—GEDGE'S PATTERN SCREW AUGER.

	3/8	1/2	5/8	3/4	7/8	1	1 1/8	1 1/4	1 3/8	1 1/2 inch.
No. 1880 Tanged	19/-	19/-	21/6	25/6	28/6	32/-	36/-	41/-	45/-	51/- per dozen.
,, 1880E Eyed	23/-	23/-	26/-	31/6	34/6	39/-	43/6	50/-	53/6	60/- ,,

No. 1872—CARPENTERS' BLACK SCREW AUGER, Tanged.

	3/8	1/2	5/8	3/4	7/8	1	1 1/8	1 1/4	1 3/8	1 1/2 inch.
No. 1872 Carpenters' Black Screw Augers, Tanged ...	13/-	13/-	14/-	16/-	18/6	21/-	23/6	26/-	28/6	34/- per dozen.
,, 1873 ,, ,, ,, ,, Eyed ...	18/-	18/-	19/6	22/-	24/6	28/-	31/6	35/-	38/6	44/6 ,,

No. 1876—SCOTCH SCREW AUGER, Eyed.

	3/8	1/2	5/8	3/4	7/8	1	1 1/8	1 1/4	1 3/8	1 1/2	1 5/8	1 3/4	1 7/8	2 inch.
No. 1879 Bright Scotch Screw Augers, Tanged	19/-	19/-	21/6	25/6	28/6	32/-	36/-	41/-	45/-	51/-	56/-	62/6	66/-	71/- per dozen.
,, 1876 ,, ,, ,, ,, Eyed	23/-	23/-	26/-	31/6	34/6	39/-	43/6	50/-	53/6	60/-	64/-	72/-	77/-	85/- ,,

EDWARD PRESTON & SONS, L^{TD.}

BRACES.

TRADE (E P) MARK.

REGISTERED BRACE.

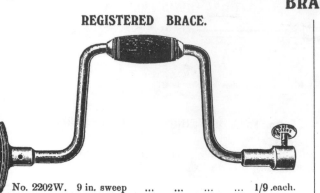

No. 2202W.   9 in. sweep   ...   .   1/9 .each.

PLAIN BRACE

HARDWOOD HEAD AND HANDLE, BALL BEARING HEAD.

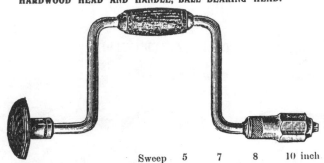

	Sweep	5	7	8	10 inch
No. 2203W.	Bright ...	2/8	2/10	3/2	3/8 each.
,, 2203WNP.	Nickel-plated	3/3	3/6	3/10	4/2 ,,

RATCHET BRACE

HARDWOOD HEAD AND HANDLE, BALL BEARING HEAD.

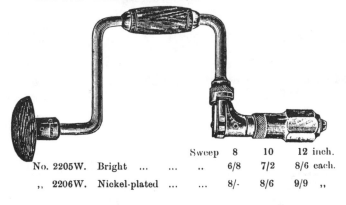

	Sweep	8	10	12 inch.
No. 2205W.	Bright	6/8	7/2	8/6 each.
,, 2206W.	Nickel-plated	8/-	8/6	9/9 ,,

2110. EXTENSION PIECE, with Thumbscrew.

10	12	14	16	18	20	24 inch.
1/6	1/8	1/10	2/-	2/3	2/6	2/9 each.

2111. EXTENSION PIECE, with Chuck.

10	12	14	16	18	20	24 inch.
1/10	2/-	2/2	2/4	2/7	2/10	3/- each.

BRIGHT BRACE

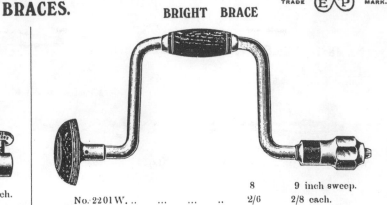

		8	9 inch sweep.
No. 2201W.		2/6	2/8 each.

BRIGHT RATCHET BRACE.

BEECHWOOD HEAD AND HANDLE.

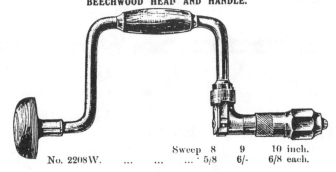

	Sweep	8	9	10 inch.
No. 2208W.	... ...	5/8	6/-	6/8 each.

BEST QUALITY BRACE.

LIGNUM HEAD.   ROSEWOOD HANDLE.   BALL BEARING HEAD.

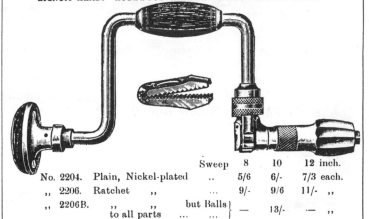

		Sweep	8	10	12 inch.
No. 2204.	Plain, Nickel-plated	..	5/6	6/-	7/3 each.
,, 2206.	Ratchet ,,		9/-	9/6	11/- ,,
,, 2206B.	,, to all parts	but Balls }	—	13/-	— ,,

AMERICAN PATTERN LATHE CHUCK.

No. 2207   ...   .   29/- per dozen.

BRACE JAWS.

No. 2209. Crocodile Pattern, N.P.
12/- per doz.

No. 2210. Plain Pattern, Bright,
9/9 per doz.

No. 2211. Plain Pattern, Nickel-
plated 11/- per dozen.

EDWARD PRESTON & SONS, L^TD.

BRACES.

BRACE, WITH THUMBSCREW.

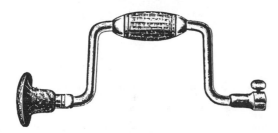

No. 2200   Brace, with Thumbscrew, 7 inch sweep   .   17/- per dozen.

COMMON THUMBSCREW BRACES.

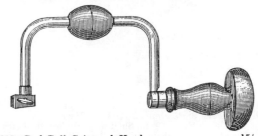

No. *2202 Red Ball Grip and Head	15/- per doz.
,, *2201 Swelled Iron Grip and Black Head ...	20/- ,,

WAGON BUILDERS' BRACE, WITH THUMBSCREW AND BALL BEARING HEAD.

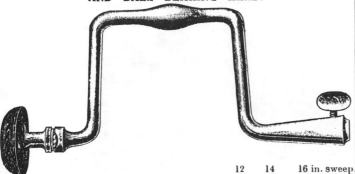

	12	14	16 in. sweep
No. 0822 Bright	8/-	8/6	9/- each.
,, 0822N Nickel Plated	9/10	10/4	10/10 ,,

WAGON BUILDERS' BRACE, WITH CHUCK AND BALL BEARING HEAD.

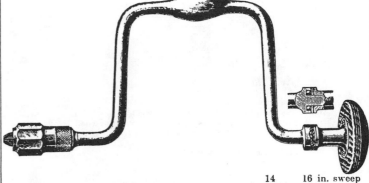

		14	16 in. sweep
No. 0823 Bright		9/9	10/9 each.
,, 0823N Nickel Plated		11/9	12/9 ,,

BEST WROUGHT SCOTCH IRON BRACE, BALL BEARING HEAD.

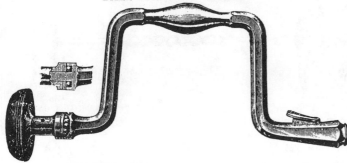

No. 0812 Bright, 9 inch sweep	12/9 each.
,, 0816 Nickel Plated, 9 inch sweep	14/- ,,

MALLEABLE SCOTCH IRON BRACE, WITH LIGNUM HEAD.

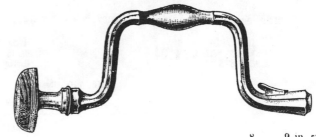

	8	9 in. sweep
No. 0820 Bright	5/	5/6 each

BRIGHT GASFITTERS' BRACE.

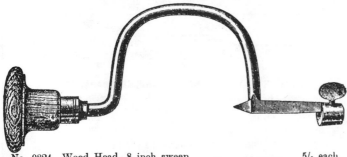

No. 0824 Wood Head, 8 inch sweep	5/- each.
,, 0825 Iron ,, ,, ,, ...	6/- ,,

*IMPORTED.

HAND RACHET BRACE.

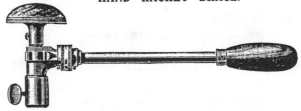

No. 0826 Bright	6/- each.
,, 0826N Nickel Plated	6/9 ,,

Can be used as an Engineers' Ratchet Brace for holes not exceeding $\frac{9}{16}$ inch diameter.

EDWARD PRESTON & SONS, LTD.

GIMLETS AND BRADAWLS.
SHELL GIMLETS.

TRADE **EP** MARK.

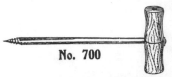
No. 700

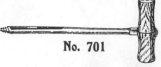
No. 701

No.	1/8	1/8 full	3/16	3/16 full	7/32	7/32 full	1/4	Assorted 1/8 to 1/4 inch.
No.	1	2	3	4	5	6	7	
No. 700 Flat Tang Shell Gimlets, Boxwood Heads ...	20/-	20/-	22/-	24/-	30/-	32/-	35/-	21/6 per gross.
„ 701C C.S Black Square Tang Shell Gimlets. Boxwood Heads ...	26/-	28/-	30/-	32/-	36/-	40/-	44/-	32/- „
„ 701 Best C.S. Bright Square Tang Shell Gimlets, Boxwood Heads ...	34/-	36/-	40/-	42/-	46/-	52/-	56/-	40/- „

No.	1/16	1/16 full	3/32	3/32 full	1/8	1/8 full	3/16	3/16 full	7/32	7/32 full	1/4	Assorted 1/8 to 1/4 inch.
No.	6°	5°	4°	3°	2°	0	1	2	3	4	5	
„ 701L Best C.S. London Pattern Shell Gimlets, Black Flat Tangs. Box & Rosewood Heads }	51/-	51/-	51/-	51/-	51/-	54/-	57/-	60/-	64/-	68/-	76/-	58/- per gross.

	1/4 full	5/16	3/8	7/16	1/2 inch.
„ 700S Flat Tang Spike Shell Gimlets, Boxwood Heads ...	4/-	5/-	6/6	7/6	9/- per doz.
„ 701S Best C.S. „ „ „ „ „ ...	5/6	7/-	8/-	9/6	11/- „

TWIST GIMLETS.

No. 703

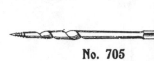
No. 705

	1/8	1/8 full	3/16	3/16 full	7/32	7/32 full	1/4	Assorted 1/8 to 1/4 inch.
No. 703 Flat Tang Twist Gimlets, Boxwood Heads ...	21/-	21/-	23/-	25/-	31/-	33/-	36/-	22/6 per gross.
„ 705C C S Black Square Tang Twist Gimlets Boxwood Heads ..	28/-	30/-	33/-	35/-	39/-	42/-	48/-	35/- „
„ 705 Best C S. Bright Square Tang Twist Gimlets, Boxwood Heads ...	40/-	42/-	44/-	48/-	54/-	58/-	62/-	43/- „
„ 705H „ „ „ „ „ Assorted Boxwood, Ebony, and Rosewood Heads	—	—	—	—	—	—	—	45/- „

No.	1/16	1/16 full	3/32	3/32 full	1/8	1/8 full	3/16	3/16 full	7/32	7/32 full	1/4	Assorted 1/8 to 1/4 inch.
No.	6°	5°	4°	3°	2°	0	1	2	3	4	5	
„ 705L Best C.S. London Pattern Twist Gimlets, Black Flat Tangs, Box & Rosewood Heads}	53/-	53/-	53/-	53/-	53/-	56/-	60/-	68/-	76/-	84/-	92/-	64/- per gross.

	1/4 full	5/16	3/8	7/16	1/2 inch.
„ 703S Flat Tang Spike Twist Gimlets, Boxwood Heads ...	4/6	5/6	7/-	8/-	9/6 per doz.
„ 705S Best C.S. „ „ „ „ „ ...	6/6	8/-	9/6	10/6	12/- „

No. 708
BREWERS' SHELL GIMLETS.

No. 710
BREWERS' TWIST GIMLETS.

No. 707
BEST C.S. AUGER GIMLETS.

No. 708 Best ... ... 8/6 per doz.
„ 708S 2nd Quality ... 7/6 „

No. 710 Best ... ... 9/- per doz.
„ 710S 2nd Quality ... 8/- „

	1/8	3/16	1/4	5/16	3/8	7/16	1/2 in.
No. 707	6/-	6/6	7/-	7/9	8/6	9/6	10/6 doz.

Assorted, 1/8 to 3/8 in., 7/- doz.

BELLHANGERS' GIMLETS.
No. 712.

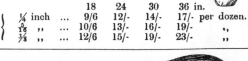

No. 712 Best Bellhangers' Gimlets, Boxwood Heads ... ...

		18	24	30	36 in.
{	1/4 inch ...	9/6	12/-	14/-	17/- per dozen.
{	5/16 „ ...	10/6	13/-	16/-	19/- „
{	3/8 „ ...	12/6	15/-	19/-	23/- „

No. 716.
BEST WARRANTED BRADAWL BLADES.

No.	1	2	3	4	5	6	
Length	1	1¼	1⅜	1½	1¾	2 in.	Ass'd 1 to 2 in.
W.G.	15	14	13	12	11	10	
	7/-	7/6	8/-	8/6	10/-	12/6	8/6 per gross.

No. 716L Assorted Large, 1½ to 2¼ inch ... 11/- „
„ 716F Flooring, Assorted, 2¼ to 3 inch ... 17/- „
„ 716C Cabinet Awls, Assorted, 16 to 18 W.G. 8/- „

POLISHED ASH OR BEECH HANDLED BRADAWLS.

No. 0230 Round Assorted, 1 to 2 inch ... 25/- per gross.
„ 0230P „ „ Pinned Handles ... 32/- „
„ 0229 Oval „ „ ... ... 29/- „
„ 0229P „ „ Pinned Handles .. 36/- „

BOXWOOD HANDLED BRADAWLS.

No. 0309 Round Assorted 1 to 2 inch ... 35/- per gross.
„ 0309P „ „ Pinned Handles ... 42/- „

EDWARD PRESTON & SONS, LTD.

GENTLEMEN'S OAK TOOL CHESTS—COMPLETE.

TRADE (EP) MARK.

IRON GLUE POTS.

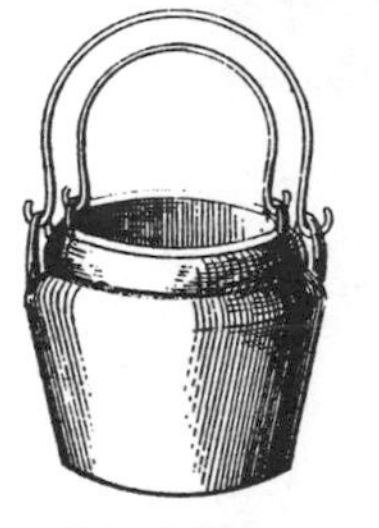

No. 0799.

No.	Pint.	Each.	No.	Pint.	Each.
8o	$\frac{1}{8}$	1/5	1	$1\frac{1}{4}$	3/8
7o	$\frac{3}{16}$	1/7	2	$1\frac{1}{2}$	4/3
6o	$\frac{1}{4}$	1/9	3	2	5/6
5o	$\frac{5}{16}$	2/2	4	$2\frac{1}{2}$	6/9
4o	$\frac{3}{8}$	2/4	5	3	8/-
3o	$\frac{9}{16}$	2/8	6	$3\frac{1}{2}$	9/-
2o	$\frac{3}{4}$	3/-	7	4	10/-
0	1	3/4	8	5	11/-

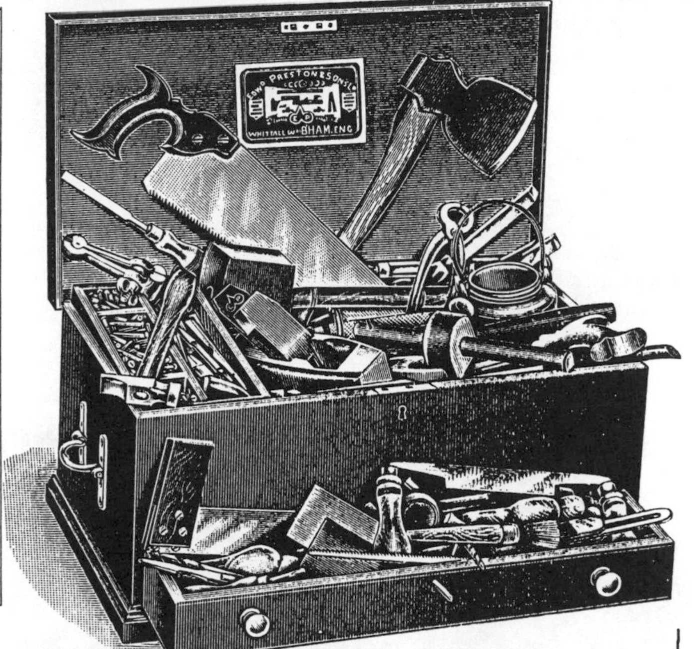

A.—10/6 each, contains

Hand Saw	Gimlet
Hammer	Chisel
Mallet	Gouge
Pincers	Turnscrew, &c.
Brad Awl	

Size of Chest $9\frac{1}{2}$ x $4\frac{1}{4}$ x $2\frac{3}{4}$ inches.

B.—13/6 each, contains

Hand Saw	Brad Awl
Hammer	Chisel
Mallet	Gouge
Pincers	Turnscrew
Gimlet	Rule, &c.

Size of Chest 11 x $4\frac{3}{4}$ x $2\frac{3}{4}$ inches.

C.—15/- each, contains

Hand Saw	Square
Hammer	Brad Awl
Mallet	Gimlet
Pincers	Marking Awl
Chisel	Punch
Gouge	Turnscrew
File	Rule, &c.

Size of Chest $12\frac{1}{2}$ x 5 x 3 inches.

No. 000.—16/- each, contains

Hand Saw	Gimlet
Hammer	Chisel
Mallet	Gouge
Pincers	Turnscrew
Brad Awl	Furniture, &c.

Size of Chest $13\frac{1}{2}$ x $5\frac{1}{4}$ x 3 inches.

No. 00.—19/- each, contains

Hand Saw	Chisel
Hammer	Gouge
Mallet	Turnscrew
Pincers	File
Two Gimlets	Rule
Two Brad Awls	Furniture, &c.

Size of Chest $14\frac{1}{2}$ x $6\frac{1}{2}$ x $3\frac{1}{2}$ inches.

No. 0.—26/- each, contains

Hand Saw	Gouge
Hammer	File
Mallet	Marking Awl
Rule	Punch
Pincers	Turnscrew
Two Gimlets	Square
Two Brad Awls	Compasses
Chisel	Furniture, &c.

Size of Chest 15 x 8 x $3\frac{1}{2}$ inches.

No. 1.—33/- each, contains

Hand Saw	Three Files
Hatchet	Oil Stone
Hammer	Marking Awl
Mallet	Punch
Rule	Turnscrew
Pincers	Spokeshave
Two Gimlets	Square
Two Brad Awls	Claw Wrench
Chisel	Furniture, &c.
Gouge	

Size of Chest 16 x $8\frac{1}{2}$ x 4 inches.

No. 2.—42/- each, contains

Hand Saw	Oil Stone
Hatchet	Marking Awl
Hammer	Punch
Mallet	Turnscrew
Rule	Spokeshave
Pincers	Square
Three Gimlets	Claw Wrench
Three Brad Awls	Pliers
Two Chisels	Compasses
One Gouge	Furniture, &c.
Three Files	

Size of Chest 17 x 9 x $4\frac{1}{2}$ inches.

No. 3.—54/- each, contains

Hand Saw	Three Gimlets
Hatchet	Three Brad Awls
Hammer	Three Chisels
Mallet	Two Gouges
Rule	Three Files
Pincers	Oil Stone
Marking Awl	Pliers
Punch	Compasses
Two Turnscrews	Lock Saw
Spokeshave	Plane
Square	Furniture, &c.
Claw Wrench	

Size of Chest 18 x $9\frac{1}{2}$ x 5 inches.

No. 4.—68/- each, contains

Hand Saw	Punch
Hatchet	Two Turnscrews
Hammer	Spokeshave
Mallet	Square
Rule	Claw Wrench
Pincers	Pliers
Four Gimlets	Compasses
Four Brad Awls	Lock Saw
Four Chisels	Plane
Three Files	Marking Gauge
Two Gouges	Glue Pot and Brush
Oil Stone	Furniture, &c.
Marking Awl	

Size of Chest 19 x $10\frac{1}{2}$ x $6\frac{3}{4}$ inches.

No. 5.—86/- each, contains

Hand Saw	Spokeshave
Axe	Square
Hammer	Claw Wrench
Mallet	Pliers
Rule	Compasses
Pincers	Lock Saw
Five Gimlets	Plane
Five Brad Awls	Marking Gauge
Five Chisels	Glue Pot and Brush
Three Gouges	Drawing Knife
Four Files	Cutting Punch
Oil Stone	Scraper
Marking Awl	Bevel
Punch	Furniture, &c.
Two Turnscrews	

Size of Chest 20 x 11 x 8 inches.

No. 6.—102/- each, contains

Two Saws	Four Files
Axe	Oil Stone
Two Hammers	Marking Awl
Mallet	Two Punches
Rule	Three Turnscrews
Pincers	Two Spokeshaves
Six Gimlets	Square
Six Brad Awls	Claw Wrench
Six Chisels	Pliers
Four Gouges	Compasses
Lock Saw	Drawing Knife
Smooth Plane	Cutting Punch
Jack Plane	Scraper
Marking Gauge	Bevel
Glue Pot and Brush	Furniture, &c.

Size of Chest 21 x $11\frac{1}{2}$ x $8\frac{3}{4}$ inches.

No. 7.—120/- each, contains

Three Saws	Pincers
Axe	Six Gimlets
Two Hammers	Six Brad Awls
Mallet	Six Chisels
Rule	Four Gouges
Four Files	Lock Saw
Oil Stone	Smooth Plane
Marking Awl	Jack Plane
Two Punches	Two Gauges
Three Turnscrews	Glue Pot and Brush
Hand Vice	Drawing Knife
Two Spokeshaves	Cutting Punch
Square	Scraper
Claw Wrench	Bevel
Pliers	Furniture, &c.
Compasses	

Size of Chest 22 x 12 x $9\frac{1}{4}$ inches.

No. 8.—138/- each, contains

Three Saws	Hand Vice
Axe	Two Spokeshaves
Two Hammers	Square
Mallet	Claw Wrench
Rule	Two Pairs Pliers
Pincers	Compasses
Six Gimlets	Lock Saw
Six Brad Awls	Smooth Plane
Six Chisels	Jack Plane
Four Gouges	Three Gauges
Four Files	Glue Pot and Brush
Oil Stone	Drawing Knife
Marking Awl	Cutting Punch
Three Punches	Scraper, Bevel
Three Turnscrews	Chalk Line Reel
Bed Key	Furniture, &c.

Size of Chest 23 x $12\frac{1}{2}$ x $11\frac{1}{2}$ inches.

No. 9.—170/- each, contains

Three Saws	Hand Vice
Axe	Square
Two Hammers	Claw Wrench
Mallet	Two Pairs Pliers
Rule	Compasses
Pincers	Lock Saw
Six Gimlets	Smooth Plane
Six Brad Awls	Jack Plane
Six Chisels	Three Gauges
Four Gouges	Glue Pot and Brush
Five Files	Drawing Knife
Oil Stone	Cutting Punch
Marking Awl	Scraper, Bevel
Three Punches	Chalk Line Reel
Three Turnscrews	Two Mortice Chisels
Bed Key	Coach Wrench
Two Spokeshaves	Furniture, &c.

Size of Chest 24 x 13 x $12\frac{1}{4}$ inches.

No. 10.—204/- each, contains

Three Saws	Cutting Punch
Axe	Six Files
Three Hammers	Oil Stone
Mallet	Marking Awl
Rule	Three Punches
Pincers	Three Turnscrews
Six Gimlets	Bed Key
Six Brad Awls	Hand Vice
Eight Chisels	Two Spokeshaves
Four Gouges	Square
Two Pairs Pliers	Claw Wrench
Compasses	Scraper, Bevel
Lock Saw	Coach Wrench
Smooth Plane	Chalk Line Reel
Jack Plane	Brace, with 12 Bits
Three Gauges	Cutting Nippers
Glue Pot and Brush	Two Mortice Chisels
Drawing Knife	Furniture, &c.

Size of Chest 25 x $13\frac{1}{2}$ x $13\frac{1}{4}$ inches.

No. 12.—325/- each, contains

Three Saws	Lock Saw
Axe	Three Gauges
Four Hammers	Glue Pot and Brush
Two Mallets	Drawing Knife
Rule	Cutting Punch
Pincers	Scraper, Bevel
Twelve Gimlets	Chalk Line Reel
Twelve Brad Awls	Brace, with 24 Bits
Twelve Chisels	Anvil and Beck Iron
Six Gouges	Saw Set
Nine Files	Cutting Nippers
Oil Stone	Nipper Pliers
Marking Awl	Hand Shears for cutting Metal, &c.
Three Punches	Spring Dividers
Four Turnscrews	Coach Wrench
Bed Key	C.S. Chipping Chisel
Hand Vice	Spring Oil Can
Two Spokeshaves	Three Socket Chisels
Two Plated Squares	Three Mortice Chisels
Claw Wrench	Bench Vice
Two Pairs Pliers	Turning Saw Frame
Two „ Compasses	Furniture, &c.
Smooth Plane	
Jack Plane	

Size of Chest 27 x 15 x 18 inches.

EDWARD PRESTON & SONS, L^{TD}.

HANDLES.
TURNSCREW HANDLES.

No. 0321P

TRADE **E P** MARK.

No. 0322B

	For Turnscrews	3	4	5	6	7	8	9	10	12 inch.
No. 0321P	Beechwood London Pattern Turnscrew Handles, Brass Ferrules, Polished ...	3/6	4/-	4/6	5/-	5/6	6/-	6/6	7/	8/- per doz.

Assorted 5 to 8 inch, 5/6 per doz.

,, 0322B	Boxwood, Oval, Steel Cap Ferrule, Polished	4/3	5/-	6/-	6/6	8/-	10/6	11/-	12/-	13/6 ,,

Assorted, 5 to 8 inch, 7/6 per doz.

BRADAWL HANDLES.

No. 0304

FILE HANDLES.

No. 0300

No. 0304	Round Polished Beechwood Bradawl Handles, Brass Ferrules, Assorted ...	...	...	...	...	...	...	15/- per gross.
,, 0305	Oval ,, ,, ,, ,, ,, ,, ,, ...	...	...	...	...	...	...	17/- ,,
,, 0306	Round ,, Boxwood ,, ,, ,, ,, ,, ...	...	...	...	...	...	...	26/- ,,
,, 0300	Common File Handles, Steel Ferrules	...	...	...	...	...	...	11/- ,,
,, 0301	Best Quartered Wood File Handles, Solid Drawn Steel Ferrules...	...	...	...	...	...	...	15/- ,,

---

 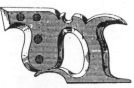 

BACK SAW HANDLES.
No. 0330 Open Handle, Polished Edges to 12 inches, 10/- per dozen.

,, 0333 Closed Handle. Polished Edges, to 14 inches, 11/6 per dozen.

HAND SAW HANDLES.

	16-22	24-26	28-30 inch.
No. 0334	8/-	9/6	— per doz.
,, B0334	12/-	13/-	14/6 ,,

SAW SCREWS.

	1	2	3	4
,, 0334S	6/-	8/-	10/-	16/- per gross.

JACK PLANE HANDLES.
No. 0331 ... ... 5/6 per doz.

,, B0331 Best ... 6/9 ,,

TRYING PLANE HANDLES.
No. 0332 ... ... 7/6 per doz.

,, B0332 Best ... 9/- ,,

ASH JOINERS' HAMMER HANDLES.

	10	12	13	14	15	16 inch.
No 0326	2/6	2/9	3/-	3/-	3/3	3/6 per dozen.

Assorted, 10 to 14 in., 2/4 ; 10 to 16 in., 2/8 ,,

No. 0326

ENGINEERS' HAMMER HANDLES.

	12	14	16	18 inches.
No. 0327	2/9	3/-	3/6	4/- per doz.

No. 0327

CHALK LINE REELS.

No 0340	Flat Beech	...	...	...	...	2/- per doz.
,, 0342	,, Box	...	...	...	...	3/6 ,,
,, 0341	Long Beech	...	...	...	...	2/3 ,,
,, 0343	,, Box	...	...	...	...	4/- ,,

Nos. 0341 and 0343

Nos. 0340 and 0342

CHALK LINES.

No. 0346	White Cotton, 20 Yards	...	...	...	30/- per gross.
,, 0347	Boiler Makers' Thin Cotton ...	...	...	...	30/- ,,
.. 0348	Hemp, 20 Yards	...	...	...	30/- ,,

EDWARD PRESTON & SONS, LTD.

CHISEL HANDLES.

TRADE MARK.

No. 0313

No. 0313S

No. 0314

No. 0320

No. 0328

No. 0329

No. 0315

No. 0316

No. 0317

No. 0318

No. 0319

No. 0330

	No. 1	2	3	4	5	6	7	8	9	Assorted	Assorted Large
Size of Ferrule	$\frac{1}{2}$	$\frac{9}{16}$	$\frac{5}{8}$	$\frac{11}{16}$	$\frac{3}{4}$	$\frac{13}{16}$	$\frac{7}{8}$	$\frac{15}{16}$	1 inch	1 to 8	5 to 9
,, Chisel	$\frac{1}{4}$	$\frac{3}{8}$	$\frac{1}{2}$	$\frac{5}{8}$	$\frac{3}{4}$	1	$1\frac{1}{4}$	$1\frac{1}{2}$	2 ,,		
No. 0313 Round Beech or Ash	19/-	20/-	22/-	24/-	25/-	26/-	27/-	30/-	34/-	24/-	28/- per gross.
,, 0313S ,, ,, ,, Scotch Pattern	19/-	20/-	22/-	24/-	25/-	26/-	27/-	30/-	34/-	24/-	28/- ,,
,, 0313B ,, Boxwood	22/-	23/-	25/-	28/-	32/-	36/-	41/-	46/-	54/-	32/-	45/- ,,
,, 0313H ,, Best Hard Boxwood	32/-	34/-	36/-	40/-	44/-	48/-	54/-	60/-	68/-	46/-	58/- ,,
,, 0314 ,, Boxwood	22/-	23/-	25/-	28/-	32/-	36/-	41/-	46/-	54/-	32/-	45/- ,,
,, 0314S ,, ,, Scotch Pattern	22/-	23/-	25/-	28/-	32/-	36/-	41/-	46/-	54/-	32/-	45/- ,,
,, 0314H ,, Best Hard Boxwood	32/-	34/-	36/-	40/-	44/-	48/-	54/-	60/-	68/-	46/-	58/- ,,
,, 0315 Octagon Boxwood	28/-	31/-	35/-	39/-	42/-	46/-	51/-	56/-	64/-	44/-	56/- ,,
,, 0315H ,, Best Hard Boxwood	42/6	45/-	47/6	50/-	55/-	60/-	65/-	70/-	75/-	52/6	64/- ,,
,, 0316 Centre, Ball Top, Boxwood London Pattern	35/-	38/-	42/-	46/-	52/-	58/-	64/-	72/-	80/-	50/-	64/- ,,
,, 0316H Octagon Centre, Ball Top, Best Hard Boxwood, London Pattern	45/-	47/6	50/-	52/6	57/6	62/6	67/6	72/6	77/6	55/-	66/6 ,,
,, 0320 Carvers' Pattern, Boxwood	22/-	23/-	25/-	28/-	32/-	36/-	41/-	46/-	54/-	32/-	45/- ,,
,, 0320H ,, ,, Best Hard Boxwood	32/-	34/-	36/-	40/-	44/-	48/-	54/-	60/-	68/-	46/-	58/- ,,

	No. 1	2	3	4	5	6	7				
For Chisels	$\frac{3}{8}$	$\frac{5}{8}$	$\frac{7}{8}$	1	$1\frac{1}{4}$	$1\frac{1}{2}$	2 inch.				
,, 0317 Beech Socket	21/-	23/-	25/-	27/-	30/-	33/-	36/-	Assorted 1 to 6		27/-	,,
,, 0318 Ash ,, Hooped Top	42/-	44/-	46/-	48/-	51/-	55/-	60/-	,, ,,		42/-	,,
,, 0328 ,, Double Hooped											
,, 0329 ,, ,, ,, Registered	54/-	58/-	62/-	66/-	70/-	74/-	78/-	,, ,,		66/-	,,
,, 0319 ,, ,, ,, Shipwrights'								Assorted		46/-	,,
,, 0330 Beech Mortice								,,		46/-	,,
,, 0332 Ladies' Carving Pattern, Assorted Hardwoods							,, $\frac{7}{16}$ to $\frac{5}{8}$			18/-	,,

EDWARD PRESTON & SONS, LTD.

PLUMBERS' TOOLS.

THREE-SQUARE SHAVE HOOKS.

No. 1509. Best, Beechwood Handles ... 13/6 per dozen.
,, 1509S. 2nd Quality ,, ,, ... 11/6 ,,

BRASS BLOW PIPES.
TINNED MOUTH END.

		8	9	10	12 inch.
No. *2282.	Ball End ...	5/6	6/-	7/-	8/6 per dozen.

No. 0649. PLUMBERS' SOLDERING IRONS.

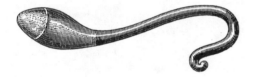

1/1 per lb.

No. 0652. MELTING POTS.

4	5	6	7	8	9 inch.
	18/-	25/-	35/-	55/-	per dozen.
15.	21/-	27/-	37/-	50/-	60/.

No. 0653. STEEL PIPE BENDING BOLTS.

12	14	16 inch.
18/-	21/-	24/- per dozen.

HEART SHAPE SHAVE HOOKS.

No. 1510. Best, Beechwood Handles ... 13/6 per dozen.
,, 1510S. 2nd Quality, ,, ,, ... 11/6 ,,

No. 1512 and 1513. WASHER CUTTERS.

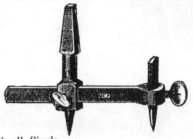

No. 1512.	Small, Single	...	...	...	...	3/6 each.
,, 1513.	Large, ,,	...	...	...	...	4/6 ,
,, 1514.	,, Double	...	...	...	...	6/6 ,,

COPPER BIT SOLDERING IRONS, Rivetted.
No. 0656

	6	8	10	12	14	16	20	24	28	32 oz.
No. 0656	26/-	32/-	35/-	44/-	48/-	54/-	64/-	74/-	84/-	94/- per doz.

No 0656H. Hatchet shape—Prices as above.

Weights given are of the Copper Bits.

Prices subject to fluctuations of Copper.

No. 0650. LEAD LADLES.

		2	2½	3	3½	4	4½	5	5½	6 inch.
No. 0650.	Best	5/-	6/-	7/-	9/-	11/-	13/-	15/-	18/-	21/- per doz.
,, 0651.	2nd Qual.	4/6	5/-	5/6	6/6	8/-	10/-	12/-	14/-	17/- ,,

PIPE OPENERS.

		¾	1	1¼	1½ inch.
No. 0654.	Plain Nose	...	16/-	17/-	21/-	22/- per dozen.
,. 0655.	Screw ,,	...	18/-	20/-	22/-	24/- ,,

* Imported.

EDWARD PRESTON & SONS, L^{TD.}

PLUMBERS' TOOLS.

BOXWOOD BOSSING MALLETS.

	1¾	2	2¼	2½	2¾	3	3½ inch.
No. 0361A. Ash Handle	14/-	15/-	17/-	19/-	20/-	22/-	30/- per doz.
,, 0361B. Cane ,,	16/-	17/-	19/-	21/-	22/-	24/-	32/- ,,

TINMEN'S MALLETS.

	2	2¼	2½	2¾	3	3½ inch.
No. 0357. Boxwood	13/-	15/-	17/-	19/-	23/-	28/- per dozen.
,, 0357B. Beechwood	9/-	10/-	11/-	12/-	14/-	16/- ,,

DRESSERS.

	1¾	2	2¼	2½ inch about.
Size No.	1	2	3	4
No 0362B. Best, Boxwood	28/-	33/-	39/-	48/- per dozen.
,, 0362C. 2nd Quality ,,	20/-	25/-	30/-	35/- ,,

BOSSING STICKS.

	No. 1	2	Asst'd.
No. 0363B. Best, Boxwood	27/-	33/-	30/- per dozen.
,, 0363C. 2nd Quality ,,	23/-	27/-	25/- ,,

SETTING-IN STICKS.

	No. 1	2	Asst'd.
No. 0364B. Best, Boxwood	23/-	26/-	24/6 per dozen.
,, 0364C. 2nd Quality ...	17/-	20/-	18/6 ,,

BENDING STICKS.

	No. 1	2	Asst'd.
No. 0365B. Best, Boxwood	30/-	34/-	32/- per dozen.
,, 0365C. 2nd Quality ,,	23/-	26/-	24/6 ,,

BOXWOOD TURNPINS.　### BOXWOOD BOBBINS.

No. 0338.　**No. 0348.**

	¾	1	1¼	1½	1¾	2	2¼	2½	3	3½	4 inch.
No. 0338)											
,, 0348)	1/6	2/-	2/6	3/6	4/6	5/6	7/-	9/-	15/-	20/-	26/- per dozen.

BOXWOOD CHASE WEDGES.

	2	2½	3	3½	4 inch.
No. 0339. With Iron Ferrule	13/-	15/-	18/-	23/-	28/- per dozen.

MANDRILLS.

12 inches long up to 2 in. dia.; 15 inches over 2 inch.

No. 0384. PARALLEL.　**No. 0385.** REDUCING.

1	1¼	1½	2	2½	3 inch.
20/-	23/-	27/-	32/-	37/-	55/- per dozen.

1	1¼	1½	2	2½	3 inch.
20/-	23/-	27/-	32/-	37/-	55/- per dozen.

EDWARD PRESTON & SONS, LTD.

MALLETS.

TRADE (E P) MARK.

GENTLEMENS' MALLETS.

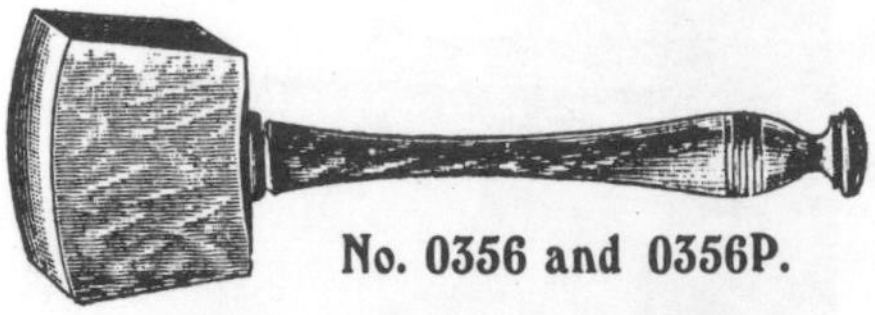

No. 0356 and 0356P.

		$3\times2\frac{1}{2}$	$3\frac{1}{2}\times2\frac{3}{4}$	4×3	$4\frac{1}{2}\times3\frac{1}{2}$	$5\frac{1}{4}\times4$	$5\frac{3}{4}\times4\frac{1}{2}$	inch.
No. 0356.	Beechwood	9/6	12/-	15/-	18/-	22/6	27/6	per dozen
,, 0356P.	Polished	11/9	15/-	17/9	20/6	25/9	31/-	,,

JOINERS' MALLETS.

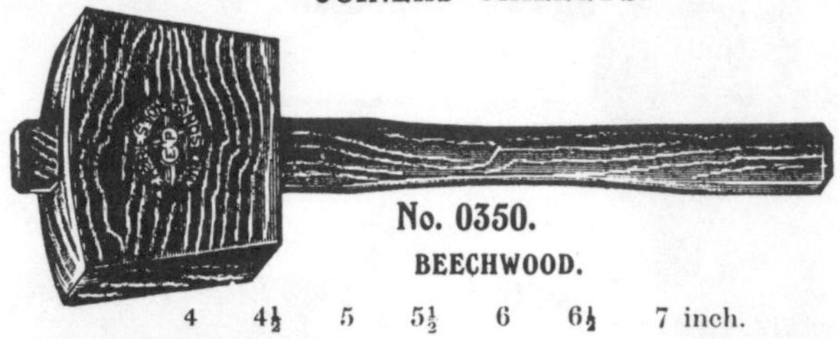

No. 0350.

BEECHWOOD.

4	$4\frac{1}{2}$	5	$5\frac{1}{2}$	6	$6\frac{1}{2}$	7 inch.
17/-	19/6	21/-	23/6	25/6	28/-	30/- per dozen.

CARVERS MALLETS.

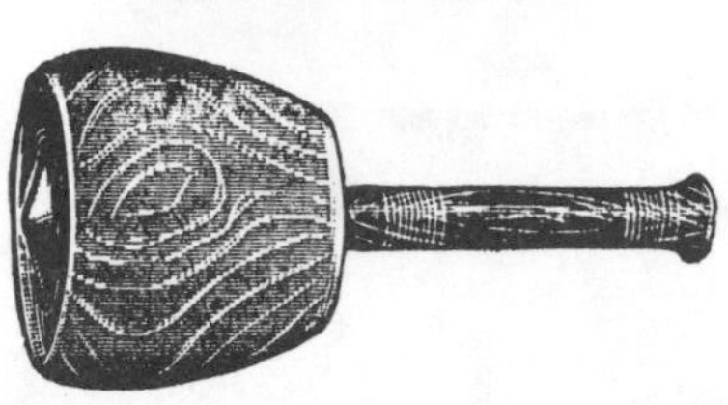

			3	$3\frac{1}{2}$	4	$4\frac{1}{2}$ inch.
No. 0358A.	Beechwood	...	16/-	17/6	19/3	20/9 per dozen.
,, 0358B.	Boxwood	...	40/-	44/9	52/3	60/- ,,

STONEMASONS' MALLETS.

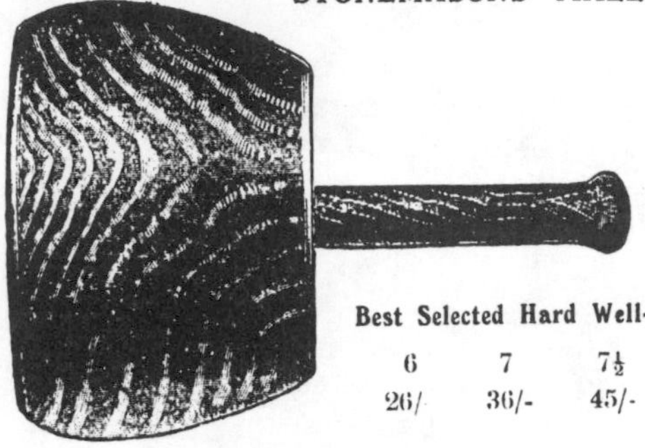

No. 0358.

Best Selected Hard Well-Seasoned Beechwood.

6	7	$7\frac{1}{2}$	8 inch.
26/	36/-	45/-	51/- per dozen.

SHIP CAULKING MALLETS.

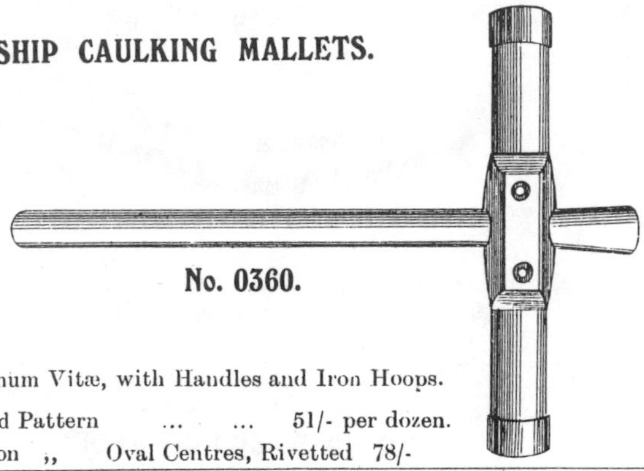

No. 0360.

Best Lignum Vitæ, with Handles and Iron Hoops.

No. 0359. Round Pattern ... ... 51/- per dozen.
,, 0360. London ,, Oval Centres, Rivetted 78/-

CARPENTERS' WOOD BENCH SCREWS.

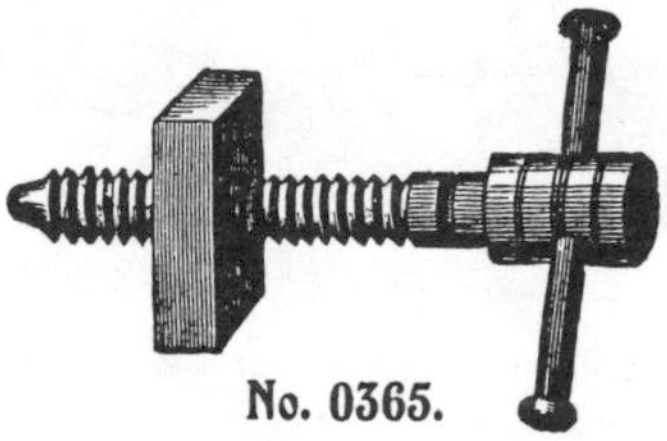

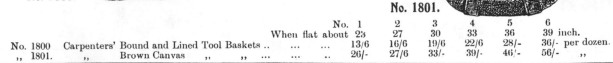

No. 0365.

	2	$2\frac{1}{4}$	$2\frac{1}{2}$	3 inch.
No. 0365 Best Quality Steamed Beech Screws,	30/6	37/6	45/-	76/- doz.
No. 0365C. Carpenters' Wood Bench do.			$2\frac{1}{2}$ in.	28/- per doz.

CARPENTERS' TOOL BASKETS.

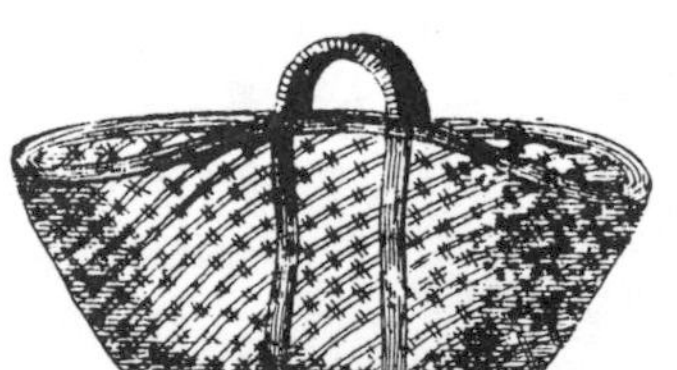

No. 1800.

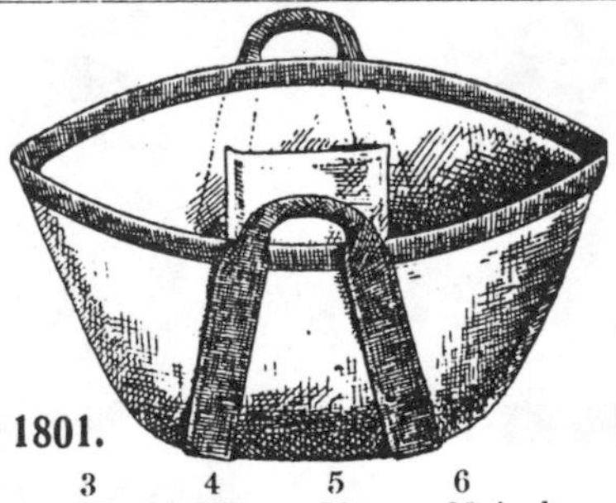

No. 1801.

	No.	1	2	3	4	5	6
	When flat about	23	27	30	33	36	39 inch.
No. 1800	Carpenters' Bound and Lined Tool Baskets	13/6	16/6	19/6	22/6	28/-	36/- per dozen.
,, 1801.	,, Brown Canvas ,, ,, ...	26/-	27/6	33/-	39/-	46/-	56/- ,,

NAME STAMPS.

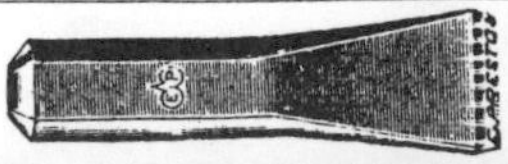

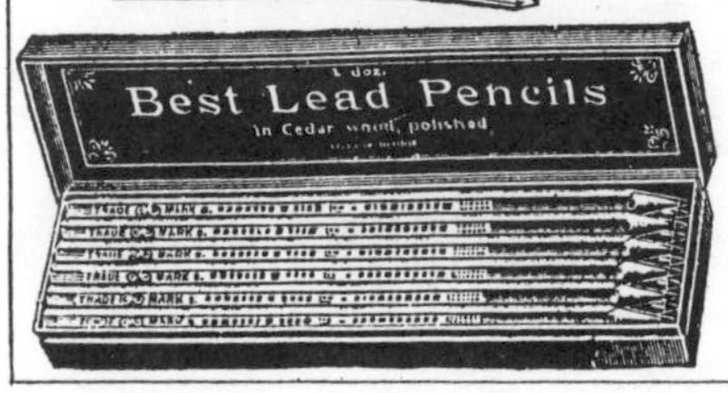

No. 1814. Joiners' Name Stamps, for Wood. $\frac{1}{8}$ inch Letters, this size, **E. PRESTON,** 4d. per letter.
,, 1814S. ,, ,, for Wood or Metal ,, ,, ,, 5d. ,,

		$\frac{1}{16}$	$\frac{1}{8}$	$\frac{3}{16}$	$\frac{1}{4}$	$\frac{5}{16}$	$\frac{3}{8}$	$\frac{7}{16}$	$\frac{1}{2}$ inch.
,, 1815.	Sets of Figures (9 to Set) ...	3/-	3/6	5/6	6/6	9/-	10/6	12/-	15/- per set.
,, 1816.	,, Letters (27 to Set) ...	9/-	9/6	12/-	15/-	19/-	24/-	30/-	36/- ,,

The above are for Stamping Wood or Metal.

No. 1817. Carpenters' Oval Polished Cedar Pencils ... ... 13/- per gross.
,, 1818. ,, Unpolished ,, "Eagle" ... 10/- ,,
,, 1819. Polished Yellow Hexagon Cedar Pencils .. ... 15/- ,,

EDWARD PRESTON & SONS, LTD.

LIGHT EDGE TOOLS.

FIRMER CHISELS.

No. 1890
CAST STEEL FIRMER CHISEL.

No. 1891
HANDLED CAST STEEL FIRMER CHISEL.

	1/16	1/8	3/16	1/4	5/16	3/8	7/16	1/2	5/8	3/4	7/8	1	1 1/8	1 1/4	1 3/8	1 1/2	1 5/8	1 3/4	1 7/8	2 in.
No. 1890 Cast Steel Firmer Chisels ...	4/3	4/8	4/3	4/3	4/6	4/9	5/3	5/6	6/-	6/6	7/6	8/-	10/-	11/-	12/-	13/6	15/-	16/6	18/-	20/- doz.
,, 1891 Do. 0313 Beech or Ash Handled																				
,, 1891S Do. 0313S Scotch Pattern Beech Handled	6/9	6/9	6/9	6/9	7/-	7/3	7/9	8/-	8/6	9/-	10/-	10/6	12/9	13/9	15/-	16/6	18/6	20/-	21/6	23/6 ,,
,, 1891B Do. 0314 Round Boxwood Handled																				
,, 1891C Do. 0320 Boxwood Carvers Handled	8/6	8/6	8/6	8/6	8/9	9/-	9/6	9/9	10/3	10/9	12/-	12/6	15/-	16/-	17/-	18/6	20/6	22/-	•23/6	25/6 ,,
,, 1891L Do. 0316 London Pattern Octagon Boxwood Handled	9/6	9/6	9/6	9/6	9/9	10/-	10/6	10/9	11/3	11/9	13/-	13/6	16/-	17/-	18/6	20/-	22/-	23/6	25/-	27/- ,,

	1/16 to 1	1/8 to 1	1/8 to 1 1/4	1/16 to 1 1/2	1/4 to 1 1/2	1/8 to 2	1/4 to 2 in.
,, 1895 Cast Steel Firmer Chisels, in Sets of 12 Assorted	5/8	5/8	6/3	7/-	7/6	9/4	9/9 per set.
,, 1895A Do. 0313 Beech or Ash Handled							
,, 1895S Do. 0313S Scotch Pattern Beech Handled	8/2	8/2	8/9	9/9	10/3	12/-	12/6 ,,
,, 1895B Do. 0314 Round Boxwood Handled							
,, 1895C Do. 0320 Boxwood Carvers Handled	10/2	10/2	10/9	11/9	12/3	14/-	14/6 ,,

No. 1894
CAST STEEL BEVELLED EDGE FIRMER CHISEL.

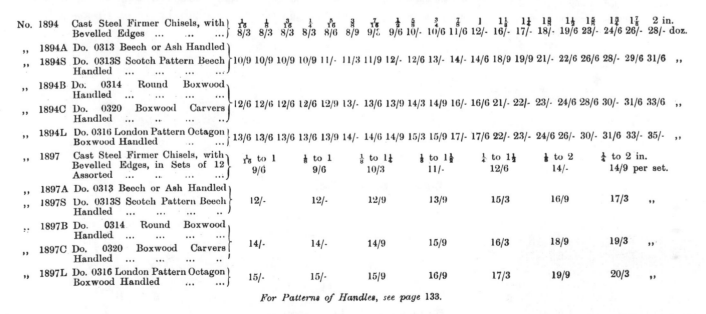

No. 1894L
CAST STEEL LONDON OCTAGON HANDLED BEVELLED EDGE FIRMER CHISEL.

	1/16	1/8	3/16	1/4	5/16	3/8	7/16	1/2	5/8	3/4	7/8	1	1 1/8	1 1/4	1 3/8	1 1/2	1 5/8	1 3/4	1 7/8	2 in.
No. 1894 Cast Steel Firmer Chisels, with Bevelled Edges	8/3	8/3	8/3	8/3	8/6	8/9	9/3	9/6	10/-	10/6	11/6	12/-	16/-	17/-	18/-	19/6	23/-	24/6	26/-	28/- doz.
,, 1894A Do. 0313 Beech or Ash Handled																				
,, 1894S Do. 0313S Scotch Pattern Beech Handled	10/9	10/9	10/9	10/9	11/-	11/3	11/9	12/-	12/6	13/-	14/-	14/6	18/9	19/9	21/-	22/6	26/6	28/-	29/6	31/6 ,,
,, 1894B Do. 0314 Round Boxwood Handled																				
,, 1894C Do. 0320 Boxwood Carvers Handled	12/6	12/6	12/6	12/6	12/9	13/-	13/6	13/9	14/3	14/9	16/-	16/6	21/-	22/-	23/-	24/6	28/6	30/-	31/6	33/6 ,,
,, 1894L Do. 0316 London Pattern Octagon Boxwood Handled	13/6	13/6	13/6	13/6	13/9	14/-	14/6	14/9	15/3	15/9	17/-	17/6	22/-	23/-	24/6	26/-	30/-	31/6	33/-	35/- ,,

	1/16 to 1	1/8 to 1	1/8 to 1 1/4	1/16 to 1 1/2	1/4 to 1 1/2	1/8 to 2	1/4 to 2 in.
,, 1897 Cast Steel Firmer Chisels, with Bevelled Edges, in Sets of 12 Assorted	9/6	9/6	10/3	11/-	12/6	14/-	14/9 per set.
,, 1897A Do. 0313 Beech or Ash Handled							
,, 1897S Do. 0313S Scotch Pattern Beech Handled	12/-	12/-	12/9	13/9	15/3	16/9	17/3 ,,
,, 1897B Do. 0314 Round Boxwood Handled							
,, 1897C Do. 0320 Boxwood Carvers Handled	14/-	14/-	14/9	15/9	16/3	18/9	19/3 ,,
,, 1897L Do. 0316 London Pattern Octagon Boxwood Handled	15/-	15/-	15/9	16/9	17/3	19/9	20/3 ,,

For Patterns of Handles, see page 133.

EDWARD PRESTON & SONS, L^TD.

LIGHT EDGE TOOLS.
FIRMER GOUGES

No. 1892.
CAST STEEL FIRMER GOUGE.

No. 1893.
HANDLED CAST STEEL FIRMER GOUGE.

Prices are from A to E Curves.   F Curve to 1-in. 9d, above 1-in. 1/- per dozen extra.

	1/16	1/8	3/16	1/4	5/16	3/8	7/16	1/2	5/8	3/4	7/8	1	1⅛	1¼	1⅜	1½	1⅝	1¾	1⅞	2 in.
No. 1892. Cast Steel Firmer Gouges	5/3	5/3	5/3	5/3	5/6	5/9	6/3	6/6	7/-	7/9	8/9	9/3	11/6	13/-	14/-	16/-	17/6	19/6	21/-	24/- doz.
,, 1893. Do. 0313 Beech or Ash Handled / ,, 1893S. Do. 0313S Scotch Pattern Beech Handled	7/9	7/9	7/9	7/9	8/-	8/3	8/9	9/-	9/6	10/3	11/3	11/9	14/3	15/9	17/-	19/-	21/-	23/-	24/6	27/6 ,,
,, 1893B. Do. 0314 Round Boxwood Handled / ,, 1893C. Do. 0320 Boxwood Carver Handled	9/6	9/6	9/6	9/6	9/9	10/-	10/6	10/9	11/3	12/-	13/3	13/9	16/6	18/-	19/-	21/-	23/-	25/-	26/6	29/6 ,,
,, 1893L. Do. 0316 London Pattern Octagon Boxwood Handled	10/6	10/6	10/6	10/6	10/9	11/-	11/6	11/9	12/3	13/-	14/3	14/9	17/6	19/-	20/6	22/6	24/6	26/6	28/-	31/- ,,

	1/16 to 1	1/8 to 1	1/8 to 1¼	1/8 to 1½	1/4 to 1½	1/8 to 2	1/4 to 2 inch.
,, 1896. Cast Steel Firmer Gouges, in Sets of 12 Assorted	6/9	6/9	7/6	8/3	8/9	11/-	11/6 per Set.
,, 1896A. Do. 0313 Beech or Ash Handled / ,, 1896S. Do. 0313S Scotch Pattern Beech Handled	9/3	9/3	10/-	11/-	11/6	13/9	14/3 ,,
,, 1896B. Do. 0314 Round Boxwood Handled / ,, 1896C. Do. 0320 Boxwood Carver Handled	11/3	11/3	12/-	13/-	13/6	15/9	16/3 ,,

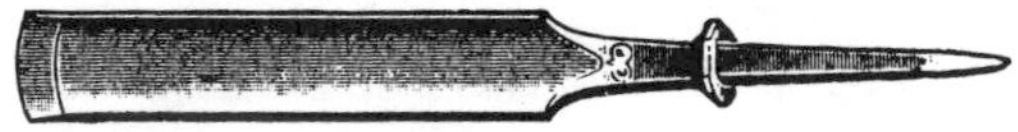

No. 1955.
CAST STEEL FIRMER GOUGE, CANNELLED INSIDE.

No. 1956C.
LONDON PATTERN SCRIBING GOUGE, HANDLED.

	1/16	1/8	3/16	1/4	5/16	3/8	7/16	1/2	5/8	3/4	7/8	1	1⅛	1¼	1⅜	1½	1⅝	1¾	1⅞	2 in.
No. 1955. Cast Steel Firmer Gouges, Cannelled inside	5/6	5/6	5/6	5/6	5/9	6/-	6/6	6/9	7/3	8/-	9/-	9/6	12/-	13/6	16/-	17/6	19/6	21/-	24/-	28/- doz.
,, 1955A. Do. 0313 Beech or Ash Handled	8/-	8/-	8/-	8/-	8/3	8/6	9/-	9/3	9/9	10/6	11/6	12/-	14/9	16/3	17/6	19/6	22/-	24/-	25/6	28/6 ,,
,, 1955B. Do. 0314 Round Boxwood Handled / ,, 1955C. Do. 0320 Boxwood Carver Handled	9/9	9/9	9/9	9/9	10/-	10/3	10/9	11/-	11/6	12/3	13/6	14/-	17/-	18/6	19/6	21/6	24/-	26/-	27/6	30/6 ,,

	1/4	5/16	3/8	7/16	1/2	5/8	3/4	7/8	1 in.
,, 1956. Cast Steel London Pattern Scribing Gouges, Cannelled inside	7/-	7/3	7/6	8/-	8/3	8/9	9/6	10/6	11/- doz.
,, 1956A. Do 0313 Beech or Ash Handled	9/6	9/9	10/-	10/6	10/9	11/3	12/-	13/-	13/6 ,,
,, 1956B. Do. 0314 Round Boxwood Handled / ,, 1956C. Do. 0320 Boxwood Carver Handled	11/3	11/6	11/9	12/3	12/6	13/-	13/9	15/-	15/6 ,,

CURVES OF GOUGES.

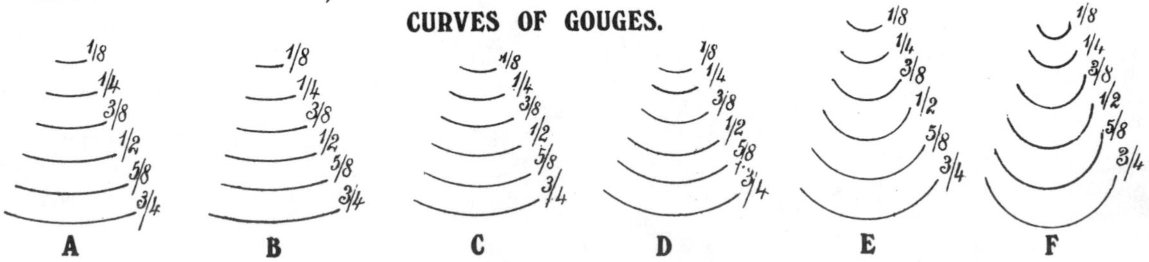

A   **B**   **C**   **D**   **E**   **F**

For Patterns of Handles, see page 133.

EDWARD PRESTON & SONS, L^{TD}.

LIGHT EDGE TOOLS.

CAST STEEL LONG THIN PARING CHISELS AND GOUGES.

TRADE **E P** MARK.

1958
LONG THIN PARING CHISEL.

No. 1958C
LONG THIN PARING CHISEL, HANDLED.

		$\frac{1}{8}$	$\frac{1}{4}$	$\frac{3}{8}$	$\frac{1}{2}$	$\frac{5}{8}$	$\frac{3}{4}$	$\frac{7}{8}$	1	$1\frac{1}{8}$	$1\frac{1}{4}$	$1\frac{3}{8}$	$1\frac{1}{2}$	$1\frac{5}{8}$	$1\frac{3}{4}$	$1\frac{7}{8}$	2 in.
No. 1958	Cast Steel Long Thin Paring Chisels (1 in. to be 9 in. to Bolster)	7/6	7/6	7/9	8/6	9/6	10/9	11/6	14/-	16/-	19/-	20/6	23/-	25/-	27/-	30/6	33/6 per dozen.
„ 1958C	Ditto 0320 Boxwood Carver Handled	12/-	12/-	12/3	13/-	14/-	15/3	16/-	18/6	20/6	23/6	25/-	28/-	29/6	32/-	35/6	39/ „
„ 1958L	Ditto 0316 London Pattern Octagon Boxwood Handled	13/-	13/-	13/3	14/-	15/-	16/3	17/-	19,6	21/6	24/6	26/6	29/6	31/-	33/6	37/-	40/6 „
„ 1959	Cast Stee' Bevel Edge Long Thin Paring Chisels	13/6	13/6	13/9	14/6	15/6	16/9	17/6	20/-	25/-	28/-	29/6	32/-	37/-	39/-	42/6	45/6 „
„ 1959C	Ditto 0320 Boxwood Carver Handled	18/-	18/-	18/3	19/-	20/-	21/3	22/-	24/6	29/6	32/6	34/-	37/-	41/6	44/-	47/6	51/ „
„ 1959L	Ditto 0316 London Pattern Octagon Boxwood Handled	19/-	19/-	19/3	20/-	21/-	22/3	23/-	25/6	30/6	33/6	35/6	38/6	43/-	45/6	49/-	52/6 „

No. 1960
LONG THIN PARING GOUGES, Cannelled Inside.

		$\frac{1}{8}$	$\frac{1}{4}$	$\frac{3}{8}$	$\frac{1}{2}$	$\frac{5}{8}$	$\frac{3}{4}$	$\frac{7}{8}$	1	$1\frac{1}{8}$	$1\frac{1}{4}$	$1\frac{3}{8}$	$1\frac{1}{2}$	$1\frac{5}{8}$	$1\frac{3}{4}$	$1\frac{7}{8}$	2 in.
No. 1960	Cast Steel Long Thin Paring Gouges, A to E Curves	12/9	12/9	13/-	13/9	14/9	16/-	16/9	19/3	22/6	25/6	27/-	29/6	34/-	36/-	39/6	42/- per dozen.
„ 1960C	Ditto 0320 Boxwood Carver Handled ...	17/3	17/3	17/6	18/6	19/6	21/-	22/-	24/-	27/6	30/6	31/6	34/6	38/6	41/6	45/6	47/6 „
„ 1960L	Ditto 0316 London Pattern Octagon Boxwood Handled	18/3	18/3	18/6	19/6	20/6	22/-	23/-	25/-	28/6	31/6	33/-	36/-	40/-	43/-	47/-	49/- „

No. 1961
REGISTERED CHISELS.

		$\frac{1}{8}$	$\frac{1}{4}$	$\frac{3}{8}$	$\frac{1}{2}$	$\frac{5}{8}$	$\frac{3}{4}$	$\frac{7}{8}$	1	$1\frac{1}{8}$	$1\frac{1}{4}$	$1\frac{3}{8}$	$1\frac{1}{2}$	$1\frac{5}{8}$	$1\frac{3}{4}$	$1\frac{7}{8}$	2	$2\frac{1}{4}$	$2\frac{1}{2}$ in.
No. 1961	Cast Steel Registered Chisels, 0329 Double Iron Hooped Ash Handled	12/-	12/-	12/3	12/6	13/3	14/6	15/9	18/9	19/9	20/9	22/-	23/3	25/3	27/3	28/9	30/3	36/-	43/- dozen.
„ 1962	Cast Steel Registered Gouges, 0329 Double Iron Hooped Ash Handled	15/-	15/-	15/3	15/6	16/3	17/6	18/9	21/9	24/9	25/6	27/-	28/3	33/3	35/3	36/9	38/3	—	— „

No. 1954
HANDLED SASH POCKET CHISEL.

		$1\frac{1}{2}$	$1\frac{3}{4}$	2	$2\frac{1}{4}$	$2\frac{1}{2}$ in.
No. 1954	Cast Steel Sash Pocket Chisels, Handled	12/-	14/-	16/-	20/-	24/- per dozen.

For Patterns of Handles, see page 133.

LIGHT EDGE TOOLS.

TRADE  MARK.

MORTICE CHISELS.

No. 1901H.
CAST STEEL MORTICE CHISEL.

	$\frac{1}{4}$	$\frac{5}{16}$	$\frac{3}{8}$	$\frac{7}{16}$	$\frac{1}{2}$	$\frac{9}{16}$	$\frac{5}{8}$	$\frac{3}{4}$ inch.
No. 1901. Cast Steel Best Joiners' Mortice Chisels	14/-	14/-	14/9	16/-	17/9	19/3	21/3	26/- per dozen.
,, 1901H. Ditto 0330 Oval Beech Handled	23/6	23/6	24/6	25/9	27/9	29/3	31/3	37/- ,,

No. 1904.
CAST STEEL SOCKET MORTICE CHISEL.

	$\frac{1}{4}$	$\frac{5}{16}$	$\frac{3}{8}$	$\frac{7}{16}$	$\frac{1}{2}$	$\frac{9}{16}$	$\frac{5}{8}$	$\frac{3}{4}$ inch.
No. 1904. Cast Steel Socket Mortice Chisels	16/6	16/6	18/-	19/6	21/-	23/-	26/-	31/- per dozen.
,, 1904H. Ditto 0318 Handled and Hooped	20/6	20/6	22/-	23/6	25/-	27/-	30/-	35/- ,,

No. 1964.
IMPROVED SOCKET LOCK MORTICE CHISEL.

	$\frac{1}{2}$	$\frac{9}{16}$	$\frac{5}{8}$ inch.
No. 1964. Improved Socket Lock Mortice Chisels...	46/-	48/-	50/- per dozen.
,, 1964H. ,, ,, ,, ,, Beech Handled	50/-	52/-	54/- ,,

No. 1907.
CAST STEEL SOCKET CHISEL.

	To $\frac{1}{2}$	$\frac{5}{8}$	$\frac{3}{4}$	$\frac{7}{8}$	1	$1\frac{1}{8}$	$1\frac{1}{4}$	$1\frac{3}{8}$	$1\frac{1}{2}$	$1\frac{5}{8}$	$1\frac{3}{4}$	$1\frac{7}{8}$	2 inch.
No. 1907. Cast Steel Socket Chisels, Blued or Black	12/3	13/-	14/-	15/-	16/6	18/3	20/-	21/3	22/9	24/6	26/6	28/6	30/6 per doz.
,, 1907A. Ditto ditto 0317 Beech Handled	14/9	15/6	16/6	17/6	19/-	21/-	22/9	24/3	25/9	28/-	30/-	32/-	34/- ,,
,, 1907B. Ditto 0318 Hooped Ash Handled	16/3	17/-	18/-	19/-	20/6	22/9	24/6	25/9	27/3	29/-	31/-	33/-	35/- ,,

No. 1908.
CAST STEEL SOCKET GOUGE.

	To $\frac{1}{2}$	$\frac{5}{8}$	$\frac{3}{4}$	$\frac{7}{8}$	1	$1\frac{1}{8}$	$1\frac{1}{4}$	$1\frac{3}{8}$	$1\frac{1}{2}$	$1\frac{5}{8}$	$1\frac{3}{4}$	$1\frac{7}{8}$	2 inch.
No. 1908. Cast Steel Socket Gouges ·	15/3	16/-	17/-	18/-	20/-	22/3	24/-	25/3	26/9	30/6	32/6	34/6	36/6 per doz.
,, 1908B. Ditto .0318 Hooped Ash Handled	19/3	20/-	21/-	22/-	24/-	26/9	28/6	29/9	31/3	35/-	37/-	39/-	41/- ,,

CAST STEEL TURNING CHISEL.

	$\frac{1}{4}$	$\frac{3}{8}$	$\frac{1}{2}$	$\frac{5}{8}$	$\frac{3}{4}$	$\frac{7}{8}$	1	$1\frac{1}{8}$	$1\frac{1}{4}$	$1\frac{3}{8}$	$1\frac{1}{2}$	$1\frac{5}{8}$	$1\frac{3}{4}$	$1\frac{7}{8}$	2 inch.
No. 1898. Cast Steel Turning Chisels (1in. to be 10¼in. over all)	6/-	6/6	7/3	8/-	9/-	10/-	11/6	13/-	14/6	16/6	18/6	20/6	22/6	24/6	26/6 per doz.
,, 1898H. Ditto Beech Handled	10/6	11/-	11/9	12/6	13/6	14/6	16/-	18/-	19/6	22/-	24/-	26/6	28/6	30/6	32/6 ,,

CAST STEEL TURNING GOUGE.

	$\frac{1}{4}$	$\frac{3}{8}$	$\frac{1}{2}$	$\frac{5}{8}$	$\frac{3}{4}$	$\frac{7}{8}$	1	$1\frac{1}{8}$	$1\frac{1}{4}$	$1\frac{3}{8}$	$1\frac{1}{2}$	$1\frac{5}{8}$	$1\frac{3}{4}$	$1\frac{7}{8}$	2 inch.
No. 1899. Cast Steel Turning Gouges (1in. to be 10¼in. over all)	7/9	8/9	9/9	10/6	12/3	14/-	15/9	17/6	20/6	23/9	26/9	29/3	31/6	35/-	38/6 per doz.
,, 1899H. Ditto Beech Handled	12/3	13/3	14/3	15/-	16/9	18/6	20/3	22/6	25/6	29/3	32/3	35/3	37/6	41/-	44/6 ,,

For Patterns of Handles, see page 133.

EDWARD PRESTON & SONS, LTD.

TRADE (EP) MARK.

PLANE IRONS.

CAST STEEL UNCUT PLANE IRONS.

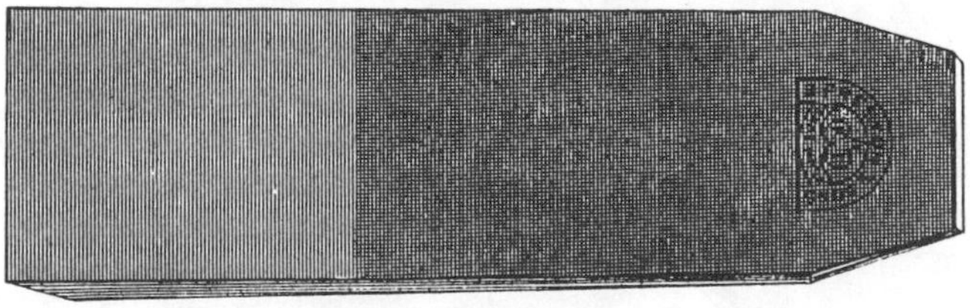

No.		To 1¼	1⅜	1½	1⅝	1¾	1⅞	2	2⅛	2¼	2⅜	2½	2⅝	2¾	2⅞	3 in.	
No. 1920	Common Plane Irons	5/7	5/11	6/-	6/8	7/-	7/3	8/-	8/6	9/9	11/-	11/6	12/9	14/-	15/6	17/-	per dozen.
,, 1921 ,, 1921R	Cast Steel Plane Irons ,, ,, ,, Round Nose } ...	8/-	8/-	8/-	8/-	8/3	9/-	9/6	10/-	11/6	12/9	13/6	15/3	17/-	18/6	21/6	,,

CAST STEEL CUT PLANE IRONS.

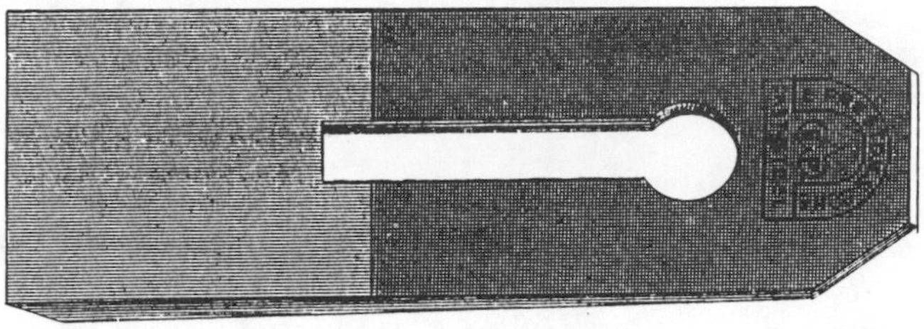

No.		To 1¼	1⅜	1½	1⅝	1¾	1⅞	2	2⅛	2¼	2⅜	2½	2⅝	2¾	2⅞	3 in.	
No. 1922	Common Cut Plane Irons	6/1	6/5	6/6	7/2	7/6	7/9	8/6	9/-	10/3	11/6	12/-	13/3	14/6	16/-	17/6	per dozen.
,, 1923	Cast Steel ,, ,, ...	8/6	8/6	8/6	8/6	8/9	9/6	10/-	10/6	12/-	13/3	14/-	15/9	17/6	19/-	22/-	,,
,, 1924	,, ,, ,, Parallel ...	11/-	11/-	11/-	11/-	11/3	12/-	12/6	13/-	14/6	15/9	16/6	18/3	20/-	21/6	24/6	,,
,, 1925	,, , ,, ,, Bright	14/-	14/-	14/-	14/-	14/3	15/3	15/6	16/-	17/6	18/9	19/6	21/3	23/-	—	—	,,

If Skew, 1/- per dozen extra.

CAST STEEL DOUBLE PLANE IRONS.

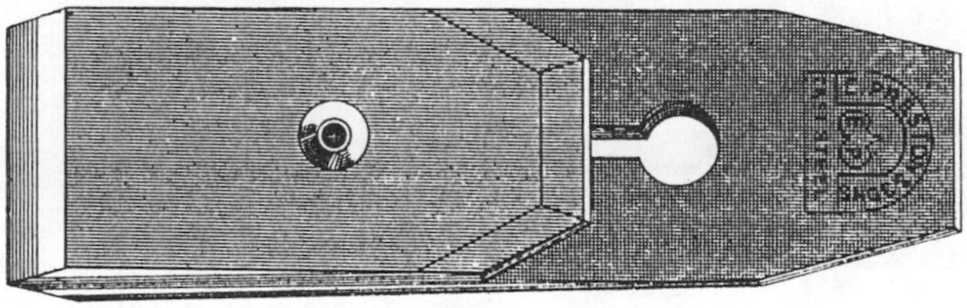

No.		To 1½	1⅝	1¾	1⅞	2	2⅛	2¼	2⅜	2½	2⅝	2¾	2⅞	3 in.	
No. 1926	Common Double Plane Irons, with Brass Nuts	14/3	15/-	15/3	15/9	16/9	17/6	19/3	21/3	22/6	24/3	26/-	29/-	32/-	per dozen.
,, 1927	Cast Steel ,, ,, ,, ,, ...	16/3	16/3	16/9	17/9	18/6	19/3	21/3	23/3	24/9	27/-	29/3	32/3	36/9	,,
,, 1928	,, ,, ,, ,, ,, ,, Parallel ...	18/9	18/9	19/3	20/3	21/-	21/9	23/9	25/9	27/3	29/4	31/9	34/9	39/3	,,
,, 1929	,, ,, ,, ,, ,, ,, ,, Bright	21/9	21/9	22/3	23/3	24/-	24/9	26/9	28/9	30/3	32/6	34/9	—	—	,,

If Skew 2/6 per dozen extra.

CAST STEEL TOOTH IRONS.

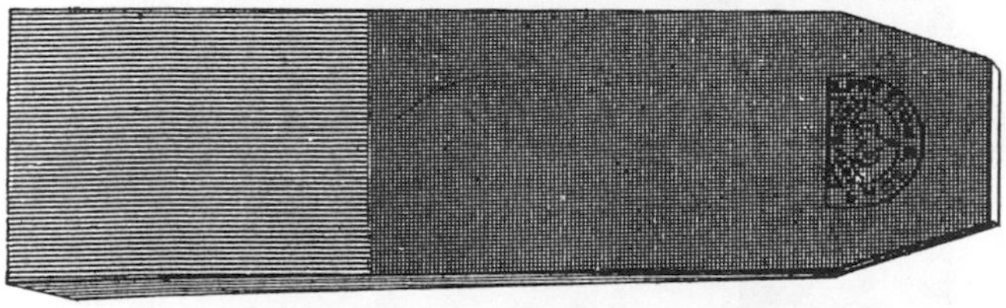

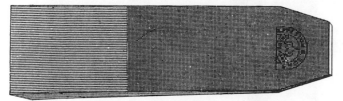

	1½	1⅝	1¾	1⅞	2	2⅛	2¼	2⅜	2½ in.	
No. 1930	12/-	12/-	12/-	13/-	14/-	15/-	16/3	17/-	18/3	per doz.

CAST STEEL TOP IRONS.

WITH SCREWS AND BRASS NUTS.

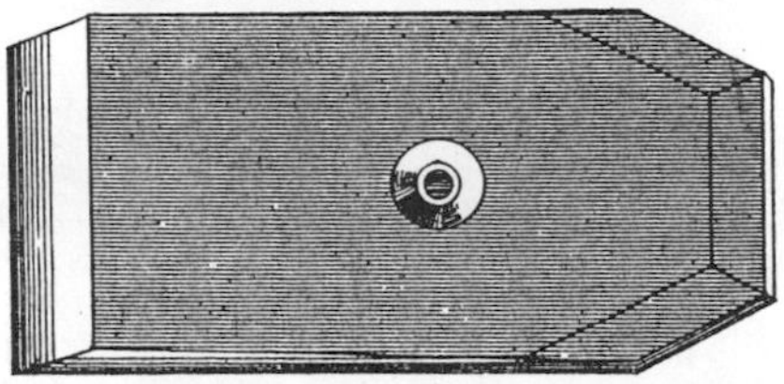

	1⅝	1¾	2	2⅛	2¼	2⅜	2½ in.	
No. 1931	5/-	5/-	5/6	5/9	6/3	6/9	7/-	per doz.

EDWARD PRESTON & SONS, L^{TD.}

PLANE IRONS.

CHARIOT IRONS.

	1	1⅛	1¼	1½ inch.
No. 1944. Bright	10/6	10/6	10/6	10/6 per dozen.

BULL NOSE IRONS.

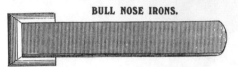

	To 1	1⅛	1¼	1½ inch.
No. 1945. Bright	8/-	8/-	8/-	9/- per dozen.

SHOULDER IRONS.

	To ¾	1	1¼	1½ inch.
No. 1946. Bright	9/-	9/-	9/-	10/- per dozen.
,, 1946S. Snecked	10/-	10/-	10/-	11/- ,,

BEST PLOUGH BITS.

No. 1947. Bright ... ... 5/4 per Set of 8. 8/- per dozen.

SOFT MOULDING IRONS.

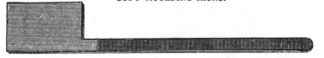

	½	⅝	¾	⅞	1	1⅛	1¼	1⅜	1½	1⅝	1¾	1⅞	2 inch.
No. 1949.	3/2	3/3	3/4	3/5	3/7	3/10	4/2	4/5	4/8	4/10	5/-	5/6	5/9 doz.

Right or Left Hand.

SQUARE RABBET IRONS.

	½	⅝	¾	⅞	1	1⅛	1¼	1⅜	1½	1⅝	1¾	1⅞	2 inch.
No. 1950.	4/4	4/6	4/7	4/8	4/10	5/-	5/2	5/5	5/8	5/10	6/-	6/6	7/- doz.

SKEW RABBET IRONS.

	½	⅝	¾	⅞	1	1⅛	1¼	1⅜	1½	1⅝	1¾	1⅞	2 inch.
No. 1951.	4/8	4/10	5/1	5/2	5/4	5/6	5/8	5/11	6/2	6/4	6/6	7/-	7/6 doz.

SASH FILLISTER IRONS.

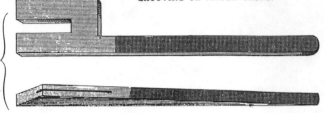

LEFT HAND.

No. 1952.	Left Hand	...	...	...	...	6/- per dozen.
,, 1952R.	Right ,,	...	...	...	...	6/- ,,

GROOVING OR MATCH IRONS.

	¼	⅜	½	⅝	¾	⅞	1 inch.
No. 1953. ...	12/-	12/-	12/-	12/-	12/-	12/-	12/- per dozen pairs.

DADO OR TRENCHING IRONS.

No. 1954. ... ... 19/- per dozen pairs.

HOLLOW AND ROUND IRONS.

	To 1	1⅛	1¼	1⅜	1½ inch.
No 1956. Square	12/-	13/-	14/-	15/-	16/- per dozen pairs.
,, 1956S. Skew	16/-	17/-	18/-	19/-	20/- ,, ,,

BEAD IRONS.

	To ¾	⅞	1 inch.
No. 1957.	10/-	11/-	12/- per dozen.

FILLISTER TEETH.

No. 1952T. ... ... 10/- per dozen.

COACHMAKERS' T RABBET IRONS.

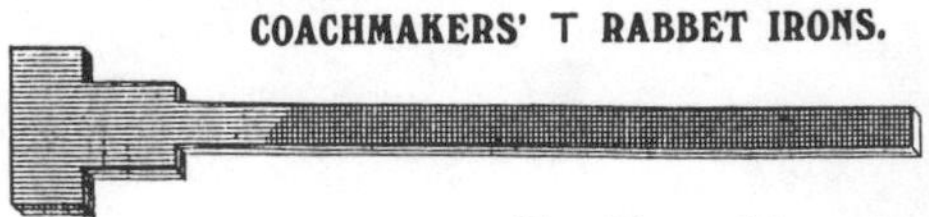

	To 1½	1⅝	1¾ inch.
No. 1955.	8/-	8/6	9/- per dozen.

Edward Preston & Sons, L^{TD.}

CARVING TOOLS.

TRADE MARK.

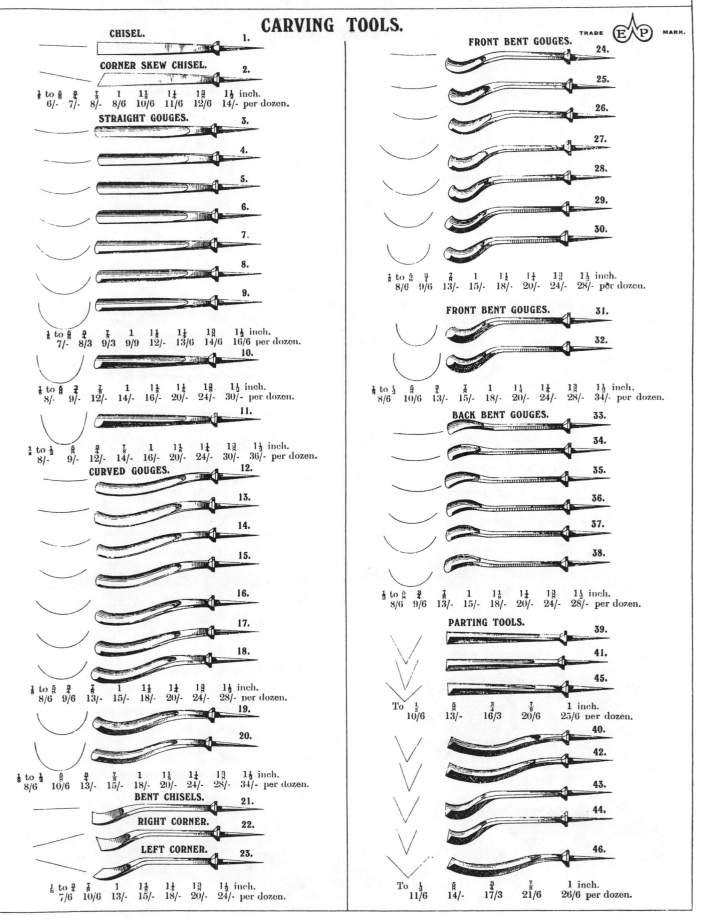

CHISEL. 1.

CORNER SKEW CHISEL. 2.

⅛ to ⅝ ¾ ⅞ 1 1⅛ 1¼ 1⅜ 1½ inch.
6/- 7/- 8/- 8/6 10/6 11/6 12/6 14/- per dozen.

STRAIGHT GOUGES. 3.

4. 5. 6. 7. 8. 9.

⅛ to ⅝ ¾ ⅞ 1 1⅛ 1¼ 1⅜ 1½ inch.
7/- 8/3 9/3 9/9 12/- 13/6 14/6 16/6 per dozen.

10.

⅛ to ⅝ ¾ ⅞ 1 1⅛ 1¼ 1⅜ 1½ inch.
8/- 9/- 12/- 14/- 16/- 20/- 24/- 30/- per dozen.

11.

⅛ to ½ ⅝ ¾ ⅞ 1 1⅛ 1¼ 1⅜ 1½ inch.
8/- 9/- 12/- 14/- 16/- 20/- 24/- 30/- 36/- per dozen.

CURVED GOUGES. 12.

13. 14. 15. 16. 17. 18.

⅛ to ⅝ ¾ ⅞ 1 1⅛ 1¼ 1⅜ 1½ inch.
8/6 9/6 13/- 15/- 18/- 20/- 24/- 28/- per dozen.

19. 20.

⅛ to ½ ⅝ ¾ ⅞ 1 1⅛ 1¼ 1⅜ 1½ inch.
8/6 10/6 13/- 15/- 18/- 20/- 24/- 28/- 34/- per dozen.

BENT CHISELS. 21.

RIGHT CORNER. 22.

LEFT CORNER. 23.

⅛ to ¾ ⅞ 1 1⅛ 1¼ 1⅜ 1½ inch.
7/6 10/6 13/- 15/- 18/- 20/- 24/- per dozen.

FRONT BENT GOUGES. 24.

25. 26. 27. 28. 29. 30.

⅛ to ⅝ ¾ ⅞ 1 1⅛ 1¼ 1⅜ 1½ inch.
8/6 9/6 13/- 15/- 18/- 20/- 24/- 28/- per dozen.

FRONT BENT GOUGES. 31.

32.

⅛ to ½ ⅝ ¾ ⅞ 1 1⅛ 1¼ 1⅜ 1½ inch.
8/6 10/6 13/- 15/- 18/- 20/- 24/- 28/- 34/- per dozen.

BACK BENT GOUGES. 33.

34. 35. 36. 37. 38.

⅛ to ⅝ ¾ ⅞ 1 1⅛ 1¼ 1⅜ 1½ inch.
8/6 9/6 13/- 15/- 18/- 20/- 24/- 28/- per dozen.

PARTING TOOLS. 39.

41. 45.

To ½ ⅝ ¾ ⅞ 1 inch.
10/6 13/- 16/3 20/6 25/6 per dozen.

40. 42. 43. 44. 46.

To ½ ⅝ ¾ ⅞ 1 inch.
11/6 14/- 17/3 21/6 26/6 per dozen.

EDWARD PRESTON & SONS, L^{TD.}

CARVING TOOLS.

TRADE  MARK.

FISH TAIL SPADE GOUGES.

No. 47.

Sweeps same as Gouges No. 3 to 9.

⅛ to ⅝	¾	⅞	1 inch.
7/6	8/9	10/6	13/- per dozen.

FISH TAIL SPADE CHISEL.

No. 48.

⅛ to ⅝	¾	⅞	1 inch.
7/-	8/3	9/3	9/9 per dozen.

LONDON CARVING KNIFE.

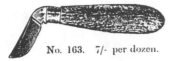

No. 159. Handled, 7/9 doz.

No. 162. 8/6 per dozen.

WHITTLE SHAPE CARVING KNIFE.

No. 160. Handled, 9/6 doz.

No. 163. 7/- per dozen.

DOG LEG CHISEL.

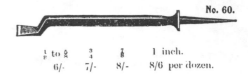

No. 60.

⅛ to ⅝	¾	⅞	1 inch.
6/-	7/-	8/-	8/6 per dozen.

MACARONI TOOLS.

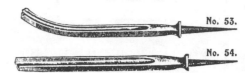

No. 53.

No. 54.

No. 54 Straight ... 14/-   No. 53. Bent ... 15/6 per dozen.

CARVING OR BUHL PUNCHES.

No. 51.

1	2	3	5	6	8	9	11	18	21	23	24

Assorted Patterns ... ... 8/- per dozen.

LADIES' or AMATEURS' CARVING CHISEL.

LADIES' or AMATEURS' CARVING GOUGE.

For Shapes and Sweeps see Carving Tools, page 143.

LADIES' or AMATEURS' CARVING TOOLS.

Ladies' or Amateurs' Carving Chisels	5/3 per dozen.
,, ,, ,, Gouges, Flat ...	6/- ,,
,, ,, ,, ,, Middle	6/- ,,
,, ,, ,, ,, Scribing ...	6/- ,,
,, ,, ,, ,, Quick ...	7/3 ,,
,, ,, ,, Straight Parting Tools	7/6 ,,
,, ,, ,, Bent ,,	8/6 ,,
,, ,, ,, Double Bent Chisels ...	7/- ,,
,, ,, ,, ,, Gouges ...	7/6 ,,
,, ,, ,, assorted in Sets of 36...	21/9 per set.
,, ,, ,, ,, ,, 48...	29/- ,,

CARVING TOOLS HANDLED.

If Beechwood Handles, 2/6   Boxwood Handles, 4/6   Rosewood Handles, 5/6 per dozen extra.

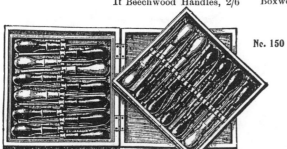

No. 150

No. 150.—Set of 24 LADIES' HANDLED CARVING TOOLS in Polished Pine Box.

LADIES' HANDLED CARVING TOOLS, in Boxes.

Sets of Ladies' Carving Tools, in Hardwood Handles.

Number of Tools in each Box	6	12	18	24	36 Tools.
No. 150. Pine Boxes ...	7/3	13/-	20/-	27/-	40/- per set.
,, 151. Oak Boxes ...	9/3	15/6	23/-	30/6	46/- ,,
,, 152. Mahogany Boxes	12/-	18/6	27/-	35/-	52/- ,,

CARVERS' SCREWS.

With Black Fly Nuts.

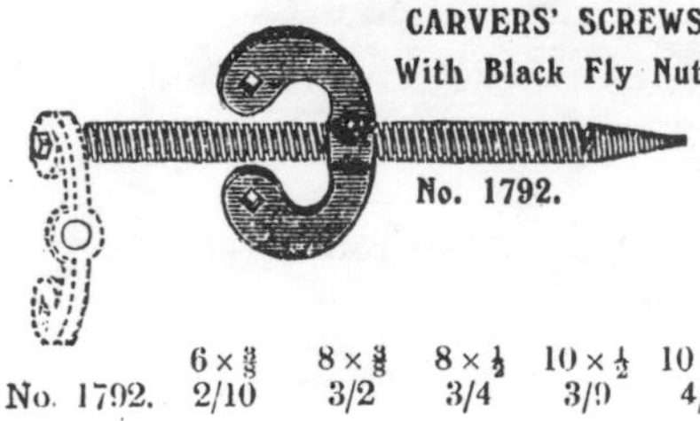

No. 1792.

	6 × ⅜	8 × ⅜	8 × ½	10 × ½	10 × ⅝	12 × ⅝ inch.
No. 1792.	2/10	3/2	3/4	3/9	4/3	4/9 each.

BEECHWOOD CARVERS' ROUTERS.

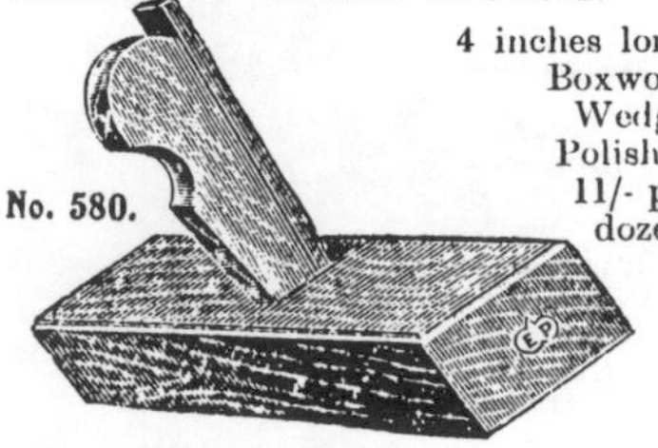

No. 580.

4 inches long. Boxwood Wedge, Polished 11/- per dozen.

CARVERS' MALLETS.

No. 0358C.

3½ inch diameter, 11/- per dozen

EDWARD PRESTON & SONS, L^{TD.}

SAWS.

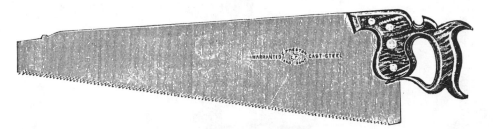

HAND, PANEL AND RIPPING SAWS.

	10	12	14	16	18	20	22	24	26	28	30 inch.
No. 1820. German Steel	24/-	28/-	34/-	40/-	46/-	50/-	56/-	62/-	64/-	70/-	76/- per dozen.
,, 1821 Cast Steel	28/-	34/-	42/-	48/-	54/-	58/-	64/-	72/-	74/-	80/-	86/- ,,

IRON AND BRASS BACK SAWS.

	10	12	14	16	18	20	22	24 inch.
No. 1822. German Steel, Bright Iron Back	48/-	52/-	56/-	62/-	66/-	68/-	74/-	80/- per dozen.
,, 1824. Cast Steel, Bright Iron Back ...	56/-	60/-	64/-	72/-	76/-	78/-	84/-	90/- ,,
,, 1826. Cast Steel, Brass Back	72/-	80/-	90/-	104/-	112/-	118/-	128/-	140/- ,,

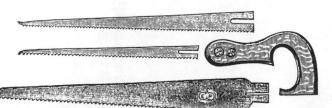

COMPASS OR LOCK SAWS.

	10	12	14	16	18 inch.
No. 1827.	15/-	18/-	21/-	24/-	27/- per dozen.

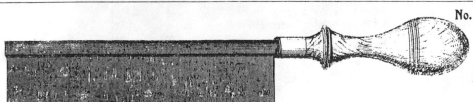

C.S. INTERCHANGEABLE SAWS.

No. 1828. Set of 3 Saws, Keyhole Compass and Pruning, with Handle... } 54/- per dozen.

No. 1842. FANCY BRASS BACK SAWS, for Wood.

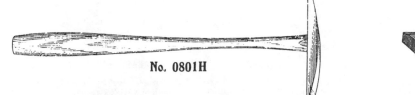

4	5	6	7	8 inch
12/-	13/6	15/-	17/-	21/- per dozen.

SAW SETTING HAMMERS AND BEDS.

No. 0801H

No. 0802

No. 0801H	C.S. Saw Setting Hammers, Handled	18/- per dozen.
,, 0801	,, ,, Hammer Heads only	16/- ,,
,, 0802	Steel Saw Setting Bed, two Bevels, with Screw Holes, 7 in. long × 1½ in. wide × ⅛ in. thick	36/- ,,

EDWARD PRESTON & SONS, LTD.

BREAST DRILLS.

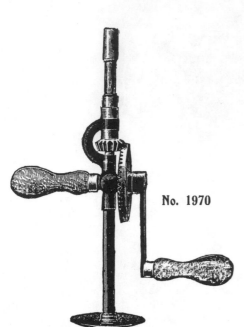

No. 1970

IMPROVED BREAST DRILL,

With 6 Drills, Assorted ⅛ to ₁⁷₆ in.

No. 1970/1 Black, with Beech Handles, length 13½ inches, 7/6 each.

No. 1970/2 Black, with Beech Handles, length 15 inches, 9/- each.

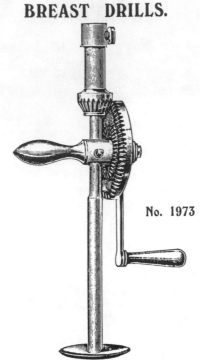

No. 1973

IMPROVED DOUBLE SPEED BREAST DRILL,

With 6 Drills, Assorted ⅛ to ₁⁷₆ in.

No. 1973 Bright all over, length 15 inches, 13/- each.

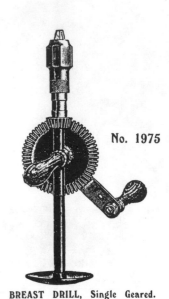

No. 1975

BREAST DRILL, Single Geared.

Japanned Red and Black, with Bright parts. 9/- each.

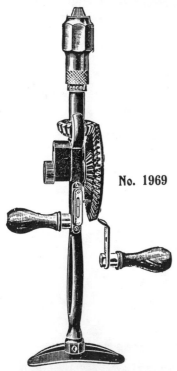

No. 1969

BREAST DRILL, Two-Speed.

Nickel Plated, Ball Thrust, Rosewood Handles, Steel Jaws, Malleable Iron Stock and Breast Plate. Each Drill is supplied with extra pair of Steel Jaws, suitable for Small Drills.

No. 1969 Ball Bearing ... ... 14/6 each.

,, 1969A Plain ,, ... 13/6 ,,

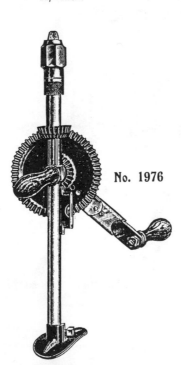

No. 1976

BREAST DRILL, Two-Speed.

Nickel Plated, Ball Thrust, Rosewood Handles, Steel Jaws, Steel Stock. Each Drill is supplied with extra pair of Steel Jaws, suitable for Small Drills, 18/- each.

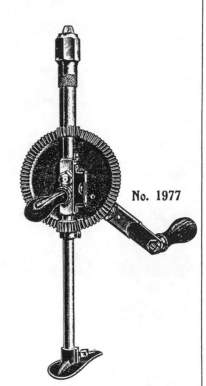

No. 1977

BREAST DRILL, Double Geared.

Ball Thrust, Steel Stock and Jaws. Each Drill is supplied with extra pair of Jaws suitable for Small Drills, Nickel Plated, 23/- each.

EDWARD PRESTON & SONS, L^{TD.}

TWIST DRILLS.

JOBBERS' OR SHORT STRAIGHT SHANK DRILLS.

WITH GRINDING LINE.

Diam. of Drills.	Length of Drills.	Price per Drill.	Diam. of Drills.	Length of Drills.	Price per Drill.
Inch.	Inch.		Inch.	Inch.	
$\frac{1}{16}$	$2\frac{1}{2}$	-/4	$\frac{19}{64}$	$4\frac{3}{8}$	1/1
$\frac{5}{64}$	$2\frac{5}{8}$	-/4	$\frac{5}{16}$	$4\frac{1}{2}$	1/2
$\frac{3}{32}$	$2\frac{3}{4}$	-/4	$\frac{21}{64}$	$4\frac{5}{8}$	1/3
$\frac{7}{64}$	$2\frac{7}{8}$	-/5	$\frac{11}{32}$	$4\frac{3}{4}$	1/4
$\frac{1}{8}$	3	-/5	$\frac{23}{64}$	$4\frac{7}{8}$	1/5
$\frac{9}{64}$	$3\frac{1}{8}$	-/6	$\frac{3}{8}$	5	1/6
$\frac{5}{32}$	$3\frac{1}{4}$	-/6	$\frac{25}{64}$	$5\frac{1}{8}$	1/7
$\frac{11}{64}$	$3\frac{3}{8}$	-/7	$\frac{13}{32}$	$5\frac{1}{4}$	1/8
$\frac{3}{16}$	$3\frac{1}{2}$	-/8	$\frac{27}{64}$	$5\frac{3}{8}$	1/10
$\frac{13}{64}$	$3\frac{5}{8}$	-/9	$\frac{7}{16}$	$5\frac{1}{2}$	1/11
$\frac{7}{32}$	$3\frac{3}{4}$	-/9	$\frac{29}{64}$	$5\frac{5}{8}$	2/-
$\frac{15}{64}$	$3\frac{7}{8}$	-/10	$\frac{15}{32}$	$5\frac{3}{4}$	2/1
$\frac{1}{4}$	4	-/11	$\frac{31}{64}$	$5\frac{7}{8}$	2/2
$\frac{17}{64}$	$4\frac{1}{8}$	1/-	$\frac{1}{2}$	6	2/3
$\frac{9}{32}$	$4\frac{1}{4}$	1/1			

STUBS' STEEL WIRE GAUGE STRAIGHT SHANK DRILLS.

Gauge Nos. of the Wire the Drills are made from	Length of Drill.	Price per Drill.	Price per Dozen.
	Inch.		
1 to 5	4 to $3\frac{13}{16}$	9d.	7/10
6 to 10	$3\frac{13}{16}$ to $3\frac{5}{8}$	8d.	7/6
11 to 15	$3\frac{9}{16}$ to $3\frac{7}{16}$	8d.	7/-
16 to 20	$3\frac{3}{8}$ to $3\frac{3}{16}$	7d.	6/6
21 to 25	$3\frac{3}{16}$ to 3	6d.	5/10
26 to 30	$2\frac{15}{16}$ to $2\frac{13}{16}$	6d.	5/2
31 to 35	$2\frac{3}{4}$ to $2\frac{7}{16}$	5d.	4/8
36 to 40	$2\frac{9}{16}$ to $2\frac{3}{8}$	5d.	4/2
41 to 45	$2\frac{5}{16}$ to $2\frac{3}{16}$	4d.	3/8
46 to 60	$2\frac{1}{8}$ to $1\frac{15}{16}$	4d.	3/2
61 to 70	$1\frac{1}{2}$ to $1\frac{5}{16}$	3d.	3/-
71 to 80	$1\frac{5}{16}$ to $\frac{3}{4}$	4d.	3/4

SETS OF DRILLS ON STANDS. Wire Drills.

No. 60 to $\frac{3}{8}$	... 36/3
No. 1 to 60	... 28/6
$\frac{1}{16}$ to $\frac{1}{2} \times \frac{1}{32}$	... 20/8
$\frac{1}{16}$ to $\frac{1}{2} \times \frac{1}{64}$	... 41/4

BIT STOCK DRILLS, for Metal or Wood,

Size ...	... $\frac{1}{16}$	$\frac{5}{64}$	$\frac{3}{32}$	$\frac{7}{64}$	$\frac{1}{8}$	$\frac{9}{64}$	$\frac{5}{32}$	$\frac{11}{64}$	$\frac{3}{16}$	$\frac{13}{64}$	$\frac{7}{32}$	$\frac{15}{64}$	$\frac{1}{4}$	$\frac{17}{64}$	$\frac{9}{32}$	$\frac{19}{64}$	$\frac{5}{16}$	$\frac{21}{64}$	$\frac{11}{32}$	$\frac{23}{64}$	$\frac{3}{8}$	$\frac{13}{32}$	$\frac{7}{16}$	$\frac{15}{32}$	$\frac{1}{2}$ inch.
Length ...	... $3\frac{1}{16}$	$3\frac{11}{16}$	$3\frac{7}{8}$	4	$4\frac{5}{16}$	$4\frac{7}{16}$	$4\frac{9}{16}$	$4\frac{11}{16}$	$4\frac{3}{4}$	$4\frac{7}{8}$	5	$5\frac{1}{8}$	$5\frac{1}{4}$	$5\frac{1}{4}$	$5\frac{3}{8}$	$5\frac{3}{8}$	$5\frac{1}{2}$	$5\frac{1}{2}$	$5\frac{5}{8}$	$5\frac{5}{8}$	$5\frac{7}{8}$	$5\frac{7}{8}$	$6\frac{1}{4}$	$6\frac{5}{8}$	$6\frac{3}{4}$ inch.
Price each ...	6d.	7d.	7d.	8d.	8d.	9d.	9d.	10d.	11d.	1/-	1/-	1/1	1/2	1/3	1/4	1/5	1/6	1/8	1/9	1/11	2/-	2/3	2/6	2/9	3/-
Price per doz.	5/-	5/6	5/6	6/6	7/-	8/4	8/8	9/4	10/4	11/4	12/-	12/8	13/8	14/4	15/8	16/4	18/-	19/-	21/-	22/-	24/-	26/8	29/4	32/-	34/4

TAPER SHANK DRILLS, with Grinding Line.

Diameter of Drills.	Length of Drills.	Price per Drill.	Diameter of Drills.	Length of Drills.	Price per Drill.	Diameter of Drills.	Length of Drills.	Price per Drill.	Diameter of Drills.	Length of Drills.	Price per Drill.	Diameter of Drills.	Length of Drills.	Price per Drill.
Inch	Inch.		Inch.	Inch.		Inch.	Inch.		Inch.	Inch.		Inch.	Inch.	
$\frac{1}{4}$	$6\frac{1}{4}$	2/-	$\frac{5}{8}$	$8\frac{3}{4}$	4/8	$\frac{15}{16}$	$10\frac{3}{4}$	9/2	$1\frac{5}{16}$	$14\frac{1}{4}$	16/-	$2\frac{1}{8}$	17	46/8
$\frac{9}{32}$	$6\frac{1}{4}$	2/2	$\frac{21}{32}$	9	5/-	$\frac{31}{32}$	$10\frac{7}{8}$	9/8	$1\frac{3}{8}$	$14\frac{1}{2}$	17/4	$2\frac{1}{4}$	$17\frac{1}{2}$	53/4
$\frac{5}{16}$	$6\frac{3}{8}$	2/4	$\frac{11}{16}$	$9\frac{1}{4}$	5/4	1	11	10/-	$1\frac{7}{16}$	$14\frac{3}{4}$	18/8	$2\frac{3}{8}$	18	60/-
$\frac{11}{32}$	$6\frac{1}{2}$	2/6	$\frac{23}{32}$	$9\frac{1}{2}$	5/8	$1\frac{1}{16}$	$11\frac{1}{8}$	10/8	$1\frac{1}{2}$	15	22/6	$2\frac{1}{2}$	19	65/-
$\frac{3}{8}$	$6\frac{3}{4}$	2/8	$\frac{3}{4}$	$9\frac{3}{4}$	6/2	$1\frac{1}{16}$	$11\frac{1}{4}$	11/4	$1\frac{9}{16}$	$15\frac{1}{4}$	27/6	$2\frac{5}{8}$	$19\frac{1}{2}$	70/-
$\frac{13}{32}$	7	2/10	$\frac{25}{32}$	$9\frac{7}{8}$	6/8	$1\frac{3}{32}$	$11\frac{1}{2}$	12/-	$1\frac{5}{8}$	$15\frac{1}{2}$	30/-	$2\frac{3}{4}$	$20\frac{1}{2}$	79/2
$\frac{7}{16}$	$7\frac{1}{4}$	3/-	$\frac{13}{16}$	10	7/2	$1\frac{1}{8}$	$11\frac{3}{4}$	12/8	$1\frac{11}{16}$	$15\frac{3}{4}$	32/6	$2\frac{7}{8}$	21	87/6
$\frac{15}{32}$	$7\frac{1}{2}$	3/2	$\frac{27}{32}$	$10\frac{1}{4}$	7/8	$1\frac{5}{32}$	$11\frac{7}{8}$	13/4	$1\frac{3}{4}$	16	35/-	3	22	104/2
$\frac{1}{2}$	$7\frac{3}{4}$	3/4	$\frac{7}{8}$	$10\frac{1}{2}$	8/2	$1\frac{3}{16}$	12	14/-	$1\frac{13}{16}$	$16\frac{1}{4}$	36/8			
$\frac{17}{32}$	8	3/8	$\frac{29}{32}$	$10\frac{5}{8}$	8/8	$1\frac{7}{32}$	$12\frac{1}{4}$	14/8	$1\frac{7}{8}$	$16\frac{1}{2}$	38/4			
$\frac{9}{16}$	$8\frac{1}{4}$	4/-				$1\frac{1}{4}$	$12\frac{1}{2}$	15/-	$1\frac{15}{16}$	$16\frac{1}{2}$	39/7			
$\frac{19}{32}$	$8\frac{1}{2}$	4/4							2	$16\frac{1}{2}$	40/10			

No. 1 Socket, 6/- each.   No. 2 Socket, 7/9 each.   No. 3 Socket, 9/- each.   No. 4 Socket, 11/6 each.   No. 5 Socket, 39/- each.

STEEL SOCKETS, for Taper Shank Drills.

These Sockets save the necessity of fitting the Drills to Machine or Lathe.

For Prices see above.

EDWARD PRESTON & SONS, L^TD.

BRAD AND SADDLERS' PUNCHES, AWLS AND NEEDLES. TRADE MARK.

CAST STEEL BRAD PUNCHES.

No. 724A.

No. 724S.	Round, Square or Oblong, Black, asst'd. ...	17/- per gross
,, 724A.	Best ,, ,, ,, ,, $\frac{1}{16}$ to $\frac{3}{16}$ in.}	22/- ,,
,, 725.	,, ,, ,, ,, ,, Bright	28/- ,,
,, 726.	,, ,, ,, ,, ,, Flooring, Black}	28/- ,,

MILLED BRAD PUNCHES.

No. 724M. Cupped Ends, Asst'd. $\frac{1}{16}$, $\frac{3}{32}$, $\frac{1}{8}$, $\frac{5}{32}$ in. ... 5/6 per dozen.

CHISEL END MARKING AWLS.

No. 728. ... 2/- per dozen.

CAST STEEL STRIKING KNIVES.

No. 729. ... 5/- per dozen.

MILLED CENTRE STRIKING KNIVES.

No. 729M. ... 5/- per dozen.

CAST STEEL HAFTED STRIKING KNIVES.

No. 731. ... 18/0 per dozen.

BEECH HANDLED MARKING AWLS.

No. 732H. ... 4/6 per dozen.

NICKEL PLATED CARPET STRETCHERS.

No. 0682.

		8	10	12 teeth.
No. 0682	.. ..	36/6	42/-	46/6 doz.
,, 0683	Handled	58/-	63/-	68/- ,,
,, 0684	Handled, with Mushroom Head	64/6	70/-	75/6 ,,

LAWYER'S BODKINS.

No. 1571.

No. 1571.	Boxwood Handled ..	8/- per dozen.
,, 1571A.	,, ,, without Eye	8/- ,,

SADDLERS' HOLLOW PUNCHES.

No. 736.

No.	1	2	3	4	5	6	7	8	9	10	11
Size	$\frac{1}{32}$	$\frac{1}{16}$	$\frac{3}{32}$	$\frac{1}{8}$	$\frac{5}{32}$	$\frac{3}{16}$	$\frac{7}{32}$	$\frac{1}{4}$	$\frac{9}{32}$	$\frac{5}{16}$	$1\frac{1}{2}$ inch.
	7/-	7/-	7/-	7/-	7/-	7/-	7/6	8/-	9/-	10/6	13/- per dozen.

No.	12	13	14	15	16	17	18	19	20	21	22
Size	$\frac{3}{8}$	$\frac{7}{16}$	$\frac{1}{2}$	$\frac{9}{16}$	$\frac{5}{8}$	$\frac{11}{16}$	$\frac{3}{4}$	$\frac{13}{16}$	$\frac{7}{8}$	$\frac{15}{16}$	1 inch.
	14/-	16/6	21/-	22/6	26/6	30/6	37/-	42/6	49/-	56/-	60/- per doz.

WAD PUNCHES.

No. 091.

$\frac{5}{8}$	$\frac{3}{4}$	$\frac{13}{16}$	$\frac{7}{8}$	$\frac{15}{16}$	1	$1\frac{1}{8}$	$1\frac{1}{4}$	$1\frac{3}{8}$	$1\frac{1}{2}$	$1\frac{5}{8}$	$1\frac{3}{4}$	$1\frac{7}{8}$	2 inch.
13/-	13/-	19/-	26/-	37/-	42/-	49/-	53/-	68/-	79/-	88/-	118/-	128/-	152/- per doz.

PINKING IRONS.

No. 0740.

		$\frac{1}{2}$	$\frac{5}{8}$	$\frac{3}{4}$	$\frac{7}{8}$	1	$1\frac{1}{8}$	$1\frac{1}{4}$	$1\frac{3}{8}$	$1\frac{1}{2}$ in.
No. 0740.	Half round, V teeth	15/-	16/-	17/-	18/-	19/-	21/-	24/-	27/-	31/- doz.
,, 0741.	,, $\frac{1}{2}$ rd. ,,	15/-	16/-	17/-	18/-	19/-	21/-	24/-	27/-	31/- ,,
,, 0742.	Angular, V teeth	16/-	17/-	19/-	22/-	24/-	27/-	29/-	32/-	36/- ,,
,, 0743.	Straight, V ,,	11/-	12/-	13/-	14/-	15/-	16/-	17/-	18/-	19/- ,,
,, 0744.	,, $\frac{1}{2}$ rd. ,,	11/-	12/-	13/-	14/-	15/-	16/-	17/-	18/-	19/- ,,

BEST CAST STEEL SAIL NEEDLES.

No. 721. Assorted, $2\frac{1}{2}$ to 4 inch ... 12/- per gross.

BEST CAST STEEL BELT AWLS.

	4	$4\frac{1}{2}$	5	$5\frac{1}{2}$	6 inch.
No. 719. ...	14/-	15/-	18/-	21/-	25/- per gross.

BEST CAST STEEL PACKING NEEDLES.

(Forged).

	3	$3\frac{1}{2}$	4	$4\frac{1}{2}$	5	6	7	8	9	10	12 inch.
No. 720.	23/-	24/-	25/-	27/-	30/-	34/-	37/-	48/-	55/-	65/-	75/- per gross.

(Machine Made).

	3	$3\frac{1}{2}$	4	$4\frac{1}{2}$	5	6	7	8 inch.
	14	13	12	11	10	9	8	7 gauge.
No. 720M.	3/-	3/6	4/6	6/-	7/6	10/6	18/-	23/- per gross.

BEST C.S. RUG NEEDLES.

No. 1543.

No. 1543.	Beech Handled, Bent or Straight ...	6/- per dozen.
,, 1543B.	Brown's Pattern Rug Needles ...	8/- ,,

BEST CAST STEEL FORGED UPHOLSTERERS' NEEDLES.

No. 722.

		6	7	8	9	10	12 inch.
No. 722.	... ...	2/6	3/-	3/9	4/6	5/-	5/6 per dozen.
,, 722M.	Machine made ...	1/8	1/9	1/10	2/-	2/3	2/9 ,,

UPHOLSTERERS' REGULATORS.

No. 722R. Assorted, 6 to 12 inch ... 4/6 per dozen.

EDWARD PRESTON & SONS, LTD.

GLAZIERS', PAINTERS' and PAPERHANGERS' TOOLS. TRADE MARK.

No. 1914. PUTTY KNIFE, SPEAR POINT.

	4	4½	5	5½	6 in.	
No. 1914 Cocoa Handled, no Ferrule ...	9/-	9/6	10/-	11/6	12/6	doz.
,, 1915 ,, ,, Brass ,, ...	11/6	12/-	13/-	14/-	15/6	,,
,, 1915E Ebony ,, ,, ,, ...	12/-	12/6	14/-	15/-	16/6	,,

No. 1915B. PUTTY KNIFE, CLIPT POINT.

	4	4½	5	5½	6 in.	
No. 1914A Cocoa Handled, no Ferrule ...	9/-	9/6	10/6	12/-	13/6	doz.
,, 1915A ,, ,, Brass ,, ...	11/6	12/-	13/-	14/-	15/6	,,
,, 1915B Ebony ,, ,, ,, ...	12/-	12/6	14/-	15/-	16/6	,,

No. 1915C. PUTTY KNIFE, CHISEL POINT.

	4	4½	5	5½	6 in.	
No. 1914C Cocoa Handled, no Ferrule ...	9/-	9/6	10/-	12/-	13/6	doz.
,, 1915C ,, ,, Brass ,, ...	11/6	12/-	13/-	14/-	15/6	,,
,, 1915D Ebony ,, ,, ,, ...	12/-	12/6	14/-	15/-	16/6	,,

No. 1918. FRENCH CHISEL KNIFE.

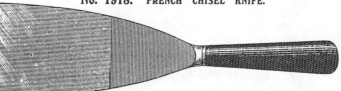

	2	2½	3	3½	4 in.	
No. 1917 Beech Handled, no Ferrule ...	—	7/-	—	—	—	doz.
,, 1918 Cocoa Handled, Ferruled ...	14/-	15/6	17/-	—	—	,,
,, 1919 Ebony ,, ,, ...	16/-	17/6	19/-	21/6	25/-	,,

PAPER HANGERS' SCRAPERS.

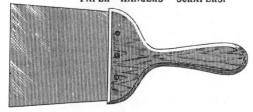

No. 1920 Beech Handled, 3½ in. Blade ... ... 9/- doz.

PAPER HANGERS' ROLLERS.

	1½	2	2½	3 in.	
No. 168 Beechwood Rollers	1/6	1/10	2/3	2/8	each.
,, 169 Brass Rollers	3/-	3/4	3/8	4/2	,,

No. 1913. HACKING KNIFE.

No. 1912 Leather Handle, 2 Rivets, Blades 4 in. ... ... 10/- doz.
,, 1913 ,, ,, 3 ,, ,, 4½ in. ... ... 12/- ,,

No. 1916. PALLETTE KNIFE.

No. 1916 Cocoa Handled, no Ferrule—

4	5	6	7	8	9	10	11	12 in.
7/6	9/6	11/-	14/6	19/-	24/-	31/-	37/-	46/- doz.

,, 1916B Balance Handles—

4	5	6	7	8	9	10	11	12 in.
9/6	11/-	14/-	18/-	21/6	27/-	36/6	42/-	54/- ,,

GLAZIERS' HAMMERS.

No. 0552. Chequered Face .. .. 31/6 doz.

GLASS CUTTERS.

No. 1536 Iron Handle ... ... 8/- doz.
No. 1541 Wood Handle ... ... 8/6 doz.
,, 1541R ,, ,, Best ... ... 16/- ,,

GLAZIERS' DIAMONDS.

	No. 1, for 16 oz.	No. 2, for 21 oz.
No. 1921 Crown or Sheet Glass	15/-	19/6 each.
	No. 4, for 26 oz.	No. 5, for 32 oz.
,, 1922 Strong ,, ,, ...	29/-	37/- each.
,, 1923 Light Plate Glass, to cut $\frac{3}{16}$ in. ... ... 46/- ,,
,, 1924 Heavy ,, ,, ,, $\frac{3}{8}$ in. ... ... 50/- ,,

GRAINING COMBS.

No. 170 4, 6, 9, 12 Teeth to the inch. 1/6 per doz. inches.
,, 171 15, 16 Teeth to the in., 2/- doz. in.
,, 172 Graduated ditto 2/- ,,
,, 173 Set of 12, in Paper Case, 3/3 set.
,, 174 ,, ,, Tin ,, 3/9 ,,

GLASS PLIERS.

	6	7	8	9 in.
No. 1925 Best Black	25/-	32/-	40/-	57/6 doz.

EDWARD PRESTON & SONS, L^{TD}.

HAMMERS.

CAST STEEL JOINERS' HAMMERS.

	1	2	3	4	5	6	7	8	9	10	
No. 1760	13/-	14/-	15/-	17/-	19/-	22/-	25/-	28/-	31/-	34/-	doz.

RIVETTING OR EXETER HAMMERS.

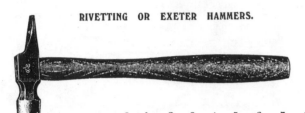

	0	1	2	3	4	5	6	7	8	
No. 1771C	11/-	12/-	14/-	16/6	19/6	22/-	25/-	29/-	32/6	doz.
,, 1771 Best ...	14/-	15/-	17/-	20/-	24/-	27/-	30/-	34/-	38/-	,,

BRIGHT KENT HAMMERS.

	0	1	2	3	4	5	6	7	8	
No. 1769	9/6	11/6	14/-	17/6	19/6	22/-	26/-	30/-	35/-	doz.

BEST SOLID KENT HAMMERS.

	0	1	2	3	4	5	6	7	8	
No. 1770	15/-	17/6	21/-	24/6	28/-	31/6	35/-	40/6	45/6	doz.

BEST CANTERBURY HAMMERS.

	0	1	2	3	4	5	6	7	8	
No. 1768	18/-	21/6	24/6	28/-	31/-	34/6	37/6	42/6	48/-	doz.

PATTERN MAKERS' FLAT PANE HAMMERS.

	Heads 4	6	8 ozs.	
No. 1764	20/-	22/-	24/-	doz.

PATTERN MAKERS' BALL PANE HAMMERS.

	Heads 4	6	8 ozs.	
No. 1766	20/-	22/-	24/-	doz.

LONDON UPHOLSTERERS' HAMMERS.

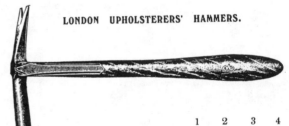

		1	2	3	4	
No. 1785 Oval Beech Handled	...	28/-	31/6	36/-	41/-	doz.
,, 1785C Round Ash Handled	...	24/6	28/-	31/6	35/-	,,
,, 1785R Ringed Handled ...	...	30/-	33/6	38/6	44/-	,,

BEST BENWELL'S UPHOLSTERERS' HAMMERS.

Oval Beech Handled.

	1	2	3	4	
No. 1793	36/-	41/-	46/-	51/-	doz.

UPHOLSTERERS' CABRIOLET HAMMERS.

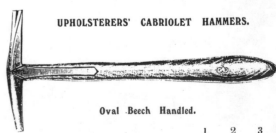

Oval Beech Handled.

	1	2	3	
No. 1794	28/-	31/6	36/-	doz.

EDWARD PRESTON & SONS, LᵀᴰD.

HAMMERS.

LATH HAMMERS.

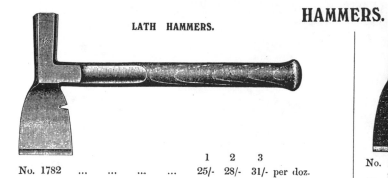

	1	2	3
No. 1782	25/-	28/-	31/- per doz.

BEST COAL HAMMERS.

Wrought Steel Face and Point.

	1	2	3	4
No. 1787	19/-	21/6	24/-	27/6 per doz.

SCOTCH CLAW HAMMERS.

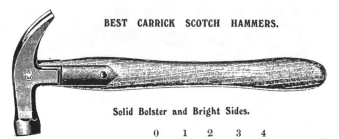

	0	1	2	3	4
No. 1783S	38/-	39/-	43/-	48/-	55/- per doz.

BEST CARRICK SCOTCH HAMMERS.

Solid Bolster and Bright Sides.

	0	1	2	3	4
No. 1783	41/-	44/-	49/-	54/-	60/- per doz.

CASE MAKERS' CLAW SPIKE HAMMERS.

No. 1783A Heads only, 16 oz., 5/- 46/- per doz.
„ 1783B Handled ... 5/- 52/- „

SOLID CAST STEEL ENGINEERS' HAMMER HEADS.

½, ¾ and 1 lb. weight, 12/- per doz.
1¼ lb. and above, 1/- per lb.

8   23   22

IRON HANDLED GROCERS' HAMMERS.

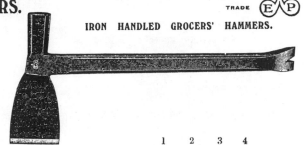

	1	2	3	4
No. 1784 Best	45/-	52/-	58/-	66/- per doz.
„ 1784C	38/-	44/-	49/-	56/- „

LADIES' TACK HAMMERS.

No. 0368 Nickel Plated	9/6 per doz.
„ 0468 Black	7/- „

No. 0370 Nickel Plated	12/6 per doz.
„ 0470 Bright	10/6 „
„ 0380 Ladies' Tack Hammers, Nickel Plated Assorted Patterns	15/- „

GENTS' BEST CLAW HAMMERS.

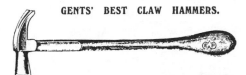

	1	2	3
No. 0551	24/-	27/-	31/- per doz.

MANCHESTER SPIKE HAMMERS.

	5	6	7
No. 1783M Handled	34/-	40/-	44/- per doz.
„ 1783O Heads	31/-	34/-	40/- „

ADZE EYE HAMMERS.

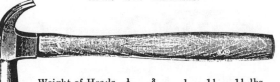

Weight of Heads	½	¾	1	1¼	1½ lbs.
	1	2	3	4	5
No. 1761	24/-	28/6	33/-	38/-	42/- per doz.

EDWARD PRESTON & SONS, LTD.

PINCERS, PLIERS and COMPASSES.

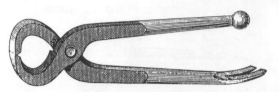

BEST TOWER PINCERS.

	6	6½	7	7½	8	8½	9	9½	10 in.	
No. 0570 ...	12/-	13/6	15/-	18/-	21/-	24/-	27/-	30/-	33/-	per doz.
,, *056 ..	9/6	10/6	12/-	13/6	15/6	—	—	—	—	,,

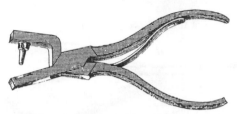

SHOE PUNCH PLIERS.

		6	6½	7 in.	
No. 0887	With any size Punch, 0 to 10	23/-	25/-	28/-	per doz.
,, 0889	Extra Punches, 0 to 10, 3/8 ... 00 000, 5/6 per doz				

IMPROVED BLACK TOWER GAS PLIERS.

		6	7	8	9	10 in.	
No. 0944	Best Cast Steel ...	30/-	34/-	41/-	48/-	58/-	per doz.
,, *0230	Solid Steel ...	21/-	25/-	30/-	38/-	46/-	,,

PLAIN BLACK COMPASSES.

		4	5	6	7	8	9	10 in.	
No. 0633	Best Black Plain Compasses ...	17/6	20/-	24/6	28/-	33/-	36/-	46/-	doz.
,, *2260	Black Plain do.	12/6	12/6	15/-	17/-	20/-	25/-	29/-	,,

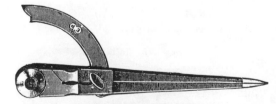

BLACK WING COMPASSES.

		5	6	7	8	9	10	12 in.	
No. 0635	Best Black Wing Compasses ...	28/-	31/-	36/-	41/-	48/-	54/-	70/-	doz.
,, *2265	Black Wing do.	20/-	24/-	28/-	32/-	36/-	42/-	60/-	,,

BEST BLACK LANCASHIRE PATTERN PINCERS.

		6	7	8	9	10 in.	
No. 0285	... ...	31/-	36/-	42/-	55/-	61/-	per doz.

No 0853L.

BEST TOWER CUTTING NIPPERS.

	6	6½	7	7½	8	8½	9	10 in.	
No. 0853	18/-	20/-	23/6	27/6	32/-	36/-	42/-	56/-	per doz.
No. 0853L	24/-		30/6		37/-		47/-	58/-	,, ,,

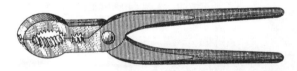

TOWER GAS PLIERS.

	6	7	8	9	10	11	12 in.	
No 0650A ..	24/	27/3	30/9	36/3	43/6	51/-	46/6	per doz.

No. 020.

TINMEN'S SNIPS.

		6	7	8	9	10	11	12 inch.	
No. 020.	Best ...	18/-	21/-	25/-	27/-	31/-	38/-	42/-	per doz.

No. 020B

TINMEN'S SNIPS.

		7	8	9	10	11	12 inch.	
No. 020B.	Best Bent Blades	28/-	36/-	40/-	45/-	50/-	54/-	per doz.

* IMPORTED.

EDWARD PRESTON & SONS, L^{TD.}

PLIERS and NIPPERS.

TRADE 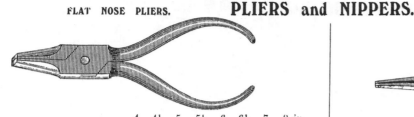 MARK.

FLAT NOSE PLIERS.

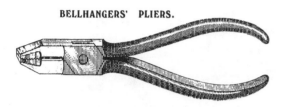

	4	4½	5	5½	6	6½	7	8 in.
No. 0161 Best Flat Nose Pliers, Black	18/-	18/-	18/-	21/-	27/-	36/-	42/-	60/- doz.
,, 0162 Best Round Nose Pliers, Black								
,, *2230 Black Flat Nose Pliers	7/6	7/6	7/6	8/9	10/-	12/-	14/6	— ,,
,, *2231 ,, Round ,, ,,								
,, *2230B Bright Flat ,, ,,	8/-	8/-	8/-	9/6	11/3	12/9	15/6	— ,,
,, *2231B ,, Round ,, ,,								

BELLHANGERS' PLIERS.

	5	5½	6	6½	7	8 in.
No. 0153 Best Bellhangers' Cutting Pliers, Black	30/-	30/-	33/-	42/-	54/-	72/- per doz.
,, *2238 Black Cutting Pliers	15/6	16/9	19/-	21/6	24/6	— ,,

ELECTRICIANS' PLIERS.

	5	5½	6	6½	7	8 in.
No. 2115 Best Black Electricians' Pliers	24/-	24/9	25/6	30/-	33/-	40/- per doz.
,, *2253 Black Electricians' Pliers	18/6	20/6	22/6	25/6	27/-	32/- ,,

ELECTRICIANS' PLIERS.

	6	7	8 in.
No. *2254 Combination Electricians' Pliers, with Insulated Handles	52/-	60/-	68/- per doz.

BURNER PLIERS.

No. 1078 Best Black Burner Pliers, 1 Hole, 6 in. ... 39/- per doz.

,, *2302 Bright Burner Pliers, 1 Hole ... ... 14/- ,,

PENDULUM PLIERS.

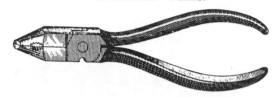

	4	4½	5 in.
No. 0159 Best Bright Pendulum Pliers	21/-	21/6	22/6 per doz.
,, *2236 Bright Pendulum Pliers	13/6	13/6	13/6 ,,

BELLHANGERS' PLIERS.

No. 096 Best Black Improved Bell Pliers, with Half Round Nose, Side Cutter and Burner Hole, 6 in. ... ... 35/- per doz.

,, *2255 Black Improved Bell Pliers, with Half Round Nose, Side Cutter and Burner Hole, 6 in. 20/- ,,

ELECTRICIANS' PLIERS.

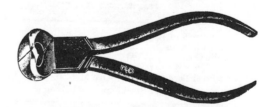

	6	7	8	9	10 in.
No. *2256 Combination Electricians' Pliers	24/-	27/6	31/6	38/6	44/- per doz.

CUTTING NIPPERS.

	4½	5	5½	6	6½	7	8 in.
No. 0505 Best Black Cutting Nippers	—	33/6	37/-	45/-	55/-	61/-	80/- per doz.
,, *2241 Black Cutting do.	22/-	22/-	24/-	26/6	30/9	34/3	45/- ,,

BURNER PLIERS.

No. 1076 Best Bright Burner Pliers, 2 Hole, 5 in. ... 39/- per doz.

,, *2301 Bright Burner Pliers, 2 Hole, 5 in. ... ... 17/6 ,,

* IMPORTED.

EDWARD PRESTON & SONS, L^{TD}.

CRAMPS.

TRADE 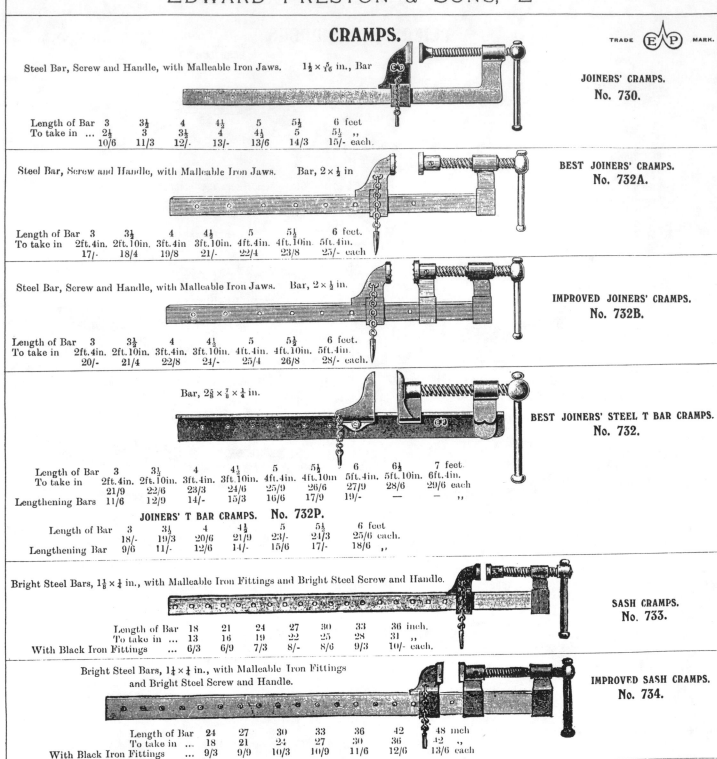 MARK.

Steel Bar, Screw and Handle, with Malleable Iron Jaws. $1\frac{1}{2} \times \frac{5}{16}$ in., Bar

JOINERS' CRAMPS.
No. 730.

Length of Bar	3	3½	4	4½	5	5½	6 feet
To take in ...	2½	3	3½	4	4½	5	5½ ,,
		10/6	11/3	12/.	13/-	13/6	14/3	15/- each.

Steel Bar, Screw and Handle, with Malleable Iron Jaws. Bar, $2 \times \frac{1}{2}$ in

BEST JOINERS' CRAMPS.
No. 732A.

Length of Bar	3	3½	4	4½	5	5½	6 feet.
To take in	2ft.4in.	2ft.10in.	3ft.4in	3ft.10in.	4ft.4in.	4ft.10in.	5ft.4in.
	17/-	18/4	19/8	21/-	22/4	23/8	25/- each

Steel Bar, Screw and Handle, with Malleable Iron Jaws. Bar, $2 \times \frac{1}{2}$ in.

IMPROVED JOINERS' CRAMPS.
No. 732B.

Length of Bar	3	3½	4	4½	5	5½	6 feet.
To take in	2ft.4in.	2ft.10in.	3ft.4in.	3ft.10in.	4ft.4in.	4ft.10in.	5ft.4in.
	20/-	21/4	22/8	24/-	25/4	26/8	28/- each.

Bar, $2\frac{5}{8} \times \frac{7}{8} \times \frac{1}{4}$ in.

BEST JOINERS' STEEL T BAR CRAMPS.
No. 732.

Length of Bar	3	3½	4	4½	5	5½	6	6½	7 feet.
To take in	2ft.4in.	2ft.10in.	3ft.4in.	3ft.10in.	4ft.4in.	4ft.10in	5ft.4in.	5ft.10in.	6ft.4in.
	21/9	22/6	23/3	24/6	25/9	26/6	27/9	28/6	29/6 each
Lengthening Bars	11/6	12/9	14/-	15/3	16/6	17/9	19/-	—	— ,,

JOINERS' T BAR CRAMPS.   No. 732P.

Length of Bar	3	3½	4	4½	5	5½	6 feet
	18/-	19/3	20/6	21/9	23/-	24/3	25/6 each.
Lengthening Bar	9/6	11/-	12/6	14/-	15/6	17/-	18/6 ,,

Bright Steel Bars, $1\frac{1}{8} \times \frac{1}{4}$ in., with Malleable Iron Fittings and Bright Steel Screw and Handle.

SASH CRAMPS.
No. 733.

Length of Bar	18	21	24	27	30	33	36 inch.
To take in ...	13	16	19	22	25	28	31 ,,
With Black Iron Fittings ...	6/3	6/9	7/3	8/-	8/6	9/3	10/- each.

Bright Steel Bars, $1\frac{1}{4} \times \frac{1}{4}$ in., with Malleable Iron Fittings and Bright Steel Screw and Handle.

IMPROVED SASH CRAMPS.
No. 734.

Length of Bar	24	27	30	33	36	42	48 inch
To take in ...	18	21	24	27	30	36	42 ,,
With Black Iron Fittings ...	9/3	9/9	10/3	10/9	11/6	12/6	13/6 each

FLOORING CRAMPS.

(Bissell Pattern).
Wrought Iron Screws.

No. 1793, Cast Bodies for Joists,
2" to 4½in. ... ...} 20/- each.

,, 1794 Malleable ditto ... 27/- ,,

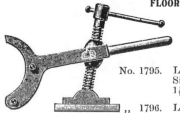

FLOORING CRAMPS. No. 1795.

Wrought Iron.

No. 1795. Light, Common Finish,
Single Prong for Joists,
1½ to 3½ inch ... ...} 25/- per pair.

,, 1796. Light, Common Finish
Double Prong for Joists,
1½ to 3½ inch ... ...} 15/- each

EDWARD PRESTON & SONS, LTD.

CRAMPS, BENCH SCREWS and HOLDFASTS.

No. 1527.

G CRAMPS. No. 1527.

Malleable Iron with Wrought Screw.

To take in	2	3	4	5	6	7	8 inch.
	2/2	2/6	2/10	3/4	4/2	5/2	6/6 each.

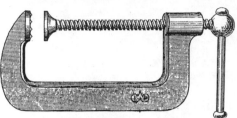

No. 1527B.

RIBBED G CRAMPS, with Vice Handle. No. 1527B.

Malleable Iron, with Wrought Screw.

To take in	4	5	6	7	8	10	12 inch.
	4/4	5/-	5/9	6/6	7/6	9/3	10/9 each.

No. 1527C.

STRONG G CRAMPS. No. 1527C.

Wrought Iron, with Vice Handle.

To take in	...	...	5	6	7	8	10	12 inch.
Diameter of Screw	...	...	$\frac{5}{8}$	$1\frac{1}{8}$	$\frac{3}{4}$	$\frac{7}{8}$	$\frac{7}{8}$	$1\frac{1}{8}$,,
			7/6	8/6	10/-	11/6	13/6	16/- each.

No. 1528.

JAPANNED CRAMPS FOR FRETWORKERS. No. 1528.

	$2\frac{1}{2}$	$3\frac{1}{2}$ inch.
	3/9	5/6 dozen.

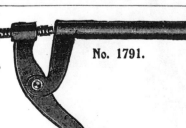

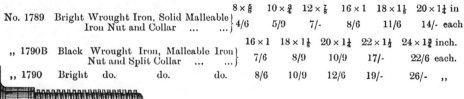

No. 1790.

CARPENTERS' BENCH SCREWS. No. 1790.

		$8 \times \frac{5}{8}$	$10 \times \frac{3}{4}$	$12 \times \frac{7}{8}$	16×1	$18 \times 1\frac{1}{8}$	$20 \times 1\frac{1}{4}$ in
No. 1789	Bright Wrought Iron, Solid Malleable Iron Nut and Collar	4/6	5/9	7/-	8/6	11/6	14/- each
		16×1	$18 \times 1\frac{1}{8}$	$20 \times 1\frac{1}{4}$	$22 \times 1\frac{1}{2}$	$24 \times 1\frac{3}{4}$ inch.	
,, 1790B	Black Wrought Iron, Malleable Iron Nut and Split Collar	7/6	8/9	10/9	17/-	22/6 each.	
,, 1790	Bright do. do. do.	8/6	10/9	12/6	19/-	26/- ,,	

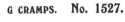

No. 1791.

BENCH HOLDFASTS. No. 1791.

Wrought Iron Pillar, Screw and Handle, with Malleable Iron Shoe and Arm.

No....	...	0	1	2	3	4
Size of Stem		$10 \times \frac{3}{4}$	$12 \times \frac{7}{8}$	14×1	$16 \times 1\frac{1}{8}$	$18 \times 1\frac{1}{4}$ in.
		6/3	7/-	8/6	10/-	12/6 each.

EDWARD PRESTON & SONS, LTD.

OIL CANS.

TRADE MARK.

No. 1804.

No. 1804A.

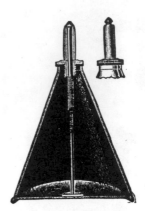

No. 1812.

No. 1810.

BENCH OIL CANS.

No. 1802 Small Tin Bottoms	...	5/- per doz.
,, 1804 ,, Brass ,,	...	6/6 ,,
,, 1804A ,, ,, ,, with Extra Large Filler	...	7/6 ,,
,, 1806 Large Tin ,,	...	7/- ,,
,, 1808 ,, Brass ,,	...	8/6 ,,
,, 1808A ,, ,, ,, with Extra Large Filler	...	9/6 ,,
,, 1812 Patent Leak-proof Brass Bottoms ..	...	9/6 ,,
,, 1810 Sewing Machine, with Long Spout	...	6/- ,,

No. 1508.

No. 1508 Bicycle Oil Can ... ... 4/- per doz.

OIL FEEDERS.

	¼	½	¾	1 pint.
No. 1813 With Patent Save All Filler	10/-	10/6	11/6	13/- per doz.
,, 1813A with "Copper" Spout ,,		11/6	12/-	13/- 14/6 ,,

No. 1968
MITRE CUTTING MACHINE.

No. 1   2
To Cut Mouldings up to 2 in., 4 in.
19/6   34/- each.

No. 1968A
"IMPERIAL"
MITRE CUTTING MACHINE.

No. 1   2
To Cut Mouldings up to 2⅛ in., 4¼ in.
21/-   36/- each.

EDWARD PRESTON & SONS, L^{TD.}

SCREW BOXES, SCRIBES, GRINDSTONES, Etc.

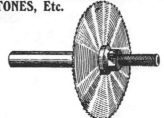

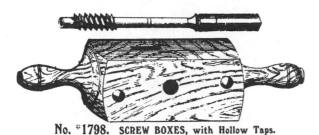

No. 1797. SCREW BOXES, with Solid Taps.

½	⅝	¾	⅞	1	1⅛	1¼	1⅜	1½	1⅝	1¾	2	2¼	2½ inch.
5/-	5/-	5/6	6/3	7/-	7/9	8/6	9/-	11/3	12/6	14/-	18/3	24/-	29/6 each.

No. *1798. SCREW BOXES, with Hollow Taps.

½	⅝	¾	⅞	1	1⅛	1¼	1⅜	1½	1⅝	1¾	2 inch.
2/8	3/-	3/3	3/9	4/-	4/9	5/6	6/6	7/9	9/6	10/9	12/9 each.

TIMBER SCRIBES.

No. 0814. Beech Handled .. .. 18/- per dozen.
,, 0815. Rosewood Handled ... ... 24/- ,,

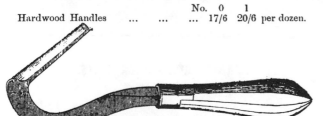

No. 0708. BEST CAST STEEL TIMBER SCRIBES.

	No. 0	1
Hardwood Handles	17/6	20/6 per dozen.

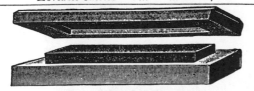

No. 0838. IMPROVED TIMBER SCRIBES.

Octagon Handle, with 3 Swan Neck Scribes, } ... 8/6 each.
Moveable Cutters ... ... }

No. 1964. SAW AND EMERY WHEEL SPINDLES.

	No. 1	2	3	4	5
Size	5 × ⁵⁄₁₆	5 × ⅜	6 × ½	7 × ⅝	8 × ¾ inch.
Spindles only...	3/-	3/6	5/-	6/-	8/- each.
Saws for ditto	3/-	3/6	4/6	5/6	7/6 ,,
Size of Saw ...	3	4	5	6	8 inch.

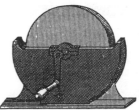

No. 1965. MOUNTED BEST GRINDSTONES,
In Low Iron Stand and Frame.

Diameter of Stone	6 × 1½	8 × 1½	10 × 2	12 × 2	14 × 2½	16 × 3 in.
		9/-	11/-	14/3	18/3	22/-	27/3 each.
No. 1965H. With Hood	11/9	14/3	17/6	21/6	26/-	32/6 ,,

Grindstones Mounted ; High Stands for foot power,
Prices on application.

No. 1961. COOPERS' STOCKED DRIVERS.

40/6 per dozen.

No. 1962. COOPERS' VICES.

No. 1	2
10/6	13/- per dozen.

No. 1963. COOPERS' CROZE IRONS.

1¼	1½ inch.
21/-	21/6 per dozen.

STOCKED OIL STONES.

Length of Stone	6	7	8	9 inch.
No. 742. *Washita in Polished Wood Stock	45/-	50/-	54/-	62/- per dozen.
,, 743. *Canadian in Plain Wood Stock ...	—	—	45/-	— ,,

OIL STONES.

No 744. *Washita No. 1	...	...	...	...	2/2 per lb.
,, 743. *Canadian ...	...	...	...	7d. ,,
,, 745. Charnley Forrest ...	...	...	...	1/- ,,
,, 746. Turkey ...	...	...	...	2/4 ,,

*Washita Slips ... ... 3/6 per lb.

Charnley Forrest Slips ... ... 5/6 per dozen.

*IMPORTED.

EDWARD PRESTON & SONS, L^TD.

HACK SAW FRAMES, METAL SAWS AND ARCHIMEDIAN DRILLS.

HACK SAW FRAMES.
~~NICKEL PLATED.~~

	8	10	12 inch.
No. *2305.	44/-	45/-	46/- per dozen.

EXTENSION HACK SAW FRAMES.
NICKEL PLATED.

No. *2306. Adjustable, 8 to 12 inch ... . 24/- per dozen.

EXTENSION HACK SAW FRAMES.
~~NICKEL PLATED.~~

No. *2307. Adjustable, 8 to 12 inch .. .. 50/- per dozen.

EXTENSION HACK SAW FRAMES.
~~NICKEL PLATED.~~

No. *2308. Adjustable, 8 to 12 inch ... ... 64/- per dozen.

HACK SAW BLADES.

	8	9	10	11	12 inch
No. 2309.	32/9	34/-	39/-	43/6	46/- per gross.

PIERCING SAW FRAMES.

	6 × 2	7 × 2½ inch.
No. *1840.	27/-	29/6 per dozen,

FANCY BRASS BACK SAWS.
FOR METAL.

No. 1841. 4½ inch ... ... 12/- per dozen.

ARCHIMEDIAN DRILLS.
Wood Handle and Head and Screw Top with 6 Drills.

No. *2272. .. .. 13/- per dozen.

ARCHIMEDIAN DRILLS.
Wood Handle and Head and Screw Top with 6 Drills.

	6	7	8	9	10	12	14 inch.
No. *2271S. ..	19/-	21/6	23/-	24/6	27/6	29/-	34/- per dozen.

*IMPORTED.

VICES.

TRADE MARK.

BEST BRIGHT STEEL TAIL VICES.

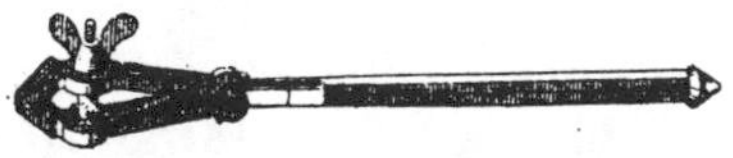

No. *2213. Solid Stem ... ... 2/9 each.
,, *2214. Hollow Stem ... ... 3/3 ,,

HANDLED HAND VICES.

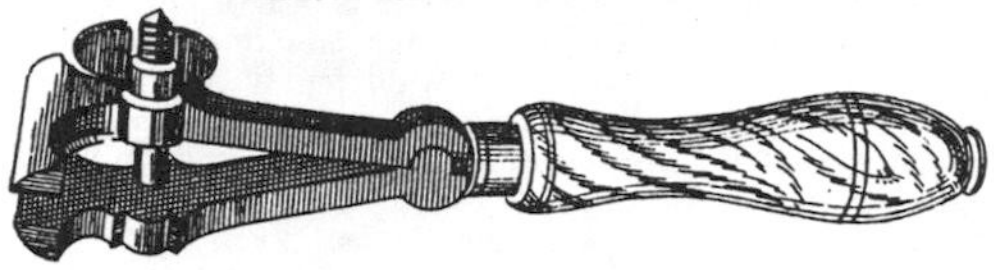

No. *2212 ... ... 3/9 each

WROUGHT HAND VICE, Steeled Jaws.

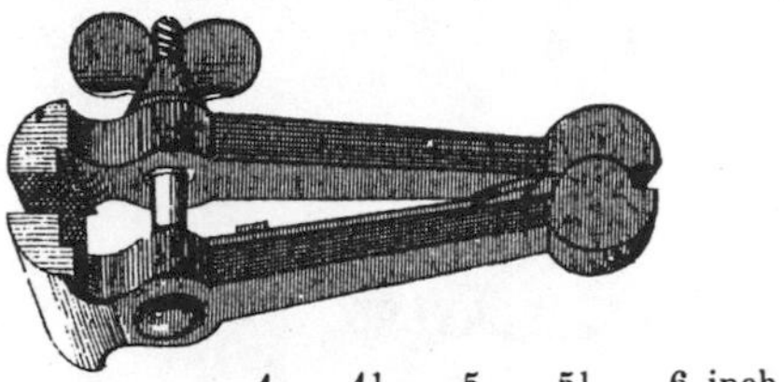

	4	4½	5	5½	6 inch.
No. *2210.	30/-	30/-	37/-	43/6	54/- per dozen.

WROUGHT BENCH VICE, Steeled Jaws,
WITH ANVIL.

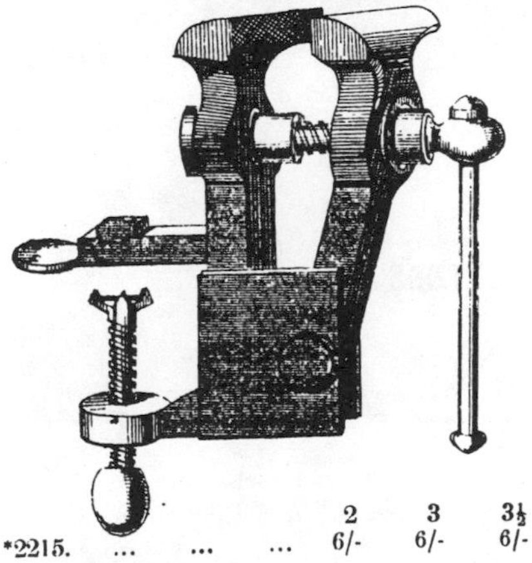

	2	3	3½	4 lbs.
No. *2215.	6/-	6/-	6/-	6/- each.

WROUGHT PARALLEL VICE.

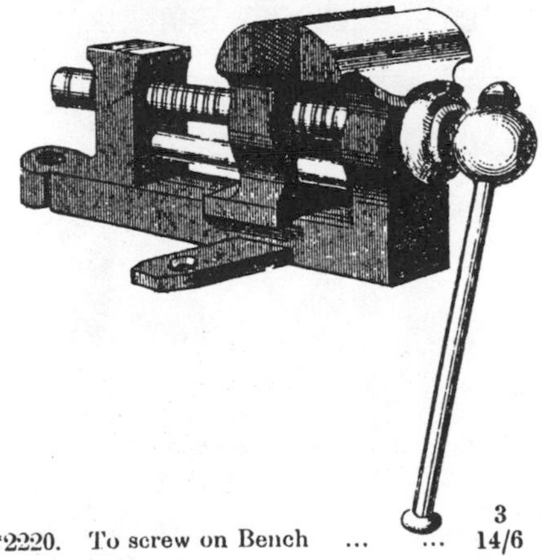

	3	4 lbs.
No. *2220. To screw on Bench	14/6	14/6 each.

* IMPORTED.

SLIDING TONGS.

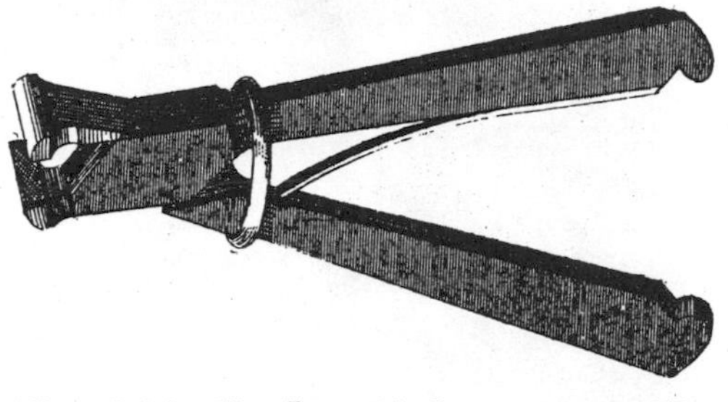

No. *2279. Bright, Vice Jaws, 5 inch ... ... 3/3 each.

No. 1967. IMPROVED PARALLEL VICE.

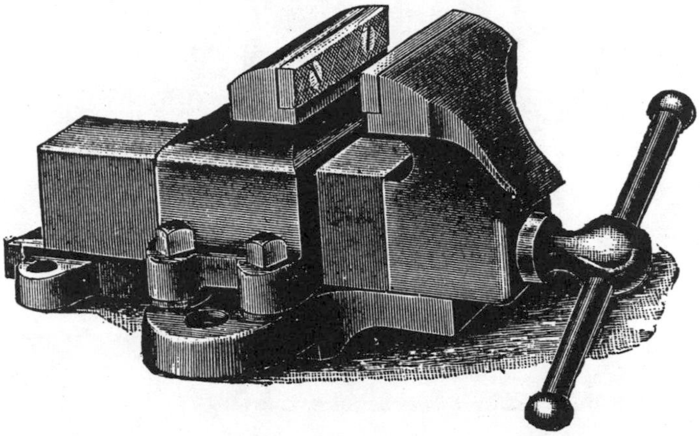

Made of Best Cast Iron, with Steel Jaws.

No. 00.	Opens 2 in.,	width of Jaw, 2¼ in. ...	8/9 each.
,, 0.	,, 2¾ ,,	,, ,, 2½ ,, ..	10/6 ,,
,, 1.	,, 3¼ ,,	,, ,, 3 ,, ...	12/- ,,
,, 2.	,, 4 ,,	,, ,, 3½ ,, ..	19/- ,,
,, 3.	,, 4¾ ,,	,, ,, 4 ,, ...	26/- ,,
,, 4.	,, 5½ ,,	,, ,, 4½ ,, ..	36/- ,,
,, 5.	,, 6¼ ,,	,, ,, 5 ,, ...	48/- ,,
,, 6	,, 7¼ ,,	,, ,, 6 ,, ..	69/- ,,

No. 1989. WOOD WORKER'S VICE.
INSTANTANEOUS JAWS.

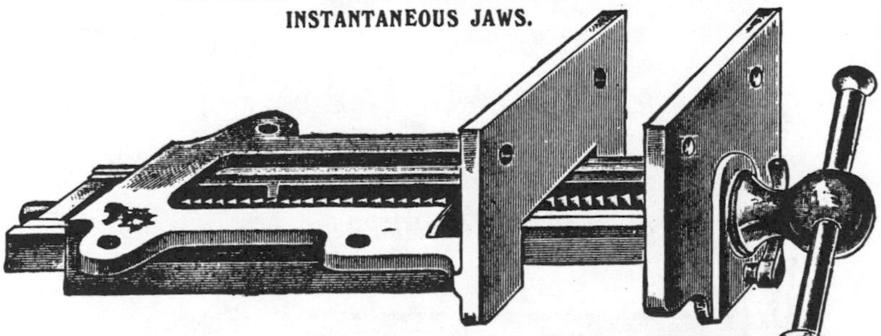

Body and Jaws of Best Cast Iron, Malleable Iron Box, Steel Hardened Nut and Steel Screw and Handle.

Width of Jaw.	Extent of Opening.	Approximate Weight.	Price.
7 inch	7 inch	20 lbs.	18/- each.
10 ,,	14 ,,	36 ,,	27/6 ,,

These Vices are made so as to obtain the requisite strength where the greatest strain occurs. The nut is hardened, thus increasing its durability and lessening friction.

The disengaging bar is in a durable holder, and a short spiral spring is used, which gives a direct pull on the bar.

The working side of the screw and nut is cut at a slight angle *inwards*, and secures them so they do not depend entirely on the pressure put upon the disengaging bar.

Edward Preston & Sons, L<u>TD</u>.

SLATERS' TOOLS.

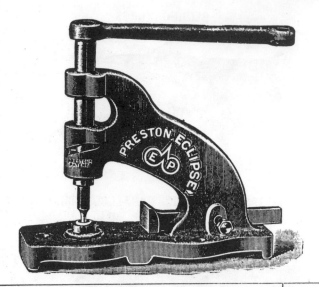

PRESTON'S "ECLIPSE"
SLATE PIERCING AND COUNTERSINKING MACHINE.

No. 1 ... 28/- each.

DRAWING QUARTER SIZE.

This Machine has great advantages over the old kind of Slate-Drilling Machines, it pierces and countersinks the hole under one operation, and is therefore quicker in work. The hole pierced is perfectly round; also the Punches and Handles are more readily removed, enabling the operator to take away the loose parts, viz:—The Handle and Punch, thus leaving the base of the press secured to the bench ready for use when next required. One end of the handle, also, is arranged to be used as a Wrench in conjunction with the Nuts which secure the Adjusting Fence, it will therefore be seen that no extra wrench is required. The Punches are made of Hardened and Tempered Steel of Best Quality, new ones may be obtained when required. The machine is well got up, being coated with Metallic Paint, which protects the Iron from rust, etc.

The Machine should not be used until it is securely screwed down.

SLATERS' HAMMERS.

EYED, WITH CLAW.

No. 1786C. ... 45/- per dozen.

BEST SLATERS' HAMMERS.

WITH CLAW.

	1	2	3
No. 1786. ...	42/-	45/-	49/- per dozen.

SLATERS' HATCHETS.

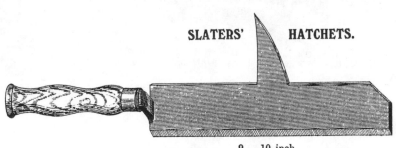

	9	10 inch.
No. 0568. ...	44/-	49/- per dozen.

SLATERS' RIPPERS.

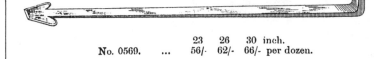

	23	26	30 inch.
No. 0569. ...	56/-	62/-	66/- per dozen.

SLATERS' DRESSING IRONS.

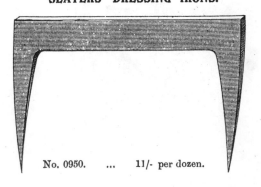

No. 0950. ... 11/- per dozen.

EDWARD PRESTON & SONS, L^{TD}.

PRESTON'S PATENT WEED EXTRACTOR.

Length 33-in. Overall.   Weight 1¼-lbs.

A simple and effective implement for ridding Lawns, Bowling Greens, etc., from Dandelions, Daisy Roots, etc.

May be had with Straight or Crutch Handles.

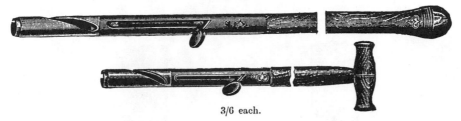

3/6 each.

INSTRUCTIONS.—Place the cutting edge of barrel over the centre of the root or weed and with a downward pressure giving at the same time a turn of the wrist. Upon withdrawing the cutter from the lawn, a plug of soil, together with the root or weed, will be found in the barrel ; remove this by means of the plunger, withdraw the weed from the plug of soil, and the plug may then be replaced in the ground, so filling up the hole made by the implement.

TOOL GRINDING REST.

No. 812

Malleable Iron, Japanned, Wrought Iron Screw with Brass Head.

1/6 each.

To take in 2⅝ × ⅜

PRESTON'S REGISTERED BROOM HANDLE TRIMMER.

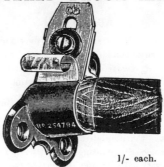

1/- each.

With the aid of this Tool, Broom and other similar handles can be fitted with great ease and rapidity.

For Ironmongers and Dealers who are in the habit of fitting the Handles on Brooms for Purchasers, the Tool will be found indispensable.

It has Screw-holes, and can be screwed up in any convenient position.

BRASS BEVEL SCREWS

(Drawings are Half Size).

No. 1436	No. 1437	No. 1438	No. 1439
No. 1436 ... 33/- per gross.	No. 1437 ... 42/- per gross.	No. 1438 .. 40/- per gross.	No. 1439 ... 42/- per gross.

No. 1439½   With Round Nut and Inch Washer, 45/- per gross.

EDWARD PRESTON & SONS, L^{TD.}

THE "VICTOR" E.P. SCAFFOLD POLE CHAIN.

This illustration represents the position the chain is in when holding ledgers.

Other connections are equally satisfactorily made

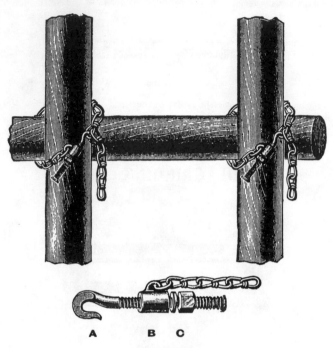

A   B   C

DIRECTIONS.

When putting this chain in use screw the nut **C** away from the hook nut **A** till stopped by the flat head at end of screw ; let the bolt **B** with chain slip down to the end (this places the chain in position desired) and fasten the hook in the link found most convenient, leaving any left over hanging loose, and screw the nut **C** towards the hook **A** until the necessary tightness is attained. Even if not screwed tight, the chain will not slip down, as the ledger causes sufficient drag to make it hold.

ADVANTAGES.

This chain has great advantages, and entirely supersedes ropes, also chains pure and simple which have to be wedged. The disadvantages attending the use of the latter are only too well known to builders, not the least of which is the wedge question With this chain no wedges are required, and the risks of the scaffold collapsing are reduced to the minimum, as a screw connection can be made so much more permanently tight and rigid than is the case when the requisite tightness is obtained by using wedges.

It is always ready for use owing to the end of screw being flat, thereby preventing the nut coming off the screw—a great consideration, and one wanting in all previous attempts in this direction.

As regards the question of rust, a fractional part of the time already spent in overhauling and attending to ropes and chains, with the accompanying driving of wedges, if devoted to occasionally painting the screw and nut with vaseline or other compound involving no great trouble, would entirely prevent their becoming rusty. By taking reasonable care the article would last years, and when the screw is worn, that portion can be renewed at a very small cost.

They are made in the following sizes—

	Nos. 1	2	3	4	
	V2	V4	V6	V8	Wire Gauge.
3 ft.	38/-	24/-	18/-	15/-	per Dozen.
6 ft.	50/-	32/-	24/-	22/6	,,
9 ft.	62/6	36/8	30/-	25/-	,,
12 ft.	75/-	47/-	37/-	29/-	,,
Breaking Strain	27	23	21	15	cwt.

These Chains can be used for lashing and other purposes.

Spanners for above for 1 in. nut at one end and ¾ in. nut at the other.
1/4 Each.

Edward Preston & Sons, Ltd.

SARDINE BOX AND TIN CAN OPENERS.

TRADE ⟨E P⟩ MARK.

These Can Openers are of Superior make and finish.

No. 1603.

SARDINE OPENERS, Bronzed "Fish" Pattern.

No. 1603/1. Blades screwed in and hardened ... 4/6 per dozen.
,, 1603/2. ,, ,, not hardened ... 4/- ,,

No. 1608.

SARDINE OPENERS, Japanned "Crocodile" Pattern.

	No. 1	2	3	
No. 1608. Blades screwed in and hardened	2/6	4/-	5/-	per dozen.
,, 1609. As 1608, but Nickel Plated ...	7/6	8/-	9/-	,,

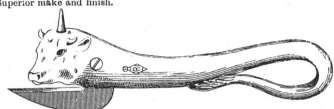

Best Bronzed "Bull's Head" MEAT TIN OPENERS.

No. 1626. Blades and Spikes screwed in and hardened 6/- per dozen.
,, 1625. ,, ,, ,, not hardened 5/- ,,

No. 1619.

SARDINE OPENERS.

No. 1619. Polished Beechwood Handle, Brass Head⎫
Blades cast in ... ...⎭ 6/- per dozen

CUCUMBER SLICERS.

No. 1555.

CUCUMBER SLICERS.

No. 1555. Boxwood Fence, with Handle, Steel Knife 10/- per dozen.

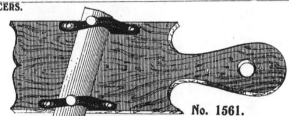

No. 1561.

IMPROVED CUCUMBER SLICERS.

No. 1561. Spring and Screws to adjust knife,⎫ 22/- per dozen.
Nickel Plated Steel Knife ... ...⎭
,, 1561W. do. do. White wood not polished 22/- ,,

ICE MALLETS and PRICKERS.

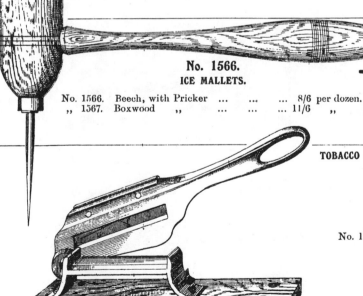

No. 1566.

ICE MALLETS.

No. 1566. Beech, with Pricker ... ... 8/6 per dozen.
,, 1567. Boxwood ,, ... 11/6 ,,

No. 1563.

HANDLED ICE PRICKERS.

No. 1563. Beech Handle ... ... 4/6 per dozen.
,, 1564. Boxwood ,, ... 6/- ,,

TOBACCO CUTTERS.

No. 1515.

TOBACCO CUTTERS.

	3	3½	4 inch.
No. 1515. Jap'd Iron Frame, Wood Stand	21/6	25/6	31/- per dozen

With Guard to Knife, 1/6 per dozen extra.

TRACING WHEELS.

SINGLE TRACING WHEELS.

No. 950. Brass Shank ... ... 5/3 per dozen.

DOUBLE TRACING WHEELS.

No. 951. Brass Shank ... ... 10/6 per dozen.

HOUSEHOLD TOOLS.

TRADE **E⚹P** MARK.

No. 101A.   SHORT HAND SAWS, Open Handles.

8	10	12	14	16 inch.
11/-	12/-	14/-	16/-	18/- per dozen.

No. 101B.   HAND SAWS, Closed Handles.

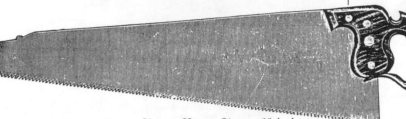

16	18	20	22	24	26 inch.
22/-	23/-	24/-	27/-	29/-	32/- per dozen.

No. 100A.   IRON BACK SAWS, Open Handles.

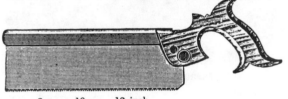

8	10	12 inch
18/-	20/-	22/- per dozen.

No. 100B.   IRON BACK SAWS, Closed Handles.

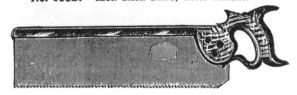

12	14	16 inch.
27/-	30/-	33/- per dozen.

No. 087.   HANDLED WOOD CHOPPERS.

No. 087.   Handled Wood Chopper   ...   ...   13/- per dozen.
 ,,   030.   ,,   ,,   better quality 17/-   ,,

No. 057.   HANDLED HATCHETS.

	No. 1	2	3	4	
No. 057	21/-	24/-	27/-	31/-	per dozen.
,, 057B Blued Heads	25/-	28/-	31/-	35/-	,,

TACK DRAWERS.

No.   40.   Beech Handle   ...   6/- per dozen.
 ,, 0739.   Hardwood Handle   15/-   ,,

No. 0583.   CAST IRON COAL HAMMERS.

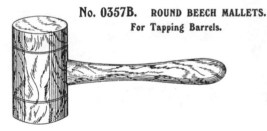

11/- per dozen.

No. 0357B.   ROUND BEECH MALLETS.
For Tapping Barrels.

3	3½	4	4½ in. diameter, 5 in. long
12/-	15/-	18/-	23/- per dozen.

No. 2000   COOKS' SAWS AND KNIVES, Beech Handles.

17/- per dozen.

MINCING KNIVES.

No. 0676.
9/6 per dozen.

No. 0672.
18/- per dozen.

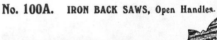

No. 0673.
31/- per dozen.

EDWARD PRESTON & SONS, L^{TD.}

CORKSCREWS.

TRADE ⓔ◊ⓟ MARK.

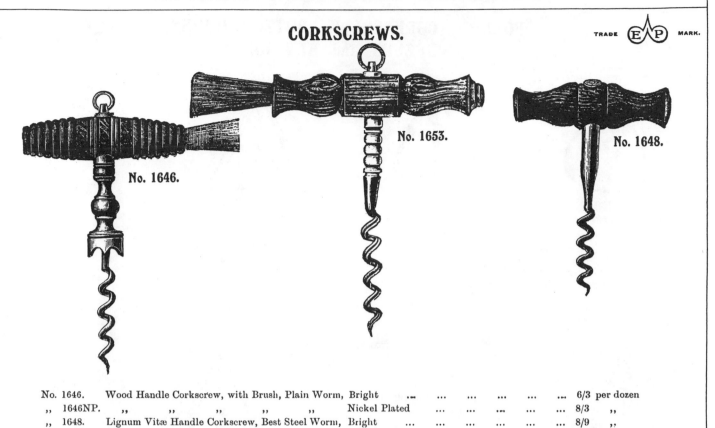

No. 1646.

No. 1653.

No. 1648.

No. 1646.	Wood Handle Corkscrew, with Brush, Plain Worm, Bright	... ... 6/3 per dozen
,, 1646NP.	,, ,, ,, ,, ,, Nickel Plated	... ... 8/3 ,,
,, 1648.	Lignum Vitæ Handle Corkscrew, Best Steel Worm, Bright	... ... 8/9 ,,
,, 1648NP.	,, ,, ,, ,, ,, Nickel Plated	... ... 11/3 ,,
,, 1653.	Best Rosewood Handle Corkscrew, ,, ,,	... ... 16/3 ,,

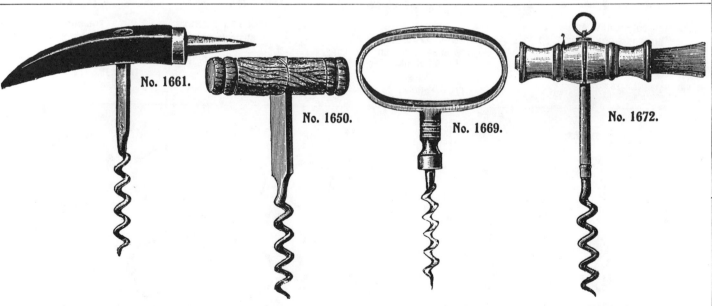

No. 1661.

No. 1650.

No. 1669.

No. 1672.

No. 1647.	Boxwood Handle Corkscrew, as 1650,	Bright ... ... 7/6 per dozen.
,, 1650.	Rosewood ,, ,,	,, ... 11/3 ,,
,, 1650NP.	,, ,, ,,	Nickel Plated... .... 12/6 ,,
,, 1661.	Buffalo Horn Handle Corkscrew, 4 inch, and Spike, Adelaide Pattern, Bright	... ... 13/3 ,,
,, 1661NP.	,, ,, ,, ,, ,, ,, ,, Nickel Plated... ...	... 15/9 ,,
,, 1661S.	,, ,, ,, ,, ,, ,, 2nd quality, Bright ...	... ... 10/9 ,,
,, 1666.	Bronzed Iron Handle Corkscrew, as 1669, but plain worm	,, ... 7/6 ,,
,, 1669.	,, ,, ,, ,, ,, with Patent Worm	,, ... 8/9 ,,
,, 1672.	Bone Handle Corkscrew, with Brush	,, ... 15/- ,,
1672NP.	,, ,, ,, ,,	Nickel Plated.. ... ... 16/3 ,,

Edward Preston & Sons, Lᵀᴰ.

FOLDING CORKSCREWS, BUTTON HOOKS, TWEEZERS and KEY RINGS.

TRADE **EP** MARK.

No. 1694
FOLDING CORKSCREW.
Plain Worm.

Bright Steel ... ... 6/- per doz.
Nickel Plated ... 7/6 ,,

No. 1695
FOLDING CORKSCREW.
Patent Worm.

Bright Steel ... ... 8/9 per doz.
Nickel Plated ... 10/9 ,,

No. 1696
FOLDING CORKSCREW.
Plain Worm.

Bright Steel ... ... 8/9 per doz.
Nickel Plated ... 10/9 ,,

No. 1697
FOLDING CORKSCREW.
Best Cut Bow, Plain Worm.

Bright Steel ... 13/9 per doz.
Nickel Plated ... 16/3 ,,

No. 1704

FOLDING CORKSCREW AND BUTTON HOOK.

Plain Worm.
Bright Steel ... 12/6 per doz.
Nickel Plated ... 16/3 ,,

No. 1713
BONE HANDLED BUTTON HOOK.
3/9 per dozen.

No. 1715
WHITE BONE HANDLED BUTTON HOOK.
Scale Tang.
5/- per dozen.

No. 1705
FOLDING POCKET BUTTON HOOK.

Bright Steel ... 6/- per doz.
Nickel Plated ... 7/6 ,,

No. 1709
FOLDING POCKET BUTTON HOOK.

Bright Steel ... 12/6 per doz.
Nickel Plated ... 14/6 ,,

TWEEZERS.

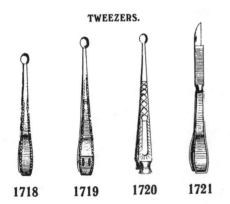

1718   **1719**   **1720**   **1721**

No. 1718 Common Fancy Tweezers 2/6 doz.
,, 1719 Good ,, ,, 3/6 ,,
,, 1720 Best ,, ,, 4/3 ,,
,, 1721 ,, ,, with
File and Knife ... 7/6 ,,

KEY RINGS.

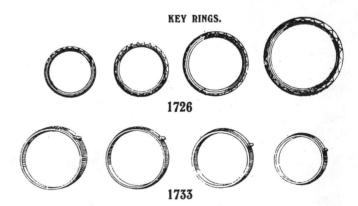

1726

1733

1722 Plain Round Split Key Rings, 1 doz. on a card, assorted 1, 1⅛, 1¼, 1⅜ in. dia., 8d. per card.
1726 Fancy Cut ,, ,, ,, 1 ,, ,, ,, ,, ,, ,, ,, ,, 1/6 ,,
1733 Best Hoop ,, ,, ,, 1 ,, ,, ,, ,, ,, ,, ,, ,, 2/6 ,,
1734 Strong Round ,, ,, ,, ... ,, 1⅛ 1¼ 1½ 1⅝
1/6 2/3 3/- 3/9 per dozen.

Drawings about Half Size.

EDWARD PRESTON & SONS, L^{TD}.

BRASS BLOW LAMPS AND BLOW PIPES.

 TRADE MARK.

The Lamps have a Brass Spring Clip which slides up and down the body of the Lamp, to which a Blow Pipe is attached, and by this means the pipe is adjustable.

The Lamp should be charged with cotton waste, using methylated spirits for light, and naptha for heavy work.

No. 1 and 2 Blow Pipes will be found very generally useful for brazing small work. In use they are attached to a gas fitting with a rubber tube of suitable length. They are fitted with an air tube to take a small rubber tube and mouthpiece.

No. 3 Blow Pipe is suitably fitted for using with bellows and gas.

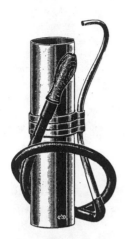

No. L1.   19/- per dozen,

No. L2.   25/- per dozen.

No. L5.   53/- per dozen.

No. L3.   35/- per dozen.

No. L4.   45/- per dozen.

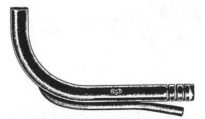

No. P1.   24/- per dozen.

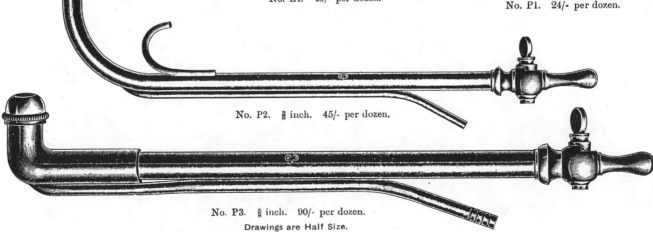

No. P2.   ⅜ inch.   45/- per dozen.

No. P3.   ⅝ inch.   90/- per dozen.

Drawings are Half Size.

EDWARD PRESTON & SONS, LTD.

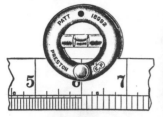

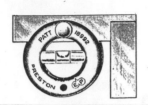

CIRCULAR POCKET SPIRIT LEVEL.

(Ashton's Patent).

This Level is made of Aluminium, 1¾-in. in diameter and round in section, with top and bottom grooves.

It is specially adapted for carrying in the vest pocket, weighing only 1 oz., and is very readily attached to a square or a straight steel rule of any length.

If attached by the bottom groove to a straight steel rule, it may be used as an ordinary level, or by the top groove as a soffit level for overhead work, or it may be attached to a square, and will then form a plumb level (*see drawings opposite*).

Drawings are Half Size of Levels.

No. 1089 Circular Aluminium Pocket Levels ... ... 24/- per dozen.
" 1089C " " " " in Leatherette
  "Covered Card Cases" ... ... 28/- "

PRESTON'S REGISTERED GROOVING OR DEPTHING ROUTER.

This is a very useful tool for Pattern Makers, Cabinet Makers, Carpenters, etc., for smoothing the bottoms of grooves and depressions below the surface of small woodwork.

The Cutting Irons may be used either in the centre, as shown in the drawing, or either knob may be removed, when the Cutting Iron can be inserted and used for getting close into corners.

Drawing is Half Size.

No. 1397 .. .. 2/6 each.

CARPENTERS' IRON BOUND MALLETS.

Malleable Iron Frame, with Beech Handle and ends, which may be renewed when worn.

	No. 1	2	2½	3	4
Size of Frame	2⅝	3	3⅜	3⅝	4 inch.
No. 1466 Iron Frame	23/-	27/-	34/-	40/-	50/- per dozen.
" 1467 Brass "	34/-	39/-	48/-	54/-	66/- "

STONE CARVERS' COMPOSITION DUMMIES.

		2¼	3	3½	4 lbs. (about).
No. 166 Beech Handled	... ...	2/9	3/-	3/6	4/- each.

RABBETING GAUGE.

A very useful small tool for Fretworkers and Amateurs for rabbeting small picture frames, &c.

No. 1511 Brass Stem and Adjustable Fence, with Steel
  Cutter, Beech Handled ... ... 11/6 per dozen.

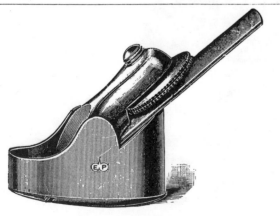

GUN METAL PLANES, for Violin Making.

These are made in Five Sizes, with Flat and Round Faces, and are fitted with One Plain and One Toothed Iron to each Plane.

F means Flat, R Round Face.

Width of Irons	...	...	...	$\frac{5}{16}$	$\frac{7}{16}$	$\frac{9}{16}$	$\frac{11}{16}$	$\frac{13}{16}$ inch.
Flat	No. 1F	2F	3F	4F	5F			
Each	...	3/-	3/3	3/9	4/6	5/6		
Round	No. 1R	2R	3R	4R	5R			
Each	...	3/3	3/6	4/3	5/6	6/-		

Drawing is Full Size of 4 R Plane.

ADDENDUM TO CATALOGUE NO. 18

The following four pages are reproductions of several price correction sheets, as well as new items added to the **PRESTON** line shortly after the issue of the catalogue in 1909.

DRAPERS' ROUND AND FLAT YARD MEASURES.

The Board of Trade Regulations, of October 1st, 1907, require that after January 1st, 1908, all wooden Yard Measures used for trade purposes to be tipped with metal at each end.

These Yard Measures are manufactured in accordance with above regulations and officially stamped at extra cost, *see note below*

No. 787.   DRAPERS' ROUND YARD MEASURES.

No. 785 Beechwood, ½-in. Round Yard Measure, Brass Capped at each end, marked parts of yard ... ...   8/- per dozen.

„ 786   „   as No. 785, but marked parts of yard and inches in 8ths ... ...   9/- „

„ 787 Boxwood, best quality, tapered ½-in. to $\frac{7}{16}$-in., Round Yard Measure, marked parts of yard and inches in 8ths   12/- „

„ 788   „   as No. 787, but thin tapered $\frac{7}{16}$-in. to $\frac{5}{16}$-in ... ...   12/- „

If less than half dozen of any No. is ordered, 1/- per dozen subject extra to above prices is charged.

NOTE.—To cover official stamping by the Weights and Measures Authorities, a charge of 3/4 per dozen subject extra to above prices is made.

N°20

Supplement to Page 35.

EDWARD PRESTON & SONS.

GLAZIERS' LATHS AND T SQUARES.

GLAZIERS' LATH, No. 652.

1¾ in. wide and ⅛ in. thick.

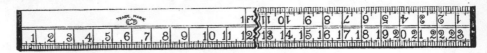

24″	30″	36″	42″	48″	60″	72″	
11/6	16/6	20/6	23/6	27/6	41/-	58/-	per dozen.

GLAZIERS' T SQUARE, No. 651.

24″	30″	36″	42″	48″	60″	
20/6	23/6	26/6	32/-	36/-	52/6	per dozen.

Preston (E∧P) Registered Brass Cap Plated Head
GLAZIERS' T SQUARE, No. 651 P.

24″	30″	36″	42″	48″	60″	
34/6	37/6	40/6	46/-	50/-	66/6	per dozen.

In place of the thin strip of brass fixed along the inner edge of the T square head, a substantial capping of channel-section brass is introduced : the head is therefore more amply protected, and is also greatly strengthened by this innovation, while adding nothing to the cost of the T square over the old method of plating the head.

ON SALE BY

Supplement to Page 46.

WE BEG TO ADVISE THE FOLLOWING

REDUCED AND REVISED PRICES

—— OF ——

SPIRIT LEVELS, LEVEL TUBES, AND PLUMBS & LEVELS.

Trade Mark.

Established 1825.

JULY 1st, 1910.

EDWARD PRESTON & SONS, LTD.,

Whittall Works, BIRMINGHAM.

PAGES REFER TO OUR **No. 18** CATALOGUE.

SPIRIT LEVELS.

No. 1013. Page 51.
6″	...	9/- per dozen.
8″	...	11/3 ,,
9″	...	12/6 ,,
10″	...	14/3 ,,
12″	...	17/- ,,

No. 1018. Page 51.
8″	...	17/9 per dozen.
9″	...	20/6 ,,
10″	...	23/3 ,,
12″	...	26/9 ,,
14″	...	34/9 ,,

No. 1223. Page 51.
18″	...	48/- per dozen.

No. 1219. Pattern similar to No. 1243, Page 53, but with light top plate and tips.
8″	...	23/- per dozen.
9″	...	26/- ,,
10″	...	29/6 ,,
12″	...	34/9 ,,

PLUMBS AND LEVELS.

No. 1251. Page 54.
8″	...	29/6 per dozen.
9″	...	33/6 ,,
10″	...	37/6 ,,
12″	...	44/6 ,,
14″	...	52/- ,,

No. 1662. Pattern as No. 1062, Page 55, Mahogany.
9″	...	17/6 per dozen.

No. 1265. Page 56.
18″	...	40/- per dozen.
24″	...	50/- ,,

No. 1064. Page 56.
12″	...	18/9 per dozen.

SPIRIT LEVELS.

No. 1605. Light pattern as No. 1287, Page 57.
6″ only	10/9 per dozen.

No. 1206. Page 58.
4″	...	10/6 per dozen.

No. 1208. Page 58.
6″	...	11/6 per dozen.

SPIRIT LEVEL TUBES.

No. 1293. Page 58.
To 1½″	...	1/4 per dozen.
1¾″	...	1/6 ,,
2″	...	1/7 ,,
2½″	...	1/9 ,,
3″	...	2/- ,,
3½″	...	2/6 ,,
4″	...	2/10 ,,
4½″	...	3/2 ,,
5″	...	4/- ,,
Assorted, 1½″ to 3″	2/1 per doz.
,, 2″ ,, 3½″	2/2 ,,
,, 2½″ ,, 4″	2/5 ,,

No. 1294. Best fine, proved with lines, Page 58.
To 1½″	...	1/7 per dozen.
1¾″	...	1/9 ,,
2″	...	2/- ,,
2½″	...	2/3 ,,
3″	...	2/5 ,,
3½″	...	2/11 ,,
4″	...	3/4 ,,
4½″	...	3/10 ,,
5″	...	4/8 ,,
Assorted, 1½″ to 3″	2/6 per doz.
,, 2″ ,, 3½″	2/8 ,,
,, 2½″ ,, 4″	3/- ,,

SPIRIT LEVELS.

No. 1286. Page 59.
2½″	...	11/6 per dozen.
3″	...	13/9 ,,
4″	...	20/- ,,

The above if in case, No. 1286c, 2/- per dozen extra.

PLUMBS AND LEVELS.

No. 06c.
12″	...	19/3 per dozen.
15″	...	21/- ,,
18″	...	24/- ,,

No. 08c. Half tipped.
12″	...	25/- per dozen.
15″	...	27/9 ,,
18″	...	31/3 ,,

No. 506c. Page 60.
24″	...	30/6 per dozen.
27″	...	32/- ,,
30″	...	35/- ,,

No. 506. Page 60.
24″	...	32/6 per dozen.
27″	...	35/- ,,
30″	...	38/- ,,

No. 508. Page 60.
24″	...	39/- per dozen.
27″	...	42/- ,,
30″	...	45/- ,,

ADJUSTABLE.

No. 507. Page 62.
24″	...	42/6 per dozen.
27″	...	44/- ,,
30″	...	48/- ,,

No. 509. Page 62.
24″	...	46/6 per dozen.
27″	...	48/- ,,
30″	...	52/- ,,

No. 511. Page 62.
24″	...	55/6 per dozen.
27″	...	58/- ,,
30″	...	61/6 ,,

No. 519. Page 62.
24″	...	75/- per dozen.
27″	...	77/6 ,,
30″	...	82/- ,,

No. 521. New No. Mahogany and Baywood triple stock.
24″	...	80/6 per dozen.
27″	...	84/6 ,,
30″	...	89/6 ,,

No. 520. Page 62.
24″	...	98/- per dozen.
27″	...	102/- ,,
30″	...	107/- ,,

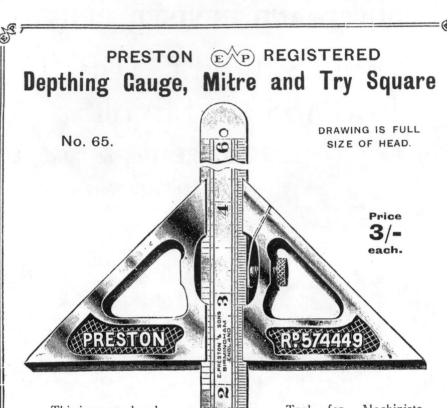
Supplement to Page 108.

TRADE  MARK.

Supplementary and Revised Price List

OF

BOXWOOD, IVORY AND BRASS RULES,

TAILORS' SQUARES, SHOEMAKERS' SIZE STICKS,

CONTRACTION LATHS, PARALLEL RULES,

HEIGHT STANDARDS, BOAT BEVELS,

SPIRIT LEVELS,

AND NEW PATTERNS OF

PLUMBS AND LEVELS,

TRAMMEL HEADS, PLUMB BOBS,

IRON PLANES,

GROOVING ROUTERS, AND DEPTHING SQUARES.

EDWARD PRESTON & SONS, LTD.,

Whittall Works, BIRMINGHAM, Eng.

LIST No. 25. *July 1st. 1912.*

EDWARD PRESTON & SONS, L^{TD}.

WE BEG TO NOTIFY THE FOLLOWING REVISED PRICES.

PAGES REFER TO OUR **No. 18** CATALOGUE.

FOUR-FOLD BOXWOOD RULES.

No.	Page 1.		
3132	... ...	1 ft. ...	4/7 per doz.

No.	Page 2.		
		2 ft.	3 ft.
3129	... ...	4/8	— per doz.
3111	... ...	7/3	— ,,
3113	... ..	8/3	— ,,
3013	... ...	8/9	10/9 ,,

No.	Page 3.		
3114	.. ...	2 ft. ..	10/- per doz.

No.	Page 5.		
		2 ft.	3 ft.
3118	... ...	14/6	17/6 per doz.

No.	Page 6.		
		2 ft.	3 ft.
3213	... ...	14/6	17/6 per doz.
3214	... ..	17/6	20/6 ,,

No.	Page 7.		
3313	... ...	2 ft. ...	16/6 per doz.
3413	... ...	,, ...	24/6 ,,

No.	Page 12.		
3220	... ...	4 ft. ...	32/3 per doz.
3221	... ...	,, ...	33/3 ,,
3316	... ...	,, ...	52/6 ,,
3375	... ...	,, ...	35/- ,,

For Drawings and Description of above Coach-makers' 4 ft. 4-fold Rules see page 5 of this List.

No.	Page 13.		
3248	... ...	1 ft. ...	23/6 per doz.
3088	... ...	,, ...	23/6 ,,

CALLIPER GAUGES.

No.	Page 13.		
3044	... ...	3 Inches ...	11/3 per doz.
3045	... ...	4 ,, ...	15/6 ,,

THREE-FOLD BOXWOOD RULES.

No.	Page 19.		
1080	... ...	2 ft. ...	6/6 each.
1081	... ...	,, ...	9/6 ,,

12 in. BOXWOOD and IVORY SCALES.

No.	Page 27.			
	Boxwood — per doz.		Ivory—each.	
1310	.. 20/6	0310	... 11/3	
1311	... 20/6	0311	... 11/3	
1312	... 20/6	0312	... 11/3	
—	.. —	0321	... 11/3	
—	.. —	0322	... 11/3	
—	.. —	0323	... 11/3	
—	.. —	0324	... 11/3	
—	.. -	0314	... 11/3	
—	.. -	0320	... 11/3	
1307	... 20/6	0307	... 11/3	
—	... —	0319	... 11/3	
1300	... 20/6	0300	... 11/3	
1308	... 20/6	0308	... 11/3	
1301	... 20/6	0301	... 11/3	
1302	... 20/6	0302	... 11/3	
1303	... 20/6	0303	... 11/3	
1304	... 20/6	0304	... 11/3	
1305	... 20/6	0305	... 11/3	

FOUR-FOLD IVORY RULES.

No.	Page 31.		
0168	... ...	3 ft. .	27/- each.
0176	... .		31/- ,,

No.	Page 33.		
0178	... ...	3 ft. ...	34/- each.
P0178	... ...	,, ...	35/- ,,

TAILORS' SQUARES.

No. 649.   Page 45.

Light Pattern Folding for Dressmakers.

24 × 18	27 × 18
26/6	32/- per doz.

No. 658.   Page 45.—Fixed Squares.

18	21	24	27	30 in.
24/-	26/-	29/3	35/-	42/- per doz.

SHOEMAKERS' SIZE STICKS.

Page 47

Nos. 710, 711, 712, 713 & 714 are now obsolete.

BOXWOOD CONTRACTION LATHS.

No.	Page 49.		
739	... ...	2 ft. ...	29/3 per doz.

EBONY PARALLEL RULES.

No. 508.	Page 50.		
6 in.	... ...	6/-	per doz
9 in.	... ...	12/6	,,
12 in.	... ...	17/-	,,
15 in.	... ...	21/6	,,
18 in.	... ...	25/6	,,
21 in.	... ...	30/6	,,
24 in.	... ...	36/-	,,

SPIRIT LEVELS.

No. 1255.	Page 54.		
10 in.	... ...	42/6 per doz.	

No. 1250.	Page 54.		
8 in.	... ...	26/6 per doz.	
9 in.	... ...	29/6	,,
10 in.	... ...	32/6	,,
12 in.	... ...	37/6	,,

No. 1265.	Page 56.		
14 in.	... ...	29/-	per doz.
16 in.	... ...	40/-	,,
18 in.	... ...	42/6	,,
20 in.	... ...	48/-	,,

No. 1064.	Page 56.		
10 in.	... ...	17/- per doz.	

No. 1600.	Page 57.		
6 in.	... ...	30/-	per doz.
8 in.	... ...	40/-	,,
10 in.	... ...	48/-	,,

7 in., 9 in. and 12 in. not now made.
NOTE.—No. 1601 is now obsolete.

No. 1602.	Page 57.		
6 in.	... ...	35/6	per doz.
8 in.	... ...	44/6	,,
10 in.	... ...	53/6	,,
12 in.	... ...	62/6	,,

7 in. and 9 in. not now made.
NOTE.—No. 1604 is now obsolete.

No.	Page 59.		
1088C	... ...	9 in. ...	66/- per doz.
1088CW	... ...	,, ..	69/3 ,,

BOAT BUILDERS' BEVELS.

No.	Page 74.		
1104	... ...	12 in. ...	11/6 per doz.
1204	... ..	,, ...	15/- ,,
1105	... ...	,, ...	11/6 ,,
1205	... ...	,, ...	15/- ,,

EDWARD PRESTON & SONS, LTD.

TWO FEET, THREE FEET and 1 METRE FOUR-FOLD BOXWOOD RULES.

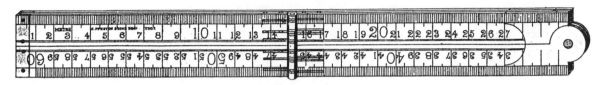

3115 L. & M.

Half Size Drawing shewing inside of No. 3115 Rule marked Millimetres.

We give below prices of Boxwood Rules 2 feet, 3 feet and 1 Metre Four-Fold, marked London (inches in 8ths) one side and Metre (Millimetres) other side. The 2 feet and 3 feet are marked London measure outside and Metre inside, but the 1 Metre are marked Metre outside and London inside. The Drawings of the different Nos. will be found on the respective pages of our No. 18 Catalogue.

When London and Metre Rules are required please add L. & M. to the No. (see drawing above).

Page for Drawings.	No. of Rule.	2 feet marked London and Metre.	3 feet marked London and Metre.	1 Metre marked Metre and London		Page for Drawings.	No. of Rule.	1 foot marked London and Metre.	
2	3130	4/10	—	7/9	per doz.	13	3248	25/6	per doz.
2	*3109	6/3	—	—	,,	13	3088	25/6	,,
2	3111	7/9	—	—	,,	13	3046	6 inch. 16/6	,,
2	*3113	8/9	—	12/6	,,	13	3044	3 inch. 13/3	,,
3	*3114	10/6	—	14/6	,,	13	3144	4 inch. 17/6	,,
3	3115	11/9	14/-	16/6	,,	13	3776	4 inch. 29/3	,,
3	3116	13/3	—	19/6	,,	13	3777	6 inch. 35/-	,,
5	*3118	15/6	—	—	,,				
5	3119	18/6	—	22/6	,,				
5	*3120	20/6	23/6	24/6	,,				
7	3313	17/6	—	—	,,				
7	3314	19/6	—	—	,,				
7	*3315	22/6	—	35/-	,,				
7	3414	28/-	—	—	,,				
7	3415	32/-	—	—	,,				
34	2010	11/6	—	—	,,				

The above prices are quoted for orders of not less than one dozen of each No. except those marked * which may be had in half dozens. Smaller quantities are charged slightly higher net prices.

The extra charge made for other Nos. of Rules marked London and Metre will be found on pages 8 to 12.

EDWARD PRESTON & SONS, LTD.

FOUR-FOLD BOXWOOD RULES.

Page 1

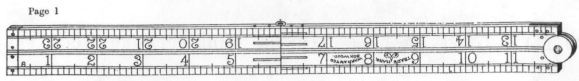

3211

No. 3211.   Round Joint, marked 8ths and 16ths, 1 inch wide   ...   .   2 feet.

5/4 per dozen.

English Measure only.

Packed in Dozens in Cardboard Boxes.

Page 6

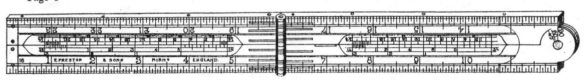

3515

No. 3515.   Three Arch Joints, Brass bound outside edges, inches in 8ths, 16ths and Scales 1⅜ inch wide   ...   2 feet.

29/3 per dozen.

Packed in Half-dozens in Cardboard Boxes.

Page 8

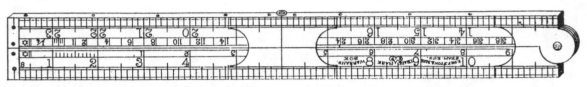

3081

No. 3081.   Arch Joint, Brass bound outside edges, inches in 8ths, 16ths, 10ths and 12ths, 8 Drawing
Scales, 1³⁄₁₆ inch wide   ...   .   2 feet.   3 feet.

31/-   44/- per dozen.

Packed in Half-dozens in Cardboard Boxes.

Page 10

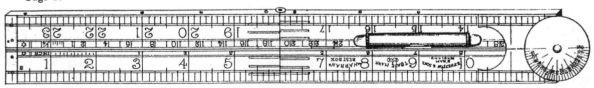

3316 L.

No. 3316 L.   Arch Joint, with Spirit Level, Brass bound outside edges, inches in 8ths, 16ths, and 10ths
Scales, Degrees on Brass Plate, 1½ inch wide   ...   .   2 feet.   3 feet.

46/9   54/6 per dozen.

Packed in Half-dozens in Cardboard Boxes.

Drawings are Half Size.

EDWARD PRESTON & SONS, L^{TD.}

TRADE **EP** MARK.

FOUR FEET FOUR-FOLD BOXWOOD RULES for COACHMAKERS and MOTOR BODY BUILDERS.

Inches marked in 8ths and 16ths.   French Polished.

Page 12.

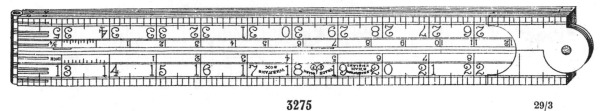

3275   29/3

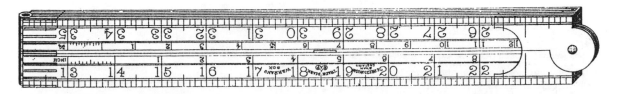

3221   33/3

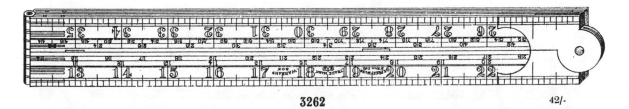

3262   42/-

MOTOR BODY BUILDERS' RULE.

Marked Metre in Millimetres inside.

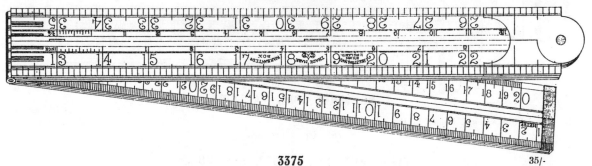

3375   35/-
4-feet.

No. 3271.	Arch Joint, inches in 8ths, 16ths, and Scales	...	...	...	1⅜-inch wide	29/3	per dozen.
,, 3275.	,,	,,	,,	,,	... ...	1½ ,,	29/3	,,
,, 3220.	,,	,,	,,	,,	Edge plates to small joints...	1⅜ ,,	32/3	,,
,, 3221	,,	,,	,,	,,	,, ,, ...	1½ ,,	33/3	,,
,, 3616.	,,	,,	,,	,,	Brass bound edges outside ...	1½ ,,	52/6	,,
,, 3221S	,,	,,	,,	,,	with 12-inch brass slide ...	1½ ,,	58/6	,,
,, 3261.	,,	Extra Best, with Steel Tips, and Steel Plates in joints			...	1⅜ ,,	37/-	,,
,, 3262.	,,	,,	,,	,,	,, ...	1½ ,,	42/-	,,
,, 3375.	,,	Inches in 8ths, 16ths and Scales, and Millimetres inside for Motor Body Builders				1½ ,,	35/-	,,

Drawings are Half Size.

EDWARD PRESTON & SONS, L^TD.

PRESTON *EesEseE* BOXWOOD RULES.
TWO FEET AND THREE FEET FOUR-FOLD.
Packed in Half Dozens in Cardboard Boxes.

This Rule has very bold black figures, and is specially heavily graduated in eighths of inches.   It will be found very useful to persons with defective eyesight, or for use in badly lighted places.

Page 2.

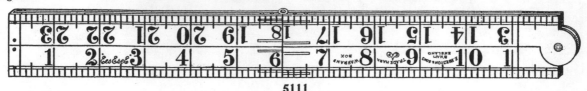

5111

No. 5111.   Square Joint, inches in 8ths, English measure only, 1⅜-in. wide   ...   ...   14/6   19/6   per dozen.

| | 2-ft. | 3-ft. |

Drawing is Half Size.

ONE FOOT TWO-FOLD BOXWOOD RULE, with SLIDE AND CALLIPER GAUGE.

Page 13.

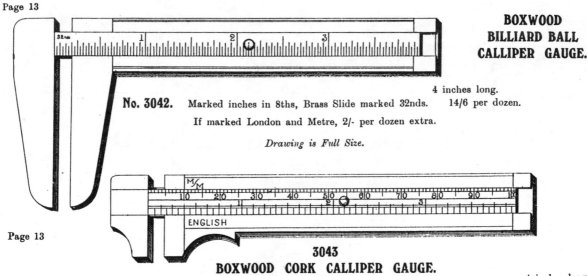

No. 3244.   Arch Joint, inches in 8ths, 16ths and 10ths. Slide marked in 32nds, 1½-in. wide, 27/3 per dozen.

If marked London and Metre, 2/- per dozen extra.

Drawing is Half Size.

3244

Page 13

BOXWOOD BILLIARD BALL CALLIPER GAUGE.

4 inches long.
14/6 per dozen.

No. 3042.   Marked inches in 8ths, Brass Slide marked 32nds.

If marked London and Metre, 2/- per dozen extra.

Drawing is Full Size.

3043

Page 13

BOXWOOD CORK CALLIPER GAUGE.

4 inches long.
18/- per dozen.

No. 3043.   Brass Slide marked inches in 16ths and Millimetres   ...   .

Drawing is Full Size.

TWO FEET TWO-FOLD BRASS RULES.
Marked inches in 8ths and 16ths.

Page 34

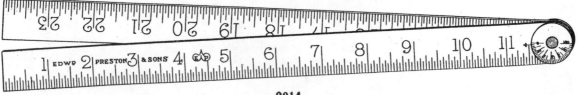

2014

No. 2014.   Two Feet Two-Fold Flexible Brass Rule, Degrees on Joint   ...   .   ⅞ inch wide.   15/6 per dozen.

Drawing is Half Size.

EDWARD PRESTON & SONS, L^{TD.}

HEIGHT STANDARDS, for Use in SCHOOLS, INSTITUTIONS, SURGERIES, &c.

These are substantially made articles, and well adapted for their purpose. They are accurately graduated, and are French Polished.

Page 49.

PRESTON'S REGISTERED SCHOOL PATTERN HEIGHT MEASURING STANDARD.

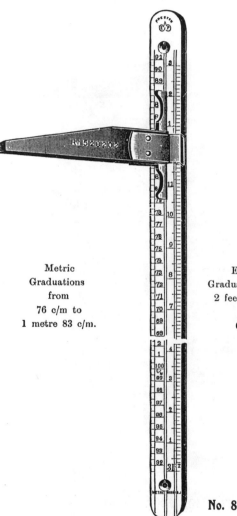

Metric
Graduations
from
76 c/m to
1 metre 83 c/m.

English
Graduations from
2 feet 6 inches
to
6 feet.

No. 828.

No. 828—Boxwood School Pattern Height Measuring Standard, 46 inches long, 1 inch wide × $\frac{5}{16}$ inch thick, to fix on door, wall, or other suitable position. With Mahogany Sliding Arm and Registered Clip, which allows of the arm being detached entirely from the Standard and placed out of danger when not in use. Marked on one side inches in 8ths and metre in half centimetres.

3/9 each.

HEIGHT MEASURING STANDARD.

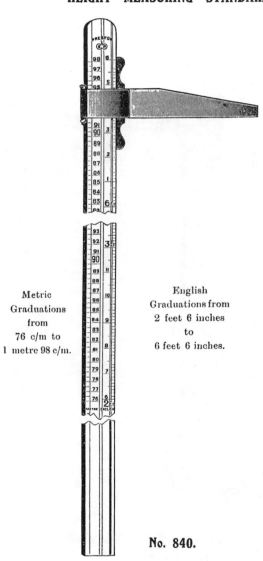

Metric
Graduations
from
76 c/m to
1 metre 98 c/m.

English
Graduations from
2 feet 6 inches
to
6 feet 6 inches.

No. 840.

No. 840—Boxwood Standard, 6 feet 9 inches long × 1¼ inch wide × $\frac{1}{2}$ inch thick with Boxwood Sliding Arm, marked one side inches in 8ths from 2 feet 6 inches to 6 feet 6 inches and metre in half centimetres from 76 c/m to 1 metre 98 c/m.

10/6 each.

EDWARD PRESTON & SONS, L^{TD}.

HEIGHT STANDARDS, for Use in SCHOOLS, INSTITUTIONS, SURGERIES, &c.

Swivel Patterns.   **French Polished.**

Page 49.

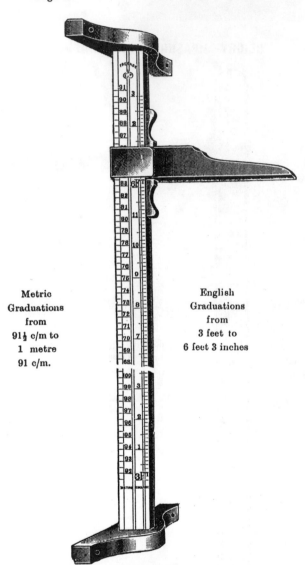

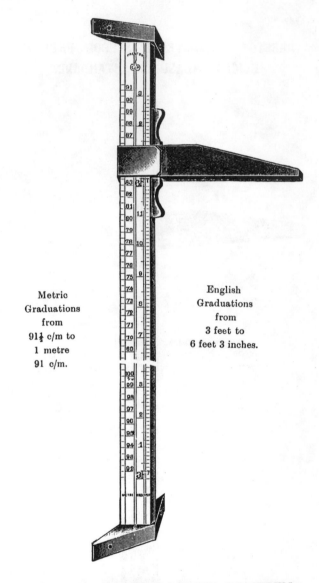

Metric
Graduations
from
91½ c/m to
1 metre
91 c/m.

English
Graduations
from
3 feet to
6 feet 3 inches

Metric
Graduations
from
91½ c/m to
1 metre
91 c/m.

English
Graduations
from
3 feet to
6 feet 3 inches.

No. 826.   BOXWOOD HEIGHT MEASURING STANDARD.

44 inches long × 1 inch wide × $\frac{9}{16}$ inch thick, with Boxwood
Sliding Arm and Mahogany Brackets for fixing to door, wall,
or other suitable position.   The Standard swivels in the
brackets, thus allowing it to be turned out of danger when not
in use.   Marked one side inches in 8ths and metre in half
centimetres.   8/6 each.

No. 825.   This is exactly as No. 826, but marked inches in
8ths only. 8/- each.

No. 827.   BOXWOOD HEIGHT MEASURING STANDARD.

44 inches long × 1 inch wide × $\frac{9}{16}$ inch thick, with Mahogany
Sliding Arm and Brackets as described under No. 826.   Marked
one side inches in 8ths and metre in half centimetres.   5/6 each.

No. 831.   This is exactly as No. 827, but marked inches
in 8ths only.   5/- each.

EDWARD PRESTON & SONS, L<u>TD</u>.

PLUMBS AND SPIRIT LEVELS,

Page 60.

With Best Proved Tubes.   French Polished.

No. 522.

These Plumbs and Levels have Two Plumb Glasses, each set in the same way in plumb holes, thus enabling the user to plumb below or above without moving the position of the level.

	36	42	48	inch.
No. 522. Double Plumb and Level, Brass Arch Top Plate, Side Views, Hardwood Stock, Polished	68/-	80/-	94/-	per dozen.

Page 60.

No. 523.

No. 523.   Plumb and Level, Brass Arch Top Plate, Side Views, Mahogany Stock, Polished, with one Rounded End, may be used with Plumb Bob and Line   ...   .   42 inch, 78/- per dozen.

Page 74.

PRESTON NEW PATTERN BRASS TRAMMEL HEADS, with STEEL POINTS.

These Trammel Heads are of Best Quality and Finish, made of Brass, with Hardened Steel Points, and are supplied with special attachment for holding an ordinary lead Pencil.

They will take a Bar $\frac{1}{2}$-in. deep × $\frac{3}{4}$-in. wide, and are constructed so that the strain during the operation of striking circles is on the <u>width</u> of the bar.

No. 1432   ...   .   3/- per pair.

Page 75.

PRESTON NEW PATTERN BRASS PLUMB BOB.

This is a New Shape Plumb Bob to which we have introduced a Loose Steel Point, which can be screwed into the head of the Bob when not in use and may be carried in the pocket without fear of damage.

The approximate weight of the Bob is 5 oz.

No. 1407   ...   .   15/- per dozen.

EDWARD PRESTON & SONS, L^{TD.}

PRESTON PATENT IRON BULL NOSE RABBET AND RIGHT AND LEFT HAND FILLISTER PLANE, with Fence and Stop.

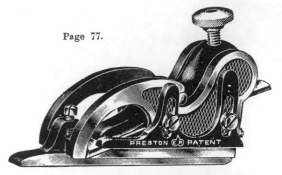

Page 77.

JAPANNED WITH BRIGHT PARTS.

Drawing is about half size over all.

This is a very handy small Wood-workers' Tool. It is made on the principle of our well-known No. 1347 Bull Nose Plane (page 77 No. 18 Catalogue), and is supplied with adjustable and detachable fence and stop.

The fence is attachable to the bottom of the Plane, and is adjustable for forming a Right or Left Hand Fillister.

The stop is attachable to either side of the Plane, and is adjustable for varying depths of rabbet.

Both fence and stop may be entirely detached, and the Plane used as an ordinary Bull Nose Plane.

The Fence is adjustable from ⅛-in. to ½-in. and the stop to ⅜-in.

No. 1347 F ... . 4/6 each.

PRESTON PATENT ADJUSTABLE SMOOTH PLANE.

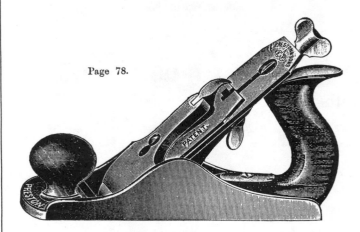

Page 78.

We wish to draw special attention to this Tool.

The Plane is made entirely of **malleable iron**, thus having great advantages over the ordinary **cast** iron Planes.

The irons are bright and parallel, of best cast steel, No. 8 W.G. thick, so that the Plane may be used on all kinds of hardwoods with satisfactory results to the user.

The cutting iron is adjustable by means of the Preston Patent Adjustment, and is also supplied with a novel form of lateral or side adjustment.

The Plane being of **malleable iron**, and having the combination adjustments mentioned, constitutes it a most unique and desirable tool.

When considering the cost of this tool it should not be compared with the cheap cast-iron Planes, but rather with the Steel Dovetail patterns, as it will do equal work with the latter, having thick irons, and being of malleable metal. When these points are considered, together with the fact of the Plane having in addition Patent Adjustments to the cutting iron, the cost will be found very reasonable, being about 20 per cent. less than Steel Dovetail Planes.

No. 1340. 10 inches long, 2¼ inch Cutting Iron ... 18/- each.

PRESTON PATENT LINING OR STRINGING ROUTER.

Page 97.

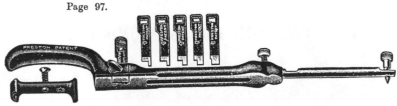

No. 1398 ... ... 4/- each.

This tool is similar to No. 1396 (page 97, No. 18 Catalogue), and will do the same work, but is supplied, in addition to the six cutters, with a round adjustable sliding rod, which is provided with two screwed holes and a removable pointed screw pin. This pin may be inserted in either hole and the rod adjusted according to desire. This combination will be found very useful when inlaying curves. When using the tool for curves, the fence should be entirely removed.

Cutting Irons 4d. each.

MOTOR BODY MAKERS' JIGGER, QUIRK OR GROOVING ROUTER FITTING.

Page 98.

This is made of Steel, and is a very handy little tool for cutting grooves for metal Panels It has four screw holes, and may be screwed on to any wooden holder by the user.

No. 612 ... ... 2/6 each.

EDWARD PRESTON & SONS, L^{TD.}

PRESTON REGISTERED DEPTHING GAUGE, MITRE AND TRY SQUARE.

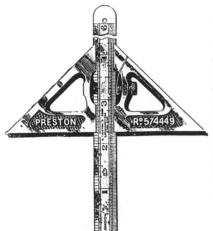

Drawing is Half Size.

Page 108.

This is a very handy Tool for Machinists, being a combined Depthing Gauge with a 6in. Steel Rule, ½in. wide, graduated on two edges, one edge in 16ths and the other edge in 32nds of inches. In combination with the Rule, which is adjustable to varying depths, the Tool may be used as a Mitre Square, and also as an ordinary Try Square. The drawing is half size of head, which is nickelplated.

No. 65 ... 3/- each.

PRESTON REGISTERED DEPTHING GAUGE, MITRE, TRY, T AND CENTRE SQUARE.

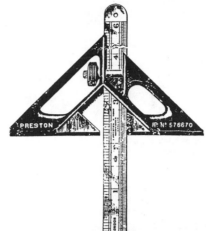

Drawing is Half Size.

Page 108.

This Tool will be appreciated by all Machinists. The Rule forming the Depthing Gauge is 8 inches long over all, and will enable the user to depth holes down to 6 inches. It is ½ inch wide, and graduated on two edges, one edge in 16ths and the other edge in 32nds of inches.

The Tool is adapted for use as a Mitre Square, a Try Square, a **T** Square, and also as a Centre Square. The drawing is half size of head, and the Tool is japanned with bright parts.

No. 66 ... 4/- each.

DRAWINGS SHEWING VARIOUS WAYS IN WHICH No. 66 DEPTHING GAUGE MAY BE USED.

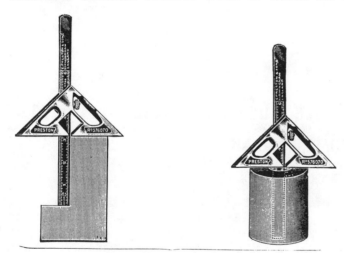

As a Depthing Gauge.

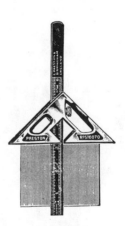

As a T Square.

As a Centre Square.

As a Mitre Square.

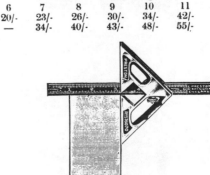

As a Try Square.

TINMEN'S SNIPS.—Page 152.

No	6	7	8	9	10	11	12 inch.
020	20/-	23/-	26/-	30/-	34/-	42/-	48/- per doz.
020B.	—	34/-	40/-	43/-	48/-	55/-	65/- ,,

EDWARD PRESTON & SONS, LTD.

PRESTON PATENT ADJUSTABLE IRON GROOVING or DEPTHING ROUTER.

NICKEL PLATED.

Page 168.

Fig. 1.

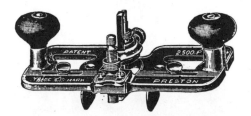

Fig. 2.

This will be found a very useful tool to Carpenters, Pattern Makers, Cabinet Makers, Staircase Makers and Woodworkers generally for depthing and smoothing the bottoms of grooves and cavities below the surface of woodwork.

Two Cutting Irons are supplied (one $\frac{5}{16}''$ and $\frac{7}{16}''$) with each tool, these are held in position on the upright grooved supports by means of the collar and milled head screw, they may be used in the position as shewn in the drawing (Fig. 1), or fixed and used in the groove on reverse side of centre support.

For working close into corners either of the knobs may be removed and the cutting iron fixed on one of the end supports, see drawing (Fig. 2).

The cutting irons may be adjusted by the milled nut to the various depths required ; when adjusting the cutting iron slacken the milled head screw of collar.

Drawings are about $\frac{1}{4}$ size.

No. 1399 P ... ... 5/6 each.

PRESTON PATENT ADJUSTABLE IRON GROOVING OR DEPTHING ROUTER PLANE.

NICKEL PLATED.

Page 168.

VIEW SHEWING BOTTOM OF ROUTER PLANE.

This tool is similar to our No. 1399 P, but we have added an important improvement in the shape of an adjustable milled head screw pin and lock nut ; this screw pin is placed in front of the cutting iron and thus forms a rest and mouth so that the tool works in the form of a **Router Plane**; whatever depth is required to be cut the adjustable pin can be screwed out to the same depth as the cutting iron and locked in position.

To compensate for the wear of the cutting iron through sharpening, the tool is provided with an adjustable sliding front, by means of which the user may always ensure a fine mouth, the result being that **shavings** are cut, as with a plane, instead of chippings.

The tool is also provided with right and left hand moveable fences.

Drawings are about $\frac{1}{4}$ size

No. 2500 P ... ... 7/6 each.